POCKET ADVENTURES

GERMANY

Henk Bekker

HUNTER

HUNTER PUBLISHING, INC,
130 Campus Drive, Edison, NJ 08818
732-225-1900; 800-255-0343; fax 732-417-1744
www.hunterpublishing.com

Ulysses Travel Publications
4176 Saint-Denis, Montréal, Québec
Canada H2W 2M5
514-843-9882, ext. 2232; fax 514-843-9448

Windsor Books
The Boundary, Wheatley Road, Garsington
Oxford, OX44 9EJ England
01865-361122; fax 01865-361133

ISBN 13: 978-1-58843-596-5
ISBN 10: 1-58843-596-2

Cover photo: Schloss Neuschwanstein (© www.romantishestrasse.de)
Index by Nancy Wolff

Maps by Toni Carbone, © 2007 Hunter Publishing, Inc.

1 2 3 4

Table of Contents

WITHDRAWN

MAPS

Introduction

Germany is a large country of wide contrasts. From the beaches of the North and Baltic Seas to the Bavarian Alpine peaks and from the forest-covered hills of the Black Forest to the nightspots of Berlin, it has much of interest to the international traveler.

For centuries, culture has played an important role in German society. Large cities have opera houses and symphony orchestras while even small villages have musical and other cultural societies. Germany is the land of Bach, Beethoven, Goethe, Schiller, and other artists that influenced Western culture. Culture is easy to enjoy in Germany with frequent performances at relatively low prices.

Germany is also a country with amazing architectural treasures. It has some minor Roman and Carolingian monuments, but it is with the Romanesque and Gothic that German building craft really came to the fore. The influence of the Renaissance was limited but Baroque and Rococo are well represented. More modern styles including Art Nouveau, Bauhaus, Modern, and Post-Modern can also be found especially in German cities. Air raids in World War II ruined most German cities – many

rebuilt the damaged buildings while others elected to rebuild in modern style. Half-timbered houses (*Fachwerk*) make some of the most favored and romantic townscapes and are often seen as typical German and typical medieval.

Fachwerk

The long tradition of dividing inheritances gave Germany literally hundreds of small states and principalities, each with its own palaces and residences. More than 20,000 castles and castle ruins are scattered throughout the country. Often the largest palaces and churches are found in what are now small and insignificant towns.

Germany is more than arts and culture. It is also a paradise for outdoor enthusiast. Hiking is the most popular activity in Germany with thousands of marked trails. Cycling is also popular with many dedicated cycling routes. Canoeing and kayaking are possible on many rivers and lakes. Skiing and other winter sports are possible in the Bavarian Alps and many parts of the Mittelgebirge. Germany also has amazing natural beauty with mountains such as the Bavarian Alps and forested hills such as the Black Forest popular recreational areas.

Sanssouci Palace, Postdam

The book starts with **Berlin**, Germany's capital, largest city, and most interesting destination. It has more than 170 museums, three opera houses, an enormous cultural variety, and gripping modern history. An interesting daytrip is to royal residences in nearby **Potsdam**.

Saxony (*Sachsen*) is one of the most densely populated states in Germany, but has natural beauty especially in the Saxon Switzerland area south of Dresden. Its two major cities, Dresden and Leipzig, are tourist magnets. Dresden is restoring its pre-1945 Baroque appearance and in addition to the marvelous architecture, Dresden has some excellent museums and art collections. The immediate appeal of Leipzig is less obvious but it is a great city to visit – it gives the impression of a lived-in city rather than an artificial tourist attraction. For those interested in the Reformation, Lutherstadt-Wittenberg is an interesting stop between Leipzig and Berlin.

Thuringia (*Thüringen*) is closely associated with German literature through the Weimar classical movement led by Goethe and Schiller. In addition to Weimar, Erfurt has a wonderfully preserved medieval town center and Eisenach has the Wartburg, the most German of castles.

Erfurt town center

Northern Germany is popular with domestic tourists, but the appeal for foreign visitors is more limited. **Hamburg** is Germany's second-largest city and premier port. It is a spread-out city with mostly modern, low-rise buildings and much water and greenery. The lovely medieval town center of Lübeck with several brick Gothic buildings makes for a particularly rewarding daytrip.

Similarly, Central Germany has less obvious attractions. **Frankfurt** is a modern city with continental Europe's busiest airport and tallest buildings.

The **Rhine valley** is one of Germany's prime tourist attractions. The most interesting part of the valley is between Speyer, with the largest Romanesque cathedral in Germany, and Cologne (*Köln*), with the largest Gothic cathedral in the world. In between is the Rhine of legend with a castle or castle ruins every mile. The equally beautiful Mosel River is a meandering stream in a steep, narrow valley. Trier has the largest collection of Roman monuments in Germany.

Baden-Württemberg is a favored holiday destination. Heidelberg with its majestic castle ruin is a must-see for most foreign visitors to Germany. The Black Forest is the largest forested

Altes Rathaus, Munich

area in Germany and has many picture-perfect towns and valleys. It is hugely popular with hikers and cyclists. Baden-Baden is the most elegant town in Germany.

Bavaria (*Bayern*) is the most popular holiday destination for domestic and foreign travelers alike. Apart from Berlin, **Munich** (*München*) is the most interesting German city. It has a vast range of cultural offerings including excellent art museums and spectacular, mostly Baroque, royal palaces. It is also the natural home of beer with many historic beer halls, many beer gardens, and of course Oktoberfest. In the north of the state is Franken with important historic cities such as Würzburg, Bamberg, and Nürnberg. Regensburg and Passau on the banks of the Danube have interesting historic centers that escaped damage during World War II. The Romantic Road is a popular holiday route that passes romantic sites including Rothenburg ob der Tauber, the most romantic of all Germany's medieval-look towns. The Bavarian Alps have the most spectacular scenery in Germany. Its natural beauty is enhanced by castles, churches, monasteries, and historic towns.

◆ History

Key Events

German history is complex and somewhat confusing. The following will help keep important events in context.

■ *100 BC-AD 400: Romans occupy parts of Germany, mostly west of the Rhine and south of the Danube.*
■ *800: Charlemagne is crowned Roman Emperor.*

- *9th to 12th centuries: Romanesque (Romanik) architecture.*
- *962: Otto II is crowned German Roman Emperor. What later became known as the Holy Roman Empire of the German Nation lasted until 1806.*
- *13th to 16th centuries: Gothic (Gotik) architecture. The oldest surviving half-timbered (Fachwerk) houses are from this period, although many of these "medieval" buildings actually date from the 16th to 18th centuries.*
- *1517: Martin Luther's 95 Theses initiates the Lutheran Reformation.*
- *1520-1620: Renaissance architecture.*
- *1618-48: Thirty Years' War devastates and depopulates large areas of Germany. Peace of Westphalia (1648) left Germany with around 350 independent political entities.*
- *17th and 18th centuries: Baroque (Barok) and Rococo (Rokoko) architecture.*
- *1688-97: Palatine War of Succession sees French troops destroy most towns and castles in the Rhineland and Palatinate.*
- *1756-63: Seven Years' War confirms the rise of Prussia as the fifth European power.*
- *1792-1815: Napoleon redraws the European and German political map. The Holy Roman Empire of the German Nation comes to a formal end in 1806. Germany is reduced to about 40 political states.*
- *19th century: Romanticism (Romantik) and Historicist architecture. After 1871, "Founding time" (Gründerzeit/ Wilhelmine) architecture followed by Art Nouveau (Jugendstil).*
- *1870-71: Franco-Prussian war ends with the foundation of the (Second) German Empire dominated by Prussia.*
- *1914-18: First World War ends with Germany defeated and the end of the monarchy.*
- *1919-1933: The ill-fated Weimar Republic fails to cope with economic and political upheaval.*

- *1933-1945: The Nazi era (the Third Reich) ends in the carnage of World War II. Germany is totally defeated, occupied, partitioned, and reduced in size.*
- *1949-1989: Germany divided into a democratic West Germany and a communist East Germany.*
- *1989: A peaceful revolution (Die Wende) ends the East German regime.*
- *1990: Germany re-unites and Berlin resumes as capital.*

History Time Line

Early History

500,000 BC: Homo Heidelbergiens showed evidence of human-like life in Germany around 500,000 years ago.

200,000-40,000 BC: Neanderthals lived near Düsseldorf.

10,000 BC: Homo Sapiens arrived in Germany.

800 BC: Celtic tribes moved into southern Germany.

100 BC-AD 400: Romans occupy parts of Germany, mostly west of the Rhine and south of the Danube.

AD 9: Germanic tribes defeated three divisions of the Roman Army.

800: Charlemagne (Karl der Große, 768-814) crowned Roman Emperor by the pope. His empire included most of present day France, Germany, Switzerland, Belgium, the Netherlands, and northern Italy.

911: The East Franks elected Konrad I (911-918) as king to firmly set Germany on a separate development course from France.

The Holy Roman Empire

918-1024: Ottonian (Saxon) dynasty.

962: Otto II crowned German Roman Emperor.

1024-1125: Salian (Frankish) dynasty.

1138-1254: Hohenstaufen dynasty. Friedrich I Barbarossa (1152-1190) introduced the title Holy Roman Emperor ("of the German Nation" was added later).

1356: The Golden Bull specified the electors of the German king as the archbishops of Trier, Mainz, and Cologne, as well as the rulers of Bohemia, Brandenburg, Saxony, and the Palatinate.

1438-1806: Austrian Habsburg dynasty.

1517: Martin Luther questioned the practices of the Roman Catholic Church and started the Protestant Reformation.

1555: Peace of Augsburg established Lutheran Protestantism as an equal to Roman Catholicism.

1618-1648: Thirty Years' War – the most devastating war in German history.

1648: The Peace of Westphalia reduced Germany to 350 states.

1688-97: War of the Palatinate Succession. French troops destroyed most Rhine castles and towns.

1740-86: Friedrich II der Große (Frederick the Great) established Prussia as the fifth European power.

1756-63: Seven Years' War.

1801: Peace of Lunéville – Germany temporarily lost all territories west of the Rhine to France.

1806: Emperor Joseph disbanded the Holy Roman Empire of the German Nation, in part to prevent Napoleon from claiming the title.

The Unification of Germany

1815: Congress of Vienna. Prussia and Bavaria vastly expanded. Germany reduced to about 40 states.

1848: Attempts to form a democratic confederacy of German states failed.

1866: Prussia defeated Austria in a brief war to become the undisputed preeminent power in Germany.

1870-71: Franco-Prussian War. Prussia, supported by all of Germany, defeated France.

1871: 25 German states united as the German Empire with the Prussian king crowned Wilhelm I, Emperor in Germany.

1914-1918: First World War.

1918: Kaiser Wilhelm II forced to abdicate and the German Republic proclaimed.

The Weimar Republic & the Nazi Era

1919: The Weimar Republic proclaimed with an ultraliberal constitution.

1922-23: Runaway inflation.

INFLATION OUT OF CONTROL!

The Weimar Republic had to deal with drastic inflation as an immediate result of the war and the high war reparations. The price of bread increased from 1 mark in December 1919 to 3.90 marks two years later. In December 1922, a loaf of bread cost 163 marks, and a year later 399,000,000,000 marks. At one stage, workers were paid daily by the wheelbarrow load and then ran to shops before the value dropped even more.

1932: Nazi party of Adolf Hitler became the largest party in a fragmented parliament.

1933: Adolf Hitler appointed chancellor. Reichstag (parliament) burnt down – Communists and other parties banned. Trade unions banned. Undesirable books burned. Nazis became only legal party.

THE THREE REICHS

The Nazis frequently referred to their regime as the Third Reich that would last a thousand years. The Second Reich was the German Empire from 1871-1918. The First Reich was the Holy Roman Empire of the German Nation. It ended in 1806, but different interpretations are possible on its origins. Usually 962, the crowning of Otto II, is considered the start of this empire, but if the crowning of Charlemagne in 800 is used, the first Reich lasted a thousand years. In the end, the Third Reich lasted about 12 years but the damage to Germany's reputation may continue for a thousand years.

1934: Hitler became *Führer* (leader) and Chancellor of the Reich.

1935: Nürnberg laws took away Jewish citizenship rights.

1938: All-out pogrom against Jews started. Jews were stripped of property and herded into concentration camps.

1938: Annexation of Austria and Sudetenland.

1939-1945: World War II.

1945: Hitler committed suicide. Germany totally defeated, occupied, partitioned, and reduced in size.

Post-WW II Germany

1945: Germany divided into four zones of occupation and Berlin into four sectors occupied by the USA, Britain, France, and the Soviet Union.

1948-49: Berlin blockade. The Soviet Union blocked western road access to Berlin. The western allies supplied West Berlin via airlift.

1949: The three western sectors united to form the Bundesrepubik Deutschland (Federal Republic of Germany) with Konrad Adenauer as Chancellor and sleepy, provincial Bonn as temporary capital. In the East, the Soviet Union created the Deutsche Demokratische Republik (German Democratic Republic) as part of its East European sphere of influence.

1961: East Germany erected the Berlin Wall to prevent citizens fleeing to richer West Berlin.

1972: West German Chancellor Willy Brandt accepted that East Germany functioned as a separate state and concluded a treaty of friendship.

1989: East Germans increasingly fled to the west via Hungary. Peaceful street protests in East Germany. Inner German border opened on November 9.

1990: Germany reunited on October 3. Federal capital returned to Berlin.

◆ Culture

Germany has a long tradition of producing high culture, with many famous composers and writers. The huge number of small states in centuries past ensured that there were ample patrons and courts that needed musicians and other performers. Classical music and theater remain very popular in modern-day Germany and

Dürer, self-portrait

attending cultural events is very much in the preserve of the middle classes. Ticket prices are often astonishingly low.

During summer, most regions arrange a summer concert season with many open-air events. Castles, monasteries, palaces, and churches are popular venues in addition to dedicated concert halls. Regional tourist offices have details on events and often make reservations too.

Although German art, music, and literature go back to the earliest beginnings of the empire, the post-Reformation works are of most interest to most foreign travelers. The best-known German painters are Albrecht Dürer, who brought the Renaissance to Germany, and Lucas Cranach the Elder, the master painter of the Reformation. Most larger towns and all cities have art museums – often with astonishingly high-quality collections. Contemporary art is also very popular with many commercial galleries in addition to the vast number of art museums.

◆ Geography

Germany is a central European state with an area of 139,221 square miles. It is at most 528 miles long and 384 miles wide.

It has a varied geography. The highest parts are the Bavarian Alps in the south. The highest mountain peak is the Zugspitze at 9,715 ft, near Garmisch Partenkirchen. Most of Bavaria is rolling hills up to the River Danube – the only major river in Germany that drains to the south rather than northwards.

Most of Germany from the Black Forest to the Harz is covered by the *Mittelgebirge* (Middle Mountains), a series of minor massifs that are mostly lower than 1,600 ft. Despite its lack of height, it does not lack in natural beauty.

The Harz is the highest and northernmost of the Mittelgebirge. From here to the North and Baltic Sea most of Germany is a flat plain. Despite the lack of geographic features, the area is beautiful, very green, and with many minor roads often tree-lined. Berlin is in the heart of these plains.

Germany has several major rivers. The most famous is the Rhine, which forms part of the natural border with Switzerland and France. The Rhine is fairly straight-flowing, but its tributaries tend to meander wildly. The Neckar curls through Baden-Württemberg while the Main makes several wide s-curves through Franken and Hesse before its confluence with the Rhine at Mainz near Frankfurt. The Mosel is similarly a meandering stream with a valley as dramatic and full of history as the much larger Rhine.

The Elbe is a mighty, slow-flowing river. It enters Germany near Dresden where the Saxon Switzerland area has some of the wildest and most bizarre mountain landscapes in Germany. The Elbe drains most of eastern Germany before flowing into the North Sea at Cuxhaven, downstream from Hamburg. The Rivers Oder and Neisse form Germany's post-1945 border with Poland.

◆ Climate

 Germany has mostly a moderately cool, but temperate climate. The plains at the eastern parts of the country can get cold and windswept. The northern coastal regions tend to be windy year-round. The central parts can be snow-covered for long stretches in winter, but have generally mild summers. The south experiences more extremes, with the Black Forest particularly sunny and the Rhine Valley area usually warmer than surrounding areas.

Rainfall is fairly evenly divided throughout the year and ranges from an annual 20 inches in the north to around 60 inches in the center and south. Some parts of the Alps receive more than 80 inches per year.

The most pleasant months to travel are generally May and June or September and October. In some years, July and August get uncomfortably hot, especially as German buildings are generally built with winter in mind and without air conditioning.

◆ Flora & Fauna

Germany's natural vegetation can be surprisingly lush for a country with such a temperate climate. The most typical tree is the oak, which is found all over the country. Natural oak and beech forests are common in the Mittelgebirge area, with pine found mostly on the higher slopes of the Black Forest, Harz Mountains, and the Bavarian Forest, as well as the poorer soil of northern Germany. Wild berries and mushrooms are often poisonous.

Germany has a wide variety of wildlife, although the largest animals are deer and wild boar. Animals such as wolfs, lynxes, and wildcats only survive in natural parks and are rarely seen.

Birdlife is more common, especially species that live in the ample forested areas. Others, such as storks, are seen in the sparsely populated northern regions.

Decades of strict environmental regulations led to an improvement in water quality in most German rivers and lakes. In response, the number of species living in the waters has also increased in recent years with salmon again living in the Rhine.

◆ Government

Germany is a federal democracy consisting of 16 states (Länder). Parliament consists of the directly elected Bundestag (Lower House) and the Bundesrat (Upper House) that represents the Länder. The President (Bundespräsident) is elected by the Bundesversammlung (Bundestag plus representatives from the Länder) and is a largely ceremonial role. The Kanzler (Chancellor) has the real power and is elected by the Bundestag.

Around half the Bundestag is directly elected to represent specific constituencies while the rest are elected based on parties' national popularity. A party needs a minimum of 5% of the national vote to be represented in parliament. (A lesson learned from the Weimar Republic where a plethora of minor parties and independent representatives made government impossible.)

Post-1945 politics have been dominated by two major parties: the left-leaning Social Democratic Party (SPD) and the right-leaning Christian Democratic Union (CDU). Most governments ruled in coalition with the Free Democrats (FDP), a generally pro-business, liberal party. Elections in September 2005 were inconclusive and led to a grand coalition of the CDU and SPD, led by Angela Merkel (CDU), Germany's first female chancellor.

◆ The Economy

 Germany is the world's third-largest economy and the second-largest trading nation in the world. Following World War II, Germany experienced an economic boom – the Wirtschaftswunder – that saw annual growth of 8% between 1951 and 1961.

Manufacturing still contributes around a third of the economy with the so-called Mittelstand – companies, often family-run, with less than 100 employees – especially important. Around two-thirds of the economy consists of service industries. Agricultural, fisheries, and mining lobbies are vocal but actually rather unimportant.

The integration of the communist East German economy into the market-orientated West German one has progressed remarkably slowly. Even to the casual visitor, East Germany is still clearly poorer (and cheaper). National unemployment levels are just below 10%, but are above 20% in most of the former East.

◆ Top Attractions

Destinations

 Berlin is Germany's largest and most interesting city. It has something for everyone from its excellent museums to its risqué nightlife. It has high culture and a vibrant underground music scene.

Munich (Bavaria) is an interesting city with many historic venues, beer gardens, and a high quality of life. It has excellent art galleries and one of the largest technology museums in the world.

Dresden (Saxony), once known as the Florence on the Elbe, is recovering some of its original Baroque splendor. In addition to the excellent museums, and the Semper Opera House, the city is also convenient for daytrips into the beautiful Saxony Switzerland area.

Leipzig (Saxony) is an interesting city unwilling and unable to hide its communist-era buildings. It is less tourist-oriented than many others but has excellent museums and cultural offerings. The revolution against the communist regime started here and the Forum of Contemporary History is one of the most interesting museums in Germany.

The **Rhine Valley** (Rhineland-Palatinate) is a popular destination with a castle or castle ruin every mile or so in the Loreley Valley. Whether traveling the valley on boat, by road, or on foot, it is a region sure to impress with its natural beauty and cultural delights.

The **Romantic Road** (Bavaria) is Germany's most popular holiday route, passing numerous mostly small and very romantic towns and locations. Rothenburg ob der Tauber is chronically overcrowded but remains Germany's most beautiful walled medieval town.

Rothenburg ob der Tauber

The **German Alpine Route** (Bavaria) offers Germany's most beautiful natural scenery. It runs the full length of the Bavaria Alps from Lindau on the Bodensee to Berchtesgaden near

Salzburg. En route, it passes several famous sights including Mad King Ludwig's castles, the Wieskirche, and Kloster Ettal.

The **Black Forest** (Baden-Württemberg) is Germany's largest forested area with superb natural beauty and ample outdoor adventure options.

Cologne (North Rhine Westphalia), for a thousand years the largest city in Germany, has the world's largest Gothic cathedral, a dozen Romanesque churches, excellent art museums, and the most refreshing beer in the country.

Great Museums

- *Gemäldegalerie (Berlin)*
- *Pergamonmuseum (Berlin)*
- *Pinakothen art galleries (Munich)*
- *Wallraf-Richartz-Museum (Cologne)*
- *Deutsches Museum (Munich)*
- *Zwinger & Green Vault (Dresden)*
- *Forum of Contemporary History (Leipzig)*
- *Zeughaus (Berlin)*
- *German National Museum (Nürnberg)*
- *Federal Art Space (Bonn)*
- *Rheinisches Landesmuseum (Trier)*
- *Luther Museum (Lutherstadt Wittenberg)*

Great Cathedrals & Churches

- *Cologne Cathedral (Gothic)*
- *Speyer Cathedral (Romanesque)*
- *Trier Cathedral (Roman, Romanesque, Gothic, Baroque)*
- *Marienkirche in Lübeck (brick Gothic)*
- *Passau Cathedral (Gothic, High Baroque)*
- *Regensburg Cathedral (Gothic)*
- *Wieskirche (Bavarian Rococo)*
- *Frauenkirche in Dresden (Baroque)*
- *Frauenkirche in Munich (Gothic)*

Great Castles

The German term *Burg* can be translated as castle or fortress, while *Schloss* can be translated as castle or palace. In this guide, a *Schloss* that can laugh off a few cannonballs is referred to as a castle. A *Schloss* where cannonballs would ruin the porcelain and stuccos is translated as a palace.

- *Burg Eltz (Rhineland-Palatinate)*
- *Wartburg (Thuringia)*
- *Marksburg (Rhineland-Palatinate)*
- *Schloss Heidelberg (Baden-Württemberg)*
- *Festung Königstein (Saxony)*
- *Schloss Neuschwanstein (Bavaria)*
- *Schloss Sanssouci (Brandenburg)*
- *Munich Residenz (Bavaria)*

Burg Eltz

Travel Information

◆ Fast Facts

Population

Around 82 million, and 9% of the population is foreign. Two-thirds of Germans are at least notionally Christian with equal numbers Protestant (Lutheran) and Roman Catholic.

Location

Germany is in central Europe and borders Denmark and the North and Baltic Seas in the north; the Netherlands, Belgium, Luxemburg, and France in the west; Switzerland and Austria in the south; and the Czech Republic and Poland in the east.

Major Cities

Almost 90% of Germans live in cities, but cities are relatively small. The five largest are:

Berlin – 3.4 million
Hamburg – 1.7 million
Munich – 1.3 million
Cologne – 960,000
Frankfurt am Main – 660,000

Time Zone

Central European Time (Greenwich Mean Time plus one hour, or Eastern Standard Time plus six hours).

◆ Orientation

When to Go

Germany is best visited between May and October. The school holiday season in July and August should be avoided as prices increase and popular sights are crowded. One week before or after the high season can make a major difference in the number of visitors, though not much in terms of weather. But the holiday season is a good time to visit major cities where hotel prices can drop to mid-winter levels.

Winters can be bleak and grey and much of the natural beauty of the country will be hidden. Many non-winter sports regions may close down for the winter season. However, Advent is a beautiful time of year, with all towns lit up and Christmas markets a major draw.

Customs & Immigration

 US and Canadian citizens may enter Germany for up to 90 days with a valid passport.

Germany is part of the Schengen Agreement allowing travel across European borders without further customs or immigration controls. However, you may at any time inside Germany and other Schengen states be requested to produce proof of identity. (Switzerland, the Czech Republic, and Poland are not members of the Schengen Agreement and have full border controls with Germany.)

Penalties for smuggling illegal drugs are severe. If carrying prescription drugs, it is sensible to bring the prescription with and do not bring more than actually needed for the duration of the vacation.

◆ Transportation

Getting Here

 By Rail: Germany has good railway connections to neighboring countries. From France, the easiest entry is via Strasbourg, while high-speed trains from Paris currently pass through Belgium to Cologne. A direct high-speed link between Paris and Frankfurt is due for completion in 2007. High-speed rail connections are also available from Brussel, Amsterdam, Switzerland, and various parts of Austria. Connections from the Czech Republic and Poland are improving, but mostly on slower trains and night trains on these routes are best avoided. The Eurostar from London connects with other high-speed trains in Brussels.

By Bus: Bus services are available from many European cities and are often the cheapest way to travel to Germany. One of the largest operators is **Deutsche Touring**, Am Römerhof 17, 60486 Frankfurt am Main, ☎ 069-790-350, www.deutsche-touring.de, which operates jointly with **Eurolines**, www.eurolines.com. It is usually only possible to take international journeys.

Berlin Linienbus, www.berlinlinienbus.de, has many services from European cities to various destinations in Germany.

 By Air: Germany is well served by many airlines, with Frankfurt International Airport the busiest on continental Europe. Most intercontinental flights arrive in Frankfurt, while Munich Airport has the largest number of European destinations. Lufthansa has the largest number of direct and non-stop flights from the USA and Canada but many American and Canadian carriers have direct flights. Most larger cities have European and domestic connections.

A growing number of European budget airlines is taking to the sky. Always double check the airports budget airlines use – they are often less convenient and farther away than the main airport.

 On Water: A ferry service from Harwich (Britain) to Cuxhaven is available a few times per week. Several ferry services are available from Scandinavia and other Baltic Sea ports – see *Hamburg* chapter for details.

Getting Around

 By Rail: Germany has a well-developed railway network with comfortable, high-speed trains often the best way to travel between cities. Although it is no longer possible to set your watch according to a German train's arrival time, trains generally do run on time.

German trains can be classed in two categories: Fernverkehr (Long Distance) and Nahverkehr (Local). This distinction is important for discount tickets. Long Distance trains are faster, usually more luxurious, and cost more. They have the prefixes ICE (InterCity Express), IC/EC (InterCity/EuroCity) – the trains are the same but the latter crosses the German border), and D (Schnell/Fast trains).

The Nahverkehr (local trains) carry the prefixes (listed in order of speed – the further down the list the more stops!) IRE (InterRegioExpress), RE (RegionalExpress), RB (Regionalbahn), and S (S-Bahn). In some cases the U-Bahn, trams, and buses are also included in rail tickets.

Tickets can be bought on board most trains, but never on the S or U-Bahn, but no discounts are available. It is generally best to buy tickets prior to boarding from the Internet, ticket counters, or machines.

Several options are available to save on German railway tickets.

- **Internet:** *It is possible to book and print virtually all German rail tickets online at www.bahn.de. The site is also an invaluable tool for planning journeys and calculating budgets. Last-minute deals are often available on the internet.*

- **Children:** *Children under 15 years always travel for free when accompanied by at least one parent or grandparent. Children older than 6 years must be added for free to the adult's ticket at time of booking. Otherwise, children pay half the adult price. A seat can be reserved for the children as well at the normal rate of €3.*

- **Rail Passes:** *For international travelers, several rail passes are available. Passes can be a good deal, especially if one-way travel is used for which normal discounts are not available. Ticket prices are available on www.bahn.de making both time and budget planning easier.*

  If the travel involves only Germany, the best deal is the German Rail Pass. It is available for four to 10 days within any month. It can be for first and second class, with twin passes for two traveling together and youth passes for those under 25, slightly cheaper. Eurail passes in all variations are also valid in Germany. Passes are best bought outside Europe – most are available locally but at a surcharge and only from select railway stations.

- **Sparpreis:** *Sparpreis tickets are available for round-trip journeys only and must be booked at least three days in advance to obtain a discount of 25%. If a Saturday night stay is* included, the discount becomes 50%. Additionally, the exact trains for both journeys must be booked in advance. When reservations are made at the same time, the first passenger pays the normal price (with discount) and up to four additional passengers pay only half of what the first one pays. Cancellation options are limited. The discounts are available for all classes of service but the number of tickets available per train is restricted.

- **Schönes-Wochenende Ticket:** *Schönes-Wochenende (Nice Weekend) tickets cost €30 per day and are valid either on Saturday or on Sunday from midnight to 3 am the following morning. It costs €30 and allows up to five passengers unlimited travel nationwide on Nahverkehr trains in Second Class.*
- **Länder-Tickets:** *Länder-Tickets are available in the separate federal states and allow for unlimited travel on Nahverkehr trains in Second Class within the different states. They are available on weekdays from 9 am to 3 am the following day. They cost between €21 and €26 and can cover up to five people traveling together. Single tickets for individual travelers are available for some of the states and cost around €15.*

 Although trains are generally the most pleasant way to get around Germany, buses are often cheaper and a private car is more convenient.

 By Bus: Bus services run between many cities in Germany, but the operators are often small, making it hard to book seats from a distance. One of the largest operators is **Berlin Linienbus**, www. berlinlinienbus.de. Although most buses end up in Berlin, it is also possible to book shorter distances on these buses.

 By Car: Trains are often the best choice if only cities are visited, but having a car is a pleasurable way of seeing more of the country. It is usually cheapest to reserve a car from abroad. Rental cars picked up from airports and stations carry a surcharge.

Driving in Germany presents little difficulty. The road signs are generally international and drivers receive ample training. Roads are mostly in very good condition and well signposted. However, bear in mind that, although all roads are numbered, many road signs only refer to the next town without giving the road numbers.

Germany has the largest highway network after the USA. The famous Autobahnen (Highways) sometimes are without speed restriction, but often are so crowded that speeds drop to a crawl. Speed restrictions on Autobahnen are generally between 100 and 130 km/h (60-78 mph). Autobahnen have the prefix A before the number and use blue road signs.

Dual carriageways that are not official Autobahnen use yellow road signs and have a speed restriction of 120 km/h (72 mph) if not otherwise restricted. These roads usually have a prefix B (Bundes/Federal road). On other country roads that have the prefix B or L (Länder/State road), the speed restriction is 100 km/h (60 mph), but often a lower speed is imposed.

In town, the speed restriction is 50 km/h (30 mph), if not otherwise stated. The restriction applies as soon as the town is entered – yellow signs are posted with the town name – without any further announcement of the speed limit. In residential areas, the speed limit is often 30 km/h (18 mph).

When arriving in towns, follow the directions to the Historische Altstadt (historic Old Town) or Zentrum (center). It is usually best to park in parking garages on the edges of the Old Town area.

 By Air: Flying inside Germany is seldom a sensible option for tourists. It is possible to cover long distances that are not well served by the high-speed railway network, but few tourists would want to go from say Rostock to Munich in an hour. Domestic flights are generally expensive with discount flights widely advertised but very hard to actually book.

 By Boat: Most major rivers and lakes have boat trips. These are usually day excursions and relevant operators are listed at respective destinations.

Longer multiple-day trips are available, with one- to two-week cruises particularly popular on combinations of the Rhine, Main, and Danube, and on the Elbe. Two large, multiple-day riverboat cruise operators are **Viking River Cruises**, 21820 Burbank Boulevard, Woodland Hills, California 91367, ☎ 1-877-668-4546, www.vikingrivercruises.com, and **Peter Deilmann Cruises**, 1800 Diagonal Rd, Suite 170, Alexandria, VA 22314, ☎ 01-800-348-8287, www.deilmann-cruises.com.

Public Transit: Germany generally has a very good, if pricey, public transportation network and, in cities, virtually every place can easily be reached without a private car. In most cities, tickets need to be validated before boarding trains and usually once you board buses and trams. The validation stamp must be on the front of the ticket; when in doubt stamp both sides. Some cities, including Frankfurt, require single tickets to be bought shortly before boarding and do not require revalidation. Riding without a ticket results in on-the-spot fines of at least €30 and eviction from the train at the next station. Most cities have day tickets that are money-savers if the system is used more than twice.

By Taxi: Taxis usually do not roam the streets and are either found at a taxi stand or ordered by telephone. Almost any shop, restaurant, or hotel will be willing to order one. Taxis can be expensive but often make sense for groups of three or four. The fare is always per meter in city limits but a price is often agreed upon if traveling outside city limits or long distances. With very few exceptions, taxis are beige, so as to cut down on potential illegal operators. Although the percentage of operators using Mercedes Benz cars is declining, it is still common to find yourself in the back of a new Mercedes limousine.

 Emergency Numbers: *For the police dial 110; for the fire brigade and ambulance dial 112.*

◆ Embassies & Consulates

USA

American travelers in need of consular assistance should contact the **Embassy of the United States**, www.usembassy.de,

Neustädtische Kirchstr. 4-5, 10117 Berlin, ☎ 030-83-050. The Consular Section is at Clayallee 170, 14195 Berlin. For American Citizen Services routine calls, ☎ 030-832-9233; in emergencies only, ☎ 030-83-050.

The **American Consulate General** in Frankfurt, Gießener Str. 30, 60435 Frankfurt am Main, ☎ 069-75-350, also deals with most consular matters. The American consulates general in Düsseldorf, Munich, Leipzig, and Hamburg offer more limited services.

Canada

The **Canadian Embassy** is in the Internationalen Handelszentrum, Friedrichstraße 95, 10117 Berlin, ☎ 030-203-120, www.kanada.de. Canada has consulates in Düsseldorf, Hamburg, Munich, and Stuttgart, but contact the Embassy in Berlin first.

◆ Money Matters

Currency

Germany uses the euro (€), which is divided into 100 cents (c). The euro comes in €5, €10, €20, €50, €100, €200, and €500 notes and in €1 and €2 coins. Cents are available in 1, 2, 5, 10, 20, and 50 c coins.

Former German Marks (DM) and pfennigs can only be exchanged at a branch of the German Bundesbank (Federal Reserve).

Money

In Germany, the normal bank cash card is also a debit card and the preferred way of paying. Credit cards can be used in most shops, hotels, and restaurants, but some, especially in rural areas, may insist on cash. Using ATMs generally gives the best exchange rate and the lowest cost. Check with your bank before leaving whether your card and PIN are valid abroad. Some foreign banks have agreements with German banks allowing for lower service charges.

Following the introduction of the euro, exchange bureaus have declined dramatically in number, but are available at main stations and airports. Traveler's checks are seldom used in Germany and often incur hefty service fees.

Avoid the €100, €200, and €500 notes – they are often refused in smaller establishments, especially when trying to use them for small payments. The €50 note is the most frequently forged – they often enter circulation at vending machines when travelers try to change them for smaller notes. Hold on to €1 and €2 coins – although most vending machines accept notes, coins are easier.

All Germans have EC (Electronic Cash) cards. They work like a debit card but are not the same as a credit card. Establishments that accept EC cards do not necessarily accept Visa, MasterCard, or American Express.

Taxes

Value Added Tax (Mehrwertsteuer/MWST) is usually 16% (due to increase to 19% in 2007) but is always included in advertised prices. Non-European travelers can reclaim some tax when departing from the European Union for goods purchased in shops participating in the VAT refund scheme. These stores have an English brochure explaining the finer details – note that the goods must be shown at customs on departure before the tax can be reclaimed. VAT on hotels, food, and services consumed while in Europe is not refundable.

In Germany, any prices advertised must include all taxes. In some spa towns, a spa tax may be added to the hotel price, but this seldom exceeds €2 per adult per night.

A deposit may be charged separately on drinks sold in plastic bottles or cans – this is currently between 15 c and 25 c. The system is still in flux and sometimes this deposit can only be reclaimed at the shop where the bottle was purchased. However, it is increasingly possible to reclaim the deposit at any shop selling the same kind of drinks.

Tipping

Tipping is less frequent than in most Anglo-Saxon countries. In restaurants, service is generally included and rounding up to the next euro or round number is acceptable. Tipping 10%, except in upscale international places, is generous but appreciated. Give the tip directly to the server, or when no change is expected say, "Thank you" or "Danke schön" when handing over the payment. Leaving money on the table is sometimes considered rude, but not the ultimate insult as it is in some other parts of Europe.

Similarly, for taxi drivers, round up to the next euro or round number. Tip bellhops in hotels around €1 per bag. Often it will be refused in embarrassment. Don't tip anyone else.

◆ Food & Drink

 German food and drink are generally familiar to the western palate. German food generally is not particularly fattening, although it can be hearty, especially in rural areas.

Although the trend is towards a standard three-meal day, the traditional five-meal day is still popular. This involves breakfast, usually eaten at home, of bread or cereal with yoghurt, cheese, eggs, etc. A second breakfast is often enjoyed around 9 or 10 am, shortly after hitting the desk or shops and it usually involves a sweet pastry. Lunch usually takes an hour between noon and 2 pm and is often the main meal of the day. *Kaffee und Kuchen* (coffee and cake) is an almost sacred tradition and enjoyed around 3 pm. Dinner is fairly early and mostly between 6 and 8 pm.

Beer is still hugely popular in Germany and every town has its own breweries and specialties. The number of national brands is limited and those with an international presence are few. *Apfelsaftschorle*, a mixture of apple juice and soda water, is probably the most popular non-alcoholic drink served in Germany. It is low in calories and socially acceptable on any occasion. Although other soft drinks and colas are generally available, it is seldom drunk with a meal. Although all municipal water is safe to drink, and actually has higher safety requirements than bottled water, many Germans prefer to drink bottled water. Do not expect tap water to be served in restaurants. Water, beer, soft drinks, and *Schorle* usually cost about the same in restaurants, with beer often slightly cheaper. Wine, both domestic and imported, is also available by the glass in most establishments.

◆ Electricity

Electricity is 230V, 50 Hz. Two round-pin plugs are used. Some hotels may have 110V flat-pin plugs for shavers, but do not bargain on it.

◆ Media

Surprisingly little is published inside Germany in English. In major cities, English magazines and newspapers are generally available from bookstores – the main station is a good place to look.

The *International Herald Tribune* is fairly easy to obtain.

English radio and television are also rare. Many satellite and cable services carry BBC News and CNN at most. Even in top hotels, it is unlikely that non-news programs will be available in English.

◆ Medical

Germany has an excellent health care system with more doctors than the country actually requires. Medical insurance is a precondition for entering Germany – it is best to first check with your own insurance company to see if international travel is included in your policy.

Doctors and pharmacists generally speak good English. Consultation hours are short but emergency services are, of course, available 24 hours.

All medicine, even aspirin and cough syrup, can only be bought from pharmacies (*Apotheke*). Price controls were recently relaxed but in general, prices are still virtually the same everywhere. Pharmacies are very common and always identified by a large, red "A."

It is wise to bring prescription medicine, as well as the original prescription, with you, but do not carry more medicine than actually needed for the duration of a trip.

◆ Restrooms

German restrooms are invariably clean, well equipped, and often have an attendant present. Restrooms are often charged for in fast-food restaurants, shopping malls, and gas stations. *Gebührenpflichtig* means the charge is compulsory; otherwise, it is up to the discretion of the user. A minimum of 25c is usually requested but most people give more.

According to German law, any restaurant where people can sit down must have at least three restrooms – one each for staff, women, and men. (In some regions, establishments with fewer than 12 seats are exempted from this requirement.) This helps to explain the popularity of *Stehcafés* (literally "standing cafés"), where patrons can stand and eat but not sit down. They usually do not charge for the use of restrooms by patrons.

Restrooms in museums and hotels are invariably free and very clean. International symbols are usually used, but otherwise "*Herren*" means men and "*Damen*" means ladies.

◆ Shopping

Germany's famously restrictive shopping hours have been relaxed in recent years. Shops are generally allowed to open from 8 am to 8 pm, but are closed on Sunday. Only bona fide souvenir shops are allowed to open on Sundays – washing machines and vacuum cleaners adorned with "Souvenir from Berlin" stickers have thus far failed to impress any judge. Shops in railway stations and airports are not bound by the same restrictions. Shops in rural areas sometimes close for lunch and are unlikely to open on Saturday afternoon.

◆ Telephones

Cellular phones bought outside Europe generally do not function in Germany. Public phones are available, but many require a designated charge card rather than cash. Many hotels still levy enormous surcharges on telephone use, including fixed charges for otherwise toll-free numbers.

It is usually worth using an international carrier such as ATT when phoning internationally. For the best savings, buy discount telephone cards from telephone shops, usually in the station area. The line quality is sometimes not the best but the savings can be huge.

Telephone numbers are of unequal length and use an area code followed by the specific number. The telephone number of a major business is often shorter than its fax number. When dialing from abroad, use country code 49 and drop the first zero of the regional code. If not using a discount carrier, dial 00 from inside Germany to make international calls.

◆ Mail

Stamps can be bought from post offices, many hotels, and often from souvenir shops. For postcards the standard rate for German and European destinations is €0.45 and for all other destinations €1.

German addresses are typically three lines: person/company name, street name with number, ZIP code (PLZ) and town name. If the addressee's name is not on the mailbox, the mail will not be delivered. If sending mail to someone staying with friends or family, ensure that the house occupant's name is also on the envelope.

◆ Dates & Time

 In Germany, time is always written using the 24-hour clock, e.g. 8:30 is always in the morning and 20:30 is at night. In spoken German, the 12-hour clock is more common.

Dates are written as year.month.day, or day.month.year, or day.month. Therefore, 2006.08.06, 06.08.2006, and 06.08 are all August 6, 2006. The names of the months are close to English - Januar, Februar, März, April, Mai, Juni, Juli, August, September, Oktober, November, and Dezember. Days of the week are Montag, Dienstag, Mittwoch, Donnerstag, Freitag, Samstag, Sonntag. The first two letters are used in abbreviations.

◆ Costs

Accommodations

HOTEL PRICES

€	. . . . Up to €50 per night
€€	. . . . €50 to €100
€€€	. . . . . €101 to €150
€€€€	. . . . . . Over €150

The scale at left is used throughout the book. It is the charge per double room, including all taxes. The rate refers to the rate the average guest can expect on non-event nights, rather than the rack rate.

German hotels are generally lower priced than in other Western European countries. Major cities are much cheaper than, for example, Paris or London.

German hotel prices are often quoted per person rather than per room. Fortunately, the quoted price always includes all taxes, with the exception of spa taxes, which are usually charged only in small towns and rarely exceed €2 per person per night. Except for luxury hotels, breakfast is usually offered for free. That means exactly that – not taking breakfast gives no discount. In cities, parking is generally charged separately and usually around €16, but more at some top hotels.

Hotel prices are generally lowest in November and January to March, except of course in winter sports areas. In many cities, four nights for the price of three are offered during this period. Major cities also have hotel bargains in July and August when Germans tend to travel to the countryside and coast. Hotel prices in cities are often the highest in September and October, months favored for visiting cities, The weather may be fine at that time, but bad weather is less disastrous than when visiting the countryside. Hotels that cater mostly for business travelers often have spectacular discounts over weekends. Sometimes that applies to the entire city, but often different hotels in the same area have different target clienteles and price accordingly. Avoid visiting cities for tourism purposes while major conferences or shows (*Messe*) are on – prices may quadruple.

The official star rating system for hotels is largely useless for travelers and is based on things like the size of the room and number of rooms with private bathrooms. It gives little indication on the quality of the establishment or service. Major hotel reservation services such as the German-based Hotel Reservation Service (HRS), www.hrs.com, use their own ratings instead. It is worth checking directly with hotels to see if they will match the price of discount agencies. Often you may get a better room if you book directly with the hotel.

Restaurants

RESTAURANT TIPS

Service in German restaurants can sometimes be shockingly bad. Upon arrival, find your own seat. Never wait to be seated – the servers are way too busy ignoring the patrons who are already seated to pay attention to new arrivals. It is quite common to share a table with strangers at busy times – no small talk except bon appetite (*Mahlzeit*) and goodbye is required.

At the end of a meal, tell the server *Bitte zahlen!* (Pay, please). It often takes an astonishingly long time for the bill to be produced. When in a hurry, ask for the bill when the coffee arrives.

Restaurants are generally open from 11 am to late at night. It is not uncommon, especially in rural areas, for restaurants to close between 2:30 and 5 pm. In rural areas, Gaststätten are open throughout the day on Sunday to cater for hikers and other visitors on day excursions.

With the notable exception of Berlin, service in the former East German states is actually much better than in the former West German ones!

RESTAURANT PRICES	
€	Less than €10
€€	€10 to €20
€€€	€21 to €35
€€€€	Over €35

Germany has a wide range of restaurant types. At the bottom end of the scale is the **Imbiss**, where take-out snacks such as sandwiches, sausages, and Döner Kebab can be bought. One step up is the **Stehcafé** (€) – literally standing café, as high tables are provided but no chairs. These are usually linked to bakeries or delis and are a convenient place for a fast and often cheap meal or coffee.

Fast food restaurants (€) such as McDonalds and Burger King are also popular and generally look just as they do back home. Self-service restaurants are usually found in department stores.

The most popular restaurants in Germany are termed **Gaststätte** (€-€€) – a mix of restaurant, inn, and bar. They are generally informal, serving mostly local dishes and offer the best value. The daily specials advertised outside on black-boards are usually the best deals and served fastest. In rural areas, as well as along country roads and hiking trails, Gaststätten are found with great frequency.

Coffee shops (€-€€) in all shapes and sizes are popular in Germany. Coffee is usually served strong. **Formal restaurants** (€€-€€€€) are mostly found in cities and the better ones are often in hotels.

◆ Sightseeing & Events

Sightseeing and cultural events in Germany can be surprisingly cheap. Top museums seldom cost more than €5 and discount tickets are usually available to tourists who plan to see several sights in the same area. Paying €10 or more to enter is the absolute exception and more common for high-technology, multimedia shows rather than traditional museums and cultural venues.

The admission fees listed in this guide are the maximum payable. This is what healthy, solo travelers generally between 25 and 55 can expect to be charged. Discounts are usually available for children, scholars, students, the legally unemployed, disabled, senior citizens, and families – proof of status is required and the discount should be asked for when purchasing the tickets. The specific rules for Ermäßigt (reduced) prices differ from place to place.

◆ Holidays

Public Holidays

In Germany, vacation days are determined by the individual states. Most vacations are linked to the religious calendar, with the southern states generally following Catholic holidays and northern states the Protestant ones. Southern states generally have more holidays. On holidays, the opening hours for Sunday are usually followed, but that is not always the case and not for all holidays. Expect most places to be closed over Christmas and New Years and often over Easter as well. (Holidays listed without dates move annually according to the church calendar.)

- *January 1 – New Year's Day*
- *January 6 – Three Kings' Day/Epiphany (only in Baden-Württemberg, Bavaria, and Saxony-Anhalt)*
- *Good Friday*
- *Easter Monday*
- *May 1 – May Day*
- *Asuncion (Thursday)*
- *Pentecost (Monday)*
- *Corpus Christi (only in Baden-Württemberg, Bavaria, Hesse, North-Rhine-Westphalia, Rhineland-Palatinate, and Saarland)*
- *October 3 – Day of National Unity*
- *October 31 – Reformation Day (only in Brandenburg, Mecklenburg-Vorpommern, Saxony, Saxony-Anhalt, and Thuringia)*
- *November 1 – All Saints' Day (only in Baden-Württemberg, Bavaria, North-Rhine-Westphalia, Rhineland-Palatinate, and Saarland.*
- *December 25 & 26 - Christmas*

Festivals & Major Events

Germany's celebratory year starts just seconds after midnight on January 1 with an incredible amount of fireworks and runs through the year to Christmas Eve.

January and February see **Carnival**-related celebrations mostly in the Roman Catholic parts of the country, with celebrations especially jovial in the Rhineland. Festivities in the Black Forest are almost pagan. Parades are held in many towns and cities on Fasching Dienstag (Shrove Tuesday/Mardi Gras) or the preceding weekend.

In March, the strong beer season celebrates the end of **Lent** and the reopening of many beer gardens.

Religious parades during **Easter** and **Pentecost** are common in the mainly Roman Catholic areas with processions in Bavaria particularly colorful.

From May to October, an amazing number of **summer cultural festivals** are arranged throughout Germany. Open-air performances are particularly popular. Large fireworks displays are common, with the Rhine in Flames series the best known.

On the second weekend in July, Berlin is invaded by the **Love Parade**, the world's largest techno-music festival. Despite a decline in attendance in recent years, those over around 25 would be wise to avoid the capital for the weekend.

The **Museumuferfest** (Museum Bank Holiday) in Frankfurt, the last weekend of August, is one of the largest festivals in the country and combines popular entertainment with cultural events.

Wine harvest festivals are scheduled, mostly in August and September, throughout the wine-producing areas (many non-wine-producing cities happily participate too).

Munich's famous three-week **Oktoberfest** is mainly held in September and ends the first Sunday in October.

On November 11, which is **St Martin's Festival**, children parade throughout the country in honor of Germany's patron saint.

Advent, the four weeks leading up to Christmas, is one of the loveliest seasons in Germany. Christmas decorations, often remarkably tasteful, are seen in all shops, many towns, and private residences. Most towns have Christmas markets at least on weekends and many cities have markets running during the whole Advent period. Musical concerts, even classical music, are scheduled throughout the month.

Christmas is celebrated on the evening of December 24. Expect businesses, shops, and restaurants to close around noon, if they open at all that day. Rooms in large hotels of major cities often go for very little, while smaller establishments may be closed for the season or insist on reservations from Christmas through New Year's.

◆ Adventures

Germany is a country rich in historic and cultural sights. However, it also has a pristine natural environment and outdoor activities are very popular.

Hiking (*wandern*) is, after reading, the most popular activity in Germany. It is particularly popular on Sundays when half the population seems to be rambling through the woods. On a Sunday, you'll never walk alone. *Gaststätten* have especially long hours on Sunday with warm meals available at all hours. Hiking maps are available from all bookshops and tourist information offices. Public transportation often makes circular routes unnecessary. Long-distance hikes are popular, with luggage transfers possible.

Cycling is also popular, with many dedicated cycling routes and most roads open to cyclists as well. Cycling maps are available from all bookshops and tourist information offices. Bicycles can usually be rented from shops close to train stations. Cyclists have the same rights and obligations as drivers and can also be fined for ignoring traffic rules.

◆ Special Interest

Senior Citizens: Germans are generally frequent travelers and few age groups are more actively on the road than the senior citizens. Senior citizens, usually over 55, can expect all kinds of discounts when traveling in Germany. But the discount should be asked for when paying or making reservations and proof of age may be requested.

More often than not, senior citizens qualify for reduced admission fees (Ermäßigt) which can mean a saving of 30 to 50% at many sights. Some hotels and other service providers also provide discounts.

Senior citizens frequently use the railways. Young Germans tend to respect the aged and few old people ever have to haul their own luggage into a train or up to the overhead bins. It is rare having to actually ask for help.

Children: For many reasons, Germans have famously few children, but the tourism industry is not to blame. Children under 15 travel for free on German railways when accompanied by a parent of grandparent. Children and students pay reduced admission everywhere.

Most hotels allow children up to 16 years to stay free in their parents' room. Separate rooms are often available at a steep discount. Many hotels have family rooms. Most restaurants have child seats, although baby-changing tables are not always guaranteed.

Disabled: Facilities for disabled travelers range from excellent to very limited. Many historic sights are completely inaccessible to the disabled. Some towns and regions have made considerable efforts to improve accessibility, though. It is a good idea to contact the local tourist information offices and inquire about options – many have special brochures with information on the accessibility of sights, restaurants, and hotels.

◆ Information Sources

Tourist Information: Tourist information is available from the German National Tourist Board (Deutsche Zentrale für Tourismus), Beethovenstrasse 69, 60325 Frankfurt am Main, Germany, www.germany-tourism.de. In the USA, contact the German National Tourist Office, 122 East 42nd Street, New York, NY 10168-0072, ☎ 212-661-7200 or 800-651-7010, fax 212-661-7174, www.cometogermany.com.

It is also useful to contact the tourist office of the state, listed in each chapter, before narrowing it down to relevant smaller regions and towns. Not all tourist offices are prepared to mail information internationally, but most have useful websites.

Internet: Most German towns have official websites, usually as www.townname.de. A dash (-) is usually, but not always, used in town names with spaces, e.g., www.bad-homburg.de. The German characters ä, ö, ü, and ß are written as ae, oe, ue, and ss in Internet addresses.

◆ Language

English is widely understood in Germany even if many Germans are unable to express themselves in English. In most hotels and restaurants English-speaking staff can be found. In particularly popular tourist areas such as Bavaria, English is widely spoken. Guided tours are mostly in German, but ask for an English-language sheet when buying tickets, not at the start of tours.

Although English and German are sister languages, many English speakers find German grammar and pronunciation difficult. German words can be famously long, as a single concept is usually written as a single word. Nouns are always written with a capital.

German is a phonetic language and all letters are pronounced. The *Umlauten* ä, ö, and ü change the sound of the vowel, while ß is pronounced like a single "s." These letters can also be written as ae, oe, ue, and ss, but the reverse is not true. Not all instances of "ss" can be written as ß and Goethe, for example, is never written as Göthe. Also, note that alphabetically the vowels with an Umlaut should be listed as ae, oe, and ue, so for example Düsseldorf should precede Duisburg.

In this guide, the 1998 language rules are followed. For the sake of simplicity, German nouns and verbs are not declined when used in a mostly English sentence. Similarly, tautology, such as Wartburg Castle and Königssee Lake, may occur for the benefit of non-German speakers.

A Few Useful Words

Following are some words that will help in reading signs and maps.

Ausgang	Exit
Auto	Car
Bahn	Train/railway
Bahnhof –	Station
Benzin	Gas/fuel for a car
Berg	Mountain
Bitte	Please
Brücke	Bridge
Burg	Castle/fortress
Danke (schön)	Thank you
Denkmal	Memorial
Dom	Cathedral
Eingang	Entrance
Fachwerk	Half-timbered

Fähre	Ferry
Fahrrad	Bicycle
Flughafen	Airport
Fluss	River
Frei	Free
Gaststätte	Restaurant (inn)
Geschlossen	Closed
Hauptbahnhof	Main railway station
Ja (wohl)	Yes
Kein zutritt	No admission/do not enter
Kirche	Church
Kloster	Monastery
Kreuz	Cross
Markt	Market (square)
Meer	Sea/ocean
Nein	No
PKW	Car
Platz	Square
Rathaus	Town Hall
Schloss	Castle/palace
See	Lake
Straße	Street
Straßenbahn	Tram
Tankstelle	Gas station
Weg	Way/road
Zug/züge	Train/trains

Berlin

Berlin emerged from the shadows of the Cold War as an exciting destination. Half a century of division left the city with much duplication in terms of museums, galleries, entertainment, and general visitors' facilities. Although this duplication contributes to the city's current state of near-bankruptcy, it is a source of undiluted joy for visitors to the German capital.

Berlin is the most interesting and most diverse of all German cities. It is probably most famous for its division during the Cold War and seeing related sights such as the Brandenburg Gate, Checkpoint Charlie, and a few surviving pieces of the Berlin Wall are priorities for many visitors. Berlin has more than 170 museums covering all genres. After four decades of division, some collections are now again united into world-class presentations. Highlights include the superb Gemäldegalerie (Paintings Gallery) and the excellent Pergamon Museum.

The Adlon Hotel

The return of the federal government to Berlin in the 1990s, led to several grandiose building projects such as the huge, modern Chancellery and the very popular, domed Reichstag that houses the German parliament. While many modern buildings sprung up in the former no-man's land, several historic buildings are finally being restored. Most of the fabulous Museum Island is either just restored or will be over the next couple of years. The luxurious Adlon Hotel was rebuilt to resemble its pre-War appearance. Unter den Linden, Friedrichstraße, and the Gendarmenmarkt are again vying for the heart and soul of the city.

Berlin is easy to enjoy. It is not all museums, galleries, and history. It is a great city to stroll in and enjoy the monuments and monumental structures. It is a city that caters for all tastes in culture. It has three opera houses and 135 theaters. Its nightlife is recouping some of the fame of the go-go 1920s and '30s. Everything, from Mahler to underground heavy metal is available in this city. It also plays host to the annual Love Parade – the world's largest technotronic music festival.

Berlin is a large city. With around 3.4 million inhabitants, it is twice the size of Hamburg, Germany's second-largest city. Geographically, it is huge – 23 miles from north to south, and 27 miles east to west. The area of 347 sq miles is about nine times that of Paris. However, tourist Berlin is much smaller and easily manageable on foot or with public transportation.

HISTORY

- 1237 – First written reference to Berlin.
- 1411 – The Hohenzollern family awarded the Margrave of Brandenburg. Soon after erected the Stadtschloss (City Castle) in Berlin as the principle residence of the family until the forced abdication of Kaiser Wilhelm II in 1918.
- 1618-1648 – Thirty Years' War. Berlin reduced to an insignificant town of 6,000 inhabitants.
- 1701 – Brandenburg and Prussia united as the Kingdom of Prussia.
- 1740-86 – Frederick the Great (Friedrich der Große) established Prussia as the fifth European power. Fought the War of Austrian Succession and the Seven Years' War. Built Sanssouci and Neues Palais in Potsdam.
- 1800 – Berlin, with 200,000 inhabitants, became the third-largest city in Europe.

- 1871 – Berlin became the capital of a united German Empire.
- 1945 – The "eyeless city," 75% of central Berlin destroyed during World War II. Berlin, an island in Soviet-occupied East Germany, divided into four sectors of occupation.
- 1948-9 – Berlin Blockade: the Soviet Union blocked Western road access to Berlin. West Berlin supplied via air bridge.
- 1949 – West Berlin became part of West Germany; East Berlin became capital of communist East Germany.
- 1961 – East Germany erected the Berlin Wall to prevent citizens fleeing to the richer West Berlin.
- 1963 – President JF Kennedy proclaimed "Ich bin ein Berliner!"
- 1989 – On November 9, the East-West border opened and East Germans streamed into West Berlin.
- 1990 – On October 3, Germany reunited.
- 1999 – Berlin resumed its role as German capital.

BERLIN WALL - FIRST VERSION

In the early 18th century, King Friedrich Wilhelm I had a wall built around the city to prevent young male Berliners from fleeing the city to avoid military conscription. To the king's disgust, his own art-loving son tried to flee for that very purpose. The king planned to execute him but was persuaded otherwise by his court. The prince, later referred to as Frederick the Great, was jailed, while his accomplice faced the firing squad.

◆ Getting Here

 By Rail: Berlin has frequent fast rail links to all major German centers. At least hourly trains are available to Hamburg (1h30), Leipzig (1h30), Dresden (2h), Frankfurt (4h), and Munich (6 to 7 hours). Journey times are steadily shortened as more of the former

East German railways are upgraded to the high-speed network. The most dramatic changes in coming years should be on the link to Munich.

Zoologischer Garten Station, mostly referred to as "Zoo," was the main station in West Berlin and still functions in that capacity. Most intercity trains arrive here, although many also continue to the Ostbahnhof. A new Hauptbahnhof (main station) is being constructed at Lehrter, and will no doubt be open by the time you read this.

 By Road: Good Autobahnen allow for easy and fast traveling times from all parts of Germany. The AVUS part of the Autobahn to the southwest of Berlin was Germany's first stretch of Autobahn.

Often the cheapest way to reach Berlin is by bus. The **Berlin Linienbus**, www.berlinlinienbus.de, has a vast network to many parts of Germany and the rest of Europe. The Zentrale Omnibusbahnhof (ZOB), or Central Bus Station, is at the Messe exhibition grounds and convenient to S-Bahn station Witzleben as well as several bus lines.

SIGHTSEEING TOUR BY PUBLIC BUS

Of particular note are bus lines 100 and 200. These were designed with tourists in mind, offering grand views from the top of the double-decker buses. Both routes start at Zoo Station, with Route 100 running through Tiergarten via the Reichstag, past the Brandenburg Gate, down Unter den Linden, across Museum Island, past the Television Tower, and terminating soon after Alexanderplatz. Bus 200 also departs from Zoo Station but runs south of the Tiergarten via the Kulturforum and Potsdamer Platz to join Route 100 at Unter den Linden on Friederichstraße. It continues deeper into East Berlin than does Route 100. Virtually all the sights of Berlin are no more than a short walk from either route.

 By Air: Despite being the capital of a united Germany for more than a decade, there still are surprisingly few direct flights to Berlin – most intercontinental flights to Germany still go to Frankfurt. Direct flights from Berlin Tegel to the USA are available on Delta (Newark) and Continental (JFK).

Berlin has two airports, sharing the same information line, ☎ 0180-500-0186, and www.berlin-airport.de. Most flights from Western Europe arrive at **Tegel** (TXL), 4.8 miles north of the city. Bus transfers cost €2.20, with X9 taking 20 minutes to Zoo station and TXL 25 minutes to Unter den Linden. Taxis to the center cost around €20.

Most other flights, including budget airlines, fly to the less conveniently located **Schönefeld** (SXF), 11 miles southeast of the City. A free shuttle bus transfers passengers to the nearby railway station, with connections to the center taking around 40 minutes. Often more convenient is express bus SFX, which runs every 30 minutes between 6 am and 8 pm to Wittenbergplatz (near Zoo Station) and Potsdamer Platz. Schönefeld is expanding and from around 2011 will be the only airport in Berlin.

◆ Information Sources

Tourist Information: Berlin Tourist Information, ☎ 030-250-025, www.btm.de, has three major locations in Berlin: Europa Center, close to the Zoologischer Garten station, inside the Brandenburg Gate, and in the basement of the Fernsehturm at Alexanderplatz.

A BERLIN WELCOMECARD

The tourist office, S-Bahn ticket offices, and many hotels sell the WelcomeCard. It allows unlimited travel on public transportation in Berlin and Potsdam for €16 (48 hours) or €22 (72 hours). It also gives discounts on many attractions. A spectacular deal is the **Schaulust Museum Pass** – unlimited entry on three consecutive days to 70 top museums for a mere €15.

◆ Getting Around

Public Transportation: Berlin has an excellent public transportation network, combining buses, trams, underground (U-Bahn), and commuter trains

(S-Bahn) into a single ticket system. Most lines have no services between 1 and 4 am, but some do on weekends, and night buses with restricted schedules run all week.

Tickets can be bought from machines (most have English) or from the driver at stops without machines. Tickets must be validated before boarding trains or onboard buses and trams. A *Kurzstrecke* (three train or six bus stops) costs €1.20. A single ticket costs €2.20 and is valid for two hours in zone AB – transfers, interruptions and round-trip trips are allowed. It is generally worth buying a *Tageskarte* (unlimited day ticket) at €5.60 should you plan to use the system more than twice. The honor system is generally used, but buses must be boarded in the front and tickets shown after 8 pm.

By Taxi: Taxis have a fairly good reputation but can be pricey. The base rate is €2.50. When going only a short distance – up to 1.2 miles or five minutes, whichever comes first – it costs €3, but only if you tell the driver Kurzstrecke (short distance) when boarding. Taxis can be hailed, but more easily found at stands nears stations or hotels. You can also ask any shop, restaurant, or hotel to call a taxi for you. There are several companies, but **Würfel-Funk** has a toll free number, ☎ 0800-222-2255.

◆ Sightseeing

For the last 50 years or so, Berlin was without a real center, making it still relatively hard to get a grip on the layout of the city. For the sake of simplicity, the sights below are grouped into six geographic areas: the areas around Zoo Station and Tiergarten in the former West Berlin; Unter den Linden, Museum Island, and Friederichstraße in the former East Berlin; and Potsdamer Platz, mostly in no-man's land during the Cold War.

When sightseeing, bear in mind that distances in Berlin can be large. Walking is not a realistic option from Zoo to Unter den Linden, for example, but walking is the best option once you're in a specific area.

Berlin has more than 170 museums; some are mentioned under the specific geographical areas, but they're described in more detail in the special museum section that follows.

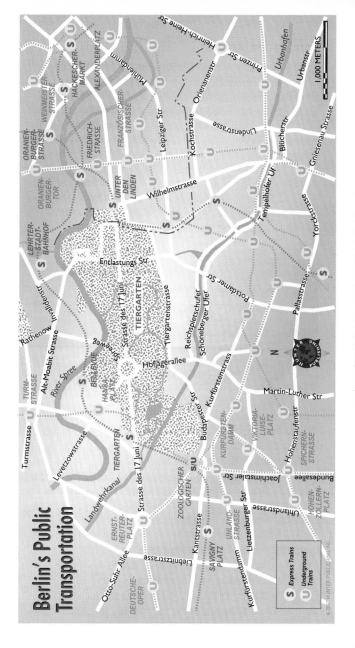

Berlin's Public Transportation

Zoo Station Area

The **Zoologischer Garten Station** area, more often simply referred to as Zoo Station, used to be the commercial heart and life of West Berlin. It is still a bustling area at all hours, but some of the glamour has faded as most investments during the 1990s were ploughed into the newly fashionable areas of East Berlin. However, in recent years, the area again experienced growth, with new hotels and upgraded shopping facilities.

Kurfürstendamm

Right in front of Zoo Station is Breitsheidplatz, a popular meeting and hangout place for people of all ages. From here, two of Berlin's busiest shopping streets spread out, the wide, tree-lined **Kurfürstendamm** to the west and **Tauentzienstraße**, with the famous Kadewe store, to the east. The Kurfürstendamm was laid out as a four-line boulevard similar to the Champs Elysées by Otto von Bismarck. Although Germany has more memorials to Bismarck than any other single figure, Berlin – typically – denied him up to the present a statue on the one street where he really wanted one!

One of the enduring symbols of West Berlin, the **Kaiser Wilhelm Gedächtniskirche** (Kaiser Wilhelm Memorial Church), **Breitscheidplatz**, ☎ 030-218-5023, www.gedaechtniskirche. com, was built at the end of the 19th century and almost completely destroyed during World War II. After the war, it was decided to leave the bombed-out tower as a reminder of war's destructiveness. A small, very modern church and tower of blue glass bricks was built next to it between 1959 and 1961. English services are held Sundays, usually at 10 am. The modern church is open daily from 9 am to 7 pm. The Memorial Hall in the bombed-out tower,

Kaiser Wilhelm Gedächtniskirche

Berlin

which has some remarkably intact mosaics depicting events in the life of the Kaiser, is open Monday to Saturday from 10 am to 4 pm. Admission is free.

Behind the Memorial Church is the 1960s **Europa Center**, the glitziest shopping center in town when the city was still split. Nowadays, it appears a bit dated, although some of the almost 100 boutiques and other small shops are still popular, especially with the younger crowd. Inside is a 43-ft water clock; the revolving Mercedes Benz star on the roof is a three ft taller.

Berlin's **Zoologischer Garten** (Zoological Gardens), Hardenberger Platz, ☎ 030-254-010, is home to more than 1,400 species, including pandas. It is large by European standards and a pleasant divergence from more serious sightseeing. The main entrance is directly opposite Zoo Station with a side entrance across the road from the Europa Center. It is open daily from 9 am until dark (latest entry 6:30 pm). Admission is €10.

Tiergarten

Tiergarten is a 714-acre park in the heart of Berlin. In the 17th century, it was a hunting ground of the Elector, but during the

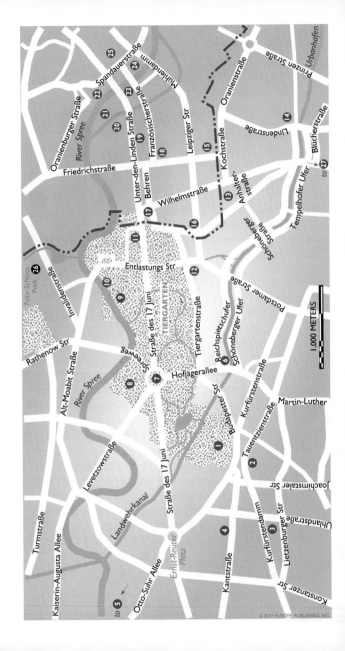

Berlin Sights

N

19th century it was converted to its present English-style park. It is a popular venue for outdoor activities of all kinds.

THE BERLIN WALL

After the war, the West Berlin border was 93 miles long, of which 64 miles was fenced off by the infamous Berlin Wall. Construction of this steel-reenforced concrete wall started on August 13, 1961, and it was maintained up to November 9, 1989. During this period, 5,075 persons succeeded in escaping over or underneath the wall; 176 died during escape attempts. The wall was between 11 and 14 feet high and had 302 guard towers.

One of the enduring images of the Cold War is the Brandenburg Gate isolated in no-man's land behind the impregnable Berlin Wall. Nowadays, only four sections of the wall remain, none near the Brandenburg Gate. The longest piece is the .8-mile stretch, now called the **East Side Gallery**, in Mühlenstraße near the Ostbahnhof. It was painted by famous artists after the *Wende*, the peaceful revolution and the unification of Germany in 1990. More accessible are the stretch at the Topographie des Terors near Checkpoint Charlie, and a very small piece at Stresemannstraße near Potsdamer Platz.

Probably the most interesting part is in **Bernauerstraße**, near Nordbahnhof. Here parts of the defenses behind the wall are also preserved. The **Berlin Wall Documentation Center**, Bernauerstraße 111, ☎ 030-464-1030, www.berliner-mauer-dokumentationszentrum.de, has interesting multimedia displays on the history of the wall. It is open Wednesday to Sunday from 10 am to 5 pm. Admission is free.

Just south of the park is the **Bauhaus Archive-Berlin**, Klingelhöferstraße 14, ☎ 030-254 00 20, www.bauhaus.de. The Berlin archives cover all stages of the Bauhaus School of Design from 1919 until its forced demise in 1933. The personal belongings and collections of drawings and books from the estates of Walter Gropius, Georg Muche, and Herbert Bayer are housed here. The museum is open Wednesday to Monday from 10 am to 5 pm. Admission is €4.

A wide boulevard cuts through the park, ending at the Brandenburg Gate. It is called **Straße des 17**. Juni (Street of 17 June) to commemorate the 1953 uprising of East German workers against the communist regime. The uprising received no backing from the Western powers and was brutally put down by Soviet forces. In the center of a large roundabout is the almost 230-ft-tall **Siegessäule** (Victory

Siegessäule

Column) at Großer Stern, ☎ 030-391-2961, with a gold-plated statue of Victory, completed in 1873 shortly after the unification of Germany. It originally stood in front of the Reichstag, but the Nazis had it moved to the middle of the Tiergarten in anticipation of victory parades to come. Open daily from 9:30 am to 6:30 pm. Admission is €2.20.

GODDESS OF PEACE OR VICTORY?

The bronze Quadriga of four horses and Irene, the goddess of peace, by Gottfried Schadow, was placed on the Brandenburg Gate in 1794. In 1806, Napoleon had the bronze dismantled and carted to Paris as war bounty. In 1814, the work returned, a staff and iron cross were added, and Irene became Nike, the goddess of victory. During the Second World War, the Quadriga was damaged. It took a rare instance of East-West cooperation to replace the Quadriga because the casts of the original were in West Berlin, while the Brandenburg Gate was in the East. The communist regime considered the iron cross a symbol of German militarism and left if out. During restoration work in 1991 the iron cross returned.

Schloss Bellevue in Spreeweg was built in the 18th century by the younger brother of Frederick the Great. It is the official residence of the president of Germany and not open to the public. The gardens may be visited when the president is not in residence.

Nearby, in John Foster Dulles Allee, is a **Glockenspiel** (Carillon) with 68 bells, one of the largest in Europe. It plays daily at noon and 6 pm. Free concerts are held Sundays at 3 pm between May and 3 October, and at 2 pm on Advent Sundays and Christmas Day.

The **Bundeskanzleramt** (Chancellery) is an enormous, modern square building on the banks of, and even crossing, the River Spree. It is a bit of an embarrassment of riches but a very impressive sight, in stark contrast to the low-key federal structures previously built in Bonn.

Built between 1884 and 1894 to house the Imperial

The Bundeskanzleramt

parliament, the **Reichstag**, Platz der Republik, ☎ 030-2273-2152, www.bundestag.de, burned down in 1933. Hitler blamed the communists and used the opportunity to ban them, as well as several others, from parliament. He thereby obtained a majority and seized power. Since 1998, the restored building, with a new larger glass dome designed by Sir Norman S Forster, housed the **Deutscher Bundestag** (German Federal Parliament). Two spiral walkways lead to the top of the glass dome, offering fine views of Berlin. A mirrored glass cone makes it possible to look into the Bundestag, the lower house of the German parliament. The hugely popular dome is open daily from 8 am to midnight, with the last admission at 10 pm. Mornings before 9 am and afternoons around 5 pm are generally less crowded. Admission is free, but expect airport-style security. Although currently still a must-see venue in Berlin, if time is limited and the lines are long, few would regret spending time elsewhere instead.

Unter den Linden

The **Brandenburger Tor** (Brandenburg Gate), Pariser Platz, is the symbol of Berlin. Built between 1788 and 1791, it was damaged, but not destroyed, during World War II. It has since been restored various times – the last restoration, to repair the damage done by the previous three restorations, was completed in 2002. It is the only remaining gate of the original 14 that provided access to the city.

The Brandenburg Gate

After years of quibbling over the site and design of the **Holocaust Memorial**, Cora-Berliner-Straße 1, ☎ 030-2639-4336, www.stiftung-denkmal.de, it has finally been completed on a site south of the Brandenburg Gate. The memorial, designed by Peter Eisenman, consists of huge concrete slabs – some as high as 15 ft – placed in close proximity to each other so walking solo will be the only way through.

 A handy brochure, "Discover Jewish Berlin," is available from the tourist office.

In 1647, the Great Elector planted six rows of lime trees along the road connecting his city palace and the Tiergarten. The road, about two-thirds of a mile, soon became known as **Unter den Linden** (Under the Lime Trees). The Nazis once cut the trees down, planning to replace them with Nazi banners, but protests were so livid even the masters of the Third Reich had to yield and replace the trees. Unter den Linden stretches from the Brandenburg Gate to Museum Island. Several cafés and restaurants of all price ranges line the street, together with embassies, fashionable shops, souvenir stalls, and luxury car showrooms.

The **Hotel Adlon** faces the Brandenburg Gate at Pariser Platz. It originally opened in 1907 as the first grand hotel of an international standard in Berlin. It became the residence of choice for visiting royalty, politicians, entertainers, and other wealthy visitors. Marlene Dietrich was discovered here. Greta Garbo desired to be left alone here. Einstein was a guest. Hitler and the Nazis generally shunned it and as a result, it became known as Little Switzerland during the Nazi era. It miraculously survived the bombings of World War II, but burned down shortly afterwards under still unexplained circumstances. Shortly after the fall of the Wall, the Kempinski Group acquired the site and successfully erected a copy of the original. It opened in 1996 and again became the best temporary address in town.

The Hotel Adlon

The new French and British **Embassies** are nearby. The new American one, supposed to be constructed between the Adlon and the Brandenburg Gate, is still in a planning phase. However, the most interesting embassy building on Unter den Linden is the Russian Embassy at Number 63-65. It is in a Neo-Classical, monumental Stalinist style and was one of the first major buildings erected in East Berlin after World War II. Nowadays the red, white and blue Russian flag is flown, but the hammer and sickle can still be seen on some detailing.

The **Deutsche Guggenheim Berlin** at Unter den Linden 13-15, 10117 Berlin-Mitte, ☎ 030-202 09 30, www.deutsche-guggenheim-berlin.de, houses alternating exhibitions from Modernism to contemporary art. It is open daily from 11 am to 8 pm (10 pm on Thursdays). Admission is €3; free on Monday.

Berlin has three major universities, four academies of arts, and 10 universities of applied sciences, but the most famous and oldest is **Humboldt University**, Unter den Linden 7. More than 20 Nobel Prize winners studied here. Famous students included Marx, Engels, Lenin, and the Grimm brothers. Einstein taught here. The original buildings were erected during the reign of Fredrick the Great. His equestrian statue in front of the main building was originally banished to Sanssouci Park in Potsdam by the communist regime.

Bebelsplatz was one of the sites where the Nazis burned books by undesirable authors. To commemorate the event a small window in the floor in the center of the square looks down on a room with empty bookshelves. Nearby, signs quote the famous words by German poet Heinrich Heine: "Where books are burned soon people will also burn." His works were also banned due to his Jewish heritage.

St Hedwigskatedrale (St Hedwig's Cathedral), Bebelsplatz, ☎ 030-203-4810, was built between 1747 and 1773 as a Roman Catholic church following Frederick the Great's annexation of Catholic Silesia. It was the only church constructed by him – he was very much in favor of freedom of religion as well as the freedom to pay for your own house of prayer. It is built in a style resembling the Pantheon in Rome. Opening hours are weekdays from 10 am to 5 pm and Sundays from 1 to 5 pm.

The **Staatsoper**, Unter den Linden 5, www.staatsoper-berlin.org, was constructed in 1742 and is considered by many the most beautiful building that Frederick the Great erected in Berlin. Early in World War II, it burned down after

Staatsoper (© bildTeam Berlin)

an air raid, but was rebuilt in a rush to restore morale and the new Oper was ready for bicentennial celebrations. It was bombed again in 1945 but rebuilt. Of the three opera houses in

Berlin, this one is the oldest and most popular. Tours are €4 – times are posted at the door.

Across the road is the **Classical Neue Wache**, Unter den Linden 4. It changed designations several times but is currently the official German memorial for the victims of war and tyranny worldwide. It has a copy of a famous sculpture by Käthe Kollwitz of a mother mourning over her dead child.

The 1695 **Zeughaus** (Armory) is the oldest building on Unter den Linden. It houses the **German Historic Museum**, which should be open by the time you read this.

Museuminsel

Museum Island was the center of Berlin during the Hohenzollern era. The area housed not only their principal residence and church, but, from the mid-19th century onwards, five large Neo-Classical museum buildings. (See *Museums* below for more on these.)

MUSEUMPASS

Admission charges for museums in Berlin are generally low. The **Schaulust Museen Berlin** card, more commonly known simply as the **Museumpass**, offers unlimited entry to 70 museums on three consecutive days for only €15. The list includes all the National Museums in Berlin and all museums listed below, unless otherwise noted. It is available from the museums, the tourist office, and some hotels.

The **Berliner Dom** (Berlin Cathedral), Am Lustgarten, ☎ 030-2026-9119, was constructed between 1894 and 1905 in a Neo-Renaissance style and is the largest 19th-century Protestant building in Germany. The vault, hardly worth seeing, contains the sarcophagi and gravestones of 100 Hohenzollerns. Short organ concerts are offered on some afternoons – schedules are posted at the entrance. The church is open from April to September, Monday to Saturday, from 9 am to 8 pm, Sundays and public holidays from noon to 8 pm. October to March, it closes at 7 pm. Admission is €5.

Across the road from the Dom was the location of the **Stadtschloss** (Town Palace), the principal residence of the Hohenzollern family since the 15th century. The palace survived World War II with remarkably little damage, but was demolished by the East German regime in 1950. Plans are currently afoot to rebuild the palace.

Across the Spree River is the gleaming copper **Palast der Republik** (Palace of the Republic). This amazing building housed the East German parliament from 1975 onwards. It was a true people's palace, with cultural forums and even a fitness center. Shortly after the *Wende* (the Change), the unification of Germany in 1990, the building was closed to clean up asbestos used during construction. It has since been decided to destroy the building. However, only when it is actually demolished will that be certain!

Nikolaikirche

The origins of Berlin are in the **Nikolaiviertel** (Nicholas Quarters). Many of the buildings here were already restored during the communist era. The **Nikolaikirche** (Nicholas Church), Poststraße 13, ☎ 030-2400-2162, dates back to 1220, although it was altered to Late Gothic in the 15th century. It is the oldest church in Berlin. It is open Tuesday to Sunday from 10 am to 6 pm. Nearby is the red-brick **Berlin Rathaus** (Town Hall).

Berlin's highest structure is the 1,207-ft **Fernsehturm** (Television Tower), Panoramastraße 1A, ☎ 030-242-3333, www.berlinfernsehturm.de. It was built using Swedish technology and opened in 1969. The rotating restaurant Telecafé at 678 ft offers the best aerial views of Berlin, with a complete turn every half-hour. It also offers a chance to experience a bit of East Germany as it was in the '70s. The observation platform is open from March to October daily, 9 am to 1 am, and November to February, 10 am to 12 pm. Admission is €7.

With the pre-war hotspots of Unter den Linden and Friedrichstraße being too close to the Wall for comfort, the government of the German Democratic Republic planned **Alexanderplatz** to become the life and soul of East Berlin. Today this huge square and the large square socialist-style buildings in the immediate vicinity are often devoid of human life and a depressing sight. Karl-Marx-Allee is lined with communist-era monumental buildings. A few blocks away are examples of the huge, low-rise apartment blocks known as *Plattenbau*, which were favored by the communist-era central planners.

Friedrichstraße

Gendarmenmarkt is one of Berlin's most beautiful public squares. It has two similar looking cathedrals dating from the early 18th century as well as the 1818 **Konzerthaus** (Concert Hall), home of the Berlin

Gendarmenmarkt

Philharmonic Orchestra. A statue of Friedrich Schiller is in front of the hall.

The **Deutscher Dom** (German Cathedral), Gendarmenmarkt 1, ☎ 030-2273-0431, was destroyed during World War II but rebuilt in the 1990s. The outside followed the original design, but the inside is thoroughly modern and used as an exhibition space by the German Parliament. The exhibition is open on Tuesdays from 10 am to 10 pm, Wednesdays to Sundays 10 am to 6 pm (7 pm in June, July and August). Admission is free.

The **French Cathedral** (Französischer Dom), ☎ 030-229-1760, www.franzoesischer-dom-berlin.de, was built for the Huguenots who had fled France and were welcomed in Prussia in the late-17th century. The tower houses a Huguenot museum and a lookout platform. The cathedral and lookout platform are open daily from 9 am to 7 pm, the museum Tuesday to Saturday from noon until 5 pm, Sunday from 11 am to 5 pm.

The presence of the Huguenots also gave rise to the lovely **Quartier** area between the square and Friedrichstraße. These three blocks house very upmarket stores, including a Galleries Lafayette and are well worth seeing even if you're not on a shopping spree.

Checkpoint Charlie gained notoriety as one of the places where the Cold War was at its hottest. Although not the only crossing point, it was the best known. The famous scene of a Russian tank speeding up, then breaking sharply to stop barely inches from the bor-

Checkpoint Charlie

derline occurred here. Today the guardhouse of the West is still in place but as a monument and background prop for tourist pictures. The large signboard, "You are leaving the American Sector," is a copy – the original is in the Museum Haus am Checkpoint Charlie. (See *Museum* section below for details.)

A good 15 minutes walk from here, but absolutely worth it, is the **Berlin Jüdisches Museum** (Jewish Museum). (See *Museum* section for details.)

Berlin

Potsdamer Platz

Potsdamer Platz was the densest traffic point in pre-war Berlin. It had the first traffic light in Germany – a copy can be seen. It was heavily bombed during the war, then was in no-man's land for four decades, and only developed again in the 1990s. It is very modern now, with the tallest buildings in Berlin.

The most impressive is the **Sony Center**, which houses not only Sony's European headquarters but also several restaurants and the impressive **Berlin Film Museum**. The magnificent roof has been described as tent and sail-like, but is actually intended to represent Mt Fuji.

Nearby is the **Kulturforum** (Cultural Forum) with several museums and concert halls. The most impressive is the **Gemäldegalerie** (Picture Gallery) and the 1960s **Philharmonie**, home of Germany's most famous symphony orchestra, the Berlin Philharmonie.

It is possible to follow the line of the former Berlin Wall from Potsdamer Platz towards Checkpoint Charlie. En route is an interesting open-air exhibition, **Topographie des Terrors** (Topography of Terror), Niederkirchnerstraße 8, 10963 Berlin, ☎ 030-2548-6703. It documents the history of the Nazis' Secret Police, the SS, and other security operations of the Third Reich. The exhibition is mainly photos and a permanent museum will eventually be built. Behind the exhibition is a large remaining part of the Berlin Wall. The site is open daily, October to April from 10 am to dusk (6 pm at the latest), rest of the year 10 am to 8 pm. Admission and English audio guides are free. (The nearby **Finanzamt** is the only Nazi-era building in Berlin that survived virtually intact.)

Museums & Galleries

Berlin has more than 170 museums and art galleries, ranging from prehistoric archeological finds to contemporary art. The most important collections are in the 16 National Museums in Berlin but some others are also well worth a visit. Split for more than half a century, the various collections of East and West Berlin are again being united into single world-class exhibitions.

National Museums in Berlin (Staatliche Museen zu Berlin – SMB)

The 16 SMB museums are located in different areas but all share the same visitors' contact information: Berlin State Museums, ☎ 030-2090-5555, www.museen-berlin.de. Opening hours are Tuesday to Sunday, from 10 am to 6 pm (minor exceptions are noted where applicable).

On Thursday, the Neue Nationalgalerie, Gemäldegalerie, Pergamonmuseum, Alte Nationalgalerie, Ägyptisches Museum, and Antikensammlung im Alten Museum are open until 10 pm with free admission after 6 pm.

The 16 SMB venues are clustered in four major geographical centers, Museum Island (€12), Kulturforum (€8), Charlottenburg (€6), and Dahlem (€6). The admission fees give access to all museums in the area for the day. Children up to 16-years old have free admission.

If time or interest is limited, give priority to the **Pergamon Museum** and the **Gemäldegalerie**.

Museum Island

The traditional location of museums in Berlin is on the northern half of Museum Island, recently declared a UNESCO World Cultural Heritage Site. Up to 70% of the buildings here were destroyed during World War II and major construction work is being undertaken to repair and refurbish the museums. All museums here are either closed or will be for reconstruction work during the next five years.

Alten Museum zum Berliner Dom, Museum Island

Berlin

MUSEUM REBUILDING

These major museums will be closed during the following periods:

Neues Museum . . . . until end 2009
Altes Museum . . . . from 2008 to 2010
Pergamonmuseum . . . . from 2008 to 2010

The oldest museum here is the appropriately named **Altes Museum** (Old Museum), Lustgarten, which has been in existence since 1830. The permanent collection consists mainly of Greek and Roman art and sculpture. The main attraction – Etruscan art – will only be on display after completion of the rebuilding.

The **Ägyptisches Museum und Papyrussammlung** (Egyptian Museum and Papyrus Collection), recently moved from Charlottenburg to the top floor of the Altes Museum. (It will move to the Neueus Museum around 2009.) It is a collection of royal ancient Egyptian art from around 3,000 BC up to the Roman Period. The works of art from the time of King Akhenaton (around 1340 BC) are internationally famous. The limestone and plaster bust of Queen Nefertiti, with its original bright, unretouched colors, is a continuous source of fascination and arguably the most famous Egyptian piece in Germany.

The **Neues Museum** (New Museum) was virtually destroyed during World War II and has been under reconstruction since 1986. Once completed, it will house the Egyptian collections as well as the Museum of Pre- and Early History, currently in Charlottenburg.

The **Alte Nationalgalerie** (Old National Galley), Bodestraße, houses a collection of 19th- and early 20th-century art. Both German and French artists from this period are well represented.

The Neo-Baroque building of the **Bode Museum**, entrance from Monbijou Bridge, should be reopened after renovations by the time you read this. It houses the Museum of Late Antiquity and Byzantine Art, the Numismatic Collection, a collection of painting and sculpture from the Middle Ages to the late-18th century, and a children's gallery.

The monolithic building of the **Pergamonmuseum**, Am Kupfergraben, opened in 1930 and currently houses several museums and collections – all included on the same admission ticket. These are the true jewels in the crown of Berlin's vast collections. Complete temples, market gates, and processional streets are rebuilt here. The **Classical Antiquities Collection** includes the Pergamon Altar with a second-century BC Hellenic frieze depicting the battle between the gods and the giants. An outstanding example of Roman art is the Market Gate of Miletus. The **Museum of Islamic Art** includes, in addition to smaller items of applied arts, large works such as the Mschatta Façade from eighth-century Jordan, the 17th-century Aleppo Room of painted wood paneling, and wall ceramics. The **Museum of Ancient Near Eastern Antiquities** includes the Ishtar Gate, a magnificent blue-tiled Processional Way, and the façade of the throne hall of King Nebuchadnezzar II (604-562 BC). Further exhibits from Sumeria, Babylonia, Assyrian, Iraq, Syria, and Turkey complete this display of 6,000 years of history. Admission to the Pergamonmuseum includes an excellent free audio guide

in English. If you have time for only one museum in Berlin, make it this one.

Berlin

Kulturforum

At the southeast corner of the Tiergarten, a mere two blocks from the ultramodern high-rise buildings of Potsdamer Platz, is the Kulturforum. This area houses, among others, the Philharmonie concert hall, the State Institute of Musicology together with the Museum of Musical Instruments, the Berlin branch of the National Library, and several national museums.

Amor Victorious (Caravaggio)

The largest and most important museum here is the superb **Gemäldegalerie** (Picture Gallery), Matthäikirchplatz, which opened in 1998 to display works from previously divided collections. It is one of the largest and most impressive collections of European paintings from the 13th to 18th centuries in the world. Around 1,500 works are on permanent display, including works by Bruegel, Dürer, Rembrandt, Vermeer, Rubens, Rafael, Titian, and Caravaggio. The main gallery has 72 rooms, divided into two main sections: Italian paintings and Dutch-German paintings. An octagonal room is at the center of the museum displaying some of the 16 works by Rembrandt. Comfortable footwear is recommended – seeing all the rooms requires a 1.3-mile walk. Thursdays open until 10 pm.

In the same building as the Gemäldegalerie are the **Kunstgewerbemuseum** (Applied Arts) and the **Kupferstichkabinett** (Museum of Prints and Drawings). The former exhibits European arts and crafts from the Middle Ages to the present, including costumes, furniture, porcelain, and gold and silversmith work. In the basement is an exhibition of 20th-century industrial products. The Kupferstichkabinett is a graphic collection with 80,000 drawings and more than half a million printed graphic sheets. The collection includes works by Dürer, Breughel, Rembrandt, and Picasso. If seen separately from other museums admission is €4 for each of these museums. On weekends, both are open only from 11 am.

The oldest building in the Kulturforum is the 1968 **Neue Nationalgalerie**, Potsdamer Straße 50. The building was designed by Mies van de Rohe of the Bauhaus school and houses Expressionists, Bauhaus, New Objectivity, and post-1945 art.

Not in the Kulturforum itself, but just a short subway ride away, is the **Hamburger Bahnhof Museum for Contemporary Art**, Invalidenstraße 50-51, near S-Bahn station Lehrter. It exhibits post-1960s works ranging from paintings, sculpture, and graphics to multimedia, room and light installations from the second half of the 20th century. Featured artists include Andy Warhol, Roy Lichtenstein, Anselm Kiefer, and representatives of minimalist art. The bookshop is impressive too. On weekends open only from 11 am and Saturday open until 10 pm. Admission is not included with the rest of the Kulturforum and is €8.

Charlottenburg

Schloss Charlottenburg

While the city was divided, the Baroque Palace Charlottenburg was a major attraction in West Berlin. However, since Die Wende, it has lost much of its appeal to the more elaborate palaces in Potsdam and some of its collections have moved to other parts of the city as well. The area still houses several major national museums, although in coming years two more are heading Museum Island's way.

Schloss Charlottenburg, Luisenplatz, ☎ 0331-969-4202, is the largest remaining Hohenzollern palace. It represents court art and culture in the Brandenburg-Prussian monarchy from the 17th to 19th centuries. The Old Palace is open Tuesday to Friday from 9 am to 5 pm, and weekends from 10 am to 5 pm. Admission is €8 and includes a compulsory guided tour. The New Wing is open Tuesday to Friday from 10 am to 6 pm and weekends from 11 am to 6 pm. Admission is €5. (A two-day pass for Charlottenburg and Potsdam palaces is available at €12.)

The **Museum für Vor- und Frühgeschichte** (Pre- and Early History), Langhans Building next to Charlottenburg Palace, houses a major collection of European and Ancient Near East artifacts from the earliest beginnings to the early Middle Ages. A highlight of the collection is works of gold, ceramics, and weaponry from the legendary city of Troy, rediscovered by Heinrich Schliemann in 1870. The display of Germanic jewelry from the migration period is also impressive. The entire museum will move to Museum Island in 2009.

The **Heinz Berggruen Collection**, Westlicher Stülerbau, Schlossstraße, consists of a collection of paintings and sculpture from the Modernist period. More than 70 pieces by Picasso form the center of the exhibition that also includes works by Klee, Cezanne, Matisse, and Van Gogh. On weekends, it is open only from 11 am.

Dahlem

The third-largest museum complex in Berlin is located somewhat off the beaten track in Dahlem, in the southwestern corner of the city. The focus here is on non-European cultures. The first three museums are housed in the same complex at Lansstraße 8 close to U-Bahnstation Dahlem Dorf.

The **Museum für Indische Kunst** (Indian Art) covers over 3,000 years of Indian art and culture with sculpture and reliefs in bronze, stone, and terracotta documenting the different religions from the subcontinent. In addition, a large collection of wall paintings and sculptures from Buddhist cave monasteries and temples along the Silk Road is on display.

In the **Museum für Ostasiatische Kunst** (East Asian Art) fine and applied arts from China, Korea, and Japan are exhibited in three individual country-specific galleries surrounding a central hall with Buddhist items common to all three cultures. The museum has an outstanding collection of calligraphy as well as Japanese woodcut prints.

With more than a half-million items, the **Museum für Völkerkunde** (Etnology) has one of the largest collections of its kind in the world. The focus is on pre-industrial cultures, mainly outside Europe. Permanent displays are augmented by frequently changing temporary exhibitions. The museum also has a large collection of sound recordings and documentary photographs taken by European explorers at the end of the 19th century.

In contrast to the other museums in Dahlem the nearby **Museum Europäischer Kulturen** (European Cultures), Im Winkel 6-8, focuses on Europe itself. The emphasis is on themes common to different cultures in Europe. Pictures play a major role in the exhibits, especially the way pictures moved away from religious and official institutions into common people's homes and everyday lives.

Other Museums

The **Zeughaus Historisches Museum** (German History), Unter den Linden 2, ☎ 030-20 30 40, www.dhm.de, houses a permanent exhibition on German history from the Middle Ages to the present. It has a collection of over 700,000 items. Excellent temporary exhibitions on a wide range of topics are housed in the annex designed by I.M. Pei. Exhibitions here are open daily from 10 am to 6 pm and

Karl der Grosse (Albrecht Dürer)

admission is generally around €2; Monday free. The permanent exhibition should be open by the time you read this.

The **Filmmuseum Berlin**, Sony Center am Potsdamer Platz, Potsdamer Straße 2, ☎ 030-300-9030, www.filmmuseum-berlin.de, explains the history of the German film industry with a strong emphasis on the early days when Berlin could still challenge Hollywood. The permanent collection includes the estate of Marlene Dietrich – several dresses as well as her travel luggage (not up to modern aviation limits!) are on display. *Das Kabinett des Dr Caligaris* is screened non-stop and some of Leni Riefenstahl's brilliant documentaries, used to great effect by the Nazi propaganda machine, are shown. Opening hours are Tuesday to Sunday from 10 am to 6 pm (Thursday until 10 pm). Admission is €6. (Museumpass not valid.)

At the famous Checkpoint Charlie is the very interesting and popular **Mauermuseum** (Wall Museum), Friedrichstr. 43-45, ☎ 030-253-7250. It focuses on the Berlin Wall and the role of Berlin in the Cold War but newer exhibitions cover non-violent struggles for human rights throughout the world. The most popular exhibits include radios, cars, and wind surfers used during escape attempts from East Germany. The original sign "You are leaving the American sector" is inside the museum – the one outside is a copy. Opening hours are very convenient: daily from 9 am to 10 pm. Admission is a rather steep €9.50 and museum passes are not valid. The museum is interesting and very popular but, given the steep admission price, you may leave wondering if they could have shown more – especially if you have visited the excellent free Forum of Contemporary History in Leipzig.

Jüdisches Museum (Jewish), Lindenstraße 9, ☎ 030-2599-3300, www.jmberlin.de, is the largest of its kind in Europe and drew over a million visitors in its second year of existence. The zinc-plated building was designed by Daniel Libeskind. This is not primarily a holocaust museum, but rather covers all aspects of Jewish history and culture in Germany. It is open daily from 10 am to 8 pm (until 10 pm on Mondays). Admission is €5 and you should expect airport-style security. A small kosher restaurant is on the premises.

◆ Cultural Events

No German city has more cultural offerings than Berlin. The half-century of division left many parallel structures and, despite the city's dire finances, no politician dares touch cultural institutions for fear of being branded a cultural philistine.

Berlin is the only city in the world with three large and widely known opera houses. Another 135 theaters offer entertainment ranging from high culture to stand-up comedy. Musicals, revues, varieté, cabaret, comedy, opera, classical music, and theater are staged all over Berlin.

The most famous high-culture venues in the former West are the **Philharmonie** and **Kammermusiksaal**, Herbert von Karajanstraße 1, ☎ 030-2548-8132 – the home of the famous Berlin Philharmonic Orchestra, and the **Deutsche Oper Berlin**, Bismarckstraße 35, ☎ 030-343-8401. In the former East, in lovely restored historic venues, are the **Konzerthaus Berlin**, Gendarmenmarkt 2, ☎ 030-20309-2101 – home of the Berlin Symphonic Orchestra, the Staatsoper, Unter den Linden 5, ☎ 030-2035-4555, and the **Komische Oper Berlin**, Behrenstraße 55, ☎ 030-4799-7400.

Tickets are often priced reasonably, but a surcharge is often required for prior bookings. The Tourist Office can make reservations, often at no fee, either in person or by phone at ☎ 030-250-025. Reservations can also be made at www.ticketonline.de.

Listings of events are available from the tourist office, and free publications can be found in most hotels, including city guides.

Berlin

BRANDENBURG SUMMER CONCERTS

In 1990, shortly after the *Wende*, a group of West Berliners, long isolated from their provincial neighbors, started to organize concerts in historic Brandenburg venues. The Brandenburg Summer Concerts are held on Sundays from June to September, usually accompanied by a sightseeing program. Bus transfers are available from Berlin to the respective venues. For reservations, contact the Kartenbüro der Brandenburgischen Sommerkonzerte, Tempelhofer Weg 39-47, 10829 Berlin, ☎ 030-7895-7940, www.brandenburgische-sommerkonzerte.de.

Since 1951, Berlin has hosted the **Berlinale**, one of Europe's largest film festivals. However, seeing a movie in Germany in English is often a challenge as virtually all movies are dubbed into German. Berlin is, fortunately, one of the few German cities where English movies can be seen fairly regularly. Listings with OmU means the movie has original sound with German subtitles and OF means original version. The best bet for English movies is CineStar in the Sony Center, Potsdamer Platz, ☎ 030-2606-6400, www.cinestar.de.

Virtually all theater and shows are in German only, but English stand up comedy is scheduled every third Tuesday of the month in **Kookaburra**, Schönhauser Allee 184, ☎ 030-4862-3186, www.comedy-club.biz.

◆ Shopping

Berlin has good shopping opportunities and the newly fashionable shops in the old East are especially popular with the well-heeled. Some of the best shops are still in the former West.

West

The **Europa Center**, Tauentzienstraße 9, ☎ 030-2649-5851, www.24ec.de, used to be the glitziest shopping center in West Berlin, but has grown a bit stale of late. It contains about 100 businesses, including many small boutiques and restaurants.

KaDeWe (Kaufhaus des Westens), Tauentzienstraße 21-24, ☎ 030-21-210, www.kadewe.de, is a large department store dating back to the early 1900s. It sells almost 400,000 items and is the largest department store in continental Europe. It has the largest food department in Europe, selling 33,000 items, including 400 kinds of bread. Around 80,000 visitors per day mean that it is always crowded.

Kurfürstendamm, www.kurfuerstendamm.de, is lined with restaurants and shops selling mainly clothes, books, and jewelry. It is the most famous shopping street in West Berlin, but **Wilmersdorfer Straße** actually has a longer tradition and is the place where Berliners themselves are more likely to shop.

Mitte

For all its fame and beauty, **Unter den Linden** itself has surprisingly few shops. The largest shop here is **Automobile Forum**, ☎ 030-2092-1200, the massive show room of the Volkswagen group, that includes not only VW, but also Skoda, Seat, Bugatti, a nd Bentley. Around the corner is **Audi Forum**, Friederichstraße 83, ☎ 030-2063-5200.

The best shops are in the side streets, especially in **Friedrichstraße**, www.friedrichstrasse.de, and the **Gendarmenmarkt** area. **Quartier 206**, Friedrichstraße 71, ☎ 030-2094-6240, is a lovely three-block shopping center. There are high-class boutiques and equally stylish marble furnishings here. It is worth seeing even if you're not shopping. It is connected through basement passages to **Galleries Lafayette**, Friedrichstraße 76, ☎ 030-209-480, which has some small bistros in the basement in addition to the more traditional department store on the upper floors.

Potsdamer Platz has many shopping opportunities, including the **Sony Style Store**, Potsdammer Straße 4, as well as **Arkaden**, ☎ 030-255-9270, a mall with more than 120 shops and restaurants.

The area around **Hackescher Markt** on the north bank of the Spree River is newly fashionable and a popular meeting place. In addition to the many restaurants and bars, the recently restored Art Nouveau **Hackescher Höfe** complex is particularly popular. The cheerful, green figure used in East Germany at

Ampelmann

traffic lights, the Ampelmännchen, has a cult following. The **Ampelmann Gallerie Shop**, Hackesche Höfe 5, Rosenthaler Straße 40, ☎ 030-4404-8809, www.ampelmann.de, sells souvenirs of all kinds adorned with this figure.

The **Nikolaiviertel**, near Museum Island, has manysmall shops selling mainly clothes and art. The area, the oldest in Berlin, has been beautifully restored and is a pleasant place to stroll in even when not on a shopping spree.

Antiques

Berlin has a surprising number of antique shops offering fair prices due to the concentration of competition in the same geographic areas. In Charlottenburg, around 30 shops are located in **Suarezstraße** (U-Bahn station Sophie-Charlotte-Platz). Many antique shops are in the side streets around **Nollendorfplatz**. In Mitte, under the covered arches of the S-Bahn railway at Friederichstraße, around 60 antique dealers take part in an **antiques market**, ☎ 030-208-2655. In contrast to most other shops, this market is open on Sunday but closed on Tuesday.

Flea Markets

Flea markets (*Trödelmarkten*) are popular in Berlin and mostly held on weekends. The **Kunst und Nostalgiemarkt** (Art and Nostalgia Market) at the Kupfergraben near the Pergamon Museum has mostly arts and crafts. The **Trödelmarkt** at Straße des 17. Juni, near Tiergarten S-Bahn stop, sells everything from art to second-hand clothes. Both markets are open weekends from 11 am to 5 pm.

If the above two markets are too mainstream try the one at **John-F-Kennedy Platz** in Schöneberg. However, the funkiest market is deeper in the old east at **Boxhagener Platz**, near U-Bahn station Frankfurter Tor. Both are open Sundays from 9 am to 4 pm.

◆ Adventures

On Foot

City Walks: Berlin Insider, ☎ 030-692-3149, www.insidertour.com, and Berlin Walks, ☎ 030-301-9194, www.berlinwalks.com, offer daily four-hour walks of Berlin's most famous sights, with native English-speaking guides. Both operate similar schedules and routes. Reservations are not required. The tours start at Zoo Station at 10 am and 2:30 pm (from November to March mornings only) at €12 per person. Insider meets in front of the McDonalds, or 20 minutes later at Hackescher Markt S-Bahn station in front of Coffee Mamas. Berlin Walks meets at the Taxi Stand at Zoo Station or 20 minutes later at the Irish Pub inside Hackescher Markt S-Bahn Station.

In addition, theme tours are offered during the summer such as tours of the Third Reich and Nazi sights, the Soviet occupation and Cold War sights, as well as Jewish Berlin.

On Wheels

By Bicycle: Fahrradstation, ☎ 0180-510-8000 or 030-2045-4500, has several rental shops scattered through Berlin. Generally, the most convenient are in the Hackeschen Höfen, ☎ 030-2838-4848, and in Bahnhof Friedrichstraße, ☎ 030-2045-4500.

Berlin Insider, ☎ 030-692-3149, www.insidertour.com, conducts four-hour cycling tours of Berlin's most famous sights. From May to September, the tour starts at 10:30 am (July and August also at 3 pm) from Friedrichstraße Station's Fahrradverleih-shop. The tour price of €20 includes the bicycle rental fee. Reservations are recommended, as the group size is restricted.

A pleasant do-it-yourself cycling tour is the 10.8-mile **Mauerradweg** (Wall Cycling Route). It follows part of the route of the former Berlin Wall from U-Bahn station Bornholmer Straße to U-Bahn station Schlesisches tour. En route are remaining pieces of the wall at the Bernauer Straße memorial, Topographie des Terrors, and the East Side Gallery, as well as famous sights such as the Brandenburg Gate and Checkpoint Charlie. The route is in the process of being signposted and a free pamphlet with the route is available from the tourism office.

Bicycles may be taken on the S- and U-Bahn as well as trams, but that requires an additional **Fahrradticket** (bicycle ticket).

Velo taxis operate on four routes: Kurfürstendamm, Tiergarten, Unter den Linden, and Potsdamer Platz. Simply flag one down, or pre-book at ☎ 0172-328-8888, www.velotaxi. com. The fare is €2.50 per kilometer.

Trabi Safari: Trabi, the nickname of the Trabant, was the most "popular" car produced in East German. Popular, not due to demand, but because it was often the only one available. The smoking, polluting, two-stroke-engine, plastic-bodied cars disappeared from the roads of East Germany as soon as people could get their hands on second-hand Golfs and Opels from the West.

However, **Trabi Safari**, ☎ 030-2759-2273, www.trabi-safari.de, has 15 Trabants available for rent on 45- and 90-minute "Trabi Safaris" through Berlin. An experienced driver shows the ropes – there is more to driving one than turning the key – and then the 15 proceed in convoy from Gendarmenmarkt through Berlin. Trips are scheduled daily from 10 am to midnight and cost from €12 per person. (You can pollute Dresden with a Trabi as well.)

On Water

Berlin is a water-rich city with several lakes, canals, and the confluence of the Rivers Spree and Havel inside the city borders. It has 120 miles of waterways and, with almost a thousand bridges, more than any other European city including Amsterdam and Venice. In addition to regular pleasure cruises and commercial traffic, most of these waters are open to private water sports activities.

Pleasure Cruises: Several companies offer sightseeing cruises on the rivers and canals of Berlin. Although different tours and routes are offered, virtually all stop at the Schlossbrücke at Museum Island and/or Haus der Kulturen der

Welt. Prices are from around €5 and up, but there is little price variation between companies for tours of equal length. Unless you have a specific itinerary in mind, simply board the first boat to depart. Most have night and dinner cruises as well.

The better-known companies include **Stern und Kreis Schiffahrt**, ☎ 030-536-3600, www.sternundkreis.de; **Reederei Bruno Winkler**, ☎ 030-349-9595, www.ReedereiWinkler.de; and **Reederei Riedel**, ☎ 030-691-3782, www.reederei-riedel.de.

Sailing & Houseboats: Houseboats can be rented in Berlin for cruises in the city, as well as the water-rich surrounding areas. Private charter boats are allowed to moor up to 24 hours at 14 public areas of Berlin for free. For all of Berlin, and for some parts of Brandenburg State, a sports boat license is required for boats stronger than 5 HP. It is best to clear with the rental agents that foreign licenses are accepted prior to reservations.

Several sailing schools are located on the lakes inside Berlin. Many rent out sailing boats as well as motorboats by the hour or day. If required, most can arrange for a skipper and crew. The organizations listed below are all located in the west of Berlin, where 12 miles of the Havel River and lakes can be sailed unhindered by bridges or sluices between Spandau and Potsdam.

Marina Lanke-Berlin, Scharfe Lanke 109-131, 13595 Berlin, ☎ 030-3620-0990, www.marina-lanke.de.

Segelschule Hering, Bielefelder Straße 15, 10709 Berlin, ☎ 030-861-0701, www.segelschule-hering.de.

Yachtcharter Martin, Nauheimer Straße 43, 14197 Berlin, ☎ 0171-544-6131, www.yachtcharter-martin.de.

In the Air

Air Service Berlin, ☎ 030-5321-5321, www.air-service-berlin.de, has several off-beat offers, including the only seaplane in Berlin, a single engine "Duck 01" that takes off from the Spree River and then circles the sights of Berlin. Flight duration is around 30 min and cost is €120. From Berlin-Schönefeld airport, 45-minute flights in a Rosinenbomber (DC3) that was used during the Berlin Airlift of 1948 cost around €130. Helicopter flights range from €50 to €120. A few small Zeppelin aircraft fly throughout Germany. When in Berlin, 45-minute flights cost around €300 and 70-minute flights €400.

Berlin High Flyer, in Ebertstraße close to Potsdamer Platz, is one of the world's largest helium balloons. Every 15 minutes, if the air is calm, it shoots 492 ft up in the air, giving fantastic views of Berlin. No reservations are taken, but ☎ 030-2266-78811 gives the wind report. In summer, the balloon is in operation from Sunday to Thursday, 10 am to 10 pm, Friday and Saturday from 10 am to 10:30 pm; in Winter from Sunday to Thursday, 11 am to 6 pm, Friday and Saturday, 11 am to 7 pm. Each ride is €20.

◆ Where to Stay

Berlin has no shortage of hotels and, with the exception of major events, hotel rooms are generally on discount

HOTEL PRICES	
€ . . . . Up to €50 per night
€€ . . . . €50 to €100
€€€ . . . . . . €101 to €150
€€€€ . . . . Over €150

throughout the year. Hotel prices are about half of what a similar room would cost in London and at least a third less than in Paris.

Mitte & East Berlin

The **Adlon Kempinski**, right next to the Brandenburg Gate, is the best temporary address in Berlin. The original Adlon miraculously survived World War II, but burned to the ground soon after. Following the reunification of Germany, the Kempinski group rebuilt the hotel in the original style. It reopened in 1996 to great acclaim. The famous, rich, and beautiful people stay and eat here. Bedrooms are spacious and very luxurious; the more expensive ones have views of the Brandenburg Gate. Camera-toting sightseers are generally not welcome. Unter den Linden 77, 10117 Berlin, ☎ 030-226-10, fax 030-2261-2222, www.hotel-adlon.de. (€€€€)

The **Grand Hyatt** is a very modern design in harmony with the ultra-modern buildings of Potsdamer Platz. Rooms are luxurious and stylish with a minimalist look. The swimming pool, on the top floor, has superb views. The hotel is popular with film stars, as befits its close location to the Berlin Film Museum. Marlene Dietrich Platz 2, 10785 Berlin, ☎ 030-2553-1234, fax 030-2553-1235, www.hyatt.com. (€€€€)

Grand Hyatt

WOMEN ONLY

Conveniently located in between the Brandenburg Gate and Potsdamer Platz is **Intermezzo**, a hotel for women and for boys under 12. Rooms are simply furnished, but prices are hard to match in this area. Gertrud-Kolmar-Straße 5, 10117 Berlin, ☎ 030-2248-9096, fax 030-2248-9097, www.hotelintermezzo.de. (€€, for singles €)

Westin Grand

The **Westin Grand** is well located in the heart of Berlin at the corner of Unter den Linden and Friedrichstraße. The high glass roof impresses, as does the pleasant ambiance. Friedrichstraße 158, 10117 Berlin, ☎ 030-20-270, fax 030-2027-3362, www.westin.com. (€€€€) The **Hilton** is next to the Gendarmenmarkt, with many rooms offering views of the square. Mohrenstraße 30, 10117 Berlin, ☎ 030-20-230, fax 030-2023-4269, www.hilton.com. (€€€-€€€€)

The **Maritim proArte** is a modern avant-garde designer hotel in the heart of central Berlin. It offers an interesting and more modern-look alternative to the number of more traditional luxury hotels in the area. Friedrichstr. 151, 10117 Berlin, ☎ 030-203 35, fax 030-2033-4209, www.maritim.de. (€€€/€€€€)

The **Mercure Hotel & Residenz am Checkpoint Charlie** combines modern architecture with a classical sandstone building. Rooms are large and well furnished; some with balconies. Checkpoint Charlie and the Mauermuseum are just two blocks away. Schutzenstr. 11, 10117 Berlin, ☎ 030-206-320, fax 030-2063-2111, www.mercure-checkpoint-charlie.de. (€€€/€€€€)

The **Arte Luise Kunsthotel**, close to the Reichstag, offers an interesting alternative to cookie-cutter chain hotels. Even in a city where designer and art hotels are in vogue, the Arte Luise is refreshingly different. Each room is designed by a

Lobby, Arte Luise Kunsthotel

different artist so the décor ranges from ultra-modern to rather kitschy. Each room style is shown on the website. Rooms on the third floor are more basic with shared toilet facilities. The hotel is next to a busy railway line, but noise is less of a problem in the new annex building. Luisenstraße 19, 10117 Berlin, ☎ 030-284-480, fax 030-2844-8448, www.kuenstlerheim-luise.de. (€€/€€€; €/€€ for more basic rooms)

CHILDREN ONLY

Need a break from the kids? **Kinderisland** can take care of children under 14, from three hours to a week. Overnight stays, from 7 pm to 9 am, cost €59 per child. A 24-hour service is available. Children can be picked up by limousine with bodyguard anywhere in Berlin. Baby-sitting can also be arranged at your hotel or residence. Sightseeing tours for children and children's parties are also available. The staff is conversant in 12 languages. The institution is supported and monitored by the Berlin authorities. Two further children's hotels are planned for Frankfurt and Munich and should be open in 2007. Eichendorfstraße 17, 10115 Berlin, ☎ 030-4171-6928, fax 030-4171-6948, www.kinderinsel.de. (€€)

Hotel Unter den Linden is the only tourist class hotel on Berlin's most famous boulevard. Despite having been renovated since the Wall came down, it still offers some of the dubious charm of a communist-era establishment. Staff has been described as indifferent and uninterested. Still, the hotel offers a brilliant location at a reasonably low price. Unter den Linden 14, 10117 Berlin, ☎ 030-238-110, fax 030-2381-1100, www.hotel-unter-den-linden.de. (€€/€€€€)

The **Intercity Hotel**, at the Ostbahnhof, offers comfortable, well-equipped rooms at reasonable prices. Am Ostbahnhof 5, 10243 Berlin, ☎ 030-293-680, fax 030-2936-8599, www.berlin.intercityhotel.de. (€€-€€€)

Nearby, the **Ibis Ostbahnhof** offers excellent value for money. The hotel is modern, with clean, functional rooms and furniture. An der Schillingbrücke 2, 10243 Berlin, ☎ 030-257-600, fax 030-2576-0333, www.accor-hotels.com. (€-€€)

West

The privately run **Grand Hotel Esplanade** is the top hotel in the former western part of Berlin. The building is a thoroughly modern design and the hotel is filled with modern art. Lützowufer 15, 10785 Berlin, ☎ 030-254-780, fax 030-254-788-222, www.esplanade.de. (€€€€)

Suite, Grand Hotel Esplanade

The **Palace Hotel** is a very luxurious spot next to the Europa Center. Rooms are individually furnished, and many have views of the adjacent zoo or Kaiser Wilhelm Gedächtniskirche.

Berlin

Corner Suite, Palace Hotel

Budapester Straße 45, 10787 Berlin, ☎ 030-250-20, fax 030-2502-1119, www.palace.de. (€€€€)

The **Swissôtel** is a high-rise, post-modern design facing Berlin's most famous shopping boulevard. While many new luxury hotels opened in the former eastern parts of Berlin, this 2001 hotel is one of very few new luxury hotels in the former West Berlin. The location is superb and the glass exterior impresses as much from the outside as the inside. Augsburger Straße 44, 10789

The Swissôtel

Berlin, ☎ 030-220-100, fax 030-220-102-222, www.swissotel.com. (€€€€)

Kempinski Hotel Bristol

The **Kempinski Hotel Bristol** is a West Berlin institution that during the Cold War hosted most famous visitors, ranging from President Kennedy to film stars. The original hotel was destroyed during the war but rebuilt in the 1950s. It was recently refurbished to the most modern standards. Kurfürstendamm 27, 10719 Berlin, ☎ 030-884-340, fax 030-883-6075, www.kempinski.com. (€€€€)

The **Inter-Continental** is a favorite with politicians and entertainers. This hotel has a quiet location next to the Berlin Zoo and close to public transportation. The east wing is more modern, but all rooms are luxuriously furnished. Budapester Straße 2, 10787 Berlin, ☎ 030-260-20, fax

Inter-Continental

030-2602-2600, www.ichotelsgroup.com. (€€€/€€€€)

Brandenburger Hof

The **Brandenburger Hof** is a very pleasant luxury hotel in a former 19th-century palace with a Classicist façade. The luxurious bedrooms have Bauhaus-look furnishings. Eislebener Straße 14, 10789 Berlin, ☎ 030-214-050, fax 030-2140-5100, www.brandenburger-hof.de. (€€€-€€€€)

Despite an anonymous exterior, the **Crowne Plaza Berlin City Center** has comfortable rooms and a friendly, competent staff. Rooms are modern and spacious with individual air conditioners, bar fridges, coffee makers, and irons. The location is close to Berlin Zoologischer Garten station, bus lines, and underground stations. Kadewe and the Kaiser Wilhelm Memorial Church are a block away. Nürnbergerstr. 65, 10787 Berlin, ☎ 030-210-070, fax 030-213-

Crowne Plaza Berlin City Center

2009, www.cp-berlin.com. (€€/€€€)

The **Best Western Hotel Boulevard** is a block from Zoologischer Garten station and has simple but comfortable rooms. The rooftop breakfast room has views of the Kaiser Wilhelm Gedächtniskirche. Kurfürstendamm 12, 10719 Berlin, ☎ 030-884-250, fax 030-8842-5450, www.hotel-boulevard.com. (€€/€€€)

In the **Hollywood Media Hotel**, the décor is very much Hollywood. Rooms are comfortably furnished. Apartments are also available. The hotel has its own

Hollywood Media Hotel

movie theater. Kurfürstendamm 202, 10789 Berlin, ☎ 030-889-100, fax 030-8891-0280, www.filmhotel.de. (€€€)

The Ku'Damm 101 is a designer hotel with sleek, modern furnishings. Rooms have large windows and the 7th floor breakfast room offers grand views over Berlin. Kurfürstendamm 101, 10719 Berlin, ☎ 030-520-0550, fax 030-520-055-555, www.kudamm101.com. (€€-€€€)

Nearby, at the far end of Kurfürstendamm, is the popular **Holiday Inn Garden Court**. The hotel is somewhat sterile, but well appointed and well regarded in this price class. Reservations well in advance are recommended. Bleibtreustr. 25, 10707 Berlin, ☎ 030-880-930, fax 030-8809-3939, www.holiday-inn.com. (€€)

Camping

There are several campgrounds in the outskirts of Berlin. However, most are inconvenient for public transportation. Facilities are generally good, but nothing exciting.

Camping Gatow is to the southwest of the city. It has 80 lots for tourists and 80 for long-term campers. It is open year-round. Kladower Damm 213-217, 14089 Berlin-Gatow, ☎ 030-365-4340, fax 030-3680-8492.

DCC Camping am Krossinsee is 18 miles southeast of Berlin. It is in a wooded area next to a lake, with 288 lots for tourists and around 200 for long-term campers. It is open year-round. Wernsdorfer Straße 38, 12527 Berlin-Schmöckwitz, ☎ 030-675-8687, fax 030-675-9150, www.dccberlin.de.

◆ Where to Eat

Berlin has around 6,000 restaurants and bars catering to all tastes and price classes. Unfortunately, with the

RESTAURANT COSTS	
€	Less than €10
€€	€10 to €20
€€€	€21 to €35
€€€€	Over €35

exception of the pricier establishments, Berlin restaurants have a well-earned reputation for indifferent and generally mediocre service. Service has improved in recent years, but it is still best to have low expectations. Reservations are advisable for dinner in the top restaurants.

 When US President John F Kennedy proclaimed "Ich bin ein Berliner" in 1963, he effectively said "I am a jelly donut." The inclusion of the article "ein" (a) changed the meaning of the noun from a citizen of Berlin to its most famous baked item.

Mitte

Unter den Linden

Unter den Linden, Berlin's grandest boulevard runs from the Brandenburg Gate to Museum Island and en route offers both top-end and basic restaurants. For a full view of the Brandenburg Gate, the Pariser Platz **Starbuck's**, across the road from the famed Adlon Hotel, is impossible to beat and will be easier on the wallet than anything else in the direct vicinity.

The **Lorenz Adlon**, Unter den Linden 77, ☎ 030-2261-1960, in the majestic Adlon Hotel, is arguably the best restaurant in Berlin. This small, elegant restaurant is on the second floor and has views of the Brandenburg Gate. The predominantly French food is served on Wedgewood porcelain accompanied by Christoffle silver. The wine list is extensive and service first-class. The restaurant is open for dinner only and closed on Sunday and Monday. (€€€€)

Lorenz Adlon

The Quarré

The **Quarré**, Unter den Linden 77, ☎ 030-2261-1555, is an elegant, luxury restaurant with a terrace on the ground floor of the Adlon Hotel. Food is international and new light German cuisine. It is more accessible than the Lorenz, but with similar views and an equally extensive wine list. (€€-€€€€)

Also on Pariser Platz, next to the French Embassy, is **Margaux**, Unter den Linden 78, ☎ 030-2265-2611, www.margaux-berlin.de. (Entrance from Wilhelmstraße.) This elegant, mod-

Margaux

ern restaurant serves French cuisine ranging from classical dishes to avant-garde. The extensive wine list beats that of the Adlon and apparently includes bottles over €10,000. (€€€€)

Café Einstein, Unter den Linden 42, ☎ 030-204-3632, is a branch of a famous similarly named Viennese-style coffee shop in West Berlin. (€-€€)

Café Einstein

Inside a building used by the German parliament is **Lindenlife**, Unter den Linden 44, ☎ 030-206-290-333, www.lindenlife.de. The cuisine is light, new German and a large variety of wine from the Rhineland Palatinate is available. It is popular with politicians and the media – a good choice for a quick, upscale lunch. (€€)

Brasserie No 12, Unter den Linden 12, ☎ 030-2061-9999, is a small brasserie serving small meals in addition to drinks at very low prices right in the heart of Berlin's most famous boulevard. Most of the food seems pre-cooked but the location is grand and the prices minimal. (€)

The best choice for food in the immediate vicinity of the Museum Island, is the **Kaiserstuben**, Am Festungsgraben 1, ☎ 030-2061-0548. The modern restaurant serves nouvelle cuisine. With only 16 seats, reservations are usually required. (€€€€),

Adjacent is the equally elegant **Die Möwe**, Am Festungsgraben 1, ☎ 030-2061-0540, www.restaurant-moewe.de. It serves nouvelle cuisine and classical dishes. Live music on Monday nights. (€€-€€€€)

A generally more affordable, but still pleasant alternative is the **Operncafé im Opernpalais**, Unter den Linden 5, ☎ 030-202-683. It is on the side of the Opera house in a former palace of the crown princess. It has one of the largest cake selections in Berlin. The terrace is popular in summer, the interior spacious and elegant at all times. The Sunday brunch (€€€) is accompanied by live jazz. (€-€€)

Farther down Karl Liebknecht Straße towards Alexanderplatz, the heart of the former East Berlin, is the Fernsehturm, the

Berlin

highest structure in Berlin. The revolving **Telecafé**, Panoramastraße 1, ☎ 030-242-3333, is located on the viewing platform of the television tower. Food is only average and is overpriced, but the continuously changing views are the best in town. (€-€€)

Zur Letzen Instanz

Zur Letzen Instanz, Waisenstraße 14-16, ☎ 030-242-5528, serves Berlin and Brandenburg specialties. It claims to be the oldest guesthouse in Berlin and therefore draws many tourists, although the chancellor also uses it occasionally to entertain foreign dignitaries with traditional food. (€€)

Gendarmenmarkt Area

Refugium, Gendarmenmarkt 5, ☎ 030-229-1661, www.refugium-bln.de, is the only restaurant on the Gendarmenmarkt itself. Although in the vaulted cellars of the French Cathedral, the cuisine is light German. The outdoor seating is particular popular. (€€-€€€)

Brasserie am Gendarmen-markt, Taubenstraße 30, ☎ 030-2045-3501, www.brasserieamgendarmenmarkt.de, is a popular brasserie across the road from the Concert Hall. Outdoor seats give an excellent view of the Gendarmenmarkt. (€€-€€€)

Brasserie am Gendarmenmarkt

The **Hilton Hotel**, Mohren-straße 30, has several dining options. **Fellini**, ☎ 030-202-30, is an elegant Italian restaurant with an extensive wine list. (€€-€€€) **Trader Vic's**, ☎ 030-2023-4605, serves Polynesian, Asian, and French cuisine. (€€-€€€)

Lutter und Wegner, Charlottenstraße 56, ☎ 030-2029-5410, www.lutter-wegner-gendarmenmarkt.de, serves excellent German and Austrian cuisine. The wine list is around a thousand labels strong. According to legend, *Sekt*, the German term for sparkling wine, was coined here. (€€€-€€€€)

The elegant French department store **Galleries Lafayette**, Französische Straße 23, ☎ 030-209-480, has several small bistros in its basement. Most serve French food but an international selection is also available. (€-€€)

In the adjacent, even more luxurious mall, the **Café and Bistro Quartier 206**, Friederichstraße 71, ☎ 030-202-9540, serves small meals in the basement as well as at a few tables on the ground floor. Meals are simple but tasty. The stylish black leather seats and elegant surroundings belie the pleasantly low prices. (€-€€)

Potsdamer Platz

Facil, Potsdamer Straße 3, ☎ 030-590-051-234, www.facil-berlin.de, on the fifth floor of the Madison Hotel, is an elegant, modern restaurant serving Mediterranean cuisine. Light floods in from the large windows and glass roof. (€€€€)

Facil

In the Grand Hyatt is the equally upmarket **VOX**, Marlene Dietrich Platz 2, ☎ 030-2553-1772. It has an open show kitchen serving international cuisine with strong Mediterranean influences. It also has a sushi bar. (€€€-€€€€)

The Sony Center has several restaurants, but always popular is the **Lindenbräu**, Bellevuestraße 3, ☎ 030-2575-1280. This beer garden serves Bavarian brew and food. (€€)

Diekman im Weinhaus Huth, Alte Potsdamer Straße 5, ☎ 030-2529-7529, is in the only pre-World War II building on Potsdamer Platz. This elegant restaurant serves French and nouvelle cuisine. (€€-€€€)

Berlin

Tony Romas, Marlene Dietrich Platz 2, ☎ 030-2529-5830, specializes in spareribs and other American steakhouse specialties. (€€-€€€)

West

Top-End Restaurants

First Floor Restaurant

The elegant, luxurious **First Floor Restaurant, Hotel Palace**, Budapester Straße 45, ☎ 030-2502-1020, serves mainly French food. Despite the somewhat uninspired name, this is one of the highest-rated restaurants in Berlin, with a wine list to match. (€€€€)

Hugos, Budapester Straße 2, ☎ 030-2602-1263, is a first-class restaurant located on the 13th floor of the Hotel Intercontinental offering splendid views of the city. The restaurant is modern and elegant, serving nouvelle cuisine with French flair. It has an excellent wine list. (€€€€)

The Grill in the Kempinski Hotel Bristol, Kurfürstendamm 27, ☎ 030-884-340, serves international cuisine with large selections of German and French food. The restaurant is luxurious, as befits the famous location. (€€€€)

The Prussian-style **Die Quadriga**, Hotel Brandenburger Hof, Eislebeener Straße 14, ☎ 030-2140-5650, is a luxurious restaurant in the Hotel Brandenburger Hof. The restaurant

Die Quadriga lounge

has Frank Lloyd Wright-designed furniture. The cuisine is mainly French. Gault Millau praised the wine list as one of the best in Germany. The restaurant is only open on weeknights. (€€€€)

Kurfürstendamm

Kurfürstendamm is lined with shops and eateries. The better restaurants are just off the main drag and often inside luxury hotels. For people-watching the cafés and outdoor restaurants on the main street itself are hard to beat.

There are several dining options in the Europa Center, though, like the center itself, several seem past their prime. **Daitokai**, Tauentzienstraße 9 -12, ☎ 030-261-8090, www.daitokai.de, is clearly one of the exceptions. It is a first-class Japanese restaurant, specializing in Teppan-yaki prepared at the table, but sushi is, of course, also available. Servers wear kimonos. (€€€-€€€€)

Also in the Europa Center, but several notches lower on the price scale is the **Mövenpick**, ☎ 030-264-7630, part of the Swiss restaurant group. It has mainly Swiss specialties but also a large selection of steaks and a good fresh salad bar. (€-€€)

Leysieffer, Kurfürstendamm 218, ☎ 30-885-7480, is a cake and chocolate shop, but it has a few tables and chairs in a small dining area across the narrow alley. In summer, it has more outdoor seating. The cakes served are excellent and a small bistro-style menu is available. (€-€€)

Although there are some Starbucks branches in Berlin, Germans generally prefer their coffee strong and similar local competition is all over the Ku-Damm. The best is **Kaffee Einstein** with branches at Kurfürstendamm 50, Savigny Platz, and inside the Peek and Cloppenburg store in Tauentzienstraße 19.

In the passage behind Kranzler is a branch of **Tony Romas**, Kurfürstendamm 22, ☎ 030-88877-3648. It has English-speaking servers and English menus available on request. It's a good alternative if you feel like a burger but Berlin's plethora of McDonalds and Burger King franchises simply won't do. (€€€)

The **Kadewe** department store, Tauentzienstraße 21-24, ☎ 030-21-210, www.kadewe.de, is a gourmet's delight. It has the largest gourmet food selection in Europe and many small, bar-style bistros serving delicacies from all over the world. The cafeteria-style restaurant on the top floor serves excellent food and other traditional, but pricier options are also available inside the shop. (€-€€€)

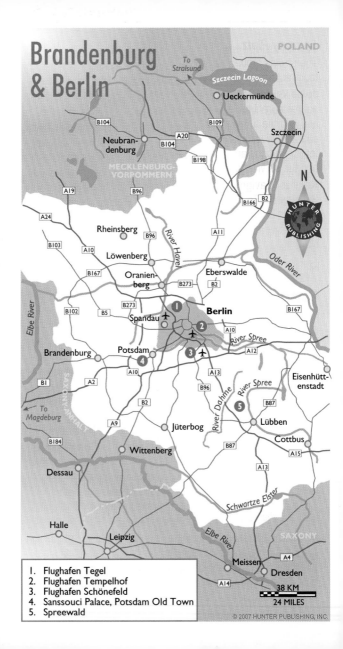

Brandenburg & Berlin

POLAND

To Stralsund

Szczecin Lagoon

Ueckermünde

B104

B109

A20

B104

Szczecin

Neubran-
denburg

B198

MECKLENBURG-
VORPOMMERN

N

A19

B96

B166

B2

HUNTER
PUBLISHING

A24

Rheinsberg

B96

River Havel

A11

Oder River

B103

Löwenberg

A10

B167

Oranien-
berg

Eberswalde

B273

B2

B102

B5

B273

Berlin

B167

Spandau

1

Elbe River

2

River Spree

Brandenburg

Potsdam

3

A10

A12

SAXONY-ANHALT

4

A10

A13

Eisenhütt-
enstadt

B1

A2

B96

River Dahme

River Spree

To
Magdeburg

B2

5

B87

A9

Jüterbog

Lübben

Cottbus

B184

Wittenberg

B87

A15

A13

Dessau

Schwartze Elster

Halle

Elbe River

SAXONY

Leipzig

Meissen

A4

38 KM

Dresden

A14

24 MILES

1. Flughafen Tegel
2. Flughafen Tempelhof
3. Flughafen Schönefeld
4. Sanssouci Palace, Potsdam Old Town
5. Spreewald

© 2007 HUNTER PUBLISHING, INC.

Savigny Platz

The streets around Savigny Platz have long been popular for their restaurants and bars.

Jules Verne, Schlüterstraße 61, ☎ 030-3180-9410, is a pleasant restaurant two blocks from Savigny Platz. The décor is limited and the furniture simple, but the food is great. The menu changes weekly and a wide range of international fare is offered. Portions are big, the food tasty, prices moderate to low, and the service friendly. (€€-€€€)

Next to Savigny Platz S-Bahn station, **Zwölf Apostel**, Bleibtreustraße 49, ☎ 030-312-1433, serves some of the best pizzas in Berlin. It is justifiably popular, making reservations for dinner recommended. Prices are low, with business lunches starting from €5. (€-€€)

◆ Daytrips from Berlin

Potsdam

Internationally, Potsdam, the state capital of Brandenburg, is best known for the Potsdam Conference, held here at the end of World War II to decide the fate of defeated Germany. However, in Germany it is better known as the Prussian Versailles. The town has been the favored royal residence of the Hohenzollern family since the 17th century and 17 of these palaces survived.

 Tip: *If visiting Potsdam on a daytrip, restrict yourself to Park Sanssouci. A full day is not enough to see all the sights here, so give preference to Schloss Sanssouci, the Orangerie, and Neues Palais. During the high season, tickets for Schloss Sanssouci sell out in minutes. Consider reserving in advance by joining the Tourist Information Office's guided tour.*

Information Sources

 Tourist Office: The tourist information office is at Alten Markt, Friedrich-Ebert-Straße 5, 14467 Potsdam, ☎ 0331-275-580, www.potsdam-tourismus.de.

Transportation

Potsdam can be reached from Berlin Zoologischer Garten station in around 15 minutes on the twice-hourly Regional Express or less frequent InterCity trains. S-Bahn S1 runs from central Berlin to Potsdam in around 40 minutes. Potsdam is part of the larger Berlin public transportation network – day tickets for Zone C are required and are valid on the S-Bahn, but *not* on the other trains.

In Potsdam, Bus 695 runs from the Hauptbahnhof to Park Sanssouci and stops behind Schloss Sanssouci, Orangerie, and Neues Palais, among other places. Bus 694 is convenient to Park Babelsberg and Bus 692 runs along the western edges of Neuer Garten. It is a fair walk from the station to the parks so using public transportation is sensible, as a lot of legwork will be required inside the parks themselves.

Sightseeing

■ Sanssouci Park & Palaces

The main sights in Potsdam are concentrated in Park Sanssouci – a huge 740-acre park originally laid out by Frederick the Great, with several palaces and other buildings of note. Most of the park and palaces are UNESCO World Cultural Heritage Sites.

VISITOR'S INFORMATION

The park itself is open during daylight hours and admission is free. Picnicking is not allowed on the lawns but there are many benches. Food and drink is not generally available inside the park – it is best to bring a picnic lunch from the station.

The individual prices at the various sights quickly add up, making one of the bewildering arrays of combination tickets worthwhile. A **Premium Day Ticket**, only available from the Sanssouci Palace ticket counter, for €15, allows access on *two* consecutive days to all the buildings in Sanssouci Park, as well as all others managed by the Prussian Palace and Gardens Foundation Berlin-Brandenburg. These include virtually all sights in Potsdam as well as Charlottenburg Palace in Berlin,

Oranienburg, and Rheinsberg Palace. A €12 **Day Ticket**, available from all ticket offices, gives the same privileges, but excludes Sanssouci Palace.

All the palaces are managed by Stiftung Preußische Schlösser und Gärten Berlin-Brandenburg, Besucherzentrum, Postfach 60 14 62, 14414 Potsdam, ☎ 0331-969-4202, www.spsg.de.   The guided tour by the Potsdam Information Office is the only English guided tour allowed in Sanssouci and the only way to guarantee entry into the palace.

Schloss Sanssouci

The most important building in the park is the small, but magnificent, Rococo summer residence erected by Frederick the Great in 1747. He called it *Schloss Sanssouci* – French, which was his preferred language, for "without a care." Here, Frederick hoped to leave the problems of state behind and pursue his own personal interests, especially in music and philosophy. Although the business of state soon followed him here, he increasingly preferred Potsdam to Berlin. He spent time here entertaining enlightened thinkers such as Voltaire and luring musicians, including Johann Sebastian Bach's son Carl Emmanuel, to his court. During Frederick's time only men stayed at court during summer and a Ladies' Wing was not added until a century later.

Schloss Sanssouci, ☎ 0331-969-4190, is open all year, Tuesday to Sunday from 9 am to 5 pm, but closing at 4 pm from November to March. Visitors are restricted to 2,000 per day and the palace can only be seen on a guided tour in German. Reservations must be made in person on the given day, then you have to wait until the appointed time to enter. Admission is €8. The Ladies Wing as well as the Palace Kitchen can be seen only on weekends from mid-May to mid-October from 10 am to 5 pm. Frankly, neither is worth the time or the €1 charge each.

Strolling through the park or visiting the nearby **Bildergalerie** (Picture Gallery), ☎ 0331-969-4181, is a better way to spend time while waiting for a tour. It was also built by Frederick the Great, as the first museum building erected for that purpose in Germany. The collection consists mainly of Baroque paintings of the Dutch, French and Italian schools. The gallery is open mid-May to mid-October from Tuesday to Sunday, 10 am to 5 pm. Admission is €2.

Orangerie

The **Orangerie** (Orangery), ☎ 0331-969-4280, same opening hours as the Picture Gallery, was built in 1851-64. It is best approached from the center of the park. This is a long walk, with numerous steep stairs, but the views are rewarding. In the park, at the edge of the palace grounds, is an equestrian statue of Frederick the Great – it is a copy of the one on Unter den Linden in Berlin. During the communist regime, Frederick and all things Prussian were initially out of fashion and the original Berlin statue was banished to this park. The palace requires another short guided tour (€3) that includes the Raphael Rooms – unfortunately, they have only copies. The tower has an observation platform with magnificent views of Potsdam and is visited without a tour (€1).

Nearby is the **Historic Windmill**, originally erected 1787-1791, but burned down in 1945. It was rebuilt in 1993 to house a museum on milling, a lookout tower, and the Sanssouci Visitors' Center.

Strolling from Schloss Sanssouci to the **Neues Palais** (New Palace), ☎ 0331-969-4255, requires around half an hour. The municipal bus running along the northern edge of the park provides a viable alternative. The Baroque Neues Palais, built 1763-1769, was Frederick the Great's most

Neues Palais

opulent palace and is considered one of the most beautiful in all of Germany. It has 400 rooms behind a façade over 700 ft long. It was built at the end of the costly Silesian War, at great expense to the Prussian taxpayers, to prove that the war had not bankrupted Prussia. (Both the war and the palace nearly did.) The palace is open all year, Saturday to Thursday, from 9 am to 5 pm, but closing at 4 pm from November to March. Admission is €5. During the summer period, the €1 German guided tour is optional and an English audio guide is available. The Royal Chambers (*Königswohnung*) of Frederick the Great can only be seen during the summer season for an additional €5 on a compulsory guided tour (in German only).

In the south of the park are three more royal sights – all three are open mid-May to mid-October, from Tuesday to Sunday, 10 am to 5 pm. Arguably the most interesting is the richly gilded **Chinesisches Haus** (Chinese Teahouse), ☎ 0331-969-4222. It was built by Frederick the Great as a summer dining room and is a good example of European *chinoiserie* during the late 18th century. Admission is €1. Although the Romans never

Chinese Tea House (© TMB/Boettcher)

made it this far, faux **Roman Baths**, ☎ 0331-969-2224, were constructed between 1829 and 1840. This complex consists of Roman baths, the residence of the court gardener, a tea pavilion, and an arcade hall with rotating exhibitions. Admission is €2 or €3 during exhibitions. **Schloss Charlottenhof**, ☎ 0331-969-4228, was built between 1826 and 1829 as a residence for Crown Prince Friedrich Wilhelm. The interiors are original and the garden is famous for its roses. Admission is €4, which includes the obligatory tour in German.

■ Other Royal Sights in Potsdam

Just north of the Old Town is the **Neues Garten** (New Garden), the first English landscape garden in Prussia, which houses the last palace constructed by the Hohenzollern family. **Schloss Cecilienhof**, ☎ 0331-969-4244, was built during World War I as the apartment of the last German Crown Prince Wilhelm and his wife Cecilie. However, the palace, in the style of an English country house, is most famous as the site of the historic Potsdam conference where Harry Truman, Winston Churchill (soon to be replaced by Clement Atlee), and Josef Stalin decided much of fate of Germany at the end of World War II. The three leaders only met here and stayed in three separate villas along the nearby Lake Griebnitz. Opening hours are Tuesday to Sunday from 9 am to 5 pm, but closing at 4 pm from November to March. Admission in summer is €4 without a guided tour and €1 additional for the German-only tour. In the winter season, admission is €4 and includes the then compulsory tour. A small luxury hotel operates in part of the palace.

Also in the park is the small square **Marmorpalais** (Marble Palace), ☎ 0331-969-4246. Friedrich Wilhelm II commissioned this summer residence in 1787, as he considered himself unworthy to stay in Frederick

Marmorpalais

the Great's Schloss Sanssouci. The richly decorated early classical interior was only completed in 1845, almost half a century after his death. A large Wedgwood collection is on display. Opening hours are similar to Schloss Cecilienhof and admission is €3 in summer with tour, €2 without a tour, and €2 in winter with free compulsory German tour.

Park Babelsberg is another large English-style landscape park with royal residences. **Schloss Babelsberg**, ☎ 0331-969-4250, was built as a summer residence for Crown Prince Wilhelm, later King of Prussia and Emperor of Germany. It was his favored residence and he used it for more than 50 years. It is built in the style of an English castle and country house. The

Schloss Babelsberg

interior is Neo-Gothic, as was favored during the mid-19th century in Germany. The palace is open from April to October, Tuesday to Sunday, 10 am to 5 pm. Admission is €2.

Also in the park is the mid-19th-century **Flatow Tower**, ☎ 0331-969-4249, based on the design of the Eschenheimer Tower, a medieval city gate in Frankfurt am Main. The 1,500-ft tower with majestic views of the park, surrounding lakes, and the Old Town can be climbed on summer weekends from 10 am to 5 pm. Admission is €2.

Cultural Events

The second half of June draws music lovers to the **Musikfestspiele Potsdam Sanssouci** (Music Festival), ☎ 0331-288-8828. Classical music concerts are staged in Frederick the Great's theater in the Neues Palais, or open-air in Sanssouci Park.

Once a year, in mid-August, the **Potsdamer Schlössernacht** (Night of the Mansions) is held. On this night, Sanssouci Park is bathed in light and the palaces illuminated. Concerts and theater are staged throughout the park and the night ends with fireworks set to music.

Bach's Brandenburg Concertos are probably the most famous music associated with this region. The **Bachtage Potsdam** (Bach Days), ☎ 0331-270-6222, www.bachtage-potsdam.de, are held annually for around two weeks in August and September. Bach is played in all forms and variations, ranging from jazz versions to concerts using original period instruments.

The **Hofkonzerte** (Court Concerts), ☎ 0331-245-609, www.potsdamer-hofkonzerte.de, are staged throughout the year in different palaces in Potsdam.

Adventures

■ On Foot

Town Walks: The tourist information office arranges a combination bus and walking tour of historic Potsdam in English and German. Tours take place Tuesday to Sunday from April to October at 11 am. The rest of the year tours are arranged from Friday to Sunday by special request only. The 3½-hour tour includes a guided tour of Schloss Sanssouci, making this the only way to guarantee entry into the palace. The tour costs €26, but includes admission fees. Reservations are highly recommended.
On Wheels

By Bicycle: Potsdam is a pleasing city to cycle in. A special cycling route named "Alter Fritz," after the nickname of Frederick the Great, leads to all the major Old Town and royal sights.

Bicycles can be rented at the main station from **Cityrad Radstation Potsdam**, Babelbergerstraße 14, ☎ 0331-620-0606.

Where to Stay & Eat

The small, luxury **Relexa Schloss-hotel Ceclilienhof** recently opened in Schloss Cecilienhof, the last pal-ace built by the Hohenzollerns, and the site of the Potsdam Con-ference in 1945. The décor and furnishings of the large comfort-able rooms follow the English

HOTEL PRICES	
€ . . . . . Up to €50 per night	
€€ . . . . €50 to €100	
€€€ . . . . . . €101 to €150	
€€€€ . . . . Over €150	

RESTAURANT PRICES	
€ . . . . Less than €10	
€€ . . . . €10 to €20	
€€€ . . . . €21 to €35	
€€€€ . . . . Over €35	

country-house style of the palace. The elegant **Schloss-restaurant** (€€-€€€€€), with a terrace, serves light regional and international dishes, including a decent vegetarian selec-tion. Neuer Garten, 14469 Potsdam, ☎ 0331-37-050, fax 0331-292-498, www.relexa-hotel.de. (€€€-€€€€€)

The **Hotel am Luisenplatz** is a 25-room privately owned and managed luxury hotel. Located in a restored city palace, the ho-tel offers modern comfort and a stylish interior. Nearby, it also manages a bed and breakfast, which of-fers excellent value for money. Apart-ments are also avail-able. Luisenplatz 5, 14471 Potsdam, ☎ 0331-971-900, fax 0331-971-9019,

Hotel am Luisenplatz

www.hotel-luisenplatz.de. (€€/€€€ for hotel; €/€€ for B&B)

One of the best restaurants in Potsdam is **Specker's Gaststätte zur Ratswaage**, Am Neuen Markt 10, ☎ 0331-280-4311, www.zur-ratswaage.de. The modern, but simply furnished restaurant has been in operation since 1763. International and classical food is served. (€€-€€€):

Built in 1736, **Der Klosterkeller,** Friedrich Ebertstraßes 94, ☎ 0331-291-218, www.klosterkeller.potsdam.de, is the oldest restaurant in Potsdam. It is in the center of the Old Town, close to the Holländer Viertel and serves mainly German food. The vaulted cellar has more than 120 seats and 300 seats in the courtyard, making the restaurant popular with large bus tour parties. (€-€€)

■ Camping

Campingpark Sanssouci-Gaisberg is to the south of Potsdam on the Templiner Lake. It has modern facilities and 240 lots. An der Pirschheide / Templiner See 41, 14471 Potsdam, ☎ 033327-55-680, www.campingpark-sanssouci-potsdam.com.

Oranienburg

Oranienburg is a small town to the north of Berlin. It was long famous as the home of the first Baroque palace in Brandenburg, but since the Nazi era, it is better known for the notorious Sachsenhausen concentration camp. Due to its proximity to Berlin, it is more often than not visited on a day-trip from the capital.

Information Sources

Tourist Office: Touristen-Information, Bernauer Straße 52, 16515 Oranienburg, ☎ 03301-704-833, www.oranienburg.de.

Transportation

Oranienburg can be reached from Berlin-Lichtenberg on Regionalbahn RB12 in around 30 minutes. The S-Bahn S1, taking 50 minutes from Berlin-Friederichstraße, is often more convenient.

Sightseeing

The main reason to visit Oranienburg is to see the **Gedenkstätte Sachsenhausen** (Sachsenhausen Memorial), Straße der Nationen 22, 16515 Oranienburg, ☎ 03301-2000, www.gedenkstaette-sachsenhausen.de. Already in 1933, the Nazis built a concentration camp in the center of Oranienburg, in an unused factory, to "house" opponents of the Nazi regime in Berlin. The town camp was soon closed and eventually replaced by Concentration Camp Sachsenhausen. This camp, with around 100 smaller branch camps, housed some 200,000 people while used by the Nazis (1936-45) and 60,000 when used later by the Soviets as an internment camp (1945-50).

From 1961 to 1992, the site was a memorial, with severely skewed

Sachsenhausen

historic explanations. The killing of, for example, Jews and Roma Gypsies was blamed on capitalist demands rather than racism and anti-Semitism. However, since 1993, serious attempts have been made to restore parts of the camp and to present a more balanced view of history. Several buildings have been restored, barracks rebuilt, and excellent exhibitions created.

The huge, triangular walled-in site is open daily from mid-March to mid-October, 8:30 am to 6 pm, closing at 4:30 pm the rest of the year. The museum and all buildings are closed on Monday. Admission is free and audio guides in English are available. The site is about 20 minutes' walk from the station – the route is well marked. Alternatively, take Bus 804 from the station in the direction of Malz (stop at Gedänkstätte).

Another sight in town is **Schloss Oranienburg** (Palace), Schlossplatz 2, ☎ 03301-537-437, the oldest Baroque palace in Brandenburg. It was built in 1651 for Louise-Henriette of Orange, the Dutch-born first wife of the Great Elector. It became

Oranienburg

the favored residence of Elector Frederick III (later Frederick I, King of Prussia). Open to the public are the reception rooms as well as private apartments of the king and other nobles. Most of the decorations are in the style of the late 16th century and show life in the Prussian court around 1700. Quality art is on display, including paintings and sculpture. Opening hours are April to October, Tuesday to Sunday from 10 am to 6 pm; November to March on weekends only, 10 am to 5 pm. Admission is €4. In summer, the guided tour (€1) is optional; in winter the tour is compulsory, but free.

Adventures

■ Walking Tours

Berlin Walks, ☎ 030-301-9194, www.berlinwalks. com, conducts guided walking tours of the Sachsenhausen Concentration Camp. The six-hour tours depart from Berlin Zoologischer Garten Station, meeting at the Taxi Stand, on Tuesday and Saturday at 10:15 am. From May to September, additional tours are offered on Thursday and Sunday. The tour costs €15 plus around €5 for the train ticket.

Saxony

Saxony is one of the smaller German federal states but one with a complex history and many historic and natural sights of interest to the foreign visitor. The main drawing cards

are the great cities of Dresden and Leipzig. Dresden is famous for its Baroque architecture, making for one of the most beautiful city panoramas in Europe. Leipzig is architecturally less harmonious but an interesting city to visit. Both cities have a number of outstanding museums and galleries. The Sächsiche Schweiz (Saxon Switzerland) area near Dresden has some of the most interesting landscapes in Germany.

During the communist regime, some areas of Saxony, especially around Dresden, had trouble receiving Western radio and television. As a result, the area was known as the "valley of the clueless." However, in 1989 it was in Leipzig and not Berlin that the opposition against the communist regime began, leading to the peaceful revolution and the unification of Germany in 1990. This process is often referred to as *Die Wende* (the change).

◆ Getting Here & Around

By Rail: Dresden and Leipzig are connected in an hour by fast hourly Intercity Express (ICE) trains as well as by cheaper but slower alternatives.

Leipzig has excellent rail connections to the rest of Germany. Hourly InterCity Express (ICE) trains are available to Frankfurt am Main (just over three hours) via Weimar, Erfurt, Eisenach, and Fulda. ICE trains from Munich via Nuremberg to Leipzig take five hours and continue to Berlin (90 minutes) via Lutherstadt Wittenberg (30 minutes). ICE trains to Hamburg take around four hours.

From **Dresden**, Intercity trains to Berlin, via Berlin-Schönefeld Airport, take two hours. The same trains also connect Dresden with Prague in just over two hours. Vienna can be reached

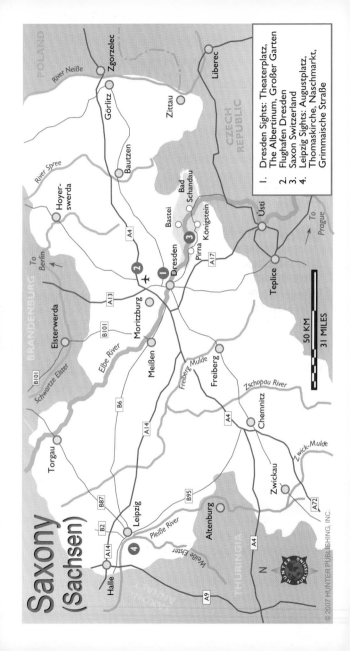

Saxony (Sachsen)

Dresden Sights: Theaterplatz,
The Albertinum, Großer Garten
1. Flughafen Dresden
2. Saxon Switzerland
3. Leipzig Sights: Augustplatz,
4. Thomaskirche, Naschmarkt,
Grimmaische Straße

50 KM

31 MILES

© 2007 HUNTER PUBLISHING, INC.

twice daily in seven hours. Most other trains to Dresden pass through, or require a change, in Leipzig.

 By Road: Saxony has a well-developed road network with Leipzig and Dresden connected by a fast Autobahn. Leipzig is on the A9, which connects Berlin and Munich, and Dresden can be reached from Berlin on the A13.

A highway is under construction between Dresden and Prague (Czech Republic) with traveling times decreasing as new sections are opened. The distance is around 90 miles.

 By Air: Both Dresden and Leipzig have excellent airports but both have only a limited number of mainly domestic flights and destinations.

Dresden Airport, Flughafenstraße, ☎ 0351-881-3360, www.dresden-airport.de, is easily reached from the city center. By train, the S-Bahn (S2) runs twice per hour, taking 22 minutes from the Hauptbahnhof. Some trains require a change at Neustadt, from where it takes less than 15 minutes. The fare is €1.50. The airport is also easily reached by car and located at the junction of highways A4 and A13. Taxis cost about €15 for the 20-minute ride.

Leipzig-Halle Airport, ☎ 0341-224-1155, www.leipzig-halle-airport.de, is halfway between Leipzig and Halle. From downtown Leipzig it is easiest to reach on the Flughafen Express, a train that runs half-hourly during peak times. It takes only 14 minutes and costs €3.20 one-way. By car, it is about 30 minutes from downtown Leipzig along the A14. Taxi fares are around €30.

 On Water: The Elbe River flows through Saxony, making arrival by boat in Dresden and Meißen possible. Cruises ranging from a few hours to several days are popular along the Elbe from Prague in the Czech Republic to Hamburg and Cuxhaven where the Elbe enters the North Sea. See the *Adventures* section for details.

◆ Information Sources

Responsible for the whole of Saxony is the Tourismus Marketing Gesellschaft Sachsen, Bautzner Straße 45-47, 01099 Dresden, ☎ 0351-491-700, www.sachsen-tourismus.de.

Dresden

Although Dresden has an 800-year history, its finest moments came during the four-decade rule of Elector Augustus the Strong (1694-1733). He was rather vain and autocratic but backed it up with good taste and built most of the Baroque structures that would transform Dresden from a provincial backwater to one of the most beautiful cities in Europe. His alchemist, Böttger, failed to produce gold but managed to produce the first porcelain in Europe, giving Augustus and his successors the funds to amass a wealth of art, which still forms the basis of Dresden's impressive State Art Collection. Dresden became known as Florence on the Elbe (Elbflorenz) and an essential stop on any European tour.

On the night of February 13, 1945, Allied air raids destroyed most of Dresden's Baroque core, killing at least 35,000 people in the process. (Dresden was crowded with refugees fleeing the advancing Russian army leading to credible claims that the exact number could have been significantly higher.) The destruction of this Baroque city, which was a purely civilian target, left a very bitter taste up to the present.

Some restoration work was done under the communist regime, notably the rebuilding of the Semper Opera, but the real restoration work only started in earnest after *Die Wende*. This allows Dresden to claim the unveiling of a "new" historic building almost every year.

◆ Information Sources

Tourist Office: Tourist information is available from Dresden-Werbung und Tourismus, Ostra-Allee, 01067 Dresden, ☎ 0351-491-920, www.dresden-tourist.de. It also has an office in the Schinkelwache in front of the Semperoper.

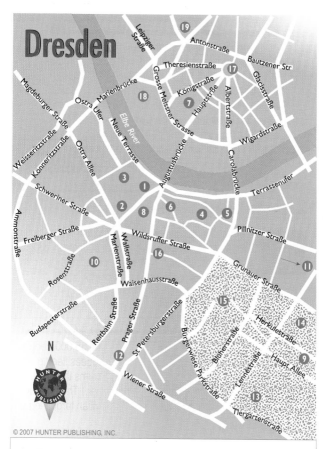

Dresden

© 2007 HUNTER PUBLISHING, INC.

1. Theaterplatz
2. Zwinger
3. Semperoper
4. Frauenkirche
5. Albertinum
6. Brühlsche Terrasse
7. Neustadt: Dreikönigskirche, Markthalle, Museum für Volkskunst, Goldener Reiter (statue of Augustus the Strong)
8. Residenzschloss (Royal Palace), Johanneum, Hofkirke, Fürstenzug
9. Großer Garten: Palais, Park Theater, puppet theater, boathouse, playground
10. Altstadt
11. Schloss Pillnitz
12. Wienerplatz, Hauptbahnhof, Filmtheater
13. Zoologischer Garten
14. Gläserne VW Manufaktur (Transparent VW Factory)
15. Blüher Park, Hygiene Museum
16. Altmarkt
17. Albertplatz
18. Japanese Palace
19. Neustadt Station

500 METERS

MONEY SAVING TIPS FOR DRESDEN

All the major museums forming part of the State Art Collection can be seen for €10 per day or €20 for the whole year. If staying two days, the **Dresden City Card** offers virtually all the museums as well as local public transportation for €19. For three days, the **Dresden Region Card** is the best option at €29: it includes all the benefits of the City Card, but also commuter transport in the whole region. This includes the S-Bahn to Meißen, Sächsische Schweiz, and Moritzburg.

◆ Transportation

Central Dresden is best explored on foot. The historic Old Town is compact with mostly pedestrian zones. Public transportation is primarily of value to get from outlying areas to the edge of the historic core.

Dresden has a well-developed public transportation network using trains (S-Bahn), trams (Strassenbahn), and buses. The S-Bahn Line 1 is particularly convenient for tourists and runs from Meißen via Dresden to Sächsiche Schweiz.

Tickets allow for transfers between bus and tram and for central Dresden cost €1.60 for up to an hour's travel. A day ticket is €4 or €13 for seven days. Tickets are bought from vending machines prior to boarding and must be validated on board.

◆ Sightseeing

Most of Dresden's tourist sights are concentrated in a small area on the outer bank of a wide curve in the River Elbe. The best view is afforded by crossing the Elbe on the Augustus Bridge from Neustadt. (It is worth repeating the crossing at various times of the day as well as at night to appreciate the different lighting conditions.)

Theaterplatz (Theater Square)

A good place to start a tour of Dresden is at Theater Square. The Neo-Renaissance **Semperoper** (Semper Opera House), Theaterplatz 2, ☎ 0351-491-1496, www.semperoper.de, is one of the best-known and most loved buildings in Dresden. It was completed in 1878 to replace a burned-down predecessor, also designed by Gottfried Semper, only to be destroyed in the

Semperoper

air raids of 1945. The Semper was rebuilt between 1977 and 1985 largely according to the original plans. The Semper is a masterpiece of 19th-century architecture, with acoustics said to exceed those of the famed Scala in Milan. The Semper is generally open weekdays from 10 am to 6 pm, with guided tours costing €5. The exact schedule is posted weekly at the entrance as it depends on rehearsal and performance times.

Saxony

DRESDEN STATE ART COLLECTION

Dresden's most famous and grandest museums and galleries are part of the Dresden State Art Collection. The collection is spread out over three buildings: the Zwinger, Theaterplatz 1, the Albertinum, Georg-Treu-Platz 2, and the Residenzschloss, Taschenberg 2. All share the same information telephone and website: ☎ 0351-491-4619, www.skd-dresden.de.

The opening hours for all are daily from 10 am to 6 pm, with the Zwinger closed on Monday. The Albertinum and the Residenzschloss are closed on Tuesday. Admission is paid separately for each exhibition but €10 covers admission to all for a day and €20 for a year. A photography permit for private use costs €5 per day for all museums – except those in the Residenzschloss. Also, note the Dresden City Ticket, which gives access to all museums and more.

If time is limited, make the Gemäldegalerie Alte Meister and the Grünes Gewölbe top priorities – not that any of the other collections disappoints.

Zwinger

Augustus the Strong planned an *Orangery* but his talented architect **Matthäus Pöppelmann** gave him a Baroque masterpiece of galleries, arcades, and pavilions instead. The resulting Zwinger became a glorious pavilion for entertainment purposes and a highlight of any visit to Dresden. Although damaged during World War II, it was largely restored by the mid-1960s. It currently houses several major museums and galleries. The museums are open Tuesday to Sunday from 10 am to 6 pm.

The Zwinger

The four pavilions of the **Zwinger** form a large rectangular courtyard with two semi-elliptical extensions. The entrance to the courtyard is via four distinct gates in the center of each of the four wings. Approaching from the Semper Opera, the **Semperbau** is the newest of the four wings. It was only completed in the mid-19th century using a High Renaissance style to the design of Semper. Most of the rest of the Zwinger was completed between 1709 and 1732 in a Baroque style. Directly opposite the Semperbau is the main entrance, the **Kronentor** (Crown Gate). It is adorned by a large crown carried by four Polish eagles, symbolizing the dual role of Augustus as Prince Elector of Saxony and King of Poland.

While facing Kronentor, to the right is the **Wallpavillon** (Rampart Pavilion), which serves as a staircase to the upper level. It is a fine symbiosis of architecture and sculpture and more art than architecture. To the right of the Wallpavillon is the French Pavilion, housing the **Nymphenbad** (Bath of the Nymphs) with a grotto, fountains, and several sensuous female sculptures. In the opposing semi-elliptical wing is the **Glockenspielpavillon**

(Carillon Pavilion). Its carillon of Meissen porcelain, although envisioned by Pöppelmann, was only completed in 1936.

The largest gallery in the Zwinger and by far the most impressive museum in Dresden is the **Gemäldegalerie Alte Meister** (Old Masters Picture Gallery). Despite losing 206 works during World War II, and having most of the collection carried off to Russia for a decade, it remains one of the richest collections of European paintings from the 15th to 18th century. The emphasis is on Italian paintings of the Renaissance and Baroque periods, with works by Giorgione, Titian, Botticelli, Parmigianino, and Veronese. The most famous work on display is Raphael's *Sistine Madonna*, featuring two adorable little angels also seen on postcards, kitsch trinkets, and wrapping paper all over town. The second main emphasis is 17th-century Dutch and Flemish art, including works by Rubens, Van Dyck, Rembrandt, Jordaens, and Vermeer. The entrance to the museum is in the archway leading from the Semper. Admission is €6.

The second major museum in the Zwinger is the **Porzellansammlung** (Porcelain Collection). It was started by Augustus the Strong, whose Asian porcelain collection comprised more than 14,500 pieces. The collection survived World War II undamaged but was transported to Russia and only returned in 1958. The core of the original collection was Chinese ceramics from the third to 17th centuries as well as Japanese Imari porcelain from around 1700. The current collection has 8,000 Meissen pieces. Entrance to the museum is from the Glockenspielpavillon. Admission is €5.

The **Rüstkammer** (Armory) is one of the world's best collections of parade weapons and costumes. It contains over 1,300 pieces displaying the pageantry of the Dresden court, knights' tournaments, and hunting. Several sets of full body armor for both men and horses are on display. Even for those with limited interest in weaponry this museum is worth a few minutes' detour. The entrance is directly across the archway from the Gemäldegalerie. Admission is €3.

It would be an error to dismiss the **Mathematisch-Physikalischer Salon** (Mathematics and Physics Saloon) as boring or too specialized. This small museum hidden in a corner of the Zwinger between Wallpavillon and Kronentor is dedicated to clocks and scientific instruments from the 16th to 19th centuries. Even the briefest of visits will be rewarding. The pieces on display are more art than science and reflect a time when the two disciplines were not strictly divided. Included is the largest collection of big globes in Germany and the world's oldest calculator, developed by Blaise Pascal in 1642. Admission is €3.

Residenzschloss

Crossing Theaterplatz from the Semper or Zwinger towards the royal residential area, one passes the 1831 **Altstädter Wache**, which currently houses a tourist information office as well as the ticket office for the Semper Opera and other entertainment venues. Across the road is the pale yellow Baroque façade of the **Taschenberg Palace** designed by Pöppelmann and given by Augustus the Strong to his mistress the Countess Cosel. It was destroyed in 1945 and only restored in 1995 to house a luxurious hotel.

Residenzschloss

One of the most important examples of Renaissance architecture in Germany is the **Residenzschloss** (Residence Castle). Although its history goes back to the 13th century, most of the castle dates from the 16th century. It was mainly left in ruins after the destruction of 1945 but reconstruction was recently completed and several museums moved back into the castle during 2004. All museums in the Schloss are open Wednesday to Monday from 10 am to 6 pm. Photography is not allowed.

The most prominent tower of the castle is the 330-foot **Hausmannturm**. Originally built in 1676 and damaged in 1945, it was rebuilt in 1991. The viewing platform is open from April to October. Admission is €2.50.

In the Grünes Gewölb

After decades as the main draw in the Albertinum, the **Grünes Gewölbe** (Green Vaults) returned to the Schloss in September 2004. It is named after its original place of safekeeping and thus nothing in the name hints that this is one of the largest and most magnificent treasury museums in the world. Most of the items were collected or commissioned by Augustus the Strong and his son. The collection includes goldsmithery mainly from the 16th and 17th centuries, works of ivory and amber, pieces commissioned by the electors, as well as a vast collection of jewelry. The public's favorite is the 1708 work by Johan Melchior Dinglinger, *State Court on the Grand Moghul's Birthday* – a diorama of 137 golden and enamel figures adorned with 4,909 diamonds, 160 rubies, 164 emeralds, and 16 pearls. It cost more than the construction of Schloss Moritzburg. From an artistic point of view, Dinglinger's *Diana Bathing* and a gilded coffee service are rated even higher. Some pieces are more than meet the eye at first glance: a cherry stone dating from 1589 is carved with 185 human heads – a strong magnifying glass brings it all to light. Admission is €6.

From September 2006, a small part of the collection, mostly jewelry, is housed in the original green vaults in the basement. Admission is a pricey €10 and is not covered by museum passes.

The two other museums in the Schloss are both highly regarded in their fields but are more specialized in nature and of lesser interest to the average visitor. The **Kupferstich-Kabinett** (Collection of Prints and Drawings) has drawings and photos dating from the 15th century to the present. The **Münzkabinett** (Coin Cabinet) displays only a selection of its 280,000 pieces. Admission to these two museums is €3 each.

In between the Elbe and Schloss is the Roman Catholic Cathedral of St Trinitatis (formerly and still commonly known as the

Dresden Hofkirche

Hofkirche or Court Church), the largest church in Saxony and the last major Baroque work in Europe. The Reformation started in Saxony and it was one of the first states formally to accept Lutheranism as the official religion. The electors of Saxony had long played a prominent role among Protestant groups in the German states but in 1697, Elector Augustus the Strong converted to Roman Catholicism, a condition for accession to the Polish throne. This left the elector without a suitable church to practice his newly adopted religion. It was only during the reign of his son, Friedrich Augustus II, that the Hofkirche was erected. It was completed in 1755, severely damaged in 1945, but restored soon after. The tower is 272 ft high and richly decorated with statues. The 53,820-sq-ft interior is mainly white with few decorations. Of special note is the processional ambulatory between the nave and side aisles – this was essential since outdoor Catholic processions, whether the ruler took part in person or not, were forbidden in Protestant Saxony. The recently restored organ was the last masterpiece of Gottfried Silbermann. Free concerts are occasionally given (the schedule is at the main entrance). Admission is free.

From the Hofkirche towards Neumarkt along Augustusstraße the outside wall of the Schloss is decorated by a massive mosaic made up of 24,000 tiles of Meißen porcelain. The 335-ft-long **Fürstenzug** (Procession of the Dukes) depicts all 35 rulers of the House of Saxe-Wettin on horseback from the first margrave of Meißen to the dukes, electors, and finally kings of Saxony in chronological order from 1125 to 1918. The mosaic survived the bombings of 1945.

Behind this wall is the **Langer Gang** (Long Hall) with a series of 22 Tuscan round-arch arcades connecting the castle with the **Johanneum**. The courtyard, **Stallhof**, was formerly the royal stables and site for knights' tournaments. Nowadays it is used for cultural events, including the medieval Christmas market – Germany's oldest. The Johanneum houses the **Verkehrsmuseum** (Tranport Museum), Augsutusstraße 1, ☎ 0351-86-440, www.verkehrsmuseum.sachsen.de; the entrance is next to the imposing Renaissance double staircase. The museum has an extensive collection of bicycles and the oldest tram in Germany. Admission is €6.

Frauenkirche

Frauenkirche by Canaletto, 1749-51

The Frauenkirche (Church of Our Lady), Neumarkt, ☎ 0351-498-1131, www.frauenkirche-dresden.de, is the true symbol and pride of Dresden. It is a High Baroque masterpiece designed by George Bähr, showing the first signs of the impending Classical revival. The church rises 312 ft and is built of Saxon sandstone. Its true architectural uniqueness is the bell-shaped stone dome, which is 77 ft in diameter and weighs 5,800 tons. The church is open for viewing Monday to Saturday from 10 am to noon and from 1 to 6 pm. Admission to the church is free. Musical performances are frequently held – some for free. Access to the dome costs €8 and is possible on weekdays between 10 am and 1 pm and 2 to 6 pm (closing at 4 pm from November to March).

THE SYMBOL OF DRESDEN

The Frauenkirche

The Frauenkirche was commissioned in 1722 by the Dresden town council. Officially, a larger church was needed but no doubt the main intention was as a snub by the Protestants to Elector Augustus I the Strong, who converted to Roman Catholicism in order to ascend to the throne of Poland. The new church was of monumental proportions with a large stone dome virtually unknown north of the Alps. For two centuries and long after the House of Saxe-Wettin lost the Polish crown, this remained the symbol of Dresden.

The church survived three days of Prussian artillery fire during the Seven Years' War as well as the initial air raids in 1945. But it collapsed on February 15, 1945 due to cracks in the pillars caused by the extreme heat of the fires. After the war, the collapsed church was left in ruins as a symbol of the destructiveness of war.

The decision to rebuild was only made in 1993. The external surface of the new church is true to the original but modern technology is employed beneath the surface to strengthen the building. Around 10,000 historic photographs were compared with 90,000 digital images of the ruins, allowing 7,000 original stones to be reused, with the largest piece weighing 95 tons. The church was re-consecrated on October 30, 2005.

The Albertinum

Nearby, on the banks of the Elbe, is the Albertinum, Georg-Treu-Platz 2, ☎ 0351-491-4619, www.skd-dresden.de. This former arsenal was converted in 1884 to a magnificent four-wing Neo-Renaissance museum. Opening hours are Wednesday to Monday from 10 am to 6 pm. Admission to the Albertinum is €5 and includes entrance to both galleries.

The **Galerie Neue Meister** (Modern Masters Gallery) is a collection of some 2,500 paintings from the 19th and 20th centuries. The gallery is famous for its collection of German Romantic painters, such as Caspar David Friedrich and Ludwig Richter, as well as German Impressionists such as Lovis Corinth, Max Slevogt, and Max Liebermann. The Nazis removed and sold on international markets several pieces from the collection, especially Expressionist and Cubist works that did not comply with the Nazi vision of art. Two triptychs by local painters survived the Nazis' wrath: Otto Dixe's *War*, illustrating the cruelty of warlike mentalities, and Hans Grundig's *The Thousand Year Reich,* a prophesy and parody of the Nazi dreams. The collection continues to expand mainly through acquisitions of local and contemporary artists.

The **Skulpturensammlung** (Sculpture Collection) has suffered from a lack of exhibition space, which will now be remedied by the move of other collections to the Schloss. The collection ranges from early Egyptian to the present. Augustus the Strong acquired a large collection of antiquities in Rome in 1728 to add to his treasures from the Renaissance and Baroque.

Sculpture Collection, Albertinum

Saxony

Brühlsche Terasse

Brühlsche Terasse

Returning to the Hofkirche from the Albertinum, the Brühlsche Terrace affords fantastic views of the Elbe and the neighborhood of Neustadt on the opposite bank. It is especially atmospheric in the early evening when most of the buildings are lit up.

Across the entrance to the Albertinum is the pleasure garden laid out by Count Brühl. Only the Dolphin Fountain and a group of sphinxes remain of his famous summerhouse, the **Belvedere**. An image in Meissen porcelain commemorates Johann Friedrich Böttger who was imprisoned under orders to produce gold but discovered the secrets of porcelain production instead.

The steps at the monument for the architect Gottfried Semper lead to the remains of the **Festung Dresden** (Dresden Fortress), George-Treu-Platz, ☎ 0351-491-4786, www.schloesser-dresden.de. This shows the bastions of the medieval city defenses. Opening hours are daily from 10 am to 5 pm (until 4 pm from November to March). Admission is €3.10.

The most beautiful building on the current Brühl Terrace is undoubtedly the **Art Academy**, with a distinctive glass cupola that is lit at night. It is locally known as the "lemon press." Close by is the Neo-Baroque **Sekundogenitur**, former residence of the second-born son to the ruling couple. It now houses a very pleasant coffee shop. A monumental staircase, with bronze sculptures representing the four times of day, leads down to the Hofkirche and to the right the Augustus Bridge crossing the Elbe to Neustadt.

Neustadt

One of the most pleasant walks in Dresden is crossing the Elbe on the **Augustusbrücke** (Bridge). The bridge offers the most magnificent views of the Baroque panorama that made Dresden famous. A stone bridge was built across the Elbe at this location as far back as 1275 but the current bridge follows the 1731 designs of Pöppelmann.

On the right bank of the Elbe is the Dresden suburb of Neustadt. It suffered less war damage and although it has few major sights, it does have pleasant Baroque, Neo-Classical, and *Gründerzeit* neighborhoods. **Hauptstraße**, www.neustadt-dresden.de, leads from the 1736 gilded, oversized equestrian statue of Augustus the Strong at the end of the bridge to Albertplatz. It is lined with shops, with the courtyards and passages on the left-hand side being particularly favored by artists and lined by intimate bars and cafés.

The **Dreikönigskirche**, Hauptstraße 23, was destroyed during the war but repaired in 1994 to resemble the exterior designed by Pöppelmann and Bähr in the 1730s. The interior is modern, but also contains one of the most important Renaissance works of sculpture in town – the *Dresden Death Dance*, designed by Christoph Walter in

Dresden Death Dance

1536 and originally part of the George Gate at the Castle.

From the Albertplatz, **Königstraße** leads back to the Elbe. This street has some of the classiest shops in Dresden and it's worth looking into the passages and courtyards. At the end of the street is the **Japanese Palace**, originally intended to house Augustus the Strong's Far Eastern porcelain collection. It currently houses two specialized museums. The **Landesmuseum für Vorgeschichte** (Pre-History), Palaisplatz 11, ☎ 0351-892-6927, has temporary exhibitions on Saxon and European archeology. It is open Tuesday to Sunday from 10 am to 6 pm. Admission is €3. The **Museum für Völkerkunde** (Ethnology), Palaisplatz 11, ☎ 0351-814-4860, displays ethnological pieces, including parts of the "electoral curiosity collection" – exotic objects collected by the electors of Brandenburg from the colonies in Africa, Asia, and Latin America. It is open Tuesday to Sunday from 10 am to 5 pm. Admission is a rather expensive €8.

◆ Cultural Events & Festivals

The main cultural draw is inevitably the **Semperoper**, but no less impressive is the modern **Kulturpalast** (Civic Center), home of the Dresdner Philharmonic Orchestra, and the **Schauspielhaus** next to the Zwinger. For reservations, contact Dresden Tourist, ☎ 0351-491-920, www.dresden-tourist.de.

Dresden hosts various annual festivals ranging from flamenco dancing to mass playing of street organs. The largest is the **Dresdner Musikfestspiele** (Musical Festival) during the first half of June. It has some 170 events in 70 locations. A three-day **Dixieland Festival** each May also draws a large audience.

Striezelmarkt

The **Striezelmarkt in Dresden** can claim to be the oldest Christmas market in Germany. It has been in existence since 1434 and has increased in size to cover more than a mile from the Hauptbahnhof all the way to the heart of Neustadt across the Elbe. The best part is inside the walls of the castle at the Stallhof. Here the market resembles that of the Middle Ages. *Stollen*, the most popular German Christmas cake, originally came from Dresden and is on sale everywhere – boxed and gift-wrapped if preferred.

◆ Shopping

The main shopping streets in Dresden are the **Prager Straße** leading from the main station towards the Old Town and the **Wilsdruffer Straße**, which crosses the Prager at the Altmarkt. On these streets, all the major shopping chains and department stores are represented.

More interesting are the higher-end boutiques and small shops in the **Neustadt** area across the Elbe. The 1899 **Markthalle** (market hall), Metzer Straße 1, ☎ 0351-810-5445, www.

markthalle-dresden.de, has been renovated and now hosts a range of small shops and a car museum rather than a normal market. High-quality food and cheese are available here but more useful to the foreign visitor is the **Weinkontor**, ☎ 0351-810-5455, which sells wine from five continents, including local Saxon wine. **Amida Spielzeuge**, ☎ 0351-810-5405, sells old-fashioned wooden and tin toys for children of all ages.

Nearby **Königstraße**, www.koenigstrasse-dresden.de, has the high-class shops of Dresden. This street, as well as the smaller streets and courtyards leading from it, has maintained its original Baroque character. Most popular are boutiques for both men and women, with jewelers, antiques, and fine arts.

A popular **flea market** is held Saturday from 7 am to 2 pm on the banks of the Elbe between Carola and Albert Bridges.

◆ Adventures

On Wheels

By Bicycle: Bicycles can be rented from the Hauptbahnhof, ☎ 0351-461-3262, or from Dresden-Neustadt station, ☎ 0351-461-5601.

By Train: Ever since the first steam engine connected Leipzig and Dresden in 1839, Saxony has been a paradise for fans of steam engines and narrow gauge trains. Dresden annually hosts the largest **Dampflokfest** (Steam Engine Festival) in Germany, attracting about 30,000 visitors each May. Contact the Dresden Tourist Office for exact details.

A popular steam train runs to Moritzburg (see *Daytrips* below). Even more accessible is the **Lilliputian Park Train**, ☎ 0351-445-6795, www.liliputbahn.de, in Dresden's Grosser Garten. It operates from April to October. This three-mile route is very much aimed at children but several other historic lines operate in Saxony. For information on these mostly off-the-beaten-track routes, contact Sachsen Tourism & Marketting, Bautzner Straße 45-47, 01099 Dresden, ☎ 0351-491-700, www. sachsen-tour.de.

Rollerblading: Up to 3,000 skaters meet from April to October on Friday nights from 9 pm to skate through the streets of Dresden. The start (and finish) is at Halfpipe, St Petersburger

Straße near the Hauptbahnhof and they follows alternating routes of around 18 miles through Dresden. The exact schedule and routes are posted at www.nachtskaten-dresden.de or by phone at ☎ 0351-484-8794. Rollerblades and safety equipment can be rented for around €5 on a first-come, first-served basis.

Trabi Safari: In Dresden, cars produced in the former East Germany are not only exhibited in museums. The Trabi, short for Trabant, was one of the most widely produced cars. It has a plastic body and noisy, polluting twin-stroke engine. For most people there was simply no alternative choice. After the *Wende*, Trabis disappeared from the streets of Germany as fast as locals could get their hands on secondhand Golfs and Opels. However, **Trabi Safari**, Theaterplatz/Schenklwache, ☎ 0351-899-0066, www.trabi-safari.de, allows you to explore Dresden driving one. In a convoy of up to eight cars, with a guide communicating via radio, you can wind your way through Dresden at speeds up to 30 km/h – it feels a lot faster! This car is not modern, so each driver gets instructions on how to operate it first and, if you do not crash it, a Trabi "driving license" is awarded afterwards. Two tours departing from Theaterplatz are available: 45 minutes cost between €12 and €18 per person and 90 minutes is between €20 and €30. Daytrips are run daily between 10 am and 6 pm. From March to November, additional night tours are scheduled between 8 pm and midnight. If you cannot fit this fun tour into your Dresden schedule, the same company helps to pollute Berlin's air in a similar way. Prior reservations are required should you need an English-speaking guide.

In the Air

Hot-Air Ballooning: Ballonfahrten Dresden, ☎ 0351-416-1700, www.ballon-dresden.de, starts from central Dresden as well as several other locations in Dresden and vicinity, including Moritzburg and Meißen.

Also offering flights from central Dresden is **Ballon-Crew Steina**, ☎ 03578-774-361, www.ballon-crew-steina.de.

On Water

Canoeing & Kayaking: Canoeing is allowed on the Elbe and many options of various lengths are available. Also contact the tourist offices in the various towns; boat rentals are available in practically every town near water.

From Dresden northwards, **Augustustours**, Bischofsweg 64, 01099 Dresden, ☎ 0351-803-3280, www.augustustours.de, offers half-day and full-day paddling tours on the Elb near Dresden. Both tours end in Meißen with the full-day (around six hours paddling) starting from Dresden and the half-day (two hours paddling) from Radebeul.

Riverboats: The **Sächsische Dampfschiffahrt**, Hertha-Lindner-Straße 10, 01067 Dresden, ☎ 0351-866-090, www.saechsische-dampfschiffahrt.de, has eight historic paddle steamers, the largest and oldest fleet in the world, with daily departures April to October from Dresden's Terassenufer in front of the Brühlsche Terasse. Most but not all cruises are on steamships. One ship goes north, reaching Meißen within two hours; it takes three hours coming back and costs €10.50 each way. Around 10

ships go south operating between various stations. Dresden to Königstein takes 5½ hours, but is two hours faster coming back, for €14.50 each way. Round-trip fares are heavily discounted, but using the train or bus one way will save time. On May 1 a **Steamship Parade** is held and the end of August sees a two-day **Steamship Festival** – written reservations are required during this period.

◆ Where to Stay

Dresden Altstadt

The **Kempinski Hotel Taschenbergpalais** opened in 1994 as the best hotel in town. The Kempinski group reconstructed Baroque Taschenberg Palace, originally built by Augustus the Strong for his mistress, the countess of Cosel, and destroyed in World War II. The exterior is pure Baroque and close to the original, while the interior is modern and furnished to the highest standards. In winter, an ice skating rink operates in the hotel's courtyard.

Kempinski Hotel Taschenbergpalais

Taschenberg 3, 01067 Dresden, ☎ 0351-49-120, fax 0351-491-2812, www.kempinski-dresden.de. (€€€€)

Hilton Dresden

The **Hilton Dresden** has a perfect location in between the Frauenkirche and the Brühlsche Terasse. This large modern hotel has all the expected comforts, although rooms are not particularly large. Lines are mostly straight and the combination of dark wood, chrome, and grey gives a modern, clean appearance. The Hilton operates several restaurants and coffee shops in the vicinity, assuring good quality and service, but at a price. An der Frauenkirche 5, 01067 Dresden, ☎ 0351-86-420, fax 0351-864-2725, www.hilton.com. (€€€-€€€€)

The **Mercure Newa** is close to the main station. Rooms are well appointed and more luxurious than the Ibis hotels, making this a more comfortable option should you need an address close to the main station. St Petersburger Straße 34, 01069 Dresden, ☎ 0351-481-4109, fax 0351-495-5137, www.mercure.com. (€€-€€€)

Nearby, are three massive 1960s-style buildings owned by the **Ibis** hotel group. The three almost identical hotels offer close to a thousand rooms. There is little to distinguish the three hotels, the rooms, or personnel. The rates are the same too. Approaching from the station, they are the **Bastei**, **Königstein** and **Lilienstein**. The location close to the station and in the heart of Dresden's main shopping street is convenient. The rooms may be uninspiring and small but so is the price. Small single rooms (€) go for a song. Prager Straße, 01069 Dresden, ☎ 0351-48-560, fax 0351-4856-6667, www.ibishotels.com. (€€)

Neustadt

Bülow Residenz

Some consider the **Bülow Residenz** as still the best hotel in Dresden. Less famous and much smaller than the Hotel Taschenberg, it is just as good in terms of luxury and quality of service. It is located in a 1730 Baroque manor house that was completely renovated in 1993. The 30 rooms are large and comfortably furnished. The hotel is in a quiet neighborhood between König and Hauptstraße. It also has the best restaurant in Dresden – one of only two Michelin star establishments in all of Saxony. Rähnitzgasse 19, 01097 Dresden, ☎ 0351-80-030, fax 0351-800-3100, www.buelow-residenz.de. (€€€-€€€€)

The modern and not particularly inspiring exterior of the **Westin Bellevue** dates from the communist era but was completely refurbished in 2000. Rooms are comfortably furnished and reasonably large. For once, Bellevue in the name does not refer to what was destroyed but rather to what is available now. The

Saxony

better rooms have spectacular views across the Elbe towards Dresden's Baroque skyline. Große Meißner Straße 15, 01097 Dresden, ☎ 0351-8050, fax 0351-805-1609, www.westin.com/bellevue. (€€-€€€€)

Camping

A very pleasant site is **Camping & Freizeitpark LuxOase** just north of Dresden near Radeberg. Closest public transportation: half a mile to bus line 305, 1.8 miles to S-Bahn station Arnsdorf-Dresden. The site is open March to October. It has space for 120 tents, motorhomes, or campers. Arnsdorfer Straße 1, 01900 Kleinröhrsdorf/Dresden, ☎ 035952-56-666, fax 035952-56-024, www.luxoase.de.

◆ Where to Eat

Zwinger – Semperoper Area

The luxurious Hotel Taschenbergpalais hosts the **Intermezzo Restaurant**, Taschenberg 3, ☎ 0351-49-120, www.kempinski-dresden.de. Like

RESTAURANT COSTS	
€	Less than €10
€€	€10 to €20
€€€	€21 to €35
€€€€	Over €35

the hotel, the restaurant is elegant but modern with first-class food and service to match. The cuisine is light Mediterranean, inspired with seasonal variations. (€€€€)

Behind the Semperoper in a former studio of the Zwinger is the **Alte Meister**, Theaterplatz 1a, ☎ 0351-481-0426, www.altemeister.net. The cuisine hints of French but the chef loves to experiment and create new innovations. The menu selection is small but varied. The restaurant itself has only 30 seats but in summer the outdoor terrace accommodates 120 more with a free view of the Semper, Zwinger, and Hofkirche. (€€-€€€€)

Also on Theaterplatz is the elegant **Italienische Dörfchen**, Theaterplatz 3, ☎ 0351-498-160, www.zugast.de/id. The name, meaning "Little Italian Town," is derived from the Italian artisans who resided here while working on the Hofkirche. In contrast, the cuisine is mostly Saxon and international with not much emphasis on Italian at all. The restaurant has several sections, with the restaurant on the second floor the most elegant. In summer, the outdoor seating is particularly pleasant, with some of the best views in town. Generally having a drink and snack here is more rewarding than a complete meal. (€-€€€)

Saxon Cuisine

It is often difficult to find traditional German restaurants in the centers of major German cities but Dresden's historic district has a surprisingly large number of restaurants offering Saxon cuisine. Three very popular restaurants share the same concept of regional cuisine in a setting of historic vaulted cellars. The décor recalls Saxony of old and the staff wears 18th-cen-

Sophienkeller

tury period costume. The largest of the three, with space for up to 400 diners, is the **Sophienkeller** in the basement of the lofty Taschenbergpalais, Taschenberg 3, ☎ 0351-497-260, www.sophienkeller-dresden.de. (€€-€€€). The other two are in the Frauenkirche district with the **Pulverturm**, An der Frauenkirche 12, ☎ 0351-262-600, www.pulverturm-dresden.de, (€-€€), in the cellar of the Coselpalais. The **Festungsmauern**, Am Brühlschen Garten 4, ☎ 0351-262-032, www.festungsmauern-dresden.de, (€-€€), is inside the former city fortifications in an incredible large barrel vault.

Slightly more up market but still unashamedly Saxon is the wine restaurant **Wettiner Keller**, Hilton Hotel, An der Frauenkirche 5, ☎ 0351-864-2860, www.hilton.com. The emphasis here is on good Saxon wine to accompany traditional hearty Saxon food. The décor is rustic and in summer, the terrace has Elbe views. (€€-€€€)

Frauenkirche & Brühlsche Terasse

Although most of the locales in this area now squarely aim at the tourist market, the variety is still good. Many of the best belong to the **Hilton Hotel**, An der Frauenkirche 5, www.hilton.

Saxony

com, assuring English menus, good quality, and service, but at a markup. The **Rossinni**, ☎ 0351-864-2855, (€€-€€€€), on the second floor of the Hilton, is one of the best Italian restaurants in the region. On the ground floor is the more informal **Bistro**, ☎ 0351-86-420, (€-€€), offering an international menu of smaller meals.

At the back of the Hilton in Terassengasse is the very pleasant **Café Antik Kunst**, Terassengasse, ☎ 0351-498-9836, which combines an antique shop with a café. You actually sit on some antiques here. The menu includes not only coffee but also small meals. (€-€€)

Inside the Sekundogenitur, the Hilton operates two cafés that more or less share the same menu and the same kitchen. The **Café Vis-à-Vis**, ☎ 0351-86-420, (€-€€), is an establishment with stylish furniture and decoration in keeping with the lovely

The Münzgasse

exterior of the former palace. The small **Splendid Espresso Bar**, ☎ 0351-86-420, (€-€€), has modern red leather seats. The atmosphere here is more relaxed, although the surroundings are still very much upmarket. Coffee and food comes at a slight premium but the quality is excellent.

The **Münzgasse** has traditionally been the place for bars and restaurants in Dresden but the fare now on offer is more international. Two interesting options are the Australian Restaurant & Bar **Ayers Rock**, Münzgasse 8, ☎ 0351-490-1188 and the Spanish **Las Tapas**, Munzgasse 4, ☎ 0351-496-0108, www.las-tapas.de. (€-€€)

◆ Daytrips from Dresden

Saxon Switzerland

Just south of Dresden, Sächsische Schweiz (Saxon Switzerland) is one of Germany's most beautiful and strangest of landscapes. The name is a bit of a misnomer as the highest peak here is only 561 m/1,840 ft high. The alternative name, Elbsandsteingebirge (Elbe Sandstone Mountains), is a better indication of what is on offer. The drenching of lakes millions of years ago combined with centuries of erosion left a landscape of strange peaks, sheer drops and straight rock faces, deep canyons, and rock formations not found elsewhere in Germany. Most of the area is protected in the Saxon Switzerland National Park.

This is a haven for outdoor fanatics, offering 720 miles of marked hiking trails, 230 miles of cycling routes, the Elbe, smaller streams, and lakes for boating, a fantastic natural theater, and a wealth of fauna and flora. In addition, there are pretty towns and mighty fortresses to explore.

Information Sources

Tourist Office: For information contact Tourbu, Am Bahnhof 6, 01814 Bad Schandau, ☎ 035022-4950, www.saechsische-schweiz.de.

Transportation

The area is easily reached from Dresden on the S-Bahn line S1. It runs every 30 minutes from Dresden, taking 35 minutes to Rathen and 41 minutes to Königstein. All stations are on the left bank of the Elbe, with convenient ferries to the opposite bank in towns without bridges. It can also be reached by boat – see *Elbe Steamers* in the *Dresden* section.

Bastei

Sightseeing: The **Kurort Rathen**, a town of only 500 inhabitants, is famous for two natural wonders made somewhat more famous through human interference. The Bastei area has some of the most spectacular scenery in the region. Fabulous views are available from the Basteibrücke (Bastei Bridge) constructed across a ravine 660 ft above the valley. The bridge is reached by a 45-minute walk from Rathen – the path close to the bridge is steep, with many stairs. Even higher, at 1,000 ft, is the viewing platform on the Bastei peak itself. On busy summer days, up to 50,000 people come to the bridge to see the sights.

An alternative way is by bus from Stadt Wehlen. **Bastei-Kraxler**, Dresdner Straße 1, 01824 Königstein, ☎ 035021-67614, runs buses that leave from the Marktplatz every hour and reach the parking area near the Bastei in 20 minutes. From here, it is just a few minutes walk to the bridge. It is also possible to take the bus four times per day from the Bastei to Königstein via Hohnstein and Bad Schandau. Journey time is just over an hour.

Also in Rathen is the **Rathen Felsenbühne** (Rock Stage), Amselgrund 17, 01824 Rathen, ☎ 035024-7770, one of the most beautiful natural theaters in Europe. It stages operas, musicals and other shows annually from May to September. During daytime, it is open to visitors for free.

Königstein

Sightseeing: On a hilltop 790 ft above the Elbe is Germany's largest fortress – **Festung Königstein**, 01824 Königstein, ☎ 035021-64-607, www.festung-koenigstein. de. Its history dates back to the early 13th century and it has been part of the Mark Meißen, later Saxony, since 1459. Its main purpose from then on was as a refuge for the Saxon court and art treasures in times of crisis. It performed this role well, as it was never conquered. During the Seven Years' War with Prussia and during the revolutionary events of 1848/49 the court hightailed it here. It also served as a prison, with the most famous inmate Johann Böttger, discoverer of European porcelain, from

1706 to 1707. In World War II, it served as a prison for captured senior officers, mainly French. Probably unknown to them, they shared the castle with the best museum pieces from Dresden. More willing overnight guests included Czar Peter I and Napoleon Bonaparte.

It is a mighty fortress, consisting of 30 buildings surrounded by a 7,200-ft outside wall. The well is 500 ft deep – literally drilled through sandstone. The more spectacular entrance to the fortress is via a steep walkway and stairs but an elevator is also available for the infirm.

The castle is located on the B172 between Pirna and Königstein. Bus 241 operates between the two towns; the castle is a short walk from bus stop Abzweig Festung. The classical approach is the half-hour walk from the town center of Königstein. Alternatively, **Bastei-Kraxler**, Dresdner Straße 1, 01824 Königstein, ☎ 035021-67614, operates the Festung Express every 30 minutes. April to October, from Königstein Reißiger Platz to the Fortress parking lot.

The castle opens daily year-round at 9 am but closes April to September at 8 pm, October at 6 pm, and November to March at 5 pm. Small parts and some shops and restaurants are closed from October to March. Admission is €4. Several dining options are available.

Adventures

On Foot

Countryside Hikes: Despite the name, Saxon Switzerland's peaks are not that high and the winters not that cold, so most hiking paths are accessible year-round. A popular 40-minute walk is from Rathen to the Bastei, with the marvelous views from the Bastei Bridge. A circular route leads back to Rathen via the Schwedische Löcher (Swedish Holes), where the local population hid from the Swedish troops during the Thirty Years' War, and the Rathen Felsenbühne (Rock Theater).

Rock Climbing: It is claimed that free climbing has its origin in Saxon Switzerland. More than a thousand peaks can be scaled here via 16,000 different routes.

Several companies offer lessons ranging from one to several days and rent equipment.

- **Outdoor Tours**, *Hauptstraße 27, 01855 Kirnitzschtal/OT Ottendorf,* ☎ *035971-56-907, www.klettern-sachsen.de.*
- **Adventure Service**, *Niederweg 10, 01814 Bad Schandau,* ☎ *035022-43-253, www.adventureservice.de.*
- **Bad Schandauer Tourismus**, *Elbsandstein Reisen, Marktplatz 12, 01814 Bad Schandau, www. elbsandsteinreisen.de.*

On Wheels

By Bicycle: One of the longest and most popular cycling paths in Germany is the 516-mile **Elbe Cycling Route**, www.elberadweg.de. It runs the full length of the Elbe from where it enters Germany south of Dresden to where it finally flows into the North Sea at Cuxhaven beyond Hamburg.

The full route is usually done over a period of two weeks. The altitude difference is a mere 200 ft, meaning cycling upstream is as easy as following the downstream route.

Nowhere is the scenery more beautiful, as the route hugs close to the Elbe, than the 45 miles between Schöna and Meißen.

Often the local or regional tourism offices arrange special packages. For the Elbe Cycling Path in Saxony the **Tourismusverband Sächsiches Elbland**, ☎ 03521-76-350, fax 03521-763-540, www.elbland.de, arranges cycling packages ranging from three to 15 nights. Packages can also be combined with canoeing, hiking, rock climbing, and other activities.

On Water

Canoeing & Kayaking: South of Dresden, **Elbe Kanu Aktiv Tours**, Elbpromenade Schandauer Straße 17-19, 01824 Königstein, ☎ 035022-50-

704, www.kanu-aktiv-tours.de, offers daily boat rental and complete packages for longer trips. The classic route is Königstein to Pirna, which takes around 3½ hours. Starting from Bad Schandau adds an hour and no extra charge. Several longer, and shorter options are available, with boat drop-off points in most towns along the Elbe.

Cultural Events

The annual **Sandstein & Musik Festival** (Sandstone and Music), www.sandstein-musik.de, schedules events from March to November. The open-air **Rathen Felsenbühne**, ☎ 035024-7770, www.dresden-theater.de, has performances ranging from opera to children's theater from April to October.

Moritzburg

Transportation

Moritzburg is reached in 25 minutes by Bus 326 or 458 (direction Radeburg/Großenhain), running at least hourly from Dresden-Neustadt station. A more interesting approach is by narrow gauge steam train – see *Adventures* below.

Sightseeing

One of the most popular day-trip destinations in Saxony is to the beautifully located **Jagdschloss Moritzburg** (Moritzburg Hunting Palace), ☎ 035207-8730, www.schloss-moritzburg.de, about nine miles to the north of Dresden. The ocher and white Baroque palace was built on an island inside an artificial pond. The current building was completed in 1736 to the design of Augustus the Strong's fa-

Jagdschloss Moritzburg

Saxony

vorite architect, Matthäus Pöppelmann, but some parts of the building are 200 years older. The symmetrical palace with four massive round towers in the four corners never fails to impress. Inside the palace is the **Baroque Museum** with period furniture, paintings, porcelain, and the world's largest collection of Baroque leather wall coverings. Opening is at 10 am year-round but closing from April to October is at 5:30 pm; November, December, and March at 4:30 pm; January and February at 4 pm. Admission is €4.10. Guided tours are €2.

Just north of the palace is the small French-style **Schlosspark** (Palace Park) but the real treat is the large **Waldpark** (Forest Park) that lies beyond. It is a fine place to stroll around and has a few interesting historic sights. The Rococo **Fassanenschlösschen** was built in the late 18th century for Elector Friedrich Augustus II and is a good example of the *chinoiserie* that was popular all over Europe at the time. Nearby is the harbor from where the nobles started boating parties. Ruins were constructed on the edge of the large pond and miniature frigates were built for mock "naval battles" to entertain the members of court.

There are six natural lakes and 25 artificial ponds in the Moritzburg area. This makes the area a haven for bird life, with around 200 species, as well as other small animals. The area is popular for hiking and cycling.

Adventures on Wheels

Narrow-Gauge Trains: The nine-mile **Loßnitzgrundbahn** between Radebeul Ost and Radeburg via Moritzburg is easily accessible and particularly popular. It crosses 17 bridges and

stops at 11 stations, but most passengers embark at Moritzburg to admire the hunting palace of Augustus the Strong. Depending on the season, there are around eight trains daily, taking an hour, with Moritzburg about halfway. Radebeul Ost can be reached in 15 minutes from Dresden Hauptbahnhof by S-Bahn Line 1. For more information contact **Oberelbe Tours**, Leipzigerstraße 120, 01127 Dresden, ☎ 0351-852-6529, www.oberelbetours.de.

About once a month, the route is covered by the **Traditionsbahn** (Traditional Train), Bahnhof Radebeul Ost, Sidonienstraße 1a, ☎ 0351-4614-8001, www.tradtionsbahn-radebeul.de, which has 19th-century-style wagons complete with wooden seats and staff in period costume. Roundtrip fare for the full route is €11, or €8 up to Moritzburg. Reservations, at no additional charge, are recommended.

Where to Stay & Eat

The small but comfortable hotel and restaurant **Churfürsteliche Waldschanke**, Große Fasanenstraße, 01468 Moritzburg, ☎ 035207-8600, fax 035207-86-093, www.churfuerstliche-waldschaenke.de, is beautifully located inside the forest and within easy walking distance of the palace and all other local sights. It dates from 1770 and was originally a gamekeeper's house for the royal forest. Some walls have hunting trophies and the original leather wall coverings. The rooms are comfortably furnished with stylish furniture. The restaurant offers local cuisine, including venison, fowl, and Saxon wine. (€€-€€€)

Inside the palace itself the **Restaurant im Barockschloss**, Im Schloss, Mortizburg, ☎ 035207-89-390, www.schlossrestaurant-moritzburg.de, offers several dining options ranging from a simple café to a stylish restaurant. (€-€€€)

Leipzig

Some observers consider Dresden's Baroque Old Town as beautiful, while some find it a bit bombastic. Since World War II, Leipzig has never been accused of either. Few cities can offer such a contrast within such a small area as the Leipzig Old Town presents.

Leipzig was heavily damaged by air raids in World War II and the scars left can still be seen – the city is a real mix of old and

Leipzig

NOT TO SCALE

© 2007 HUNTER PUBLISHING, INC.

1. Hauptbahnhof
2. Museum der Bildenen Künste
3. Museum in der Runden Ecke
4. Zum Arabischen Coffe Baum
5. Thomaskirche
6. Bosehaus, Bach Museum
7. Neues Rathaus
8. Mädlerpassage
9. Altes Rathaus, Stadtgeschichtliches Museum
10. Alte Handelsbörse, Naschmarkt
11. Zeitgeschichtliches Forum
12. Nikolaikirche
13. Leipzig University
14. Moritzbastei
15. Mendelssohnhaus
16. Neues Gewandhaus
17. Augustusplatz
18. Opernhaus
19. Grassi Museum

N

new with seemingly little planning. Within 15 minutes walk, you can see the enormous early-20th-century Hauptbahnhof, huge communist-era apartment blocks, the modern, glass-box art gallery, the Renaissance town hall, Gothic and Baroque churches, modern shopping centers, shopping streets dating back to the Middle Ages, concert halls from the 1960s, new buildings being erected, old ones being restored to their former glory, while some equally impressive looking old ones are simply going to waste. Although much has been done since the *Wende* to restore Leipzig's historic buildings, much remains to be done. Architecturally, this city is one scrambled egg that will not be unscrambled anytime soon. For the visitor, it is an incredibly interesting experience.

Leipzig played a major role in the peaceful German revolution of 1989 that led to the end of communist East Germany. It was here, rather than in Berlin, where the peaceful protest movements against the communist regime started.

◆ Information Sources

Tourist Office: Leipzig's tourist information office is across the road from the Hauptbahnhof at Richard-Wagner-Straße 1, ☎ 0341-710-4260, www.leipzig.de.

◆ Transportation

Leipzig has a very well developed public transportation system combining trains, trams, and buses. Due to the compactness of the Old Town, it is quite possible to visit Leipzig without using public transportation at all. The Völkerschlachtdenkmal is the only attraction described below that is not within walking distance of the main station.

◆ Sightseeing

Hauptbahnhof Area

Leipzig's **Hauptbahnhof** (Central Station), Willy-Brandt-Platz 7, ☎ 0180-599-6633, with 26 platforms, is the largest train station in Germany. The building dates from 1915 and was restored to its original condition in the 1990s. It is colossal: the front façade is almost 1,000 ft long and the huge glass roof is larger than three soccer fields. Back in 1915, it served both the Saxon and Prussian railway companies,

Hauptbahnhof

but separately, meaning everything is doubled, from waiting rooms to grand staircases. With 150 shops and restaurants, it is also the largest shopping center in town. All major buses and trams depart from Willy Brandt Platz in front of the station.

Close by, at Sachsenplatz, a huge glass cube 110 ft high recently became the new location of the **Museum der Bildenden Künste** (Fine Arts Museum), Katharinenstraße 10, ☎ 0341-216-990, www.mdbk.de, one of the world's great collections of European art. Highlights include early German and Dutch works, Dutch art of the 17th century, Italian art from the 15th to 18th centuries, and German art from the 18th century to the present. Opening hours are Tuesday to Sunday from 10 am to 6 pm; Wednesday from noon to 8 pm. Admission is €5.

Across the road in Katherinenstraße are a few surviving Baroque houses. The most interesting is the **Romanushaus** (1704), on the corner with Brühl. It was built by the mayor

Romanushaus

Romanus, who financed its construction with uncovered notes and spent over four decades in Königstein jail as punishment for this and other crimes. At No 11 is the **Fregehaus**, which belonged to a rich banker. It is based on a 16th-century building but was reconstructed in the early 18th century. In contrast to these, the huge communist-era apartment blocks and secondhand shops in the area remind us that this is very much a living city and not just a tourist destination.

Markt Area

The **Markt** (Market Square) is dominated by one of the most beautiful Renaissance edifices in Germany, the **Altes Rathaus** (Old City Hall), Markt 1. It was built in a record-breaking nine months in 1556 between two trade fairs. The Markt

Altes Rathaus

is the center of all festivals and still used on Tuesday and Friday for the farmers' fresh produce market.

To the south is the magnificent **Königshaus** (Kings' House) where the Saxon rulers resided when in town. It was converted into a Baroque house in 1707 and famous guests in addition to the Saxon rulers included Czar Peter the Great, Frederick the Great, and Napoleon, who said farewell to his Saxon allies from the balcony after losing the Battle of the Nations. On the opposite end of the square only the façade with sundial remained of the **Alte Waage** (Old Weigh House).

Leipzig has been an important city in Germany for centuries and therefore the **Stadtgeschichtliches Museum Leipzig** (City History Museum), Markt 1, ☎ 0341-965-130, www. stadtgeschichtliches-museum-leipzig.de, has several interesting displays. The pride of the museum are the imperial edicts related to the trade fair privileges granted to the city. The largest hall is 174 ft long and has a scale model of Leipzig made in 1823. Several Lucas Cranach paintings are on display as well as some of the 24,000 prints featuring Leipzig panoramas. Opening hours are Tuesday to Sunday from 10 am to 6 pm and

Tuesday from 2 to 8 pm. Admission is €2.50 but free on the first Sunday of the month.

Naschmarkt Area

Behind the Altes Rathaus is the **Naschmarkt,** with a statue (1903) of a young Goethe in front of the **Alte Börse** (Old Commodities Trading Exchange), the first major Baroque building in

Leipzig (1687). Goethe's stare is fixed on the **Mädler-Passage**, www.maedlerpassage.de, Leipzig's most magnificent mall. Here are several stylish shops and restaurants. The most famous is the **Auerbachs Keller**, a drinking hall and restaurant that is the setting of a scene in Goethe's most famous work, *Faust*. Large statues of Mephisto and Dr Faust mark the entrance to the cellars. Despite the glamour of the establishments in the Mädler-Pas-

Mädler-Passage

sage, in an adjacent and directly linked parallel passage, cheap socks and underwear can be bought from makeshift stalls. This Leipzig.

One of the most interesting museums in all of Germany is the **Zeitgeschichtliches Forum Leipzig (**Forum of Contemporary History), Grimmaische Straße 6, ☎ 0341-22-200, www.hdg.de. The museum displays the history of the two post-World War II Germanys, with special emphasis on the history of dictatorship, opposition, and resistance in the Soviet Occupation Zone and in the German Democratic Republic during 40 years of German division. In addition to contemporary items, there are very impressive multimedia presentations. Particularly interesting are displays showing how the same video footage was used to portray events in a completely different way on news programs in the former East and West. Several recordings of famous speeches are available to complement the hundreds of photos and documents on display. This museum is far more impressive and interesting than any of the more widely advertised, and often pricey, competing museums in Berlin. Opening hours are Tuesday to Friday from 9 am to 6 pm, weekends from 10 am to 6 pm. Admission is free.

Internationally less famous but older and larger than the Thomas Church is the **Nikolaikirche**, Nikolaikirchhof 3, ☎ 0341-960-5270, www. nikolaikirche-leipzig.de. The Gothic chancel and west towers date from the 14th century while the triple nave and galleries are early 16th century. The central tower was completed in 1555. The Classical interior dates from the late 18th century. The slender white pillars resemble palm trees and end in light green leaves. The rest of the ceiling is coffered in light pink stucco flowers. Opening hours are Monday to Saturday from 10 am to 6 pm. Admission is free.

Nikolaikirche

Saxony

The Grassi Museum Complex

Leipzig's highest concentration of museums is in the **Grassi Museum Complex** at Johannesplatz, www.grassimuseum.de. This complex was erected in the 1920s in the Expressionist style with hints of Art Deco. It was extensively damaged during World War II but reconstruction was completed in 2005.

The **Museum für Kunsthandwerk** (Arts and Crafts), ☎ 0341-213-3719, www.grassimuseum.de, has a collection of mainly European arts and crafts dating from the earliest times to the present. A special focal point is items collected during the 1920s and 1930s at the Leipzig fairs and German ceramics from the post-war period. Opening hours are Tuesday to Sunday from 10 am to 6 pm; Wednesdays until 8 pm. Admission is €4.

The **Museum für Völkerkunde** (Ethnography), ☎ 0341-973-1900, www.grassimuseum.de, with 220,000 items and around 100,000 photographs, is one of the oldest and largest collections of its kind in Europe. Opening hours are Tuesday to Friday from 10 am to 6 pm; weekends from 10 am to 5 pm. Admission is €2 but free the first Sunday of the month.

The third museum offers pleasure for both eye and ear. The **Musikinstrumentenmuseum** (Musical Instruments Museum), ☎ 0341-687-0790, www.grassimuseum.de, displays about a quarter of the 4,000 historic musical instruments belonging to the University of Leipzig. The collection is considered to be the second-most important in Europe, after the one in Brussels, and spans five centuries. Opening hours are Tuesday to Saturday from 10 am to 5 pm; Sundays and public holidays from 10 am to 1 pm. Admission is €3.

A few blocks from the Grassimuseum is the **Schumann-Haus**, Inselstraße 18, ☎ 0341-393-9620, www.schumann-verein.de. It was the residence of Robert and Clara Schumann during the first four years (1840-1844) of their marriage. It is one of the few remaining Classical buildings in Leipzig. Opening hours are short and only from Wednesday to Saturday, 2 to 5 pm.

Thomaskirche Area

From 1723 until his death in 1750 Johann Sebastian Bach was cantor of the **Thomaskirche**, Thomaskirchhof 18, ☎ 0341-960-2855, www.thomaskirche.org. Most of his cantatas, oratorios, and passions were first performed here. Felix Mendelssohn Bartholdy performed Bach's *St. Matthew Passion* here to reintroduce his work to the general public in 1841. During Bach's time,

Thomaskirche

the church interior was Baroque and richly decorated with colorful paintings and biblical verses. However, it was remodeled in a Neo-Gothic style during 1884-89 leaving the interior rather bare. After a detour in the local graveyard and the now destroyed Johanniskirche, Bach's body was finally buried here in the chancel after World War II. A statue of Bach was erected in front of the church in 1908. The church is open daily from 9 am to 6 pm and admission is free.

Frankly, the **Johann Sebastian Bach Museum** in the Bose Haus, Thomaskirchhof 15-16, ☎ 0341-913-7200, www.bach-leipzig.de, is somewhat disappointing. Bach became nationally and then internationally famous only long after his death and consequently few items can directly be attributed to his life. The Museum is on the second floor and consists mainly of information and copies of documents relating to the great composer's life. A few pieces of furniture and a Bible that belonged to Bach, as well as period instruments, are exhibited. Opening hours are daily from 10 am to 5 pm. Admission is €3.

The **Neues Rathaus** (New Town Hall), Martin Luther Ring 4-6, ☎ 0341-1230, was built at the start of the 20th century and still serves as the seat of the local government. The building was extensively restored in the 1990s and has richly decorated façades and roof structures.

One of Leipzig's most interesting museums is the **Museum in der "Runden Ecke"** (literally Museum in the Round Corner), Dittrichring 24, ☎ 0341-961-2443, www.runde-ecke-leipzig.de. It is housed in the former Leipzig head office of the feared and despised Stasi, the secret police of the German Democratic Republic. The site was known as the Round Corner due to the curvature of the building. The Stasi managed to know a lot of what the citizens were up to through a wide network of spies, illegal opening of mail, and wiretapping of phones. On display are some of the machines designed to open and close letters – up to 2,000 per day – as well as ones designed to read the contents of some without having to open the envelope. The paranoia reached far and near: after the fall of the regime, a secret, permanently staffed telephone listening post was found inside the Stasi building itself. Thousands of files that were kept on ordinary citizens are on display. Information in the museum is in

German only, but an English folder with a room-by-room description is available at the entrance. Opening hours are daily from 10 am to 6 pm. Admission is free.

The coffee shop **Zum Arabischen Coffe Baum**, Feine Fleischergasse 4, ☎ 0341-961-0060, www.coffe-baum.de, opened in 1694 and has been in continuous operation ever since. It therefore is the oldest coffee shop in the world, although a Parisian establishment disputes this. It has three coffee shops and three restaurants on the premises (see *Where to Eat* section) as well as a **Coffee Museum** (free entry) on the second and third floors. On display are all sorts of paraphernalia associated with coffee since its introduction to Europe from the East. The Coffe Baum has been popular with high society for centuries and frequent guests included literary figures such as Goethe and Lessing, as well as composers such as List, Wagner, and the Schumanns. A lesser-known work by the great composer Johann Sebastian Bach, the *Coffee Cantata*, is played constantly in the museum.

◆ Farther Afield

To commemorate the centenary of the Allied victory over Napoleon at the Battle of the Nations, the German Empire in a fit of nationalism erected the **Völkerschlachtdenkmal** (Battle of the Nations Monument), Prager Straße, ☎ 0341-878-0471, www.t-online.de/home/stadtmuseum.leipzig. The 298-ft colossus of Saxon porphyry took 15 years to build and is still

Völkerschlachtdenkmal

undisputedly the largest monument in Germany. (It is also a strong contender for the title of the ugliest monument!) There is a 200-ft-high Hall of Honor with 324 equestrian soldiers in the cupola. Another 12 soldiers, each 40 ft high, guard the outside of the building, together with a 40-ft archangel Gabriel. Some

500 steps lead to the viewing platform, with marvelous views of Leipzig and the surrounding countryside. The hall has fantastic acoustics, making it a popular venue for concerts. The **Forum 1813** right next to the monument has exhibitions on the battle, the developments in Europe leading up to the battle, as well as the suffering of soldiers during the period. Around 350 original items relating to the battle are on display and multimedia is used to bring across the horrors of the event. Beyond the reflecting pool is the **Napoleonstein** (Napoleon Stone) marking the spot where Bonaparte stood during the battle. Reenactments of the battle are staged annually in mid-October. Opening hours are daily, April to October from 10 am to 6 pm, November to March from 10 am to 4 pm. The area is most easily reached by Tram No 15, running from the Hauptbahnhof.

THE BATTLE OF THE NATIONS

In October 1813, Napoleon Bonaparte with an army of 165,000 men faced the 225,000 men of the allied armies of Prussia, Russia, Austria, and Sweden to the south of the city of Leipzig. Saxony was officially an ally of France but many soldiers changed sides during the battle. One of the largest battles in history, the Battle of the Nations, often simply referred to as the Battle of Leipzig, ensued. Initially France won and on October 16 Napoleon rang victory bells. However, with fresh reserves the Allies attacked again and scored a clear victory on October 18. Around 130,000 soldiers lost their lives during the battle and thousands more during Napoleon's hasty and chaotic retreat to France. The Battle of Leipzig finally broke Napoleon's hold on much of Europe.

The Russian **Gedächtniskirche St Alexei's** (Memorial Church) honors the 22,000 Russian soldiers as well as 16,000

Germans, 12,000 Austrians and 300 Swedish allies, who died in the battle. It is a copy of the 16th-century Kolomenskoye Church of the Ascension near Moscow. Of special note are the icon walls in the upper part of the church.

◆ Cultural Events

Leipzig is the city of Bach, Mendelssohn, Schumann, Wagner, and many others, ensuring that there is always a wide variety of musical performances on offer throughout the year. In Advent, the number of concerts is particularly high, but also in summer, when open-air performances are popular. Leipzig has an amazing amount of theater ranging from classical pieces to cabaret. It is easiest to contact the tourist office, Richard-Wagner-Straße 1, ☎ 0341-710-4260, www.leipzig.de, which has information on all the main venues.

A special annual event is the **Bachfest**, a two-week festival of about 70 concerts held in mid-May. The emphasis is obviously on Bach, but music of others is also performed. Tickets and information are available from the Bach Archive, ☎ 0341-913-7333, www.bach-leipzig.de.

Mendelssohn's music can be heard every Sunday at 11 am in the **Mendelssohn-Haus**, Goldschmidtstraße 12, ☎ 0341-127-024, www.mendelssohn-stiftung.de.

The center of the **Christmas market** is on the Market Square. However, more interesting is the small market on the adjacent **Naschmarkt**. Here, the market resembles that of the Middle Ages with old-fashioned stalls and fare far different from the sausages and potato cakes offered at the main market.

◆ Shopping

Leipzig's best-known shopping center is the **Promenaden**, with around 150 shops inside the main station. In contrast to other areas, shops here are open until 10 pm. Shops range from electronics to clothing stores and supermarkets.

The major department stores are on Neumarkt and Petersstraße. The more interesting smaller shops are in the **historic passages**, which abound in the area around the

Markt. Most famous is the **Mädler-Passage** but with fame come high prices. Better deals are found in the adjacent passages.

Antique and flea markets are popular in Leipzig. Flea markets are held the first weekend of the month: Saturday at the Hauptbahnhof Platform 24 and Sunday at the Alte Messe Hall 13. Arguably, the best market is the large antique and flea market, usually held the last weekend of the month at the Agra-Exhibition Ground (Tram Line 11 from the main station) in Leipzig-Markkleeberg, www.agra-markkleeberg.de. This market is "ohne Neuwaren" (without new goods), meaning no cheap plastic junk or discounted socks and underwear. For exact times and location, ☎ 0341-980-4817 or, on the day of the market itself, ☎ 0172-968-7629.

◆ Adventures

On Wheels

By Bus: Several companies offer bus tours of Leipzig. **Leipzig Erleben**, www.leipzig-erleben.de, and **Elke's Oldtimer**, www.elkes-oldtimer-tours.net, operate in cooperation with the Tourist Information Office from Richard-Wagner-Straße 1, ☎ 0341-710-4230. Leipzig Erleben has several daily tours to various destinations in and around the town. Elke's Oldtimer offers an interesting alternative: daily at 11 am and 2 pm it uses 1930s Parisian buses for 90-minute city tours. The afternoon tour includes a 30-minute walking tour as well.

In the Air

Hot-Air Ballooning: Sachsen Ballooning, ☎ 0341-521-5315, www.sachsen-ballonning.de, offers flight from the Völkerschlachtdenkmal and several other spots in the vicinity.

The annual **Saxonia International Balloon Fiesta** takes place at the end of July. It is one of the largest hot-air balloon gatherings in Europe. Contact the tourist office for exact dates and schedules.

◆ Where to Stay in Leipzig

The best temporary address in Leipzig is the elegant **Hotel Fürstenhof**. It has

just under 100 rooms in a reno-vated patrician house dating from 1770. Rooms are very comfortable and stylish with lots of natural light. The **Fürstenhof Restaurant** (€€€€) is one of the best in Leipzig, with light in-

ternational and nouvelle cuisine. The **Vinothek** has a large selection of Saxon, German, and international wines, as well as lighter meals. Tröndlinring 8, 04105 Leipzig, ☎ 0341-1400, fax 0341-140-3707, www.arabellasheraton.com. (€€€€)

The **Westin Leipzig** is on the top 15 floors of a 27-floor building two blocks from the station. All rooms are comfortably furnished. Most have stylish modern furniture, although some still have older and slightly worn furnishings clearly dating from the previous owners. The hotel was part of the Intercontinental group until recently and the "I"

emblems can still be seen on some of the detailing. All rooms offer spectacular views, allowing you to study from the comfort of your own bedroom the architectural mix of old, communist-era, and new that make up central Leipzig. The restaurant **Yamato** (€€€-€€€€) is one of the best Japanese dining options in Saxony. **Panorama XXVII** (€€€) on the 27th floor offers a buffet dinner by candlelight and live

Westin Leipzig

piano music on Friday and Saturday from 6:30 pm. On Sunday from 11 am to 2 pm, a brunch buffet is available. The food is mainly international and the view is one of the best in town. Gerberstraße 15, 04105 Leipzig, ☎ 0341-9880, fax 0341-988-1229, www.westing.com/leipzig. (€€-€€€€)

The historic **Seaside Park Hotel** opened in 1913 as the first grand hotel in Leipzig. The present hotel is a modern establishment behind a historic façade. The well-equipped rooms are done up in an Art Deco style. The **Oriental Express** restaurant serves dishes from the menu of the legendary train. Richard-Wagner-Straße 7, 04109 Leipzig, ☎ 0341-98-520, fax 0341-985-2750, www.seaside-hotels.de. (€€-€€€)

Seaside Park Hotel

In the same area is the **Ibis Leipzig Zentrum**. It is typical Ibis, with few frills but reasonable prices for the well maintained, modern, and clean rooms. Rooms are without mini bars and without mini bar markups. Prices remain sane during the high season. Brühl 69, 04109 Leipzig, ☎ 0341-218-60, fax 0341-218-6222, www.ibishotel.com. (€-€€)

The closest hotel to the main rail station, across the street from the west entrance, is the ever-popular **Holiday Inn Garden Court Leipzig City Center**. From the outside, it looks a bit grim, but inside it is stylish and modern. A combination of location and low prices makes early reservations advisable. Kurt-Schuhmacher-Straße 3, 04105 Leipzig, ☎ 0341-125-10, fax 0341-125-1100, www.holiday-inn.com. (€€-€€€)

Camping

Camping Am Auensee is a pleasant site in a forest to the northwest of Leipzig. It has excellent facilities and 130 lots. It is open year-round. Gustav-Esche-Straße 5, 04159 Leipzig, ☎ 0341-465-1600, fax 0341-465-1617.

◆ Where to Eat

Markt & Naschmarkt Areas

In the Altes Rathaus, the large **Café Brasserie Lotter & Widemann**, Markt 1, ☎ 0341-149-7901, is a pleasant

RESTAURANT COSTS	
€	Less than €10
€€	€10 to €20
€€€	€21 to €35
€€€€	Over €35

place for anything from coffee to a full dinner. The restaurant is divided into three sections: brasserie, restaurant, and gourmet restaurant. The latter influences even the simplest dishes in the brasserie section, making for pleasant dining with a view of the passersby on the busy Market Square. (€-€€€)

The Mädlerpassage, www.maedlerpassage.de, has one of the most famous restaurants in Germany, the **Auerbachs Keller**, Mädlerpassage, Grimmaischestraße 2-4, ☎ 0341-216-100. A young Wolfgang von Goethe frequented it as a student and used it as the setting of a scene in his most famous work, *Faust*. It still serves good food but with a tourist surcharge. The restaurant has two distinct parts, with the **Großer Keller** (€€€-€€€) open daily from 11:30 am to midnight. The **Historische Weinstube** (€€€-€€€€) is open only from 6 pm to midnight and offers more upscale food at upscale prices. Reservations for dinner are highly advisable.

Also in the Mädlerpassage but at ground level are two good French bistros. **Mephisto**, ☎ 0341-216-1050, is close to the Auersbachkeller, with the **Kümmel Apotheke Bistro**, 0341-960-8705, set deeper into the building. Both offer the same authentic French bistro-style food with good service and similar prices. (€-€€)

Across the courtyard from the Nikolaikirche is the very modern steel and glass construction of the **Medici**, Nikolaikirchhof 5, ☎ 0341-211-3878, www.medici-leipzig. The restaurant is airy, with designer chairs, small round tables, and a relaxed atmosphere. The predominantly Italian food is first-class and higher priced. (€€€-€€€€)

In stark contrast is the more traditional and very pleasant **Café Riquet**, Schuhmachergässchen 1, ☎ 0341-961-0000. It is three places in one: a wine cellar in the basement, a coffee shop on the ground floor and a good Viennese-style café to linger in on the first floor. Outside, it is instantly recognizable by the carved elephants above the door. (€-€€)

Thomaskirche Area

Across the road from the Thomaskirche are several coffee shops. **Café Concerto** (€) is a smart café with stylish red chairs. It offers mainly drinks and cakes. Next door is the **Bachstübl**, ☎ 0341-960-2382, similarly offering mostly drinks and cakes but also small snacks. Its interior is more heavily decorated in a faux-Baroque style. (€)

Other establishments in the area also use Bach's name, but visitors can almost certainly do better elsewhere. A good option is the **Thüringerhof**, Burgstraße 19, ☎ 0341-994-4999, www.thueringer-hof.de, a Leipzig institution since 1454. It is the oldest restaurant in the city and can count Martin Luther as a former patron. The cuisine is a combination of Thuringian, as is obvious from the name, and Franconian specialties. Dishes tend to be hearty, prices surprisingly low. (€-€€)

After the *Wende*, Paulaner, the Munich brewery giant, was quick to move back to its original pre-war premises in Leipzig. In between the Thomaskirche and the Barfußgässchen, the **Paulaner Leipzig**, Klostergasse 3-5, ☎ 0341-211-3115, www.paulaner-leipzig.de, has a typical Bavarian operation going: an informal beer hall, a slightly more formal and much quieter restaurant and, of course, when the weather cooperates, a beer garden. The food is a combination of Bavarian specialties and international dishes. The beer is Bavarian and only Paulaner. (€-€€)

Drallewatch Area

The Drallewatch, Saxon for "going out," has traditionally been in the narrow alleys and passages along Brühl and Fleischergasse. The area still teams with small bars and pubs as well as higher-end restaurants.

On the edge of the area is the historic **Zum Arabischen Coffe Baum**, Kleine Fleischergasse 4, ☎ 0341-961-0060, www.coffe-baum.de, with a wide range of cafés and restaurants. It has been in continuous operation since 1694. On the ground floor are two rustic restaurants (€-€€): **Lehmannschen Stube** and the **Schumann-Zimmer**, the latter named after the musical couple who frequented it. Both share the same menu consisting mainly of hearty Saxon dishes. On the first floor is the more stylish **Lusatia Restaurant** (€€-€€€€) offering Saxon and international cuisine. On the second floor are three separate **cafés** (€) in Viennese, Arabian, and French style; the cakes are good and the coffee naturally superb. Contrary to popular belief, Coffe Baum has been serving tea and alcohol since 1720, and continues to do so, but having your alcohol here anyway other than in your coffee would be a shame.

Barthels Hof

Barthels Hof, Hainstraße 1, ☎ 0341-141-310, www.barthels-hof.de, has been serving food since 1497. The complex is divided into three establishments: the Barthel's Weinschäncke (wine bar), Weber's Speisestube (informal restaurant or inn), and the Tollhardt's Zechgewölbe (vaults). Cuisine is local Saxon, ranging from light to hearty. Between 7 am and 9 am the breakfast buffet is a bargain at €6.90 including *Sekt* (sparkling wine). (€-€€)

◆ Daytrip From Leipzig

Lutherstadt Wittenberg

The major reason for visiting Lutherstadt Wittenberg is to see the sights associated with Martin Luther. Although the town itself is pretty, it is only the Luther connection that lifts it above average to make it a major tourist destination.

In the 1930s, Lutherstadt was officially added to the name to increase tourism potential. Under communism, Luther was initially out of vogue but made a strong comeback after his rehabilitation in the 1950s. Wittenberg has again become a major attraction since the unification of Germany and all sights are in magnificent condition. The Luther House, Melanchthon House, Stadtkirche, and Schlosskirche are UNESCO World Cultural Heritage Sites.

Information Sources

Tourist Office: Tourist Information Office, Schlossplatz 2, 06886 Lutherstadt Wittenberg, ☎ 03491-498-610, www.wittenberg.de.

Transportation

The train station, with the oldest surviving station building in Germany on one side and a very modern design on the other side of the track, is a 10-minute walk from the Lutherhaus.

Wittenberg is a stop for the ICE trains, 30 minutes from Leipzig and an hour from Berlin. ICE trains run around every two hours. The more frequent but slower and cheaper regional trains reach Leipzig in an hour.

Saxony

MARTIN LUTHER (1483-1546)

Martin Luther was born on November 10, 1483 in Eisleben. He studied law in Erfurt, but, after narrowly escaping a thunderbolt during a severe thunderstorm, entered the Augustine Monastery in Erfurt. He was ordained in 1507 and a year later started teaching at the university in Wittenberg.

Sometime during the 1510s, Luther concluded that the only way to eternal salvation was through faith. The selling of indulgences outraged him as his flock increasingly relied on indulgences rather than confession and a Christian lifestyle. On October 31, 1517, he wrote to his superiors deploring the practice and suggested 95 theses for debate by the church. The 95 Theses became public knowledge and copies spread through Germany in a matter of weeks.

Originally, Luther intended to change practices inside the church. He did not intend to start a new church. In 1521, he was excommunicated by the Pope and declared an outlaw at the Diet of Worms. While disguised as a knight and staying in the Wartburg Castle, he translated the New Testament into German. Apart from its influence on religion, Luther's German New Testament finally united the various regional dialects into a High German still understood and used by all German speakers.

He returned to Wittenberg in 1522 and, after that, there was no return to the old ways. Germany became split between his supporters and those of the Roman Catholic Church. Several battles were fought, some intellectual and some physical. It was only in 1555 that Emperor Charles V, the same emperor who banned Luther at Worms, agreed to freedom of religion – meaning freedom to choose either the Lutheran or Roman Catholic faith – in the German states.

Luther died while on business in Eisleben on February 18, 1546. He was buried in the Schlosskirche in Wittenberg.

In Germany, the Lutheran church is mostly referred to as the Evangelical (*Evangelische*) church. Members of this church follow the teachings of the Bible as interpreted by Luther. They do not consider themselves as followers of Luther, but rather followers of Christ.

Sightseeing

Sightseeing in Wittenberg is easy, as all the major sights are in a straight line in Collegienstraße, which turns into Schlossstraße after the Market Square.

Martin Luther in Wittenberg: The **Luthereiche** (Luther Oak) is in a small park on the corner of Collegien and Lutherstraße. In 1520, Luther burned a copy of the papal bull, which excommunicated him, and books by his opponents here. (Through the years, he burned various other copies in other towns as well. The original bull is in the state archives in Dresden.) The original oak died long ago and the current one dates from 1830.

Up the street, past the park and parts of the former city walls, is the stately mid-16th-century **Collegium Augusteum** (Augustus College). Directly behind it is the **Lutherhaus** (Luther House), Collegienstraße 54, ☎ 03491-42-030, www.martinluther.de, where Luther lived from 1508, first as a monk and from 1525 until 1544 with his wife, Katharina von Bora. The museum is one of the most interesting in Germany. It gives a very good overview of the life of Luther as well as the reasons for and the spread of the Reformation. In addition, the museum is about the only place in Wittenberg where it is openly acknowledged that Luther never nailed his 95 Theses to the church door.

Lutherhaus

Saxony

Luther's life and his move from critic to outright reformer are illustrated with more than a thousand exhibits. Of particular relevance and interest are numerous indulgences from all over Germany – the items that sparked Luther's protest in the first place. In the Lutherstube, the original wood paneling survived in the room that Luther and his family used as dining and reception room for his numerous guests. Note the "Petr" scratched on a doorsill – graffiti left by Czar Peter the Great in 1702.

The Lutherhaus is open April to October daily from 9 am to 6 pm, and November to March, Tuesday to Sunday from 10 am to

5 pm. Admission is €5. A combination ticket with the Melanchthonhaus valid for two days is available for €6).

Melanchthonhaus

Nearby is the **Melanchthonhaus** (Melanchthon House), Collegienstraße 60, ☎ 03491-403-279, with its characteristic gable. Philipp Melanchthon (1497-1560), one of Luther's closest friends and strongest supporters, lived here from 1536 until his death. The house has an interesting interior with mainly prints and panels on his life. Opening hours are the same as for the Lutherhaus. Admission is €2.50.

Practically next-door is the **Alte Universität** (Old University) that existed from 1502 to 1817. This institution drew both Luther and Melanchthon to Wittenberg, as teachers of Philosophy and Greek respectively.

Marktplatz Area: On the **Marktplatz** (Market Square) are statues of Luther (1821) and Melanchthon (1865). The large Renaissance **Rathaus** (Town Hall) was completed in 1535. Opposite is the **birthplace of Lucas Cranach** the Younger, Markt 6. Lucas Cranach the Elder lived and worked here from 1505 to 1547. The house was severely damaged by bombardments during the Seven Years' War. It was converted and the Baroque façade added in 1760.

Clearly visible from the Marktplatz but accessible from here only through a narrow alley is the **Stadtkirche St Marien** (Town Church of St Mary), Kirchplatz, ☎ 03491-403-201. It is the oldest building in town and has a famous Cranach Reformation altarpiece. Most of this Gothic church dates from the early 1400s, but parts of the towers are from the 13th century. The adjacent chapel is from 1370. Opening hours are May to October from Monday to Saturday, 9 am to 5 pm; Sunday from 11:30 am to

5 pm. November to April opening hours are Monday to Saturday from 10 am to 4 pm, Sunday from 11:30 am to 4 pm.

Marktplatz

Saxony

The **Cranach Höfe** (Cranach Courtyards), Schlossstraße 1, ☎ 03491-432-817, dates from 1506 and has about 100 rooms in which Cranach the Elder lived and worked. It is used as a museum, with a historic printing press and gallery. Open Monday to Saturday from 10 am to 5 pm, but closed on Monday from November to April. On Sunday, open from 1 to 5 pm. Admission is €3 for some exhibitions but free to most parts of the building.

The **Haus der Geschichte** (House of History), Schlossstraße 6, ☎ 03491-660-366, is a small museum dedicated to life in the former German Democratic Republic. The focus is on everyday life and the articles that were used by ordinary people. Living rooms of every decade from the 1940s to 1970s show how fashion changed even in communist times. It also has kitchens, bathrooms, and toys from various eras. On the ground floor is an exhibition of bulky radios and televisions, some with modifications to receive western broadcasts. Opening hours are Tuesday to Friday from 10 am to 5 pm and weekends from 11 am to 6 pm. Admission is €3.

The Schloss Area: At the far end of the Old Town on the Schlossplatz are the Schloss (Castle) and more famous

Schlosskirche (Castle Church). Both were built by Elector Frederick the Wise around 1500 but were damaged during wars and rebuilt differently from the originals.

The **Schloss** was changed into a citadel in 1819 after Prussia annexed among others Saxony-Wittenberg as punishment for Saxony's alliance with Napoleon. It currently houses a not particularly interesting Nature and Ethnology Museum. Of more interest are the restaurant in the cellar, the views from the garden, and the plaques in the courtyard with names of famous people associated with Wittenberg.

The **Schlosskirche Allerheiligen**, ☎ 03491-402-585, is a major tourist draw. It is on the doors of this church that Martin Luther was supposed to have nailed his 95 Theses on October 31, 1517. The church, and said door, burned down in 1760 during the Seven Years' War. The current church was constructed in 1892 and incorporated one of the original castle towers as a church tower. In 1855, the 95 Theses were cast in bronze and are seen on the door facing the square. Inside the church are the tombs of both Luther and Melanchthon. Also of note are the

Schlosskirche

bronze epitaph (1527 by Peter Vischer) of Fredrick the Wise and an alabaster statue (1537) of him kneeling in knight's armor. The pulpit, altar, baptismal font, and most other decorations date from 1892, although they are made to look older. Openings hours are the same as for the Stadtkirche.

DID HE OR DID HE NOT?

It was long believed that Martin Luther started his protest against the Roman Catholic Church when he nailed his 95 Theses to the door of the Schlosskirche. This act was confirmed by his close friend Philipp Melanchthon, who claimed to have witnessed the event.

It is now generally accepted by most historians that this event never took place. Luther's 95 Theses were written in Latin. Only the educated at the university could read Latin, thus excluding even the nobles in town, making the Schlosskirche meaningless for such a protest notice. Furthermore, Melanchthon, the chief witness, only arrived in town six months after the event. In addition, Martin Luther at this stage, and for several years afterward, was more interested in reforming the church than in creating a separate church.

Historians now accept that on October 31, 1517, Luther wrote to his church superior in Magdeburg complaining about the fact that people were buying indulgences rather than confessing their sins. He included his 95 Theses, intended for theological debate, with the letter. However, they became public knowledge and transcripts were distributed in less than two months throughout Germany. With the notable exception of the Lutherhaus museum, virtually all of Wittenberg acknowledges only the version with the Theses on the door.

Saxony

Where to Stay & Eat

The most pleasant accommodation is at the **Best Western Stadtpalais Wittenberg**. The hotel opened in 1999 in a restored mansion. Rooms are large, with all modern comforts. The restaurant **Wittenberger Hof** (€-€€€) is the town's best choice for international cui-

Best Western Stadtpalais

sine, although regional specialties are also available. Colegienstraße 56-57, 06886 Lutherstadt Wittenberg,

☎ 03491-4250, fax 03491-425-100, www.stadtpalais.
bestwestern.com. (€€-€€€)

A pleasant alternative close to the Market Square is the
Stadthotel Wittenberg Schwarzer Baer. It has been serving
food since 1520 and Luther, Melanchthon, and Cranach were
patrons. Rooms are comfortable, rather than luxurious, but still
well appointed and spacious. The historic **restaurant
Schwarzer Baer** (€-€€) serves snacks and full meals.
Schlossstraße 2, 06886 Lutherstadt Wittenberg, ☎ 03491-420-
4344, fax 03491-420-4345, www.stadthotel-wittenberg.de. (€€)

Many dining options are available on the Market Square and its
direct vicinity. An excellent option is the **Brauhaus Wittenberg
im Beyerhof**. It is a brewery and patrons are welcome to observe the brewmaster at work. The courtyard transforms into a
250-seat beer garden when the weather is good and is also the
setting for frequent concerts. The food ranges from local specialties to Mediterranean cuisine. The beer is local only and
fresh. In addition, 14 large and comfortable rooms are available
for overnight guests. Markt 6, 06886 Lutherstadt Wittenberg,
☎ 03491-433-130, fax 03491-433-131, www.brauhaus-
wittenberg.de. (€-€€)

Inside the cellars of the castle is the restaurant **Schlosskeller
Lutherstube**, Schlossplatz, ☎ 03491-580-805. The walls here
are yards thick and tables are set in all kinds of nooks and cran-
nies. The food is unashamedly old German and regional. Portions are large. Local beer and wine from the Saale region are
available. Service is fast and friendly. (€-€€)

Camping

 The **Marina-Camp Elbe** is on the banks of the Elbe
in Wittenberg across from the Lutherhaus. It is
newly built and in excellent condition with all the latest comforts. There are 100 lots for visitors. Boat
and bicycle rental, as well as simple holiday homes, are available on-site. Open from March to November. Brückenkopf 1,
06886 Lutherstadt Wittenberg, ☎ 0178-601-7665, fax 03491-
454-199, www.marina-camp-elbe.de.

Thuringia

Thuringia is the smallest of the former East German states that joined the Federal Republic of Germany in 1990. Its central location at the geographical heart of Germany allows easy access from all regions.

Thuringia, despite its small area, has more than 400 fortresses, castles, and palaces, including the magnificent Wartburg – often referred to as the German national monument. Weimar, seat of German artists such as Goethe and Schiller, is still as important a cultural site as it was in the early 19th century. Erfurt, with 204,000 inhabitants the largest city in the state, has one of the best-preserved medieval city centers in Germany.

◆ Getting Here & Around

By Rail

The major Thuringian cities are stops on the fast, luxurious ICE network, allowing fast travel times to other German cities. From Frankfurt to Eisenach requires just under two hours. From here, it is 10 minutes to Gotha and another 20 minutes to Erfurt, which is only 15 minutes from Weimar, and an hour from Leipzig. Not every ICE train stop in each city on every run, but the frequent local trains are not much slower, occasionally even faster, and always significantly cheaper.

MONEY SAVING TICKETS IN THURINGIA
The **HopperTicket** allows round-trip journeys on any regional train in Thuringia for distances up to 30 miles each way. It costs only €4.50 per person. (Erfurt to Weimar one-way would normally be €4.20!) The HopperTicket is valid weekdays after 9 am and all day on weekends.

By Road

Autobahn A4 cuts through the southern part of Thuringia giving fast access to the cities Eisenach, Gotha, Erfurt, Weimar, Jena, and Gera. At the east end, this autobahn connects to the A9 with access to Berlin and Leipzig in the north, as well as Bavaria to the south. Just west of Thuringia, the A4 crosses the A5 with access to Frankfurt and the A7 with access to Hamburg in the north and Bavaria to the south. Do not be tempted to take the B7, which runs parallel to the A4. Distances may be shorter, but this road is dog-slow, overcrowded, and runs mainly through industrial areas.

By Air

Erfurt Airport, Flughafenstraße 4, 99092 Erfurt, ☎ 0361-656-2200, www.flughafen-erfurt.de, is a minor regional airport with mainly charter and domestic flights. The airport is only three miles from the city center and can be reached in 16 minutes by Bus 99 from the main bus station, or around 10 minutes by taxi.

A more realistic option is to use **Leipzig-Halle** or **Frankfurt International Airport**.

THE THÜRINGEN CARD

The Thüringen Card, www.thueringencard.info, is available from most tourist offices as well as participating venues. It gives unlimited access and discounts to many sights and forms of transportation. Conditions vary each year, but it generally saves money when visiting more than two major participating sights per day.

◆ Information Sources

Thüringer Tourismus, Postfach 100519, 99005 Erfurt, ☎ 0361-37-420, www.thueringen-tourismus.de.

Thuringia
(Thüringen)

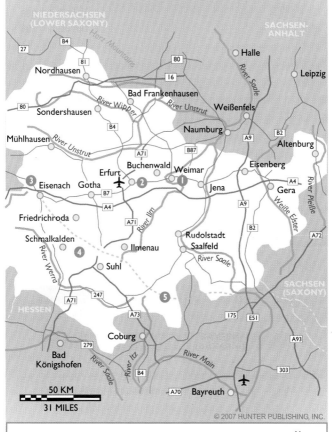

1. Weimar: Theaterplatz, Schiller & Goethe residences, Markt area, *Park an der Ilm* (Park on the Ilm), Buchenwald
2. Erfurt: Domplatz, Fischmarkt, Krämerbrucke, Nordhausen, Harz Mountains, Bad Frankenhausen, Kyffhäuser Mountains
3. Eisenach: The Wartburg, Old Town, Gotha
4. *Thuringer Wald* (Thuringian Forest)
5. Rennsteig hiking trail

Weimar

Weimar is a pretty, small town of around 60,000 inhabitants, but its fame stretches far beyond the borders of Thuringia. Foreigners generally associate Weimar with the ill-fated Weimar Republic founded here in 1919, but ruled from Berlin where it floundered in the early 1930s after the Nazis came to power.

Although never a large town, and never of real strategic importance, Weimar attracted artistic talent for centuries. During the late 18th century, under the reign of the talented Duchess Anna Amalia and later her son Carl August, the Duchy Saxe-Weimar-Eisenach reached its classical period and, for a few decades, this town of under 5,000 was the center of intellectual thought in Germany. The Duchess came to power in 1758, and acquired the services of **Christoph Martin Wieland** to educate her son. The greatest coup was inviting the brilliant young writer **Johann Wolfgang von Goethe**. He would stay in Weimar from 1775 until his death in 1832, playing a major role not only in the arts but also in the administration of the duchy. He attracted other writers, such as the dramatist **Friedrich von Schiller** and the theologian **Gottfried Herder**. These four elevated German literature to an unknown level, leading to the period referred to as the Classical. For most German tourists, and students of German, visiting Weimar is largely a pilgrimage to the sites associated with these writers.

GERMANY'S FOREMOST POET

Johann Wolfgang Goethe (1749-1832) was born in Frankfurt am Main into a rich and well-educated, middle-class family. He trained as a lawyer in Leipzig and Strasbourg but lost interest in law long before his father forced him to complete his training in Wetzlar. His experiences there led to *Die Leiden des Jungen Werther*

(*The Sorrows of Young Werther*), the biggest-selling work during his lifetime. It brought him European fame – Napoleon carried a copy on his Egyptian campaign and claimed to have read it seven times.

In 1776, Goethe visited the court of Duke Karl August in Weimar and ended up staying here the rest of his life. The duke had him elevated into the nobility – thus allowing the "von" in his surname. In addition to his writings, he was an avid scientist and geologist. As de facto prime minister, he did much to improve the administration and finances of the Duchy of Saxe-Weimar-Eisenach.

It is, of course, on his writing that his reputation is built. Initially he belonged to the *Sturm und Drang* movement, but later turned Classical. He wrote numerous plays, poems, and books. He traveled frequently and his traveling notes are in books such as *Die Italienische Reise* (*Italian Journey*) and his autobiography *Dichtung und Wahrheit* (*Poetry and Truth*). His most famous work is the epic drama *Faust* – a tragedy with a happy ending and the most likeable devil ever.

Through the centuries, Weimar also attracted other talents such as **Lucas Cranach the Elder**, who died here. **Johann Sebastian Bach** was organist and choirmaster in Weimar from 1708 to 1717. From 1848, **Franz Liszt** filled the same position.

In the 20th century, Weimar played a major role in the foundation of modern architecture and design. From 1902, **Henri van de Velde**, the Belgian exponent of **Art Nouveau**, worked in Weimar. After World War I, the **Bauhaus** was founded in Weimar under the leadership of **Walter Gropius**.

◆ Information Sources

Tourist Office: The tourist information office is at Markt 10, 99423 Weimar, 03643-240-00, www.weimar.de.

◆ Transportation

The main station is about a 20-minute walk from the historic center – taking a bus to Goetheplatz is more sensible. Bus 6 is particularly convenient, running past the Nietzsche Archive, Goetheplatz, and the Hauptbahnhof to Buchenwald.

◆ Sightseeing

At first glance, Weimar may seem like one big cele-bration of Goethe and Schiller. This is true to some extend, as Goethe especially played a dominant role in establishing Weimar as a cultural center. Weimar does not have large structures, cathedrals, or castles.

BAUHAUS IN WEIMAR

The Bauhaus was founded in Weimar in 1919 under the leadership of Walter Gropius. The group's interdisciplinary interaction between artist and artisans laid the foundation for modern architecture and design. Cubicle architectural design was not acceptable to conservative Weimar and the Bauhaus moved to Dessau in 1925. In 1932, the Nazis closed the Bauhaus, accusing leading members of being communist. Most went abroad to find more acceptance of their ideas, especially to the USA.

Reflecting the original rejection of the Bauhaus ideas, Weimar has only four Bauhaus sights – the Bauhaus Museum, the former Arts and Crafts School, the former School of Fine Arts, and the Haus am Horn. The latter three are UNESCO World Cultural Heritage Sites.

The sights here are more subtle and it takes more time to ap-preciate them. However, even for visitors with no interest in German literature, a visit to Weimar can be enjoyable.

Weimar is best explored on foot. From Goetheplatz, follow the crowds down the pedestrian mall to the sights of Weimar.

Virtually all tourist sights in Weimar are managed by the **Stiftung Weimarer Klassik** (Weimar Classics Foundation) and share the same contact details: Besucherinformation, Frauentorstraße 4, 99423 Weimar, ☎ 03643-545-401, www.weimar-klassik.de.

The interiors of many of the former houses of artists are not lit, which makes visiting on bright days desirable. In these houses, the atmosphere of a home rather than a museum is preserved, meaning very few descriptions and only a few chained-off spaces. A guided tour, or adequate guidebook, is essential for visitors interested in more than just seeing the houses and furniture. Out of conservation concerns, the number of visitors is sometimes limited during the high season.

Unless otherwise noted, opening hours for all the sights are Tuesday to Sunday, April to October from 9 am to 6 pm, November to March from 9 am to 4 pm. Admission fees are set differently for individual sights. An annual ticket, giving multiple accesses to all sights, is available at €30. A combination ticket with single entries to 15 sights, excluding the Goethehaus, is €20.

Theatherplatz

The Neo-Classical **Deutsches Nationaltheater** (German National Theatre), Theaterplatz, ☎ 03643-755-334, is the third theater built on this site. The current building was erected in 1948, following the plans of the 1908 theater, which was destroyed during World War II. Goethe and Schiller were directors here; Liszt and Wagner conducted here. In 1919, after the collapse of the German Empire at the end of World War I, the National Assembly met here to write Germany's first democratic constitution. This ultraliberal constitution almost faltered in the early 1920s, but it was the consequences of the Depression that exposed its limitations, allowing Hitler to use illegal means to grab power legally.

In front of the theater is the **Goethe-Schiller statue**, showing the two literary giants in period dress. This 1857 work by Ernst Rietschel, is arguably Germany's most famous and most pho-

Thuringia

tographed statue. Copies of the statue are found in San Francisco, Cleveland, and Milwaukee.

The **Bauhaus-Museum**, Am Theaterplatz, 03643-546-961, is located, somewhat ironically, inside a Neo-Classical building. The museum exhibits around 500 items at a time from its vast Bauhaus collection, as well as a number of Art Nouveau items by Henri van de Velde and his followers. Admission is €4.

The adjacent **Wittumspalast** (Widow's Palace), Am Theaterplatz, ☎ 03643-545-377, dates from the mid-18th century and was the town residence of Duchess Anna Amalia, from 1775 until 1807. On display are living and reception rooms typical from that period. The main draw is the *Tafelrundezimmer*, a drawing room where Goethe and other luminaries met for social and intellectual discussions. The palace opens only at 10 am. Admission is €3.50.

The Schiller & Goethe Residences

Friederich von Schiller came to Weimar in 1799 and rented various properties before acquiring, in 1802, a yellow Baroque house on the Esplanade (since renamed Schillerstraße), where he lived until his early death in 1805. The house was converted into a museum, **Schillers Wohnhaus** (Schiller's Residence), Schillerstraße 12, ☎ 03643-545-401. Although the museum was created only in 1847, 20 years after his widow's estate sold the property, family members re-

Schillers Wohnhaus

turned much of the original furniture. The complete house is furnished and decorated as it was in Schiller's time. The museum is closed on Tuesday but open on Monday. Admission is €3.50.

Germany's Foremost Playwright

Johann Christoph Friedrich Schiller (1759-1805) had a rebellious youth and intensely disliked the military positions the Duke of Württemberg forced upon him. His first play, *Die Räuber* (The Robbers), was published anonymously and first performed in 1782, in Mannheim. In the same year, he fled Württemberg and soon found his skills appreciated elsewhere.

Schiller age 21

He met Goethe in 1787 and the two eventually became lifelong friends – some say rivals – and cooperated intensively after Schiller settled in Weimar in 1799. In 1802, he was granted a noble title, allowing "*von*" (from) to be added to his name. He died in Weimar on May 9, 1805.

In contrast to Goethe, Schiller wrote plays to be performed, rather than just read. He took into consideration the limitations of the theater as well as the actors, factors Goethe famously ignored. His plays include *Don Carlos*, *Maria Stuart*, *Wallenstein*, *Maid of Orleans*, and *Wilhelm Tell*. His most famous work is *Lied an der Freude* (*Ode to Joy*), set to music by Ludwig van Beethoven in his monumental Ninth Symphony.

Two blocks away is Weimar's most popular attraction, the **Goethe-Nationalmuseum**, Frauenplan 1, ☎ 03643-545-300, which encompasses Goethe's house and a permanent exhibition. In 1792, Goethe moved into the house Am Frauenplan and lived there until his death in 1832. It remained in the hands of the Goethe family until it was opened as a permanent museum in 1885. The Goethes Wohnhaus (Goethe's Residence) is furnished almost exactly as it was in Goethe's days – he kept meticulous records and described parts of the house in detail in letters to friends and family. Many pieces are original. Goethe left an art collection of 26,511 works, 5,400 books, and around 22,000 scientific specimens; only a minute part is on display. The house is elegantly, although simply furnished. Bear Goethe's

Goethes Wohnhaus

observation in mind that excessively beautiful and over-decorated rooms are for people without their own thoughts or new ideas. Note the high desks – he preferred to write standing up. Admission is €6.

In the adjacent house is a moderately interesting **Permanent Exhibition** on the members of the Weimar Classical period, 1759-1832. The exhibition consists of art works and items associated with the various artists who worked in Weimar during the period. Admission is €2.50.

Markt Area

The Cranachhaus

On the **Markt** (Market) are the Neo-Gothic **Rathaus** (Town Hall), the Renaissance **Cranachhaus**, where Lucas Cranach died in 1553, and the mid-1930s exterior of the famed **Hotel Elephant**. In addition to the tourist information office, Markt

also has an information office for Buchenwald Concentration Camp, Markt 5, ☎ 03646-747-540.

Nearby is the **Herzogin Anna Amalia Bibliothek** (Duchess Anna Amalia Library), Platz der Demokratie 1, ☎ 03643-545-200. Currently the library has more than a million items, including the libraries of Liszt and Nietzsche. Its most famous part, a magnificent Rococo hall, was severely damaged by fire in 2004 and will be closed for several years.

Stadtkirche

Two blocks to the north of Markt is the triple-nave **Stadtkirche** (City Church), Herderplatz. The oldest parts of the church date back to the 15th century but most parts are Baroque. A large statue of Johann Gottfried Herder is on the square in front of the building. Bach and Liszt were organists here. The church has a splendid Cranach triptych. The church is open Monday to Saturday, from April to October, 10 am to noon and 2 to 4 pm, and from November to March, 11 to noon and 2 to 3 pm.

Although Goethe played a major role in the construction of the palace, in the **Schloßmuseum** (Palace Museum), Burgplatz 4, ☎ 03643-546-960, the focus for once is not on Goethe but on fine art. The museum has a large collection, spread over three floors, with works from the Middle Ages to the early 20th century. Especially noteworthy are the Cranach gallery and the ceremonial rooms. Admission is €4.50.

Park an der Ilm

The **Park an der Ilm** is a lovely landscape park stretching from the Schloss southwards along both banks of the River Ilm. On the east bank is the best-known structure in the park, **Goethes Gartenhaus** (Goethe's Garden Cottage),

Goethes Gartenhaus

Im Park an der Ilm, ☎ 03643-545-375. It is a simple, small

house with a remarkable, high steep roof. Goethe lived here from 1776 to 1782. Even after moving into town, he frequently stayed here during summer to work in the peaceful surroundings. The sparsely furnished house is open daily and admission is €3.

On the edge of the park, the **Haus am Horn**, Am Horn 6, ☎ 03643-904-054, is the only original Bauhaus-designed house in Weimar. It was built in 1923 as part of what should have become a complete Bauhaus neighborhood. Opening hours are Wednesday and weekends from 11 am to 5 pm.

In the park, near the bridge to Goethe's Garden Cottage, is a **Shakespeare statue**. It was erected in 1904 as the first statue to honor Shakespeare on the European continent. Nearby is the **Liszt-Haus**, Marienstraße 17, where Franz Liszt lived most summers from 1869 to 1886. The house is open Tuesday to Sunday from April to October, 10 am to 1 pm and 2 to 6 pm. Closed on Monday and during the winter season. Admission is €2.

The **Bauhaus University**, Geschwester Scholl Straße 8, has two UNESCO World Cultural Heritage buildings that were used by the original Bauhaus. Both were designed by Henri van de Velde around 1904 and became the seat of the Bauhaus in 1919. The university is open weekdays from 8 am to 9 pm and Saturdays from 8 am to 3 pm.

Both Goethe and Schiller found their final resting place in the mausoleum of the ducal family, the **Fürstengruft**, Historischer Friedhof, Am Poseckschen Garten, ☎ 03643-545-380. The mausoleum and adjacent Russian Orthodox church are open Tuesday to Sunday from April to October, 10 am to 1 pm and 2 to 6 pm, closing at 4 pm during the winter season. Admission is €2.

Friederich Nietzsche spent his final years, from 1897 to 1900, in Weimar with his sister. She had Henri van de Velde design the **Nietzsche-Archiv**, Humboldstraße 36, ☎ 03643-545-159, to house his works. His writings are now in the Goethe-Schiller archive and his library in the Duchess Anna Amalia Library, but the Art Nouveau interior can be seen. The museum is open Tuesday to Sunday from April to October, 3 pm to 6 pm. Closed on Monday and during the winter season. Admission is €2. From here, Bus 6 is convenient to return to Goetheplatz, the main station, or to Buchenwald.

Near Weimar: Buchenwald

Buchenwald

A mere six miles from the spiritual home of German humanism, the Nazis constructed the notorious **Buchenwald Concentration Camp**. Between 1937 and 1945, 250,000 people were interned here and around 50,000 died. Buchenwald was a work camp and not solely an extermination center. Between 1945 and 1950, the Soviet occupation forces used parts of the camp as an internment center for both Nazis and arbitrarily arrested persons. During this period, 7,000 of 28,000 prisoners died. This fact was hidden until the discovery of the mass graves during the 1990s.

The **Gedenkstätte Buchenwald** (Memorial), ☎ 03643-4300, www.buchenwald.de, is located at the original camp. Most of the camp was demolished while establishing a memorial to anti-fascist resistance. Only the foundations of the barracks and most other buildings are still visible. The gate still displays the original message: "*Jedem das Seine*" ("To each what he deserves"). A museum is located inside the former storehouse. Other buildings that survived include the crematorium, prisoners' canteen, the arrest cells, and the disinfection building.

The museum and exhibition rooms are open Tuesday to Sunday from May to September, 9:45 am to 6 pm, and from October to April, 8:45 to 5 pm. The campgrounds are open daily until nightfall. The camp can be reached from Weimar by Bus no 6 only if marked

Buchenwald inmates right after liberation in April 1945

Buchenwald – usually one per hour. Admission is free.

◆ Cultural Events & Festivals

Weimar has a rich cultural tradition and many events are scheduled throughout the year. Virtually all plays are performed in German only, but musical and dancing events, ranging from contemporary to classical, are also frequently scheduled. The Tourist Information Office has details and can make some reservations.

The Weimar **Kunstfest** (Art Festival), www.kunstfest-weimar. de, is a cultural highlight from mid-August to mid-September. Music and plays are performed on most public squares and in all theaters, including the famed German National Theater.

Weimar also arranges events during the **Thuringian Bach Weeks**, www.bach-wochen.de, staged during March and April.

The largest folk festival in Thuringia is the three-day Weimar **Zwiebelmarkt** (Onion Market) in mid-October. Apart from onions, loads of food and drink are available and live music is performed on most squares and public spaces.

◆ Shopping

Weimar is a good place to buy German literature. The town breathes literature and works are available from many bookshops as well as most museum shops. Classical works in paperback are surprisingly cheap but prices rise fast as soon as photographs and color are added. **Stiftung Weimarer Klassik**, Frauentorstraße 4, ☎ 03643-545-401, www.weimar-klassik. de, has a vast selection of books and other paraphernalia associated with the Weimar Classicists.

◆ Adventures

On Foot

Countryside Hikes: A popular hike is the 17-mile **Goethe Wanderweg** from Weimar to Schloss Kochberg. The route is marked with a "G" in Goethe's handwriting. Although Goethe usually covered the route on horseback to visit his close confidante Charlotte von Stein, he also famously walked the route in around four hours. Most hikers take significantly longer, spending time en route enjoying the scenery and visiting inns and beer gardens. A popular stop is the 128-ft covered bridge over the River Ilm at Buchfahrt. Parts of this wooden bridge and the adjacent watermill date from the 17th century.

On Wheels

By Bicycle: The **Ilmtal cy**cling route runs for 75 miles in the Ilm Valley from the Thuringia Forest to where the Ilm flows into the Saale near Bad Sulza. This route is easy and mostly asphalt. It is marked by a cyclist and a blue and green wave. An interesting alternative is the 17-mile **Feininger route**. It is runs in a circle from Weimar and passes sites frequented and sketched by the Bauhaus artist Lyonel Feininger in the 1920s.

Bicycles can be rented from **Fahrradverleih Grüne Liga**, Goetheplatz 9b, ☎ 03643-492-796, or from **Fahrrad Hopf**, Untergraben 2, ☎ 03643-202-120.

◆ Where to Stay & Eat

The most famous hotel in Weimar, and one of the best known in Germany, is the **Hotel Elephant**, centrally located on the Market Square. The first paying guests slept here in 1741 and since then luminaries such as Goethe, Schiller, Bach, Clara Schumann, Felix Mendelssohn-Bartholdy, Franz Liszt, Richard Wagner, and Tolstoy spent the night. Thomas Mann used it as the setting for *Lotte in Weimar* (translated as *Beloved Returned*). Hitler stayed and apparently did not like it much, as the Nazis had the upper floors rebuilt in the style that survived to the present. The comfort-

Hotel Elephant

able rooms are furnished with Bauhaus and Art Deco furniture. The **Anna Amalia Restaurant** (€€€-€€€€) is arguably the best in town and the **Elephantenkeller** (€€-€€€) is the most famous. The Anna Amalia offers nouvelle cuisine, mixing German and Mediterranean dishes, while the Elephantenkeller serves more traditional regional food. Markt 19, 99423 Weimar, ☎ 03643-8020, fax 03643-802-610, www.starwoodhotels.com. (€€€€)

The **Dorint Sofitel am Goethepark** is conveniently located between the Goethehaus and the Park an der Ilm. It successfully combines two historic houses with modern architecture to create a thoroughly modern interior. Rooms are comfortable and spacious. Beethovenplatz 1-2, 99423 Weimar, ☎ 03643-8720, fax 03643-872100, www.accorhotels.com. (€€-€€€€)

Dorint Sofitel

Grand Hotel Russischer Hof

In Weimar, only the Elephant has a longer tradition and more impressive guest list than the **Grand Hotel Russischer Hof**. The building dates back to 1797 and, in contrast to the Elephant, the exterior here looks the part. It is located on Goetheplatz near the National Theater and Bauhaus Museum. Rooms are comfortable, with French-style period furniture. The equally luxurious and stylish **Anastasia Restaurant** (€€-€€€€) serves international cuisine, with a large selection of Austrian and Thuringian dishes. Goetheplatz 2, 99423 Weimar, ☎ 03643-7740, fax 03643-774-840, www.russischerhof.com. (€€€€)

Ringhotel Kaiserin Augusta

Across the road from the main station, behind a historic façade, is the modern interior of the **Ringhotel Kaiserin Augusta** (previously Intercity Hotel). The hotel is well equipped and especially popular with business travelers. Rooms are not particularly large, but are comfortable, with stylish dark furniture. Carl-August-Allee 17, 99423 Weimar, ☎ 03643-2340, fax 03643-234-444, www.ringhotels.de. (€€€)

Apart from the Elephantenkeller, the most famous restaurant in Weimar is **Gasthaus Zum Weißen Schwan,** Frauentorstraße 23, ☎ 03643-202-521. It is literally around the corner from the Goethehaus, which is not surprising given that it was one of Goethe's favored restaurants for entertaining. The cuisine is hearty local specialties and the prices surprisingly moderate for such a well-known establishment. (€-€€).

Just off the Market Square is **Shakespeares**, Windischenstraße 4, ☎ 03643-901-285. It is a large, modern bistro-style restaurant with its own stage. The food is both good and reasonably priced. Open only for dinner. (€-€€)

Camping

Near Weimar, in the Ilm Valley, is the **Ilmtal-Oettern** campsite. It has 100 lots but facilities are rather basic. It is open from mid-April to October. Campingplatz Ilmtal, 99438 Oettern, ☎ 036453-80-264.

Erfurt

Erfurt, the capital of Thuringia, is a lovely, unpretentious town. It receives far fewer visitors than nearby Weimar, but is easier to enjoy. Much of the Erfurt experience is simply strolling through the beautiful streets and enjoying one of Germany's most authentic medieval city cores.

Thuringia

In 742, Erfurt was founded as a bishopric by St Boniface. Its heyday was in the 14th and 15th centuries, when trade in the woad plant, used for blue dye before the introduction of indigo, made it a rich city. Martin Luther lived here from 1501 to 1511, first as a student and then as a monk. In 1808, Napoleon Bonaparte met Czar Alexander I here for a congress lasting 17 days.

◆ Information Sources

Tourist Office: The Tourismus Gesellschat Erfurt, Benediktsplatz 1, 99084 Erfurt, ☎ 0361664-0110, www.erfurt-tourismus.de, is located in between the Krämerbrücke and the Fischmarkt.

◆ Transportation

The main train station is a five-minute walk to the south of Anger, the main shopping area at the edge of the Old Town. Frequent trains to Weimar take between 11 and 20 minutes. Trams 3, 4, and 6 run from the station through the Old Town to Domplatz and beyond.

◆ Sightseeing

Erfurt's historic center is fairly large, but the numerous beautifully decorated buildings make the city easy to enjoy and a pleasure to stroll in. A good place to start is from the massive Domplatz, the size of four football fields. It is a half-hour walk from the station – well worth it to see the interesting decorated buildings – or can be reached in minutes by tram.

Domplatz

The most impressive view in Erfurt is from the Domplatz towards cathedral hill. A wide flight of 70 stairs leads from the square to the top of the hill where the cathedral and an abbey are set in close proximity.

The **Dom St Marien** (St Mary's Cathedral), Domberg, ☎ 0361-646-1265, was originally a Romanesque basilica, constructed in 1154. The High Gothic choir was added in the 14th century and after 1455 the original nave was replaced by a Late Gothic

Domplatz from the air, with St Severikirche at far right and Dom St Marien to its left (Balloonsportclub Jena)

construction. One of the largest free-swinging bells in the world, the 1497 "Gloriosa," rings on special occasions from the central tower. The main entrance is through an interesting High Gothic portal – two doors are set obliquely to form a rare triangular portal. The current interior is mostly Baroque. The Wolfram, a bronze statue candelabra dating from 1160, is considered the oldest freestanding bronze sculpture in Germany. The stained-glass windows in the choir are 14th-century originals. The church is open from May to October, Monday to Saturday, 9 to 11:30 am and 12:30 to 5 pm, closing at 4:30 pm on Saturdays; from November to April, Monday to Saturday, 10 to 11:30 am and 12:30 to 4 pm. On Sunday, it is open from 2 to 4 pm, year-round.

The Wolfram

Thuringia

Across the road is the **St Severikirche** (St Severus Church), Severihof 2, ☎ 0361-576-960, a five-nave early Gothic hall church. Its towers have tall, sleek spire roofs – the cathedral once had similar ones – that must be any thunderbolt's dream. The interior is mostly Baroque but the real treasures are Gothic: the sarcophagus of St Severus sculpted around 1360 and the 49-ft baptismal font created in 1467. The church is only open on weekdays, from May to October, 9 am to 12:30 pm and 1:30 to 5 pm, and November to April from 10 am to 12:30 pm and 1:30 to 4 pm.

The narrow road in front of the church, Severihof, leads to the **Zitadelle Petersberg** (Petersberg Citadel), the only largely intact Baroque town fortifications in central Europe. The interesting underground passages can be seen on guided tours conducted by the tourist information office.

Fischmarkt

From the Domplatz, Marktstraße leads to the Fischmarkt (Fish Market), with its Neo-Gothic Rathaus (Town Hall). En route is the early-14th-century **Heiligengeistkirche** (Holy Ghost Church),

Fischmarkt

which, interestingly, has a triangular shape that follows the lay of the land. From the church, look down Große Arche road to see the lovely yellow Baroque façade of the **Haus zum Sonnenborn**, Große Arche 6.

In addition to the Rathaus, there are several imposing structures on the Fischmarkt, including the lovely Renaissance **Zum breiten Herd** (1584) and the **Zum roten Ochsen** (1562). On the square is a statue of St Martin, Germany's patron saint, oddly dressed as a Roman soldier.

Nearby is the **Predigerkirche**, Predigerstraße 4, ☎ 0361-562-6214, erected between 1270 and 1400 by the Order of the Mendicant Friars. In summer, it has organ concerts on most

Wednesday afternoons. The church is open April to October from Tuesday to Saturday, 10 am to 6 pm, and Sunday from noon to 4 pm. From November to March, it is open Tuesday to Saturday, 10 am to noon, and 2 to 4 pm.

Across the stream is the **Barfüßerkirche**, Barfüßerstraße 20, ☎ 0361-554-560. It was left in ruins after World War II but inside the choir is a small museum of medieval art. It is open April to October from Tuesday to Sunday, 10 am to 1 pm, and 2 to 6 pm. Admission is €2.

Krämerbrucke

Krämerbrucke

A block from the Rathaus is the Krämerbrücke (Shopkeepers' Bridge), one of Erfurt's best-known sights. It is the only bridge north of the Alps with inhabited houses – 393 ft long and lined by two rows of houses that completely cover both sides of the bridge. It dates back to 1325 and currently spans the River Gera with six arches. There are 33 buildings, including a church, at the far end. It now houses mostly antique shops and small boutiques.

The best views of the bridge are from Horngasse, which spans the river slightly to the north. Nearby is the **Augustinerkloster**

Looking down on the Krämerbrucke

(Augustine Monastery), Augustinerstraße 10, ☎ 0361-576-600, www.augustinerkloster.de, where Martin Luther lived from 1505 until 1511. The original 13th-century buildings were com-

Thuringia

pletely destroyed in 1945, but rebuilt in recent years. Most of it is used as a conference center, but the reconstructed Martin Luther cell, the lovely library, and other parts of the monastery can be seen. It is open April to October from Monday to Saturday, 10 am to noon and 2 to 4 pm, and Sunday from 11 am to 2 pm. From November to March, it is open Monday to Saturday, 10 am to noon, and 2 to 4 pm, Sunday from 11 am to 2 pm. Admission is €3.50.

Krämerbrücke leads into Futterstraße, where at No 15 Napoleon entertained the Czar in what is now know as the **Kaisersaal** (Emperor's Hall). The building houses several restaurants and conference facilities.

The **Anger** is a large square near the main station and is the heart of commercial Erfurt. It is also a major hub of the tram network. The shops on the square are all housed in large, grand buildings and the post office building here must be one of the best-looking in Germany.

◆ Cultural Events

A highlight on the Erfurt cultural calendar is **Thuringia Bach Weeks**, www.bach-wochen.de, staged during March and April. The main theme is obviously music by Bach but other composers are also played.

The **Domstufenfestpiele** (Cathedral Steps Festival), www.domstufen.de, is staged from mid-August to early September on the famous steps at Erfurt's cathedral.

In summer, the **Predigerkirche**, Predigerstraße 4, ☎ 0361-562-6214, has organ concerts on most Wednesday afternoons.

◆ Shopping

The **Krämerbrücke** has a number of small antique shops and art galleries. In many studios, the artists can be observed at work. Although the bridge is a popular tourist destination, prices remain sane.

Erfurt's wealth was built on the **woad** trade and products made from it can still be bought. Woad was used to create a blue dye.

Apart from blueprints, cosmetics (*Waidkosmetik*) are also available from many outlets, including the Tourist Office.

◆ Adventures

On Wheels

By Bicycle: Bicycles can be rented from **ADFC Fahrradverleih**, Espachstraße 3a, ☎ 0361-225-1732.

◆ Where to Stay & Eat

The **Mercure Hotel Erfurt Altstadt** is in the center of town, close to the Krämerbrücke. The hotel combined restored 16th-century buildings and a new wing into a modern, comfortable hotel. The styl-

Mercure Hotel Erfurt Altstadt

ish **Zum Rebstock Restaurant** (€€-€€€€) has international and local cuisine. Meienbergstraße 26-27, 99084 Erfurt, ☎ 0361-594-90, fax 0361-594-9100, www.accorhotels.com. (€€-€€€€)

Sorat Hotel Erfurt

Nearby is the **Sorat Hotel Erfurt**, a designer hotel with modern furnishings. Some rooms have views of the Krämerbrücke. The **Zum Alten Schwan Restaurant** (€€-€€€€) has a long tradition, but is rendered totally modern in the refurbished hotel. International cuisine and a large vegetarian selection are offered. Gotthardstraße 27, 99084 Erfurt, ☎ 0361-674-00, fax 0361-674-0444, www.sorat-hotels.com. (€€€-€€€€)

Hotel Zum Norde am Anger is a small, privately run hotel, offering a pleasant alternative to the chain hotels in the region. It is located near the Anger in the Old Town. Rooms are comfortably furnished and service is first class. The **Zum Norde Restaurant** (€€-€€€) has light, regional cuisine in an authentic Art Nouveau setting. Anger 50-51, 99084 Erfurt, ☎ 0361-568-00, fax 0361-568-0400, www.hotel-zumnorde.de. (€€-€€€€)

Adjacent to the station is the very modern **InterCity Hotel**. Rooms are not particularly large, but are stylish and well equipped. Willy-Brandt-Platz 11, 99084 Erfurt, ☎ 0361-560-00, fax 0361-560-0999, www.intercityhotel.de. (€€-€€€).

The **Hotel Ibis** is in the center of the Old Town, just minutes from the Dom. Rooms are modern and well equipped for this price class. Barfüßerstraße 9, 99084 Erfurt, ☎ 0361-664-10, fax 0361-664-1111, www.accorhotels.com. (€€)

The gourmet **Alboth's Restaurant**, Futterstraße 15, ☎ 0361-568-8207, www.alboths.de, is located at the splendid Kaisersaal, where Napoleon and the Czar engaged in diplomacy. On offer is nouvelle cuisine as well as light regional dishes. The wine list is extensive. (€€€-€€€€).

Located in one of the loveliest buildings in town, with a view of the equally impressive Rathaus, is **Paganini im Gildenhaus**, Fischmarkt 13-16, ☎ 0361-643-0692. Food is mainly Italian with some regional specialties and international dishes as well. (€-€€€)

Camping

 About 15 miles from Erfurt, in the small town of Mühlberg, is the **Drei Gleichen** campsite. It has 150 lots. A golf course and riding stables are adjacent to the site. It is open year-round but advance reservations are required from November to March. Am Gut Ringhofen, 99869 Mühlberg, ☎ 036256-22-715, fax 036256-86-801, www.campingplatz-muehlberg.de.

Eisenach

The Old Town of Eisenach suffered major damage during World War II. Under communist rule, little was spent on upkeep and many historic buildings were torn down. Things changed dramatically after the *Wende*. The most famous sights have been restored and all over town restoration and preservation work is continuing.

The main sight in Eisenach is undoubtedly the **Wartburg Castle**. The fortress perched high on a hill has been described as the most German of all castles and is often considered the national monument of Germany. In town, the main draws are the **Luther Museum** and the **Bachhaus**. Most museums in Eisenach are open seven days a week.

The Wartburg Castle

◆ Information Sources

 Tourist Office: Tourist Information, Markt, 99817 Eisenach, ☎ 03691-79-230, www.eisenach.de.

◆ Transportation

The Hauptbahnhof is a few minutes walk from the Nikolaitor and the start of the historic Old Town.

Bus No 10 runs from the station to the Wartburg. Bus No 11 is convenient for hikes starting at Hohe Sonne and the bottom parking lots of the Wartburg.

◆ Sightseeing

The Wartburg Castle

History: The Wartburg's history goes back to around 1067, when the Ludovingian family ruled Thuringia. The family was powerful enough to consider it proper to add a third floor to the main Romanesque palace building, something that was generally done only for a residence of the German king.

The most famous event in the castle's long history was in 1521, when an outlawed Martin Luther lived in the Wartburg, disguised as a knight called Junker Jörg. In only 10 weeks, he translated the New Testament from Greek into German. The Wartburg has been a drawing card for tourists ever since and pilgrims carried away his original desk splinter by splinter. The current desk on display replaced the paltry remains of the original, already at the end of the 19th century.

The Nazis loved the Wartburg and all the symbolism surrounding it. They had the golden Christian cross replaced by a swastika. However, at the end of the war the Wartburg hoisted the white flag to prevent it being damaged by the advancing American army. The Wartburg was declared a UNESCO World Cultural Heritage Site in 1999.

LEGENDS OF THE WARTBURG

Luther's Room

A favored sight in the Wartburg Castle is the wood paneled quarters where Martin Luther resided in 1521. Luther was a prolific writer producing numerous letters and manuscripts. Soon after he left the Wartburg, it became an important pilgrim's station. Martin Luther wrote that he had to fight the devil with ink. Although he meant fighting with writing, it soon became legend that an ink stain on the wall of his room was caused when Martin Luther threw an inkpot at the devil. For centuries, pilgrims scraped the ink off the wall and the authorities re-inked it when necessary. Although that practice ceased at the end of the 19th century, the legend survives to the present day.

Another famous legend is of the competition of the *Meistersänger* (troubadours) in 1206 and 1207. According to the story, six troubadours competed here in a singing competition, with the loser to lose his head. In the end the power of music triumphed and all survived. Whether the competition really took place is uncertain, but it is known that the count at that time, Hermann I, was a great supporter of cultural life and that Wolfram von Eschenbach wrote part of his 25,000-line *Parzival* here. The competition was made famous again by Wagner's opera *Tannhäuser und der Sängerkrieg auf Wartburg.*

Visiting the Wartburg Castle: There are three distinct parts when visiting the Wartburg – the palace, the museum and the Luther quarters. The **palace** can only be seen on a 45-minute guided tour in German. English brochures are available.

At the end of the guided tour, visitors are guided straight into the **museum**, which contains period pieces from the region but not actually from the Castle itself. Displays include crockery, silverware, time-keeping instruments, a large cabinet produced by Albrecht Dürer, and several famous paintings by Lucas Cranach. At the end of the museum, cross over to the **Lutherstube** (Luther's Room) or gentleman's prison where Martin Luther worked and slept during his 10-month sojourn at the Wartburg. Visitors not taking the guided tour of the castle enter the museum and Lutherstube at intervals of 15 minutes to limit the numbers inside the somewhat cramped space.

The Wartburg is a very popular destination for Germans of all ages. Even in the off-season, expect school groups and families. It is highly advisable to arrive at opening time to take the first tour of the day – seeing the crowds in the courtyard when emerging from the first tour will make you glad you did.

Luther preaching in the Wartburg

The Wartburg, Schlossbergweg 2, ☎ 03691-77-073, www.wartburg-eisenach.de, is open daily from March to October, 8:30 am to 8 pm (last tour at 5 pm), and November to February, 9 am to 5 pm (last tour at 3: 30 pm). Admission to the Castle, museum, and Lutherstube is €6.50 or €3.50 without the Castle. Reservations are not possible.

The Castle is a few minutes drive to the south of the Old Town. When the parking lot at the castle itself is full, cars are directed to parking lots at the bottom of the hill and a shuttle bus, or a steep 20-minute walk, must be taken to the Castle. During the high season children and adults weighing less than 60 kg/132 lbs can take the traditional donkey ride, ☎ 03691-210-404, to the top castle terminus. Bus No 10 runs from the Hauptbahnhof in Eisenach to the top of the hill, and Bus 11 stops at the parking lots at the foot of the hill.

From the Castle parking lot, donkey, and bus stops it is still a good 10 minutes of stair-climbing or a steep 550-yard walk to reach the first gate of the Wartburg.

Old Town Sights: The Old Town of Eisenach is not particularly pretty, but there are a few interesting sights well worth seeing. Continuing restoration work is improving the attractiveness of the Old Town. Most sights are within easy walking distance from the main train station.

Close to the train station is the **Nikolaitor** (Nicholas Gate). This huge Romanesque town gate is the only one of the original five that survived. Next to the gate is the **Nikolaikirche** (Nicholas Church), Karlsplatz, the last Romanesque construction in Thuringia (around 1180), but altered at the end of the 19th century. Opening hours are daily May to October from 10 am to noon and 3 to 5 pm. On the small Karlsplatz is an oversized statue (1895) of **Martin Luther** with three reliefs illustrating scenes from his sojourns in Eisenach.

Nikolaitor and Karlsplatz

Karlstraße leads to **Markt** (Market Square), where a fountain with a golden statue of St George slaying the dragon forms the focal point. The main building at the square is the huge **Georgenkirche** (George Church), Markt, ☎ 03691-79-230. It dates back to 1180, but most of the current church, with three levels of galleries, and the tower are Baroque. Johan Sebastian Bach was baptized here and several of his family members were the organists here, a position the great composer himself never held in his hometown. Opening hours are daily from 10 am to noon and 2 to 4 pm.

Rathaus

Two other important buildings on Markt are the Late Renaissance **Rathaus** and the Baroque **Stadtschloss** (Town Palace), erected around 1750 by the dukes of Saxe-Weimar-Eisenach. It houses the Thuringian Museum, which is indefinitely closed due to restoration work. The adjacent **Marstall**, Markt 24, ☎ 03691-670-450, houses temporary exhibitions. Opening hours are Tuesday to Sunday from 10 am to 5 pm.

Nearby, in a 14th-century half-timbered building, is the **Lutherhaus**, Lutherplatz 8, ☎ 03691-29-830, www.lutherhaus-eisenach.de. Martin Luther stayed here from 1498 to 1501 with the Cotta family, while studying Latin. The house has a museum with an exhibition on Luther's life and the history of the Reformation. Opening hours are April to October daily from 9 am to 5 pm, and November to March from 10 am to 5 pm. Admission is €2.50.

Farther up the road is the **Bachhaus**, Frauenplan 21, ☎ 03691-79-340, www.bachhaus.de. This museum is dedicated to Eisenach's most famous son, the composer Johan Sebastian Bach (1685-1750). It was originally thought that this house was his place of birth, but arguments still rage over whether that was an honest mistake, or whether the truth was hidden until the real birth house could be destroyed and the land used for other commercial purposes. Although the first museum in the world dedicated to Bach, it only opened in 1906 and has little that was used by Bach himself. Most of the exhibits are documents and prints on his life and work, with descriptions in German only. Behind the lovely garden in the back of the house is a modern glass and steel hall used for temporary exhibitions. Admission is €4 and includes a 20-minute program of Bach music, with some pieces played on period instruments. Concerts are sometimes held in the museum. Opening hours are daily from 10 am to 6 pm.

In the direction of the station, at Johannisplatz 9, is the **Schmale Haus** (Narrow House). This building, erected around 1750, is 28 ft high, but only 6.7 ft wide and thus is considered the narrowest half-timbered house in Germany.

The Schmale Haus

Higher up the hill, close to the access road to the Wartburg, is the **Reuter-Wagner-Museum**, Reuterweg 2, ☎ 03691-743-293. A popular German poet, Fritz Reuter, had the Neo-Renaissance villa built in 1866. In addition to rooms dedicated to Reuter, the villa houses the second-largest archive of Wagner works. Opening hours are Tuesday to Sunday from 10 am to 5 pm. Admission is €3.

◆ Cultural Events

Eisenach, with its important links to the Bach family, plays a central role in the **Thuringia Bach Weeks**, www.bach-wochen.de, staged in March and April. Music by Bach is the focus of these culture weeks but work by other composers is also performed.

Between May and September, concerts are often held in the Festival Hall of the **Wartburg**.

Near Eisenach are the **Burgruine Brandenburg** (castle ruins), 99819 Lauchröden, ☎ 036927-90-619. Although the ruins have nothing to do with Bach's famous Brandenburg Concertos, open-air Brandenburg concerts are held in June and July.

◆ Adventures

On Foot

Countryside Hikes: A popular three-hour, six-mile walk, is from Hohe Sonne (Bus 11 from Eisenach Station) to the Wartburg. The most beautiful part of the route is the first hour, around 2.1 miles, leading through the dramatic landscape of the narrow **Drachenschlucht** (Dragon's Gorge) to Großes A. This part has many stairs, as the height difference is about 330 ft, making the route dangerous when iced over.

◆ Where to Stay & Eat

Since 1913, the luxury **Hotel auf der Wartburg** has been the preferred address for visitors. The hotel was constructed in the style of a Thuringian castle just below the entrance to the Wartburg Castle. It has only 26 double rooms and nine singles, making early reservations essential. The **Landgrafenstube Restaurant** (€€€-€€€€) serves regional

Hotel auf der Wartburg

Thuringia

Thuringian dishes with seasonal variations and a large vegetarian selection. Smaller meals can be enjoyed on the terrace of **Café Wintergarten**, which has views of Eisenach. Auf der Wartburg, 99817 Eisenach, ☎ 03691-7970, fax 03691-797-100, www.wartburghotel.de. (€€€€)

In town, several hotels have a longer tradition. The luxurious **Steigenberger Hotel Thüringer Hof** is in a restored building dating back to 1807. Rooms are very comfortable, well appointed, and with city or forest views. In addition to the café, the elegant **Galerie Restaurant** (€€-€€€) serves regional cuisine with a large seafood selection – something rare in a region best known for its sausages. Karlsplatz 11, 99817

Steigenberger Hotel Thüringer Hof

Eisenach, ☎ 03691-280, fax 03691-281-900, www. steigenberger.de. (€€€)

Nearby, next to the Nikolai Gate, is the very pleasant **Best Western Hotel Kaiserhof**. Rooms are comfortably furnished in a romantic style. A special treat is the hotel's gourmet restaurant **Turmschäncke** (€€€-€€€€) located inside the

Best Western Hotel Kaiserhof

Nikolaitor, the only surviving medieval city gate. Regional and international dishes are complemented by a long wine list. The menu changes weekly and the restaurant is open for dinner only. Reservations are recommended. The **Zwinger Restaurant** (€€-€€€) serves Thuringian and Bavarian cuisine in a relaxed atmosphere. Wartburgallee

2, 99817 Eisenach, ☎ 03691-213-513, fax 03691-203-653, www.bestwestern.de. (€€-€€€)

On a busy pedestrian-only shopping street, between Karlsplatz and Markt, is **Café-Restaurant Alt Eisenach**, Karlstraße 51, ☎ 03691-746-088. It is less formal than the restaurants located in hotels, but still much more pleasant than other budget establishments catering to the tourist market. (€-€€)

Schlosshotel

Near the Lutherhaus is the **Schlosshotel**, a modern hotel located partly in a former Franciscan Monastery, which has a history dating back to the 13th century. Rooms are comfortable, with solid wood furniture. The large 17th-century vaulted cellars of the monastery are the setting for the pleasant and atmospheric **Schlosskeller** (€€), which serves international and local food. Markt 10, 99817 Eisenach, ☎ 03691-214-260, fax 03691-214-259, www.schlosshotel-eisenach.de. (€€-€€€)

Several dining options are available on the square in front of the Bachhaus. Many trade on the great man's name, but at **Café Konditorei Brüheim**, Marienstraße 1, ☎ 03691-203-509, at the bottom end of the square, the quality of the cakes and sweets is good enough to be worth a visit. The Bachhaus and statue are within visual range if you choose your seat well. The café is smoke-free – a rarity in this part of the world. (€)

A very pleasant alternative to staying directly in the Old Town is **Villa Anna**. It is located on a hill opposite the Wartburg, in a quiet residential neighborhood of mainly *Gründerzeit* villas. From the hotel, it is about 15 minutes walk, involving steep slopes and stairs, to the Bachhaus. Rooms are spacious, with modern furnishings, and flooded with natural light from large windows that offer wonderful views of the valley. Villa Anna, Fritz-Koch-Straße 12, 99817 Eisenach, ☎ 03691-23-950, fax 03691-239-530, www.hotel-villa-anna.de. (€€)

Camping

 The closest campsite to Eisenach is the pleasant **Altenberger See Campinpark Eisenac**h. It is on the banks of the Altenberger Lake, offering not only watersports opportunities but also hiking in the nearby forests. It has 240 lots, of which 120 are available for short-term campers. It is open from December to October. Campingpark Eisenach, 99819 Wilhelmsthal, ☎ 03691-215-637, fax 03691-215-607, www.campingpark-eisenach.de.

Hamburg

Northern Germany sees far fewer tourists than areas to the south. This is not totally surprising as the area is relatively flat with few extraordinarily interesting sights. The beaches of northern Germany are popular with German families but few foreigners would select them over what is available elsewhere in Europe.

Hamburg, Germany's second-largest city and premier port, does surprisingly little to alleviate the lack of tourism potential. The city suffered tremendously from air raids during World War II and is mostly a very modern city with liberal and independent attitudes. Hamburgers are often considered rather reserved and formal. The elegant city also seems to hide its best features. Although the quality of life here is high, most sights are low-key and the city is far less attractive for foreign visitors than, say, Berlin, Dresden, or Munich.

Hamburg is famous for its relationship to water. The mighty River Elbe flows through the city and into the largest harbor in Germany. In addition, the Alster is a huge artificial lake created in the middle of the city. The city is very green with many large parks in the central section.

Although Hamburg was founded in 808 by Charlemagne, it has very few old buildings. Most of central Hamburg was destroyed in 1842 by a major fire. A century later, during World War II, air raids killed 55,000, destroyed more than half of all houses, and 80% of port facilities. Most buildings are therefore fairly new, although some historic ones have been restored. The 19th-century Neo-Renaissance **Rathaus** is the most impressive of these buildings. Several major churches with high spires punctuate the skyline from all directions.

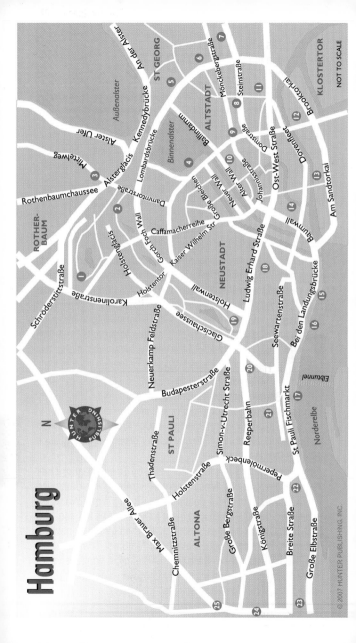

Hamburg, as a harbor city, has a reputation for seedy nightlife. Even though the **Reeperbahn**, the traditional red-light district, is a shadow of its former self, it is still internationally the best-known aspect of Hamburg. Nowadays, more respectable family entertainment options, such as musicals, are a major attraction in this area.

Lübeck, once one of the richest and largest cities in Germany, is worth a journey. Its historic Old Town is beautifully preserved and has some prime samples of brick Gothic, a style typical of the region.

◆ Transportation

By Rail

Although it's in the far northern parts of Germany, many other centers can be reached surprisingly fast by high-speed train. At least hourly connections are available to Berlin (90 minutes), Frankfurt (3h30), Cologne (4 hours), and Munich (6 hours).

By Road

By Car: Major highways from all parts of Germany lead to Hamburg. The A7 runs from Denmark via Hamburg to Hannover and eventually to Bavaria in the south. The A1 leads from Lübeck past Hamburg via Bremen to the Rühr. The A24 connects Berlin and Hamburg.

Driving in most of Hamburg is not particularly challenging and easier than in most other large German cities. In central Hamburg, a car is not particularly useful but, for outlying areas, it is a

1. Planten und Blomen
2. Alter Botanischer Garten
3. Dammtor Station
4. Alsterpavillon
5. Kunsthalle
6. Hauptbahnhof
7. Museum für Kunst
   und Gewerbe
8. St Jakobi
9. St Petri
10. Rathaus, Rathausmarkt
11. Chile-haus
12. Deutsches Zollmuseum
13. Speicherstadt
14. Diechstraße
15. Cap San Diego
16. Rickmer Rickmers
17. Landungsbrücken
18. St Michaelis
19. Museum für Hamburgische
    Geschichte
20. Operettenhaus
21. Herbertstraße
22. Fischmarkt
23. Altonaer Balkon
24. Altonaer Museum
25. Altona Station

Hamburg

viable option. Street-side parking in downtown Hamburg is very limited, but parking garages are available.

MONEY-SAVING TIP: HAMBURG CARD

The Hamburg Card (often simply **HH-Card**) allows unlimited local transportation and reduced entrance fees to many museums and attractions, as well as city tours and harbor cruises. It come in two versions: the single ticket (€7.30 for one day or €15 for three consecutive days) and a group ticket for up to five (€13.50 per day or €23.90 for three consecutive days). A bus trip and a trip to the Museum of Art and Crafts pay off the price of a single-day ticket. The card is sold at tourism offices, many hotels, and in vending machines at stations.

Visitors under 30 can save even more with the **Power-Pass**. It offers the same discounts as the HH-Card plus discounts at movies, restaurants, clubs, and discos. It is €7 for the first day and can be extended up to seven days for €3.30 per

---

 By Bus: Hamburg can easily be reached from Berlin by bus. The **Berlin Linienbus**, www. berlinlinienbus.de, departs daily at least every two hours between 7 am and 9 pm from Berlin ZOB am Funkturm to Hamburg ZOB am Hauptbahnhof. The journey takes just over three hours. Round-trip tickets are as low as €35.

Hamburg has an excellent public transportation system, which combines buses, trains, and ferries. Some express buses are classified First Class and require more expensive tickets. (The Hamburg Card includes the surcharges for first class.)

Particularly useful for tourists is Bus 36 – it runs from Rathausmarkt past most of the sights, down the Reeperbahn, and continues via Altona to Blankenese. Bus 112 connects the Hauptbahnhof with Altona via the Landungsbrücke.

By Air

 Hamburg Airport (HAM), Flughafenstr. 1-3, 22335 Hamburg, ☎ 040-50-750, www.ham.airport.de, is close to the city center. The Airport Express Bus Line 110 connects the airport every 10 minutes with Ohlsdorf station. From here U1, S1, and S11 run to downtown

Hamburg in around 20 minutes. (The S-Bahn will be connected to the airport in 2008.)

Several other bus services are available to various parts of Hamburg, including the Airport Express to the Hauptbahnhof. From Lübeck, the Trave-Liner, ☎ 0451-888-1078, operates buses directly to Hamburg Airport. Taxis from the airport to downtown Hamburg take 30 minutes and cost around €20 (according to meter).

Lübeck Airport (LBC), Blankenseer Straße 101, ☎ 0451-583-010, www.flughafen-luebeck.de, is used mostly by low-cost carriers. It is about half an hour south of Lübeck with Bus 6 connecting to the main station every 20 minutes. Shuttle buses to Hamburg are available to coincide with flight arrivals.

By Boat

Despite its famous harbor, no international ferry services serve Hamburg directly.

A regular car and passenger ferry service operates between nearby Cuxhaven and Harwich in England. **SeawaysDFDS**, Van-der-Smissen-Strasse 4, 22767 Hamburg, ☎ 040-389-030, www.dfdsseaways.co.uk, has around four sailings per week taking 15 hours.

From Travemünde, daily car ferry sailings are available to Helsinki on **Finnlines**, Einsiedelstraße 43-45, 23554 Lübeck, ☎ 0451-150-7443, www.finnlines.de, and to Trelleborg on **TT-Line**, 20422 Hamburg, ☎ 04502-80-181, www.TTLine.com. **Latlines**, ☎ 0451-709-9697, operates from Riga in Letland to Lübeck.

Information Sources

Tourist Office: Tourism information is available from Hamburg Tourismus, Postfach 102249, 20015 Hamburg, ☎ 040-300-51-333, www.hamburg-tourismus.de. It has offices at the Hauptbahnhof and at the Landungsbrücke in St Pauli.

◆ Sightseeing

Hamburg is a large, spread-out city, but the tourist area is mainly concentrated in the section bound by the Hauptbahnhof and Binnenalster, St Pauli and the Elbe River. It is generally a pleasant city to stroll in but it's a long haul from, for example, the Hauptbahnhof to St Pauli, or even the Rathaus to Speicherstadt. Buses or trains are often the best way to move between major sightseeing areas.

Rathausmarkt

Rathausmarkt is the heart of Hamburg. Gotttfried Semper and Alexis de Chateauneuf used Venice's St Mark Square as inspiration when designing the Rathausmarkt in the 1840s following the Great Fire. This is clearly seen in the Renaissance-style, white-pillared Alster Arcades. At the Kleinen Alster is a memorial for the fallen soldiers of World War I. This monument, showing the misery of war, did not please the Nazis, who erected a more belligerent monument near Dammtor station. At the south end is a memorial for the poet Heinrich Heine that replaced one destroyed by the Nazis.

Rathaus

However, the square is dominated by the magnificent Neo-Renaissance **Rathaus** (Town Hall), ☎ 040-428-312-063, built in 1886-97. The building is 364 by 230 ft with a 367-ft campanile and 647 rooms. The façade facing the square is decorated with bronze statues of 20 former emperors. The building rests on over 4,000 piles. The fountain in the courtyard commemorates the cholera epidemic of 1892 when almost 9,000 people died in just over two months. The interior of the Rathaus can only be seen on guided tours. English-language tours are conducted from Monday to Thursday at 10:15 am and 3:15 pm, and from Friday to Sunday at 10:15 am and 1:15 pm. German tours are more frequent. Admission is €1.50.

Alster

The Alster is a 500-acre lake in the heart of Hamburg formed when the River Alster was dammed. The lake is divided into the Binnenalster (Inner Alster) and the much larger Aussenalster (Outer Aster). The division is formed by the Lombard rail bridge and the Kennedy road bridge.

The **Binnenalster** is surrounded on three sides by elegant buildings that form a beautiful backdrop to the water. In summer, a fountain sprays up to 115 ft high. The most famous bank is the **Jungfernstieg**, which is lined by expensive shops.

The **Aussenalster** is mostly encompassed by parks and is a popular relaxation area. The lake itself is at most just over 6½ ft deep and popular for all kinds of water sports. The banks are suitable for walking and cycling, but even a drive by car is rewarding as several places allow views of the skyline with the four church towers and the Rathaus tower – all over 328 ft high. In summer, ferries operate on the lake, while pleasure cruises are available as long as the lake remains ice-free.

Hauptbahnhof Area

Mönckebergstraße, a major shopping street, leads from the Rathausmarkt to the Hauptbahnhof. In addition to the numerous department stores, two of Hamburg's main churches are along this boulevard.

The **Petrikirche** (St Peter's Church), Speesort 10, ☎ 040-325-7400, first mentioned in 1195, is the oldest parish church in Hamburg. The Gothic church of the 14th century was destroyed during the Great Fire of 1842 and rebuilt in a Neo-Gothic style. The tower is 432 ft high. The church suffered relatively minor damage during World War II and has many old artworks that were rescued from the fire. The lion doorknob on the left door of the main portal dates form the 14th century and is considered the oldest artwork in Hamburg. The Madonna with child dates from 1470. Concerts of religious music are scheduled on most Wednesdays at 5:15 pm. The church is open Monday to Saturday from 10 am to 6:30 pm, closing at 5 pm on Saturday. On Sunday, it is open from 9 am to 9 pm.

The nearby **Jacobikirche** (St Jacob's), Jakobikirchhof 22, ☎ 040-303-7370, has a slightly shorter history, but parts of the 1340 brick Gothic basilica survived as the oldest actual church building in Hamburg. The church was frequently changed and has elements from every century in its design. The tower is 403 ft high. The church was severely damaged during World War II, but most of the art treasures were saved. The 1693 Arp Schnitger organ with 3,880 pipes is the largest Baroque organ in Northern Germany. Opening hours are Monday to Saturday from 10 am to 5 pm.

Two blocks south of the church is the **Kontorhausviertel** (Counting House Buildings Quarter). Here, several huge brick office buildings were put up in the 1920s. The best known is the 10-story **Chilehaus**, Buchardsplatz, which was erected in 1924 for the successful trader Henry B Sloman who traded sulfur with Chile. Its decorative façade serves as a prime example of the versatility of brick.

Nearby, just south of the Hauptbahnhof, is the excellent **Museum für Kunst und Gewerbe** (Arts & Crafts), Steintorplatz 1, ☎ 040-428-542-732, www.mkg-hamburg.de. It opened in 1877 and established itself as one of Europe's leading museums for cultural history, decorative arts, design, and photography. In addition to the large collection of European items, it also has objects from the Middle East, China, and Japan. It has an impressive collection of keyboard instruments – an audio guide with sample pieces is included in the admission price. The instruments are played

Museum für Kunst und Gewerbe

during special guided tours, usually on Thursday at 6:30 pm, Saturday at 3 pm, and Sunday at 4 pm. Opening hours are Tuesday to Sunday from 10 am to 6 pm (closing at 9 pm on Thursday). Admission is €8.20.

Hamburg Kunsthalle (Art Gallery), Glockengiesserwall, ☎ 040-428-131-200, has art from the Renaissance to the modern era. It has lesser-known works from all the major artists, as well as a large modern art collection displayed in a post-modern cubic building. Although the largest collection in Northern Germany, the old masters' section is not of the same quality or depth as what can be seen in Berlin, Dresden, and Munich. However, the modern art collection is large, and especially strong on late-20th-century works. Opening hours are Tuesday to Sunday from 10 am to 6 pm (closing at 9 pm on Thursday). Admission is €8.50.

St Michaelis

St Michaelis (St Michel's Church), Englische Plancke 1a, ☎ 040-3767-8100, locally known as the Michel, is the symbol of Hamburg. The church had a rather eventful history. The first large church built here in 1647-61, was struck by lightning and burned down in 1750. Its replacement, completed in 1762, was a Baroque masterpiece. However, soldering work in 1906 caused the wooden tower to catch fire and the entire church burned down. Its re-

A concert in St Michaelis

placement, completed in 1912, was severely damaged during World War II. The current church was completed in 1952 to the designs of 1750, but used more modern building techniques, including an elevator in the tower. The tower is 433 ft high with a viewing platform at 269 ft. The church clock, with a diameter of 26.2 ft, is the largest in Germany.

Hamburg

The lovely Baroque interior seats 2,500 and is frequently used for organ concerts. The church has three organs, including a 1962 Steinmeyer organ with 6,665 pipes, a 1912 Marcussen organ with 3,562 pipes, and a Grollmann organ with 224 pipes. All three organs can be heard daily at noon. From Monday to Saturday at 10 am and 9 pm, Sunday at noon only, the tower trumpeter plays a hymn from the tower platform in all four directions.

The church is open from May to October from Monday to Saturday from 9 am to 6 pm, and Sunday from 11:30 am to 5:30 am. From November to April, it is open Monday to Saturday from 10 am to 4:30 pm and Sunday from 11:30 am to 4:30 pm. Admission to the church is free, but it costs €2.50 for the tower.

Speicherstadt

Speicherstadt

When Hamburg lost its free trade status at the end of the 19th century, it responded by creating the world's largest free harbor to facilitate trade. In the process the **Speicherstadt** was built. Here huge brick buildings formed the largest warehouses in the world. Up to 20,000 Hamburgers had to move to make way for these buildings, which then became the economic lifeline of the city. Many of these buildings, as well as large sections of the former port – the so-called HafenCity (Harbor City) – are currently being converted into office space and apartments in what is the largest building site in Europe.

The **Hamburg Dungeon**, Kehrwieder 2-3, ☎ 040-3005-1512, offers a multimedia trip through the trials and tribulations of Hamburg's past. Opening hours are daily from 11 am to 6 pm. Admission is €13.45. Advance reservations are possible, and recommended in the high season. (The show is not recommended for children under 10, and children under 14 must be accompanied by an adult.)

Miniature Wonderland, Kehrwieder 2, ☎ 040-3005-1505, has one of the largest miniature train sets in the world. The display has models from many parts of the world using 500 trains, 16,400 feet of track, 50,000 lights, and 60,000 figures. Opening hours are weekdays from 10 am to 6 pm (Tuesday until 8 pm) and weekends from 9 am to 8 pm. Admission is €9.60.

Spicy's Gewürzmuseum (Spice Museum), Am Sandtorkai 31, ☎ 040-367-989, claims to be the only spice museum in the world. It has around 800 displays including 50 spices that can be touched, smelled, and tasted. Opening hours are Tuesday to Sunday from 10 am to 5 pm. Admission is €3 (including some free samples).

Some distance away in the Baakenhafen is the **U-Bootmuseum Hamburg** (U-Boat Museum), Versmannstraße 23c, ☎ 040-3200-4934, www.u-434.de. On display is a decommissioned Russian U-434 submarine, built in 1976 and in use until 2002. Guided tours of 45 minutes are available in multiple languages. Opening hours are daily from 10 am to 6 pm. Admission is €8.

The **Deutsches Zollmuseum** (German Custom Museum), Alter Wandrahm 16, ☎ 040-300-876, has exhibitions on customs in Germany and the world. On display are customs receipts dating back to Roman times as well as confiscated goods. Some original smuggling methods are also illustrated. Opening hours are Tuesday to Sunday from 10 am to 5 pm. Admission is free.

Some of the loveliest historic buildings in Hamburg are in the **Deichstraße**. The street has been in existence since at least 1304 but most houses here actually date from the 17th to 19th centuries. Many buildings were destroyed in the Great Fire of 1842 but rebuilt on the original foundations.

Hamburg

Planten und Blomen

Dammtor Bahnhof (station), Dag-Hammarskjöld-Platz, is in a 1903 Art Nouveau glass and steel building. On the approach from downtown are a series of memorials for victims of World War II – a dispute between the Senate and the artist ended with only two of the works completed. Also in the region is the 1936 Kriegerdenkmal (War Memorial), erected by the Nazis who found the Hamburg World War I memorial at the Rathausmarkt too defeatist.

In the 1930s, a large park called **Planten und Blomen (**local dialect for plants and flowers) was laid out on the land of the former city defenses. It stretches as a wide green belt in a halfcircle from the Alster to the Elbe. Close to Dammtor is the botanical garden, as well as the largest Japanese garden in Europe. A Wasserlichtorgel (water and light organ) plays summer evenings at 10 pm (9 pm in September). It also performs at 2, 4, and 6 pm without light effects.

Still in the park, but close to St Pauli, is the **Museum für Hamburgische Geschichte** (Hamburg History Museum), Holstenwall 24, ☎ 040-428-132-2380, www.hamburgmuseum. de. It is the largest city history museum in Germany and has several scale models in addition to historic items. Particularly popular are the models of the harbor and the railway system. Opening hours are Tuesday to Sunday from 10 am to 5 pm (closing at 6 pm on Sunday). Admission is €7.50.

St Pauli

St Pauli is Hamburg's most (in)famous neighborhood. From St Pauli U-Bahn Station, the 1,900-ft **Reeperbahn** stretches westwards towards Altona. The Reeperbahn and Große Freiheit have tradi-

Reeperbahn

Along the Reeperbahn

tionally made up the red-light district of Hamburg and, in addition to sex-related shops, have around 500 bars and restaurants. It attracts 15 million visitors each year. Recent years have seen a gradual gentrification of the area, with musical shows doing very well in theaters at both ends of the Reeperbahn. Sex still sells, but middle-class and family entertainment clearly brings in bigger profits.

PROSTITUTION

Prostitution is perfectly legal in Germany, although pimping and many related activities are not. Prostitutes have their own labor unions that set working hours, rates, and work practices. They are supposed to pay tax, but politicians frequently lament the low amount of both income tax *and* value added tax that is actually forked over. However, even though legal, prostitution remains very much an underworld culture with dubious practices. Red light districts, sex shops, and related businesses are usually found in the vicinity of train stations.

During the day, the area is quiet – it only comes to life after 8 pm and then knows no official closing time. A huge police presence means that the area is safe at all hours. Halfway down the

Herbertstraße, open to men only

Hamburg

Reeperbahn is the **Davidwache** – Germany's best-known police station. In addition to being busy, it also features frequently in German films and television programs. Nearby is the **Herbertstraße**, since 1900 a closed-off street that basically is a huge brothel district. Since the mid-1980s, the street has been open to adult men only. (The prostitutes working here got tired of troops of schoolchildren and retirees strolling through with camera in hand.)

The Landungsbrücke

The Reeperbahn runs parallel to the Elbe River, which is only a few minutes walk downhill. In between St Pauli and the Landungsbrücke U-Bahn stations is a 48-ft statue of Otto von Bismarck. It was erected in 1906 to symbolize the protective power of Bismarck's mighty German Empire over the trade interests of Hamburg.

The **Landungsbrücke** is Europe's largest floating island – a 23,000-ft pontoon bridge that is a popular hangout spot, with ample benches and restaurants to sit and watch the world go by. Many future Americans departed from here to the New World. Nowadays, virtually all harbor cruises leave from here. The 656-ft-long Art Nouveau reception hall was built in 1909 – it has six archways to the pontoon, two corner towers, and cupolas.

Landungsbrücke

At the west end is the **Alte Elbtunnel** (Old Elbe Tunnel). It was completed in 1911 and connects St Pauli with the opposite bank via two 1,480-ft tiled tunnels. Elevators on both ends are used to lower cars and pedestrians by 75 ft. Cars have to pay a toll and may only use the tunnel from Monday to Saturday. (The New Elbe tunnel, part of the Autobahn A7, is 1.8 miles west of the old one and opened in 1975. It is over 1½ miles long and currently has four tunnels used by 100,000 cars per day.)

At the east end is the **Rickmer Rickmers**, St Pauli Landungbrücke Pier 1, ☎ 040-319-5959, a former East Indies windjammer. A museum is housed inside this green-and-red vessel. It was built in Bremerhaven in 1896 and confiscated off the Azores in 1916. It served the Portuguese navy up to 1962 as a training vessel and opened as a museum following restoration in 1987. Opening hours are daily from 10 am to 6 pm. Admission is €3. It has a restaurant on board.

Slightly farther upstream is the **Überseebrücke**. Visiting naval vessels often anchor here – opening hours are listed at the gangway. Permanently anchored here is the **MS *Cap San Diego***, Überseebrücke, ☎ 040-364-209, built in Hamburg in 1962 to serve the trade route to South America. It remained in service up to 1986 but the changeover to container ships made it outdated. It was then opened as a museum – the last ship built of this type. Opening hours are daily from 10 am to 6 pm. Admission is €5.

◆ Cultural Events

Hamburg has a full cultural calendar with concerts of all types scheduled throughout the year. Classical music is very popular and concerts are held in many dedicated concert halls and churches.

In recent years, Hamburg has become famous as the place to see musicals in Germany. Although the show titles are instantly recognizable, all lyrics are sung in German. The tourism office has information on most events and can make reservations at a charge similar to that of any advance ticket booking services.

◆ Festivals

The **Hafengeburts-tag** (literally, Harbor's Birthday) is one of Hamburg's greatest festivals. It celebrates the founding of the harbor on May 7, 1188. Emperor Friedrich I Barbarossa guaran-

Hafengeburtstag

teed tax-free entry for all ships from the North Sea down the River Elbe to Hamburg. The festival has many cultural and gastronomical events but the highlight is the parade of ships, with everything from historic windjammers to modern cruise ships.

◆ Shopping

Passages

 Hamburg is famous for its large number of passages, or covered malls. Most are in the triangle formed by Jungfernstieg, Fuhlentwiete, and Alsterfleet. Here you will find the majority of the top brand shops, while Mönckebergstraße near the Hauptbahnhof has top department stores. The **Karstadt** is the largest department store in Hamburg. The **Peek & Cloppenburg** has upmarket, mainly European clothes.

For top international brands such as Hermès, Giorgio Armani, and Hugo Boss, head to **Neuer Wall**. Other top brands are found nearby.

Antiques Market

A few minutes walk from the Hauptbahnhof is **Antik-Center**, Klosterwall 9 -21. Here, 39 shops sell all kinds of antiques. With so many dealers in close proximity, bargains are unlikely but neither are outrageous prices. Opening hours are Tuesday to Friday from noon to 6 pm, and Saturday from 10 am to 2 pm and 4 to 6 pm.

Flea Market

The most famous flea market in Hamburg is the **Fischmarkt** (Fish Market) in Altona, held Sunday mornings from 5 am to 10 am (mid-November to mid-March from 7 am). A huge flea market with live music and eating and drinking, it is favored by late-night revelers, who come here straight from nightspots, and by early risers. Fish is actually still sold on the sidelines, but is of decreasing importance.

◆ Adventures

On Foot

Town Walks: From April to October, the **Tourism Office** arranges a wide selection of walking tours covering many topics. The two-hour walks are mostly on weekday afternoons from 4 pm or Saturday from 2:30 pm. The schedule, with the starting point for the various walks, is available from the Tourism Office.

Stattreisen Hamburg, Bartelsstraße 12, ☎ 040-430-3481, www.statttreisen-hamburg.de, has more specialized tours in a season that runs from February to November. Some tours are in English. Prior reservations are generally not required but are essential for the popular "Beatles in St Pauli" tour.

Jogging: Innovative Sport Organisation, Goesta Gerd Dreise, Schanzenstr. 41a, ☎ 0178-660-6604, www.touristjogging.de, guides joggers through Hamburg on four routes ranging from 4.2 to six miles, taking 45 to 80 minutes. The jogging tours are generally at 8 am or 6 pm.

On Wheels

By Bicycle: Popular cycling areas are around the Alster and along the Elbe. Outside rush hours, bicycles may be taken for free on subways and all day on Elbe ferries.

Bicycles can be rented from **DB Service**, Hachmannplatz at the Hauptbahnhof, ☎ 040-319-850-475.

Several companies offer guided cycling tours to various parts of Hamburg. **Sightcycling** (SD-Bikes), Jarrestraße 29, ☎ 040-278-008-00, www.sightcycling.de, has eight different tours. Your own bicycle is required.

Bikestation, Burmesterstrasse 34a, ☎ 0178-640-1800, www.bikestation-hamburg.de, is run by a local who conducts four- to five-hour cycling tours – bicycle rental and a coffee is included in the price.

By Bus: Three bus tours operate in cooperation with the Hamburg tourism office. The **Top Tour**, www.top-tour-hamburg.de, uses open-top double-decker buses on a circular route with several hop-on, hop-off points. During the high season, buses depart every 30 minutes from 9:30 am. The **Gala-Tour**, www. gala-tour.de, is a standard 30-mile bus tour taking in all the major sights in 2½ hours. Departures are daily at 10 am and 2 pm. The **Scene Night Tour** includes a walking tour of the Reeperbahn area and a visit to a bar. It departs Friday and Saturday at 9 pm. The principal departure point for all three tours is the Hauptbahnhof/Kirchenallee. Tickets are available on the bus or from many hotels.

In the Air

 Seaplane: A seaplane, operated by **Himmelschreiber**, ☎ 040-378-341, www. himmelsschreiber.de, takes off from the River Elbe at the City Sporthafen on Baumwall. Flights depart every 45 minutes, Tuesday to Sunday from 10 am until dark. Flights last 20 minutes plus taxi time and cost €85. Children under three or weighing less than 15 kg/33 lbs fly for free.

Historic Plane: Flights over Hamburg in a JU52 depart from Hamburg Airport. Flights of 30 minutes cost around €160 per person, and 60-minute flights are €260. Reservations at ☎ 040-5070-1717.

Helicopter Flights: Helicopter Service Wasserthal, ☎ 040-5075-2114, offers helicopter flights and transfers from Hamburg Airport.

On Water

 Boat Rentals: Segelschule Pieper Sohn, An der Alster at the Hotel Atlantic, ☎ 040-247-578, rents sail, pedal, and rowboats daily, 10 am to 9 pm from April to early October.

Canal & Harbor Cruises: Boat trips in Hamburg can be divided into two distinct categories: cruises of the harbor and cruises on the Alster Lake and canals. When in Germany's largest port city, a harbor tour is considered a must. However, touring the "Fleets," the traditional canals that led to the warehouses among others, is also interesting.

Harbor Cruises: Virtually all harbor cruises depart from the Landungsbrücke. There is little to distinguish the cruises, in content or price. It is generally best to simply select the next cruise to depart, unless a particular ship is preferred. Smaller boats can go deeper into canals, while larger boats usually have better views from the top deck.

The largest operator is **HADAG**, St Pauli Fischmarkt 28, ☎ 040-311-7070, www.hadag.de. In addition to the river and harbor cruises, HADAG also runs ferry or waterbus services. These are much cheaper than the regular harbor cruises. On some routes, the Hamburg Card or other transportation cards are valid. Particularly popular is Route 62 that runs from Sandtorhöft near the Altstadt via Landungsbrücke and Altona to Finkenwerder. From here, connections to Blankenese are available via Teufelsbrück. Route 73 is also popular – it goes from Landungbrücke via the Theater im Hafen deeper into the harbor.

Alster & Fleet Cruises: Boats operate on the Alster Lake and the waterways (Fleet) of old Hamburg. **ATG**, Anleger Jungfernstieg, ☎ 040-357-4240, www.alstertouristik.de, has several boat trips daily. The main season is from May to September but cruises are available all year. There are several cruises on the lake itself but more interesting are the ones in the Fleets. The boats are narrow and small enough to enter canals inaccessible to the larger vessels operating harbor cruises. From April to September, a ferry service connects several stations on the Alster.

◆ Where to Stay & Eat

The **Raffles Hotel Vier Jahreszeiten** is a grand hotel, perfectly located on the Binnenalster. Its core is an 1897 Gründerzeit building, but rooms are modern, large, elegant, and luxurious. It has a large, exclusive spa area. The **Haerlin Restaurant** (€€€-€€€€) is one of the

HOTEL PRICES	
€ . . . . Up to €50 per night	
€€ . . . . €50 to €100	
€€€ . . . . . €101 to €150	
€€€€ . . . . . . Over €150	

RESTAURANT PRICES	
€ . . . . Less than €10	
€€ . . . . €10 to €20	
€€€ . . . . €21 to €35	
€€€€ . . . . Over €35	

best in Hamburg, serves mainly French cuisine, and offers great views of the Binnenalster. **Doc Cheng's** (€€-€€€)

Raffles Hotel Vier Jahreszeiten

serves Euro-Asian food in a faux-1920s Shanghai-style locale. Neuer Jungfernstieg 9, 20354, ☎ 040-34-940, fax 040-3494-2600, www.raffles-hvj.de. (€€€€)

The **Kempinski Hotel Atlantic** has been known as the Weiße Riese (White Giant) since it opened its doors in 1909. This elegant, luxury hotel is close to the Hauptbahnhof on the banks of the

Kempinski Hotel Atlantic

Außenalster. Rooms are modern, luxurious, and elegant – some with lake views. The **Atlantic Restaurant** (€€€-€€€€) serves nouvelle cuisine with French and Italian influences, while the **Atlantic-Mühle** (€€-€€€) offers local specialties. An der Alster 72, 20099 Hamburg, ☎ 040-28-880, fax 040-247-129, www.kempinski.de. (€€€€)

The red brick **Steigenberger Hotel** is ideally situated between the Rathaus and harbor area. The modern bedrooms are large and luxurious. The **Calla Restaurant** (€€€-€€€€) serves Euro-Asian food and is open for dinner only. The **Bistro am Fleet** (€€) is a modern restaurant serving a wide range of international dishes. Heiligengeistbrücke 4, 20458 Hamburg,

Steigenberger Hotel

☎ 040-368-060, fax 040-3680-6777, www.steigenberger.de. (€€€€)

The **Intercontinental Hotel** is on the Außenalster, with views of the lake and the city skyline. This luxury hotel has comfortable, well-equipped rooms. The **Windows Restaurant** (€€€€) serves international cuisine with a view –

it is on the ninth floor facing the lake and city and is open for dinner only. The **Hamburg Spielbank** (Casino) is inside the hotel. Fontenay 10, 20354 Hamburg, ☎ 040-41-420, fax 040-4142-2999, www.interconti.com. (€€€€)

Intercontinental Hotel

Europäischer Hof

The **Hotel Europäischer Hof** is Hamburg's largest privately managed hotel and has been in operation since 1925. It is at the Hauptbahnhof. Rooms are large and comfortable. The hotel has a large spa area with a 492-ft waterslide that goes down six stories. The room key gives access to three days of public transportation and a harbor cruise. Kirchenallee 45, 20099 Hamburg, ☎ 040-248-248, fax 040-2482-4799, www.europaeischer-hof.de. (€€€-€€€€)

The 26-floor **Hotel Radisson SAS** is Hamburg's tallest hotel. It is inside the Planten und Blomen park and connected to the Congress Center and the Dammtor Station. Rooms are well equipped and have grand views. The **Trader**

Hotel Radisson SAS

Vic's Restaurant (€€-€€€) serves Polynesian and French cuisine. (Open for dinner only.) Marseiller Straße 2, 20355 Hamburg, ☎ 040-35-020, fax 040-3502-3440, www.radissaonsas.com. (€€€-€€€€)

The **Intercity Hotel Hamburg Hauptbahnhof** opened in 2004 across the road from the Hauptbahnhof near the Mönckestraße shopping area. The hotel is modern, with well-equipped, comfortable rooms, aimed mainly at the business traveler. The room key gives free access to local transportation. Glockengießerwall 14/15, 20095 Hamburg, ☎ 040-248-700, fax 040-2487-0111, www.intercityhotel.de. (€€€)

The **Hotel Hafen** is on a hill above the Landungsbrücke, with grand views of the Elbe from most rooms. The hotel has three wings and the oldest keeps up its seafaring tradition with many maritime decorative items. The newer wing has rooms that are more comfortable. The close proximity of the hotel to the Landungsbrücke and the Reeperbahn makes it popular with those who are here to see the musicals on the Reeperbahn and across the Elbe. The **restaurant** (€€-€€€) serves international dishes and offers lovely views of the Landungsbrücke area. Limited free parking is available on a first-come, first-park

View from room at Hotel Hafen

basis. Seewarten-straße 9, 20459 Hamburg, ☎ 040-311-130, fax 040-3111-3755, www.hotel-hamburg.de. (€€-€€€)

The **Hotel Kronprinz** is next to the Hauptbahnhof and has neat rooms furnished with high-quality solid wood furniture. Some antiques are used in the public areas. Kirchenallee 46, 20099 Hamburg, ☎ 040-271-4070, fax 040-280-1097, www.kronprinz-hamburg.de. (€€)

The **Ibis** chain (www.accordhotels.com) has several hotels in Hamburg, of which three are well located for tourists. As is usual with this chain, there are few thrills, no minibars, but clean rooms, at low prices in attractive locations. (All are €€, even during event times.) The **Ibis Hamburg Alster**, Holzdamm 4-12, 20099 Hamburg, ☎ 040-248-290, fax 040-2482-9734, is near the Hauptbahnhof on the banks of the Alster. The **Ibis Altona**, Königstraße 4, 22767 Hamburg, ☎ 040-311-870, fax 040-3118-7304, is at the far end of the Reeperbahn and popular with tour groups visiting the nearby musical theater. The Ibis **St Pauli**, Simon-von-Utrecht-Straße 63, 20359 Hamburg, ☎ 040-650-460, fax 040-6504-6555, is at the east end of the Reeperbahn near St Pauli U-Bahn station.

◆ Where to Eat

In addition to the restaurants mentioned inside hotels above, Hamburg has many excellent restaurants in all price classes scattered through the city.

Anna, Bleichenbrücke 2, ☎ 040-367-014, is rustic locale with terrace near the Rathaus. It serves a wide range of dishes with a large local specialties selection. (€€€)

Across the road from the Michaelskirche is **San Michele**, Englische Plancke 8, ☎ 040-371-127. It serves Italian food, mostly from the Naples region. (€€-€€€)

Hamburg

The **Ratsweinkeller**, Große Johannisstraße 2, ☎ 040-364-153, is in the historic vaults underneath the impressive Rathaus. The restaurant is stylish and decorated with ship models and maritime items. The menu has a large selection of local specialties, but also more international fare. (€€-€€€)

Jena Paradies, Klosterwall 23, ☎ 040-327-008, is at the south end of the Hauptbahnhof inside part of a former Art Academy. A wide variety of dishes, ranging from French to Austrian cuisine, are served inside this Bauhaus-style spot. Lunch menus are particularly good value. (€-€€€).

The **Arkaden Café**, Alsterarkaden 9-10, seems to have all the elements of a tourist trap. It is in the Alster Arcade with wonderful views of the Rathaus from the terrace, or the Alsterfleet from the basement rooms. However, prices show no tourist markup, service is fast and friendly, and the bistro-style food is good. It has great breakfast options starting at 8 am – two hours before anything else in the vicinity opens for the day. (€-€€)

Camping

 Camping Schnelsen Nord is nine miles north of Hamburg. It is right next to the A7 highway (and the local Ikea) but noise levels are acceptable due to sound-reduction walls. Facilities are good. It has 150 tourist lots. It is open from April to October. Wunderbrunnen 2, ☎ 040-559-4225, fax 040-550-7334, www. campingplatz-hamburg.de.

◆ Daytrip from Hamburg

Lübeck

Lübeck is a popular daytrip from Hamburg, but few would regret staying longer. The main sight is the historic town center, which is a UNESCO World Cultural Heritage Site because it kept its original medieval layout and has around 1,000 listed buildings.

Lübeck was founded in 1143 on a strategic and relatively safe island in the Trave River. It became a free imperial city in 1226 and soon after became the center of the Hanseatic League. For the next 400 years, it was one of the richest and most powerful cities in Northern Europe. During World War II, the town suffered from air raids as early as March 1942. Following the war, the influx of refugees from the eastern provinces of Germany doubled the town's population to 200,000.

As in other cities in northern Germany, the main building material in Lübeck is brick. The massive brick structures, especially churches, are the main draw. Also interesting are the narrow alleys reminiscent of medieval times.

Transportation

Hamburg and Lübeck are connected at least hourly by trains that take about 45 minutes.

Lübeck is an easy 45-minute drive from Hamburg along the excellent Autobahn A1. The A20 gives easy access to Wismar, Rostock, and Berlin.

Information Sources

Tourist Office: Lübecker Verkehrsverein, Am Bahnhof/Linden Arcaden, Konrad-Adenauer-Straße 6, 23558 Lübeck, ☎ 0451-72-300, www. luebeck.de.

Sightseeing

The main sights in Lübeck can be seen by walking from the Holstentor into the Old Town and along Breite Straße.

■ Holstentor Area

The massive brick, twin-tower **Holstentor** (Holsten Gate), the symbol of Lübeck, was erected in 1464-78. It was actually constructed in front of the city walls and clearly more intended to flaunt the city's power and wealth than for defensive purposes. The less frequently photographed façade facing the city is artistically more impressive. It houses the **Holstentor-Museum** (Local History Museum), ☎ 0451-122 -4129. Opening hours are daily from 10 am to 5 pm, closing at 6 pm from April to October. Admission is €4. The large brick buildings south of the gate date from the 16th to 18th centuries and once served as salt stores (Salzspeicher).

A flight of stairs from Kolkstraße leads to the **Petrikirche** (St Peter's Church), Schmiedestraße, ☎ 0451-397-730. This origi-

Holstentor

nal triple-nave, mid-13th-century Romanesque church was altered to the Gothic style in the 14th century and two additional naves were added in the following two centuries. It was virtually destroyed during World War II but rebuilt. More interesting than the church itself is the view from the top of the tower. It is reached by elevator and thus one of the most popular viewing platforms in the region. Opening hours are daily from March to September from 9 am to 7 pm.

Petrikirche

■ Rathaus Area

Lübeck's two most impressive brick buildings, the Rathaus (Town Hall) and Marienkirche (St Mary's Church), are adjacent to each other along Breite Straße.

The **Rathaus** was built from 1250 onwards. It is mostly of glazed, dark brick and forms an L-shape on two sides of the Marktplatz. It has characteristic high protective walls decorated with slender turrets. On ground level, it has Gothic arcades, still

The Rathaus

used by local merchants for their intended purpose. On Breite Straße, it has a wonderful late-16th-century Dutch Renaissance external staircase. Up to 1669, the representatives of the Hanseatic League usually met in Lübeck in the Hansasaal. The interior can only be seen on a German guided tour, weekdays at 11 am, noon, and 3 pm. Admission is €2. Across the road is the famous **Café Niederegger** – see *Where to Shop & Eat* below.

THE HANSEATIC LEAGUE

The Hanse (Hanseatic League) started as a guild of traders in the 13th century, but eventually turned into a loose confederation of cities. The main aim was to facilitate trade and to keep it in the hands of the members. During the 14th and 15th century, the league was the most powerful political and economical force in Germany and northern Europe. At its height, it had over 200 member cities.

The Hanseatic League came undone during the 16th century when its power was increasingly challenged by upcoming nation states such as England and the Netherlands. It finally fell apart during the ravaging Thirty Years War. The last Hansetag was held in 1669. Although nine cities attended, the League was a spent force and never recovered.

Lübeck, the third-largest city in Germany during the 14th century, was known as the Queen of the Hanse, as it was the richest and the Hansetage were usually held here.

The monumental **Marienkirche**, Schüsselbuden 13, ☎ 0451-397-700, served as a prototype for all northern Germany's brick

Marienkirche (© Carsten Clasohm)

Gothic churches. It was constructed between 1250 and 1350 – the third-largest church in Germany and its 262-ft-long central nave, rising 126 ft, is the highest brick nave in the world. The spires are 410 ft high. The church was damaged during an air raid in 1942. During the ensuing fire, most of the interior was lost, but long-forgotten medieval wall paintings were laid bare and restored with the rest of the church. At the rear, two bells lie where they fell as reminder of the destructiveness of war. Two-hour guided tours of the towers and vaulting are conducted on Saturday from April to October at 3:15 pm, the last Saturday of the month also at 8:30 pm, and during July and August also on Wednesday at 3:15 pm. Opening hours are daily from 10 am to 6 pm.

Across the road from the church is the 1758 Baroque **Buddenbrookhaus**. It belonged to the Mann family from 1841 to 1891 and Lübeck's most famous sons, the writers Thomas and Heinrich Mann, spent several summers here. Thomas Mann, Nobel laureate

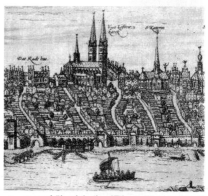

Lübeck in the 17th century

for literature in 1929, used the house as the setting for his novel *Die Buddenbrooks*, which described the life and fall of a rich patrician family. The house was virtually destroyed during the war but the façade was restored. The modern interior houses the **Heinrich and Thomas Mann Center**, Mengstraße 4, ☎ 0451-122-5407, with displays on the two writers' lives and works. Opening hours are daily from April to October, 10 am to 6 pm, and from November to March, 11 am to 4 pm. Admission is €5. (Combination tickets with the Günther Grass-Haus are €7.)

■ Northern Altstadt Area

Schiffergesellschaft

At the far end of Breite Straße is the 1535 **Schiffergesellschaft** (Seamen's Guild) house with a Renaissance exterior and a beautiful preserved interior. It is mostly wood paneled with rough wooden furniture and brass fittings as befit a seamen's tavern. It houses a popular restaurant – see below.

Across the road is the small, Gothic triple nave **Jakobikirche** (St James's Church), Jakobikirchhof 5, ☎ 0451-308-0115. More interesting than the mostly 14th-century church are the magnificently carved 16th-century organ lofts. The church is open daily from 10 am to 6 pm, but from September to April closing at dusk and on Monday.

The **Heiligen-Geist-Hospital** (Holy Ghost Hospice), Am Koberg, ☎ 0451-122-2040, founded in 1280, is one of the oldest social institutions in Europe. It originally served to take care of the sick, but gradually turned into an almshouse and later a house for the aged. Of special note are the Late Gothic wall paintings in the chapel as well as the large Gothic Langes Haus (Great Hall). It is open Tuesday to Sunday from April to October, 10 am to 5 pm, and from November to March, 10 am to 4 pm.

The **Museumskirche St. Katharinen** (St Catharine's Church Museum), König-straße, ☎ 0451-122-4180, houses modern statues inside the 14th-century church. Some wall paintings from the 14th and 15th centuries survived. Opening hours are from April to September, Tuesday to Sunday, from 10 am to 1 pm, and 2 to 5 pm. Admission is €1.

Heiligen-Geist-Hospital

Nearby is the **Günther Grass-Haus**, Glockengießerstraße 21, ☎ 0451-122-4192, www.guenter-grass-haus.de. Here the emphasis is not only on the written work of the 1999 Nobel laureate for literature, but also on his less well-known fine art works, including drawings, paintings, and sculpture. Opening hours are daily from April to October, 10 am to 6 pm, and from November to March, 11 am to 4 pm. Admission is €4. (Combination tickets with the Buddenbrookhaus are €7.)

Farther down Glockengießerstraße are several courtyards and passages (Höfe und Gänge) that housed social institutions. In the 17th century, several buildings here were erected for the poor and elderly. Of special note is the 1636 Baroque façade of the Füchtingshof (no 25).

Cultural Events

Lübeck's magnificent brick churches are frequently used for concerts. Organ music is particularly popular, but other classical music concerts are also arranged. Many church services include extensive musical recitals. The schedules are available from the **Kirchenkreis Lübeck**, Bäckerstraße 3-5, 23564 Lübeck, ☎ 0451-790-2127, www.kirchenmusik-luebeck.de.

The **Schleswig-Holstein Music Festival**, www.shmf.de, stretches over seven weeks in July and August. During this period, some 40 classical music concerts are scheduled at various venues in Schleswig-Holstein.

This festival is complemented by the **Theater Sommer Lübeck** – a series of concerts, theater, and musical productions held during the summer months. For the past decade, operettas have been an integral and increasingly the most popular part of this festival. Take a look at www.luebecker-sommeroperette.de for schedules.

Shopping

 Konditorei-Café Niederegger, Breite Straße 89, ☎ 0451-530-1126, is a Lübeck institution. The firm is most famous for producing marzipan. Its products are sold all over Germany, but only here does the selection exceeds 300 item. A museum, on the second floor, explains the almond delicacy's journey from the Orient to Lübeck and from here to the rest of Germany.

Adventures

■ On Foot

 Town Walks: The tourist office arranges guided two-hour walking tours of the city. The tour is available year-round on Sunday at 11 am. From May to October, further tours are Monday to Saturday at 11 am, and additionally at 2 pm from July to September. Participation is €4 per person or €6 to include the Rathaus.

■ On Ice

 Ice Skating: This is possible in the Altstadt in December and January. It is referred to as the "Hals-und Beinbruch" (literally, neck and leg breaking). Rental skates are available.

Where to Stay & Eat

 The best temporary address in Lübeck is the **Radisson SAS Senator Hotel**. It is in a modern building just outside the Holstentor offering great views of the Trave and the Old Town. The **Restaurant Nautilo** (€€-€€€) serves international and nouvelle cuisine and the **Kogge Restaurant** (€€-€€€) has mostly fish and Nordic specialties. Willy-Brandt-Allee 6, ☎ 23554 Lübeck, ☎ 0451-1420, fax 0451-142-2222, www.senatorhotel.de. (€€€-€€€€)

Nearby, with equally good views, but this time in the Old Town itself, is the simpler **Ringhotel Jensen**. It is in a patrician house dating back to 1307. However, rooms are modern and comfortably furnished. The **Yachtzimmer Restaurant** (€€-€€€) emphasizes Lübeck's seafaring tradition and serves regional specialties. An der Obertrave 4, ☎ 23552 Lübeck, ☎ 0451-702-490, fax 0451-73-386, www.ringhotel-jensen.de. (€€)

For local flavor, it is hard to beat the historic **Schiffergesellschaft**, Breite Straße 2, ☎ 0451-76-776. Even if not dining here, take a look inside to see the traditional wood-paneled seamen's tavern. The building dates to 1535. The food is mostly local specialties. Reservations are highly advisable. (€€-€€€).

A similar local option is **Zimmermann's Lübecker Hanse**, Kolkstraße 7, ☎ 0451-78-054, near the Holstentor. Wood beams and wooden floors add to the charm of the venue. They serve mainly seafood, but meat and a wide vegetarian selection are also available. Reservations are advisable. (€€-€€€)

Another Lübeck institution is the pleasant **Konditorei-Café Niederegger**, Breite Straße 89, ☎ 0451-530-1126 – across the road from the Rathaus. This firm made marzipan famous in Germany and the marzipan is used in many items. The café serves small meals, including several breakfast options, and very tasty cakes. The café is elegant and spread over multiple levels. Prices are pleasantly reasonable. (€-€€)

■ Camping

 Camp Lübeck-Schönbröcken is 1.8 miles from Lübeck's historic town center. It has 70 lots for tourists, with limited shade. A direct bus service is available to Lübeck. The site is open from April to October. Steinrader Damm 12, ☎ / fax 0451-893-090.

RV homes may park at **Park & Sail**, Am Fischereihafen, ☎ 04502-1300.

Frankfurt am Main

Frankfurt am Main is at the geographical heart of Germany. Its population of 650,000 makes it the fifth-largest city in Germany, but the larger Rhine Main area with nearly five million people is the strongest economic region in the country. Frankfurt is mostly a modern city, but more attention to con-

servation, arts, and cultural projects after the 1970s have done much to improve the rather dour and boring image of the city. It has several interesting historic buildings, many skyscrapers, a lovely riverfront, 38 museums, 109 art galleries, and 33 theaters.

Although some parts of Frankfurt were settled in Roman times, its modern history dates from the time of Charlemagne, who erected a Pfalz (Imperial Palace) here. Ever since, it occupied a strategic position on the major trade routes. Frankfurt has held trade fairs (*Messe*), which became the base for its wealth and fame, since the 11th century.

In 1152, Friedrich Barbarossa was elected German king. This was the first of the 33 imperial elections (out of 52) that took place in Frankfurt. From 1356, all elections were in Frankfurt and, from 1562, the formal coronations were in the Frankfurt Kaiserdom.

During World War II Frankfurt suffered several air raids that destroyed most of the Old Town and killed 6,000 people. Frankfurt's rebuilding was decidedly modern, with few of the original old buildings preserved.

Frankfurt remained the banking center of Germany and banks mainly occupy the skyscrapers that were constructed in Frankfurt during the last quarter of the 20th century. Frankfurt has 19 buildings higher than 165 ft, making it the only city in Germany

Frankfurt

WESTEND-NORD

INNENSTADT

ALTSTADT

SACHSENHAUSEN

WESTEND-SÜD

Konrad Adenauer Straße
Kurt Schumacher Straße
Alte Brücke
Gr Friedbergerstr
Fahrgasse
Eschenheimer
Oeder Weg
Stephanstr
Bleichstraße
Zeil
Mainkai
Braubachstraße
Berliner Straße
River Main
Landstraße
Anlage
Schillerstraße
Grüneburgweg
Gärtnerweg
Bockenheimer
Hochstraße
Borsenstraße
Kaiserstraße
Kaiser-platz
Museumsufer
Schaumainkai
Reuterweg
Junghofstraße
Mainzer Straße
Untermainkai
Untermain-brücke
Staufenstraße
Taunusanlage
Gutleustraße
Münchenerstraße
Kaiserstraße
Wilhelm Leuschnerstraße
Liebigstraße
Ulmenstr
Bockenheimer Landstraße
Kettenhof Weg
Guiollettstraße
Niedenau
Taunusstraße
Niddastraße
Schubertstraße
Beethovenstraße
Westendstraße
Westend-platz
Savignystraße
Rheinstraße
Friedrich Ebert Anlage
Hohenstaufenstr
Schumannstraße
Senkenberganlage
Mainzer Landstraße

N

HUNTER PUBLISHING

NOT TO SCALE

© 2007 HUNTER PUBLISHING, INC.

with a real skyline. The Commerzbank building, at 848 ft, is the tallest in Europe.

◆ Information Sources

Tourist information is available from Römerberg 27, ☎ 60313 Frankfurt, ☎ 069-2123-8800, www. frankfurt.de, or from the Hauptbahnhof.

◆ Getting Here & Around

By Rail: Frankfurt's Hauptbahnhof is the busiest in the country and offers excellent transportation connections to other cities in Germany. Daily, around 1,800 trains stop at Frankfurt Hauptbahnhof and almost half of all German trains pass through the Rhine Main area. By train, Cologne can be reached in just over an hour (three departures per hour and more from the airport). At least hourly direct trains take four hours to Berlin; 3½ hours to Hamburg, Leipzig, or Munich. Amsterdam can be reached in four hours on several trains per day.

The airport has a major railway station as well, making it often unnecessary to travel to the Hauptbahnhof before continuing to the final destination. Due to the overcrowding at the Hauptbahnhof, some long distance trains stop in Frankfurt-Süd, with S-Bahn connections to the Hauptbahnhof or elsewhere in the city.

1.	Römer	16.	Freßgasse
2.	Alte Nikolaikirche	17.	Alte Oper
3.	Historisches Museum	18.	Jüdisches Museum
4.	Schirn Kunsthalle	19.	Museum Judengasse
5.	Kaiserdom (Cathedral)	20.	Palmengarten
6.	Museum für Moderne Kunst	21.	American Consulate General
7.	Paulskirche	22.	Naturmuseum Senckenberg
8.	Liebfraukirche	23.	Eiserner Steg pedestrian bridge
9.	St Leonardkirche	24.	Museum für Angewandte Kunst
10.	Karmeliterkloster	25.	Deutsches Filmmuseum
11.	Goethehaus	26.	Deutsches Architektur Museum
12.	St Katherinenkirche	27.	Museum für Kommunikation, Städel, Liebighaus
13.	Hauptwache	28.	Hauptbahnhof
14.	Eschenheimer Turm	29.	Rothschild Park
15.	Börse		

Frankfurt am Main

Frankfurt has a very good public transportation network combining S-Bahn, U-Bahn, tram, and bus networks. For sightseeing in the Old Town, the U-Bahn is usually the most convenient. Bus 46 runs from the Hauptbahnhof along the Schaumainkai where most of the Sachsenhausen museums are located. In contrast to most other German cities, tickets must be bought only shortly before boarding and not separately validated.

By Road: Several major Autobahnen pass through the region. The A3 connects Cologne and the Ruhr area with Frankfurt, Würzburg, and farther destinations in northern Bavaria. The A5 connects northern German destinations with the Black Forest and Switzerland via Frankfurt. The A7 from Denmark via Hamburg and Hanover runs through the eastern parts of Hesse to southern Germany.

By Air: Frankfurt's Rhein-Main International Airport (FRA), ☎ 01805-372-4636, www.flughafen-frankfurt.de, is the busiest in continental Europe. Virtually all intercontinental flights to Germany arrive here and many scheduled European flights as well. The airport is southwest of the city and can easily be reached by public transportation. Taxis to downtown take less than 30 minutes and cost around €25. The fastest way is by rail. There are two train stations at the airport. The one closest to the terminal is for local transportation: take the S-Bahn from here to downtown (Hauptbahnhof) or in the opposite direction to Wiesbaden and Mainz. The Fernbahnhof serves long-distance trains including the InterCityExpress (ICE) trains. Many airlines have check-in counters at the Fernbahnhof.

◆ Sightseeing

The main sights in Frankfurt are concentrated in the Old Town center, with several museums on the opposite bank of the Main in Sachsenhausen. There are a few more sights in the surrounding Neustadt, which is still within the old city walls. Most of the skyscrapers are in the Bankerviertel, but these are best seen from a distance, especially from the banks of the river.

If time is limited, give priority to Römer and the Kaiserdom, the view of the skyline from the Eiserner Steg (a pedestrian bridge), and the Städel Art Museum.

Altstadt

The Römerberg

Frankfurt's main sights are located in the close vicinity of **Römerberg**, the physical and spiritual heart of Frankfurt since the days of Charlemagne. This huge square is the setting for all modern day festivals. The fountain (1611) has Lady Justice not blindfolded, but rather facing the Town Hall as a warning to the town council to treat the citizens fairly.

Römer is the historic Rathaus, which consists of 16 buildings that were connected through the centuries to form the town hall. The exterior is Neo-Gothic and the statues only added decades after the last emperor was crowned here. Römer was extensively damaged during World War II, but rebuilt in simplified form. The Kaisersaal is the only part of the building open to tourists. It has late-19th-century paintings of all emperors from Charlemagne to Joseph II. Note the portrait of Matthias – his coronation in 1612 is fondly remembered. Contrary to popular belief, his coronation was the only one where the fountain in the square spouted wine. Opening hours are daily from 10 am to 1 pm and 2 to 5 pm. It is often closed for official functions. Admission is €1.50.

The lovely half-timbered houses facing the Rathaus were constructed in the 1980s as copies of the originals destroyed during World War II. Most of the Old Town still looked like that in 1940. The only half-timbered building in the Old Town that survived the inferno following the air raids is **Haus Wertheym** across from the History Museum.

At the south end of the square, dividing it from the Main River, is the 12th-century **Alte Nikolaikirche** (Old St Nicholas Church), Am Römerberg, www.alte-nikolaikirche.de. Opening hours are daily from 10 am to 6 pm, closing at 8 pm from April to September. The carillon chimes daily at 9:05 am, 12:05, and 5:05 pm.

The Alte Nikolaikirche

Next to the church is the **Historisches Museum** (History Museum), Saalgasse 19, ☎ 069-2123-5599, www.historisches-museum.frankfurt.de. It has interesting displays, but unfortunately very few English descriptions. Of particular interest is the model of the Old Town, as well as a small part of Charlemagne's original Pfalz or Imperial Palace. Opening hours are Tuesday to Saturday from 10 am to 5 pm, Wednesday from 4 to 8 pm, and Sunday from 1 to 5 pm. Admission is €4.

The ultra-modern **Schirn Kunsthalle**, Römerberg, ☎ 069-299-8820, www.schirn.de, occupies the area from the Kaiserdom to Römerberg. It houses rotating exhibitions of modern art of international acclaim. Opening hours are Tuesday to Sunday from 10 am to 7 pm (Wednesday and Thursday until 10 pm). Admission depends on the exhibition but is around €6. The attached art bookshop has surprisingly reasonable prices.

The **Kaiserdom** (Imperial Cathedral) is a bit of a misnomer as it was never the seat of the bishop, but had the honorary title added after it became the church in which the German King was crowned. The Gothic church was built between 1315 and 1514, but the tower was left unfinished. A major fire in 1867 destroyed parts of the cathedral, but it was rebuilt using the original plans and this time the tower was actually completed. The bombing raids of World War II left only the shell of the church but it was soon rebuilt. The reddish interior of the church houses several works of art. From 1356, the election of the German emperor took place in the library south of the choir. The coronations were held here from 1562 to 1792. Opening hours are daily from 8 am to noon and from 2:30 to 6 pm, but open in the mornings only on Friday and Sunday. During the winter, it closes at 5 pm.

The Kaiserdom

The small **Dommuseum** (Cathedral Museum), Domplatz 1, ☎ 069-1337-6186, is attached to the church. It houses the cathedral treasures, mainly gowns and some chalices and minor reliquaries. Opening hours are Tuesday to Friday from 10 am to 5 pm and weekends from 11 am to 5 pm. Admission is €2.

European and American artworks from the 1960s form the core of the **Museum für Moderne Kunst** (Modern Art), Domstraße 10, ☎ 069-2123-0447, www.mmk-frankfurt.de. Works are rotated every six months – the display never follows a stylistic or chronological presentation. Opening hours are Tuesday to Sunday from 10 am to 5 pm, closing at 8 pm on Wednesday. Admission is €5.

Just north of the Römer, is the round **Paulskirche**, Paulsplatz. This Classical building is a post-war copy of the original, dating from 1790-1833. The first elected German parliament met here in 1848-49. The current interior is modern, with a small exhibition on German parliamentary history. A plenary hall on the second floor is used for conferences and other mostly non-religious events. Opening hours are daily from 10 am to 5 pm. Admission is free.

The **Liebfrauenkirche**, (Church of Our Dear Lady), was a former monastery church. It was destroyed in 1944, but rebuilt in the original Gothic style. It has an interesting Three-Kings Tampanum, Gothic panels, and Baroque figures saved from the ruins of the former church. It is open daily from 6:30 am to 6 pm.

The **St Leonhardkirche** (St Leonard's Church) is a Late Romanesque construction with a Gothic chancel added around 1430. Note the Romanesque spires and the Gothic frescoes and altars. Opening hours are Tuesday to Sunday from 10 am to noon and from 3 to 6 pm.

The **Karmeliterkloster** (Carmelite Monastery), Münzgasse 9, ☎ 069-2123-6276, has the largest religious mural north of the Alps. This 460-ft-long painting was done in the 15th century by Jörg Ratgeb. On the second floor are changing exhibitions, mainly photographs of historic events or themes related to Frankfurt. Opening

Karmeliterkloster mural

hours are weekdays from 8:30 am to 5 pm and weekends from 10 am to 5 pm. Admission is free.

Neustadt

Room in the Goethehaus

The **Goethehaus** (Goethe House) and **Goethe Museum**, Großer Hirschgraben 23-25, ☎ 069-138-800, www.goethehaus-frankfurt.de, focus on Goethe's early years. He was born and spent his youth here. Although almost completely destroyed during World War II, the house of Goethe's youth has been restored faithfully. Inside, the 16 rooms on four floors are furnished as in Goethe's time. A gallery has works on display from artists that influenced or inspired him. Open weekdays 9 am to 4 pm (closing at 6 pm from April to September) and weekends from 10 am to 4 pm. Admission is €5.

The **St Katherinenkirche** (St Catherine's Church) is a Late Gothic hall church with Baroque portals added in the late 17th century. It is open weekdays from 2 to 6 pm.

The Baroque **Hauptwache** was erected in 1729 but altered over the years. It was actually torn down to make way for the construction of the huge subway interchange underneath the square and then rebuilt in its original form. It houses a pleasant café serving mostly local cuisine at surprisingly reasonable prices. To the east of the square is the **Zeil**, Frankfurt's premier shopping street and claimed to be the most valuable one in Germany.

To the north is the **Eschenheimer Turm** (Tower), the loveliest of the few remaining original city defenses. The tower dates from the early 15th century and was one of 42 that protected the rich city. When Frankfurt tore down the last parts of the wall in the 19th century, a large park was created that forms a green half-circle around the Old Town. It is a favorite recreation area for locals.

The **Börse** (Stock Exchange), Börseplatz, is in a 19th-century building. As all trading is by computer, there is not much to see except the obligatory Bull and Bear statue in front of the building.

The Goethestraße

To the west of the Hauptwache is the Grosse Bockenheimer Straße. Part of the street is known as the **Freßgasse** (Gluttony Alley) due to the number of food shops that traditionally traded here. Presently most businesses here are restaurants or coffee shops. In contrast to the cafés at the Paulskirche, locals outnumber tourists by far. Parallel to the Freßgasse is the **Goethestraße** – the most expensive shopping street in Frankfurt, with all the international haute couture names.

At the end of the Freßgasse is the Opernplatz with the Late Classicist **Alte Oper** (Old Opera House), Opernplatz 1, ☎ 069-134-0400, www.alte-oper-frankfurt.de, completed in 1880. It was bombed out in

The Alte Oper

World War II and its shell was for almost 30 years the most beautiful ruin in Germany. It was restored in the 1970s and re-opened in 1981. The lovely exterior is a copy of the original, but the interior is modern and used for all kind of performances, but very seldom opera. (An excellent, modern opera house is a few blocks away.)

The park that leads from here to the River Main has several statues of famous German artists, including Beethoven and Schiller in the Taunusanlage and Goethe in the Gallusanlage. (Goethe may move to the renovated Goetheplatz in the near future.) The park also affords great views of the banking houses in the vicinity. Close to the Main is the Jewish Museum.

Frankfurt traditionally had a large Jewish community whose financial skills were absolutely necessary for the development of Frankfurt's trade and banking industry. In addition, Jews were taxed higher than other nationals and their huge tax contributions ensured that the town council opposed, often unsuccessfully, medieval pogroms. In addition to the Rothschilds, Anne Frank was born in Frankfurt and fled with her family to Amsterdam soon afterwards. The **Jüdisches Museum** (Jewish Museum), Untermainkai 14-15, ☎ 069-2123-5000, www.juedischesmuseum.de, in the former Rothschild Palace illustrates the history of Jewish settlements in Germany from the Middle Ages to the present. Opening hours are Tuesday to

Sunday from 10 am to 5 pm, closing at 8 pm on Wednesday. Admission is €2.60.

Westend

The Westend is to the west of the Alte Oper and the traditional area of bankers and diplomats. It has some of the most expensive residential property in Germany. It also has two sights worth seeing. Both are easiest to reach on foot from U-Bahn station Bockenheimer Warte.

Palmengarten Palm House

The **Palmengarten** (Palm/ Tropical Gardens), Siesmayer-straße 43, ☎ 069-2123-3939, is a huge park and botanical garden. It has the oldest botanical building in Europe – the 1869 Palm House. More recent greenhouses have plants from different climate zones. Opening hours are daily from 9 am to 6 pm, closing at 4 pm from November to January. Admission is €3.50.

Nearby is the **Naturmuseum Senckenberg** (Natural History Museum), Senckenberganlage 25, ☎ 069-75-420, www.senckenberg.uni-frankfurt.de. It is one of the largest of its kind in Europe and has an important paleontology collection. However, the fossils and rocks are upstaged by the dinosaur displays. Opening hours are daily 9 am to 5 pm, but closing at 8 pm on Wednesday and 6 pm on weekends. Admission is €5.

Sachsenhausen

Sachsenhausen is the section on the south bank of the River Main. It was not destroyed during World War II and still has large areas with 19th-century villas. During the last two decades of the 20th century, several excellent museums opened on the south bank of the Main. The museums are described below in order, moving from the Eiserner Steg downstream. If time is limited, give preference to the Städel and the Liebieghaus.

Frankfurt am Main

Eiserner Steg

Several bridges span the River Main but, if you're walking, use the **Eiserner Steg.** This pedestrian footbridge was erected in the 19th century as a private initiative to be paid for with tolls. However, the city took control of the bridge soon after its completion and opened it to all for free. It offers some of the best views of the Frankfurt skyline. In addition, it is the most convenient crossing point from the Römer area to Sachsenhausen. In summer, many outdoor cafés line the Sachsenhausen bank of the Main.

The **Museum für Angewandte Kunst Frankfurt** (Museum of Applied Arts), Schaumainkai (Museumsufer) 17, ☎ 069-2123-4037, www.museumfuerangewandtekunst.frankfurt.de, has a collection spanning 6,000 years. The emphasis is on European applied arts from the 12th century to the present, but works from other parts of the world, especially East Asia and Islamic countries are also on display. Opening hours are Tuesday to Sunday from 10 am to 5 pm, closing at 9 pm on Wednesday. Admission is €5.

The **Deutsches Filmmuseum** (German Cinema Museum), Schaumainkai 41, ☎ 069-2123-8830, www.deutsches-filmmuseum.de, has exhibitions on the development of cinema, both German and international. It exhibits various instruments used in filmmaking and projecting, as well as the development of the industry. At its heart is a theater that shows mainly art films. Opening hours are Tuesday, Thursday, Friday, and Sunday from 10 am to 5 pm, Wednesday from 10 am to 8 pm, and Saturday from 2 to 8 pm. Admission is €2.50.

The **Deutsches Architektur Museum** (German Architectur Museum), Schaumainkai (Museumsufer) 43, ☎ 069-2123-8844, www.dam-online.de, opened in 1984 as then the only museum of its kind in Europe. It has a permanent exhibition on the development of architecture from the most primitive huts to modern skyscrapers. Opening hours are Tuesday to Sunday from 10 am to 5 pm, closing at 8 pm on Wednesday. Admission is €6.

The **Museum für Kommunikation** (Communications Museum), Schaumainkai (Museumsufer) 53, ☎ 069-60-600, www.museumsstiftung.de, has displays on all matters related to mail and communication. In addition to the permanent collection, it hosts temporary exhibitions and has a large space where children can experience communication through various means. Opening hours are Tuesday to Friday from 9 am to 6 pm and weekends from 11 am to 7 pm. Admission is €2.

The **Städelsches Kunstinstitut und Städtische Galerie** (Municipal Art Institute and Gallery), Schaumainkai (Museumsufer) 63, ☎ 069-605-0980, www.staedelmuseum.de, is usually referred to as **Das Städel**. It is Frankfurt's most impressive museum, with a huge collection covering seven centuries. The old Masters' collection is particularly impressive and includes representative works by Holbein, Rembrandt, Rubens, and Vermeer. The French Impressionists, including Renoir and Monet, as well as the German Impressionists, are well represented. Modern works by Picasso, Klee, and Feininger are complemented by contemporary works. Special exhibitions are often held in an adjacent building. The most famous work is a Tischbein painting of Goethe. The Café-Restaurant Holbein is currently very fashionable. Opening hours are Tuesday to Sunday from 10 am to 5 pm, closing at 9 pm on Wednesday and Thursday. Admission is €6.

The **Liebieghaus – Museum Alter Plastik** (Museum of Ancient Sculpture), Schaumainkai (Museumsufer) 71, ☎ 069-2123-8617, www.liebieghaus.de, has an impressive range of sculpture. It displays Egyptian, Greek, and Roman antiquities, medieval sculpture, works from the Renaissance and the Baroque, Classicism, and some from East Asia. Opening hours are Tuesday to Sunday from 10 am to 5 pm, closing at 8 pm on Wednesday. Admission is €4.

◆ Cultural Events & Festivals

Frankfurt has 33 theaters, making for a busy cultural calendar. The Alte Oper alone hosts around 600 concerts per year. Music is also played in many of the churches. In summer, open-air concerts are popular. Schedules are available from the tourist office and they can also make reservations for many

Christmas market

events. The **English Theater**, Kaiserstraße 52, ☎ 069-2423-1620, www.englishtheater-frankfurt.de, performs in English only.

Frankfurt has a reputation for needing little reason to throw a party. A recent move by a politician to ban the **Opernplatz festival** (end June, early July), as it was dedicated to eating and drinking rather than to cultural events, was shouted down from all directions.

The **Mainfest**, early August, is a folk festival with rides and food stalls held at Römerberg and the Main quay. The **Rheingauer Weinmarkt** (Rheingau Wine Market) is held in the Freßgasse the last week of August. The last weekend of August also sees the **Museumuferfest** – a huge cultural festival at the museums in Sachsenshausen.

The year ends with the best festival of all – the **Christmas market**, held from end November to just before Christmas. It is the largest Christmas market in Germany, with the largest Christmas tree standing in front of the Rathaus. The heart of the market is Römerberg, but it spreads to the Main banks, the square in front of the Paulskirche, farther up the road and down much of the Zeil. Secondary Christmas markets are at the station and airport.

◆ Shopping

The high-class shops are in **Goethestraße**, which leads from the Opernplatz parallel to the Freßgasse. It has all the premier international brands.

Ordinary people shop on the **Zeil**, a huge pedestrian street that claims to be the most valuable shopping street in the country. It has mostly department stores and fashion outlets. The **Zeilgallerie**, Zeil 112, has many small, moderately priced boutiques popular with the younger crowds.

Sachsenhausen has a major **flea market** on Saturday mornings from 8 am to 2 pm. It is held in the vicinity of the Eiserner Steg. However, quality items are few and far between.

◆ Adventures

On Foot

Town Walks: Guided tours of specialized themes are conducted on weekends by **Statt-Reisen**, Rotlintstraße 70, ☎ 069-9441-5940, www.stattreisen.de.

On Wheels

By Bicycle: Frankfurt is an easy city to cycle in – it is mostly flat and there are many dedicated cycling paths. A popular longer distance cycling route is the **Mainuferweg** (Main Banks Route), which runs on both sides of the Main from Aschaffenburg to Mainz and Wiesbaden. Bicycles can be rented at the Hauptbahnhof, ☎ 069-2653-4834.

By Tourist Tram: The **Ebbelwei-Express** is a tourist tram that operates weekend afternoons on a circular route through the

Old Town and Sachsenhausen. A round-trip takes an hour but it is possible to interrupt the journey temporarily at any stop. It costs €5 and includes a bottle of apple wine or juice.

On Water

Riverboats: Primus-Linie, Mainkai 36, ☎ 069-1338-370, www.primus-linie.de, has regular cruises on the River Main departing mostly from near Römer. In addition to one- to two-hour circular cruises, dinner and dance cruises, as well as day cruises up the Main are also available.

Spas

Bad Homburg, a town to the northwest of Frankfurt, has several expensive private clinics where patients can take advantage of the health benefits of the local springs. For the casual visitor the Kur Royal and Taunus Therme offer the two most attractive, if completely different, options.

The **Kur Royal** is a day spa located inside the grand 19th-century Kaiser Wilhemsbad in the Kurpark, ☎ 06172-178-178, www.kur-royal.de. Its facilities and splendor remind the visitor why Bad Homburg was the spa of choice for the royalty of Europe before World War I. The basic Kur Royal Inclusive package goes for €25 for two hours, €40 for four, and €60 for a full day. It includes the following: a warm saltwater relaxation pool, a stone oven bath, an aromatherapy bath, a hay steam bath, a sand and light bath (a dawn-to-dusk day on the beach simulation in 30 minutes), a high-humidity Roman steam bath and, to finish, "wave dreams" – a cool down with visual effects and coordinated music. Nude bathing is not allowed – towels are supplied but not swimsuits or bathing slippers. No smoking and no under 16s. Prior reservations are required.

Just outside the Kurpark is the much more informal and cheaper **Taunus Therme**, Seedamweg, ☎ 06172-406-40, www.taunus-therme.de. It combines elements of Japanese, Finnish, and Greco-Roman culture in both its architecture and approach to the spa concept. It has an enormous outdoor pool as well as several other hot and cold pools, cascading waterfalls and bubbling hot whirlpools. Traditional Finnish saunas add Nordic charm and some go up to 113°F and 98% humidity. Most areas require swimsuits but 150 outdoor tanning spots are available in the FKK (nude) zone. The spa is open daily from 9 am to 11 pm. Admission fees include the use of all facilities. During the week, admission is €12.50 for two hours, €17 for four hours, and €24 for a full day. On weekends and holidays, add €2 to each fee.

Bad Homburg is most easily reached from Frankfurt on S-Bahn S5 – up to four connections per hour taking 20 minutes.

◆ Where to Stay

Old Town Area

The **Steigenberger Hotel Frankfurter Hof** is the grand dame of Frankfurt hotels and the premier property in

HOTEL PRICES	
€	Up to €50 per night
€€	€50 to €100
€€€	€101 to €150
€€€€	Over €150

the impressive Steigenberger portfolio. Behind the Neo-Renaissance façade is a modern hotel with a stylish interior. Rooms are comfortable, with impressive bathrooms. It is worth paying slightly more for a larger room. The hotel is halfway between the Hauptbahnhof and Old Town. It has several restaurants. The very elegant **Francois** (€€€€) serves French cuisine. The bistro-style **Oscar's** (€€-€€€) serves international fare, while **Iroha** (€€€-€€€€) has Japanese cuisine.

Do not even dream of staying here during the major exhibitions – it is booked out years in advance. Am Kaiserplatz, 60311 Frankfurt, ☎ 069-21-502, fax 069-215-900, www.steigenberger.de. (€€€€)

Steigenberger Hotel Frankfurter Hof

The **ArabellaSheraton Grand Hotel** is at the far end of the Old Town in Konstabler Wache. It is a large, very modern hotel, much flashier than the Frankfurter Hof. Décor in the elegant, large rooms ranges from Arabian to Asian and Post-Modern.

The hotel has six restaurants. The **Peninsula** (€€€) serves nouvelle cuisine with strong Mediterranean influences. Konrad-Adenauer-Straße 7, 60313 Frankfurt, ☎ 069-29-810, fax 069-298-1810,

ArabellaSheraton Grand Hotel

www.arabellasheraton.de. (€€€€)

The Hilton

The **Hilton Hotel** is next to a large park near the Alte Oper. It is a modern hotel with comfortable rooms. It has a fitness center and a large swimming pool that is under protection order. The Hard Rock is across the road. Hochstraße 4, 60313 Frankfurt, ☎ 069-133-8000, fax 069-1338-1338, www.hilton.com. (€€€€)

The **Palmenhof Hotel** is between the Old Town and the Messe, close to the Palmengarten. Rooms are very comfortable, using a combination of modern and antique furniture. The **L'Artichoc Restau-**

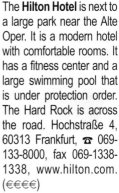

Palmenhof Hotel

rant (€€-€€€) serves nouvelle cuisine and local specialties. Bockenheimer Landstraße 89-91, 60325 Frankfurt, ☎ 069-75-0060, fax 069-7530-0666, www.palmenhof.com. (€€€)

The **Miramar Hotel** is one of very few hotels inside the Old Town itself. It is close to the Paulskirche. Rooms are functionally furnished, mostly in dark wood. Berliner Straße 31, 60311 Frankfurt, ☎ 069-920-3970, fax 069-9203-9769, www.miramar-frankfurt.de. (€€€)

The **Best Western Hotel Scala** is close to the ArabellaSheraton in the northern reaches of the Old Town. The building was recently renovated and has modern, neat rooms. Schäfergasse 31, 60313 Frankfurt, ☎ 069-138-1110, fax 069-284-234, www.scala.bestwestern.de. (€€-€€€)

Hauptbahnhof Area

The very luxurious **Steigenberger Hotel Metropolitan** opened in 2003 at the north side of the Hauptbahnhof. Rooms have all modern comforts and technology requirements for the business traveler. The

Steigenberger Hotel Metropolitan

health club has a sauna, solarium, and whirlpool. Poststraße 6, 60329 Frankfurt, ☎ 069-5060-700, fax 069-506-070-555, www.steigenberger.de. (€€€€)

Nearby is the **Manhatten Hotel**. It is a modern building with modern interior. Rooms are comfortable and well designed with modern furniture. It is close to the nightlife area. Düsseldorfer Straße 20, 60329 Frankfurt, ☎ 069-269-5970, fax 069-269-597-777, www.manhatten-hotel.com. (€€-€€€)

The **Ibis Frankfurt Friedensbrücke** is a few blocks from the Hauptbahnhof on the banks of the Main. Rooms are typically Ibis with functional furniture and few thrills. Some have good river views though. Speicherstraße 4, 60327 Frankfurt, ☎ 069-273-030, fax 069-237-024, www.ibishotels.com. (€€-€€€).

◆ Where to Eat

The **Opéra**, Opern-platz 1, ☎ 069-134-0215, is an upscale restaurant on the sec-ond floor of the Alte Oper. More

RESTAURANT PRICES	
€ . . . . Less than €10	
€€ . . . . €10 to €20	
€€€ . . . . €21 to €35	
€€€€ . . . . Over €35	

pleasant than the inside room, is the terrace with views of the Frankfurt skyline. The restaurant serves international nouvelle cuisine with strong French influences. Do not confuse the res-taurant with the pleasant, small café bistro in front of the Alte Oper. (€€€-€€€€).

Opéra Restaurant

The **Main Tower Restaurant**, Neuer Mainzer Straße 52, ☎ 069-3650-4777, is on the 53rd floor and the only restaurant open to the general public in Frankfurt's skyscrapers. It serves international cuisine with the best views in town. Dinner reser-vations are advisable. (€€-€€€).

Yours Australian Sports Bar, Rahmhofstraße 2, ☎ 069-282-100, is in the Schillerpassage near the Hilton Hotel. It is a great place for burgers and other Australian or American-style food – a much better choice than the Hard Rock next door. (€-€€)

Café Liebfrauenberg, Liebfrauenberg 24, ☎ 069-287-380, is an old-style café with pleasant service and a large selection of food and drink. It is close to the Liebfrauenkirche.(€)

Sachsenhausen

Adolf Wagner Restaurant

Inside the Städel Art Museum is **Holbeins**, Holbeinstraße 1, ☎ 069-6605-6666, a modern restaurant serving mainly international cuisine with Mediterranean influences. It is also a pleasant place for afternoon coffee and cake. It is presently very fashionable, making dinner reservations advisable. (€€-€€€)

NYC, Schweizer Straße/Hans-Thomas-Straße, ☎ 069-614-818, is a good choice for American food close to the museum area. (€)

APPLE WINE

Sachsenhausen is famous for its apple wine locales. Apple wine (Ebbelwoi) is a local specialty, but a bit of an acquired taste. It has the same alcohol

Zum Gemalten Haus

content as beer. These taverns usually serve only small meals and have a limited selection. The traditional spots are concentrated in the area between Wall, Dreieichstraße and the Main. Two taverns with good food are closer to the Museumufer: **Adolf Wagner**, Schweizer Straße 71, ☎ 069-612-565 and **Zum Gemalten Haus**, Schweizer Straße 67, ☎ 069-614-559. (€)

Frankfurt am Main

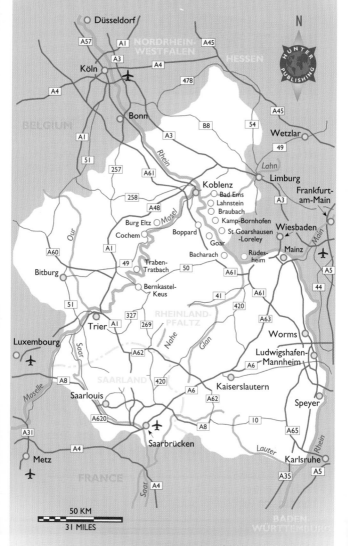

The Rhine & Mosel Valleys

50 KM
31 MILES

The Rhine &
Mosel Valleys

The Rhine Valley is on the must-see list of many visitors to Germany. The most beautiful section is from Rüdesheim to Koblenz. Along here a castle or castle ruin can be seen every mile or so. The valley is at its narrowest and the river flowing at its fastest pace. The villages are small, romantic, and picturesque. Restaurants and outdoor cafés abound.

Farther upstream are the cathedral cities of **Speyer**, **Worms**, and **Mainz**. All three towns are dominated by their Romanesque cathedrals. Speyer's remained true to the original, while the cathedrals in Worms and Mainz received Gothic additions.

Downstream is **Cologne**, a city of close to a million people. For a thousand years, up to the late-19th century, Cologne was the largest city in Germany. Its skyline is still dominated by the largest Gothic cathedral in the world, as well as by 12 Romanesque churches.

The **Mosel Valley** is for many an even more spectacular destination than the Rhine. The valley is narrower, the hills steeper, and the river meanders constantly. Villages are mostly small and picture-perfect. **Burg Eltz**, a castle that was never destroyed in eight centuries, is arguable the best-looking medieval castle in Germany. **Trier**, the largest town on the Mosel, is the oldest one in Germany and has the largest collection of Roman ruins on German soil.

◆ Getting Here & Around

By Rail: Cologne is an important railway hub with fast connections to all parts of Germany as well as to the Netherlands, Brussels, and Paris. Berlin is just over four hours away on hourly trains. At least three ICE trains per hour connect Cologne and Frankfurt Airport or Hauptbahnhof in just over an hour.

Trains run on both sides of the Rhine, with the left bank (Mainz to Koblenz) carrying slightly more traffic than the right bank (Wiesbaden via Rüdesheim to Lahnstein and Koblenz). Frankfurt am Main to Mainz or Wiesbaden takes about 45 min and Koblenz to Cologne an hour, bringing the Rhine Valley well into reach for daytrips from these larger cities. The trains between Koblenz and Mainz take one to two hours depending on the number of stops. Very few of the luxurious and fast Intercity Express (ICE) trains run through the Rhine Valley – the frequent Mainz and Frankfurt to Cologne connections now use a much faster direct route.

In the Mosel Valley, at least hourly trains run from Koblenz to Trier. The faster trains take 90 minutes and the local trains two hours. All trains stop in Cochem.

By Road: Very good highways connect the major cities in the region but the main sights in the valleys are on smaller, slower roads with little commercial or through-traffic. Mainz, Koblenz, and Cologne are major transportation hubs with intersecting Autobahn connections to all parts of Germany. The Autobahnen near the Rhine and Mosel run parallel to the rivers but without river views.

By Air: Frankfurt Airport (FRA, see Frankfurt am Main chapter) is the most convenient for much of the area. It is about half an hour by road or very frequent trains to Mainz or Wiesbaden. Cologne is a mere hour away on the fast ICE trains (around three per hour). **Hahn Airport** (HHN), ☎ 06543-509-200, www.hahn-airport.de, is mainly used by budget carriers and has seen a vast increase in European destinations served in the past two years. From Hahn, buses take half an hour to Koblenz, an hour to Mainz, and 90 minutes to Frankfurt Airport. A pre-booked rental car is a good option. **Köln-Bonn Airport** (CGN), ☎ 02203-404-001, www. koeln-bonn-airport.de, is southeast of Cologne. It can be reached by at least twice-hourly trains from Cologne Hauptbahnhof – the 21-minute journey costs €2. Taxis to Cologne take 15 minutes (€25) and to Bonn 20 minutes (€40). Bus services are available to several parts of Cologne and Bonn.

By Boat: The River Rhine and several tributaries and canals continue to play an important role in trade and transportation in most of the state. The Rhine is also popular for tourist boat trips lasting from less than an hour to several days, with Switzerland and the Netherlands favorite starting points, in addition to the ports in Germany. Boats operate mostly between April and October, with the main season from May to September.

Several companies ply the Rhine route, but the most established is **Köln-Düsseldorfer**, better known simply as **KD**, Frankenwerft 35, 50667 Cologne, ☎ 0221-208-8318, www.k-d. com. It has boats in virtually all Rhine towns and operates local sightseeing cruises as well as rides between towns. The stretch between Rüdesheim and Koblenz is particularly popular, with many daily departures. If time is limited, the best part of the route is between Kaub or Oberwesel and St Goar or St Goarhausen – this part includes the Loreley. KD has several special rates, including free trips on birthdays, half-price for over 60s on Monday and Friday, and two for the price of one on Tuesday if two bicycles are taken with. (Bicycles are always transported for free.) Passengers arriving via DB railways receive 20% discount.

Most towns have smaller competing boat companies, which usually charge slightly less but often have fewer departures.

◆ Information Sources

Tourist Offices: Information is available from Rheinland-Pfalz Tourismus, Löhrstraße 103-105, 56068 Koblenz, ☎ 0261-915-200, www.rlp-info.de. For destinations north of Koblenz, contact Nordrhein-Westfalen Tourismus, Worringer Str. 22, 50668 Köln, ☎ 0221-179-450, www.nrw-tourismus.de.

The Rhine Valley

The Rhine River is arguably Europe's most famous and most important waterway. From its source in Switzerland to its ending in the Netherlands, the river runs almost 800 miles, with the stretch from Basel downriver completely navigable. However, the romantic Rhine of castles, robber barons, and legends is primarily between Mainz and Koblenz, where the scenery is most dramatic. At first, nearly 1,500 ft wide, the river flows slowly through a broad open valley, then narrows dramatically from the Bingen until, at the Loreley rock, it is only 426 ft wide and flows at six mph.

During July and August, Rhine towns can become uncomfortably busy, but they can be surprisingly quiet just weeks prior to or after the main holiday season. During spring and autumn, when the Rhine Valley is at its prettiest, even weekends can be quiet, except during the frequent festivals held in towns along the river. In winter, many sights and towns close down for the season and the valley is often filled with fog, which can be hauntingly beautiful, but hides much of the scenery and castles that most visitors came to see.

Most of the famous castles along the Rhine, and there are many, have been ruined twice – first by invading French troops, who blew most of them up in the 17th century, and then by Rhine Romanticism, when many were rebuilt and restored during the 19th century in a false romantic notion of what medieval castles should have looked like. They are still pretty, however, and worth seeing.

If time is limited, give preference to the Loreley Valley, Cologne, and Speyer.

◆ Speyer

Speyer is an interesting town close to the more popular and famous Heidelberg. The huge cathedral, Germany's largest Romanesque structure, is worth the journey. In addition, Speyer has a lovely Old Town area and a large technology museum with full-size aircraft.

Speyer was an important city during the middle ages. It was especially favored by the Salian Emperors (1024-1125) of the Holy Roman Empire, who sponsored the construction of a monastery and other buildings. The imperial diet met over 50 times in Speyer. In 1689, French armies destroyed most of the medieval town. As a result, most of the buildings date from the Baroque period.

Information Sources

Tourist Office: Verkehrsamt Speyer, Maximilianstraße 11, 67346 Speyer, ☎ 06232-142-392, www.speyer.de.

Transportation

Speyer can be reached by frequent local trains from Heidelberg in 40 minutes and from Worms in 30 minutes. It is a 20-minute drive by car from either town.

Sightseeing

The main sight in Speyer is the domed, four-tower **Kaiserdom St Maria and St Stephan** (Imperial Cathedral of St Mary and St Stephan), the largest Romanesque building in Germany and a UNESCO Word Cultural Heritage Site. Constructed between 1030 and 1061, it withstood most of the trials and tribulations of the centuries, although it did suffer some war damage. Recent restoration work returned it to its original Romanesque condition with an airy, almost bare interior,

Speyer Kaiserdom

emphasizing the natural beauty of the architecture. Different color stones break the monotony and wall paintings color the areas above the high Romanesque arches. The large crypt houses the tombs of eight German emperors and kings. The octagonal cupola is best viewed from the raised transept. The cathedral is 440 ft long in total; the nave 344 ft long and 108 ft high, and the towers range from 216 to 232 ft. It is open Monday to Friday from 9 am to 7 pm, Saturdays from 9 am to 6 pm and Sundays from 1:30 to 6 pm. From November to March, it closes at 5 pm.

Altpörtal (© Becks)

The **Altpörtal** (old west tower) of the original 13th-century city walls of Speyer survived to the present day. At 180 ft, it is one of the highest medieval city towers built in Germany. The lower parts date from 1230, but the top floors were added later and the Baroque roof in 1708. It is possible to climb the 154 stairs to the top for spectacular views of Speyer, the Rhine, and the surrounding countryside. The tower is open from April to October on weekdays from 10 am to noon and 2 to 4 pm, weekends from 10 am to 5 pm. Admission is €1.

Maximillianstraße connects the Altpörtal with the Cathedral. Until it was destroyed by the French, this was considered one of the most impressive medieval roads in Germany. The imperial court trekked along it in splendor and it is often referred to as the **Via Triumphalis**. Today, the Via Triumphalis is mostly for pedestrians and lined with appealing cafés, outdoor restaurants, and mostly Baroque buildings.

Around 1090, the Bishop of Speyer invited Jews to settle near the cathedral. Today, little is left of the former Jewish Quarter, but the ritual Jewish bath, **Mikwe**, Judengaße, ☎ 06232-291-971, is still preserved. A barrel-vaulted staircase leads down to this bath, which is 32.8 ft below the surface. It is the oldest bath

Speyer Mikwe

and best preserved of this type in Central Europe. Open daily from April to October from 10 am to 5 pm. Admission is €1.

About 10 minutes stroll and a world away from the Cathedral and centuries past, is the **Technik Museum** (Technology Museum), Am Technik Museum 1, ☎ 06232-67080, www.technik-museum.de. The most popular exhibits relate to transportation, ranging from old cars to locomotives and airplanes that can be seen close-up and in some cases even entered for closer inspection. The crowds' favorites are a Lufthansa Boeing 747 and the cramped interior of a 150-ft-long German submarine dating from the late 1960s. The museum is open daily from 10 am to 6 pm. Admission is €10.50.

Where to Stay & Eat

The **Domhof Hotel** opened in 1990 and occupies several connected historic buildings near the Dom. Rooms are comfortable and functional. The hotel has its own brewery and guests are welcome to watch the brewing process. Bauhof 3, 67346 Speyer, ☎ 06232-13-290, fax 06232-132-990, www.domhof.de. (€€€)

HOTEL PRICES		
€ .... Up to €50 per night		
€€........ €50 to €100		
€€€ ..... €101 to €150		
€€€€ ...... Over €150		

RESTAURANT PRICES		
€ .... Less than €10		
€€ .... €10 to €20		
€€€........ €21 to €35		
€€€€........ Over €35		

The **Goldener Engel Hotel** is near the Altpörtel in the heart of the Old Town. It uses a combination of antique and designer furniture in comfortable rooms. The **Wirstshcaft Zum Alten Engel** (€-€€€) is in the vaulted cellars and serves hearty local specialties. Mühlturmstraße 5-7, 67346 Speyer, ☎ 06232-13-260, fax 06232-132-695. (€€)

The **Backmülde Restaurant**, Karmeliterstraße 11, ☎ 06232-71-577, is a block from the Altpörtal. It serves nouvelle cuisine with strong Mediterranean overtones. The wine list features around 600 labels – mostly from the Palatinate. (€€€)

The **Ratskeller,** Maximilianstraße 12, ☎ 06232-78-612, offers local specialties in the vaulted, 16th-century cellars of the Rathaus. (€-€€)

◆ Worms

Like Speyer, Worms was favored by the Salian Emperors, but the town today is best remembered for the Diet of Worms of 1521. Here, Martin Luther was invited to appear before the Imperial Parliament to revoke his opposition to the excesses of the Roman Catholic Church. He refused and claimed to have uttered the immortal words: "Here I stand for I cannot do otherwise. So help me God! Amen." The Diet's decision to outlaw Martin Luther had probably the most devastating consequences of any conference decision up to 20th century.

Most of medieval Worms was destroyed by the French in 1689 during the wars of the Palatinate succession. As a result, from the times of Martin Luther only the cathedral and a plaque remind one of the momentous events of 1521. The main reason to visit Worms is to see the cathedral.

Information Sources

Tourist Office: Information is available from the Tourist Information, Neumarkt 14, 67547 Worms, www.worms.de.

Sightseeing

The **Kaiserdom St Peter und St Paul** (Imperial Cathedral of St Peter and St Paul), Domplatz 1, ☎ 06241-6115, is a mainly Romanesque cathedral in magnificent condition following restoration works after the Second World War. It was originally erected between 1000 and 1025, but most of what is currently seen was built in the early 12th century. The cathedral is considered one of the

Worms Kaiserdom

best examples of Late Rhine Romanesque, despite some Gothic and Baroque additions. Opening hours are daily from 9 am to 5 pm, closing at 6 pm from April to October.

For centuries after the Reformation, Worms remained a multi-religion area. As a result, it was only in 1868 that the **Luther Monument** was erected in a park laid out after the destruction of the city walls. It is the largest monument in the world to honor the Reformation. At its center stands Martin Luther, surrounded by statues of followers and supporters and the names of cities and regions that played a major role in the Reformation.

One of the most famous medieval German poems is the *Nibelungenlied*. Surprisingly, this song is based at least partly on fact. The Burgundian Kingdom was established early in the fifth century in the Worms' area. The legend is filled with action heroes and betrayal of the worst kind. A famous scene in the poem has Hagen throwing the treasure of the Nibelungen in the Rhine – a statue of Hagen caught in the act is on the Nibelungen Bridge. A **Nibelungen Museum**, Fischerpförtchen 12, ☎ 06241-202-120, www.nibelungen-museum.de, opened recently in two medieval towers and part of the town wall. It uses multimedia techniques to explain the legend. English audio guides are available. Opening hours are Tuesday to Sunday from 10 am to 5 pm, closing at 10 pm on Friday. Admission is €5.50.

◆ Mainz

Mainz has a population of 180,000 and is the capital of the state of Rhineland-Palatinate. It is on the left bank of the Rhine across from the confluence of the River Main with the Rhine and thus has been of strategic importance for most of its more than 2,000 years of recorded history.

Mainz was founded in 39 BC by the Romans. It was an important city, housing at times up to 16,000 Romans. On New Year's Eve in 406 AD, the Rhine froze over and the German tribes crossed the river. Mainz was sacked and the Romans abandoned the city, which was eventually to be settled by the Franks.

By 750, Mainz was regaining importance after St Boniface, the Anglo-Saxon missionary who brought Christianity to the Germans, settled here. The archbishopric of Mainz was one of the most powerful and wealthiest posts in the German-speaking world up to secularization in the early 19th century.

Information Sources

Tourist Office: Information is available from the Verkehrsverein Mainz, Brückenturm am Rathaus, 55116 Mainz, ☎ 06131-286-210, fax 06131-286-2155, www.mainz.de.

Transportation

The sights of Mainz are concentrated in the compact Old Town, which consists mostly of pedestrian zones. The Dom is about 20 minutes walk from the main train station while the passengers from Rhine boats embark almost in the heart of the Old Town.

Sightseeing

The **Dom St Martin and St Stephan** (Cathedral), Markt 10, ☎ 06131-253-412, was begun under the auspices of Archbishop Willigud during the reign of Emperor Otto II in 975. Through the next millennium, it burned down seven times, the first time the day before its consecration in 1009. What remained today is mostly the style and construction work of the 12th and 13th centuries. Despite added Gothic features, the dominant style, especially noticeable in the dark interior, remains Romanesque. Most of the Mainz archbishops from the past millennium are buried here, with many memorial tombstones adoring the pillars of the church. The east choir is the oldest part of the church, with 6½-

Dom at Mainz

ft-thick walls. None of the original stained glass and wall paintings survived all seven fires, but the bronze doors of the main entrance are the originals. The two lion doorknobs are about 200 years newer. Opening hours are April to September on weekdays from 9 am to 6:30 pm, Saturdays from 9 pm to 4 pm, and Sundays from 12:45 to 3 pm and 4 to 6:30 pm. During winter months, the Dom closes at 5 pm, and 4 pm on Saturdays.

The nearby **Gutenberg Museum**, Liebfrauenplatz 5, 55116 Mainz, ☎ 06131-122640, www.gutenberg.de, commemorates the city's most famous son – Johannes Gensfleisch zu Gutenberg, who invented the moveable type press around 1440. The display includes two Gutenberg bibles as well as other books and scriptures of the past two millennia. Many may find the rather lifeless displays a bit academic and disappointing. Opening hours are Tuesday to Saturday from 9 am to 5 pm, Sundays 11 am to 3 pm; closed on Mondays and all official holidays. Admission is €3.

The façades of the building on **Marktplatz**, across from the Dom, are copies of the originals. However, on the south side of the Dom, stroll south along Leichhof and Augustinerstraße to see some parts of the Old Town that escaped war damage.

The **Museum für Antike Schifffahrt** (Ancient Ships), Neutorstraße 2, ☎ 06131-286-630, opened in 1994 at the southern edge of the Old Town. In 1981, while digging foundations for an extension of the Hilton Hotel, five well-preserved Roman ships were discovered under 26 ft of rubble. After treating the wood to prevent further decay, the ships were put on display in the brightly lit former Market Hall. Two full-size replicas of Roman river battleships are here, together with wrecks of the five boats, as well as three boats discovered elsewhere. The shipbuilding techniques are illustrated, as are the expansion plans of the Roman Empire. The ships are assumed to date from around 407 when the Romans had to abandon Mainz following successful attacks by Germanic tribes from across the Rhine. The museum is open Tuesday to Sunday from 10 am to 6 pm. Admission is free.

On the highest hill of old Mainz is the **St Stephan-kirche** (Church of St Stephan), Kleine Weiß-gasse 12, ☎ 06131-231640. The first church was erected here in 990 but the current Gothic church dates from the early 14th century. The church was severely damaged after a nearby gunpowder depot blew up in 1857. It was hit in three air raids during World War II and only the outer walls remained. Attempts were

St Stephankirche

made to restore the church to its Gothic origins and largely succeeded, although a lack of money necessitated a flat ceiling rather than vaults. Few of the 200,000 annual visitors notice this, as the main attractions are the stained glass windows. In the last years of his life, Marc Chagall, who never visited Mainz, created the windows for the apse and the transept and his colleague of 28 years, Charles Marq, did the rest. The predominant color is blue, to create an atmosphere for meditation, with Chagall using up to 18 tones of blue while Marc restricted himself to 10 for the north and only 8 for the south windows. This is the only church in Germany with Chagall windows and it is also the largest single work by Chagall. The church is open daily from 10 am to 12 pm and 2 to 5 pm (4:30 in December and January) but Sunday mornings are open only for services. For the best light conditions, visit in the morning.

Cultural Events & Festivals

Cultural Summer Rhineland Palatinate, Kultursommer Rheinland-Pfalz, Kaiserstraße 26-30, 55116 Mainz, ☎ 06131-288-380, www.kultursommer.de, organizes a range of events throughout the state. This program includes around 40 jazz concerts held mostly on wine estates and some 70 choral and other vocal concerts.

Villa Musica, Auf der Bastei 3, ☎ 06131-925-1800, www.villamusica.de, puts on concerts right through the year, mainly in castles and fortresses. The schedule is not restricted to the Rhineland area.

Mainz also presents a special summer program of mainly classical music in historic settings such as churches, museums, and castles. A similar program is occurs in winter with special concerts in the Christmas season. For more information, contact the Mainz Tourism Office, or Ticketbox, ☎ 06131-211-500, www.ticketbox-mainz.de.

Karneval is celebrated enthusiastically in Mainz. The traditional parades are usually held at the end of February or early March. The tourist office has details on the exact dates and route.

Adventures

On Foot

Town Walks: The Mainz Tourist Office conducts two-hour guided walks of the Old Town sights in English at 2 pm on Saturday and from April to end October also on Wednesday and Friday.

On Wheels

By Bicycle: Bicycles may be rented from **ASM Parkhaus Cityport**, ☎ 06131-225-699. There are pleasant cycling stretches along the Rhine.

Where to Stay & Eat

The **Hyatt Regency Hotel** is on the banks of the Rhine in a building that successfully combines parts of the historic Fort Malakoff and a modern glass and steel design. It is

Hyatt Regency

close to the Ancient Ship Museum, about 10 minutes stroll from the Dom. Rooms are large and luxurious. The **Bellpepper Restaurant** (€€-€€€) uses an open kitchen to produce fresh Mediterranean dishes. Malakoff-Terrasse 1, 55116 Mainz, ☎ 06131-731-234, fax 06131-731-235, www.hyatt.com. (€€€€)

Mainz Hilton

The **Mainz Hilton**, on the banks of the Rhine adjacent to the Rheingoldhalle, has the best location close to tourist attractions. The **Brasserie** (€€) serves international cuisine with strong French influences and has excellent views of the Rhine. Rheinstrasse 68, 55116 Mainz, ☎ 06131-2450, fax 06131-245589, www.hilton.com. (€€€-€€€€)

The **Hotel Hammer** is close to the Hauptbahnhof. Rooms are modern and comfortable. Bahnhofsplatz 6, 55116 Mainz, ☎ 06131-965-280, fax 06131-965-2888, www.hotel-hammer.com. (€€)

The **Ibis Hotel** is close to the Südbahnhof at the southern edges of the Old Town. Rooms are modern and functional. Holzhofstraße 2, 55116 Mainz, ☎ 06131-2470, fax 06131-234-126, www.ibishotel.com. (€€)

Camping

Camping Maaraue is idyllically located at the confluence of the Rivers Rhine and Main. It has around 100 lots, many with views of Mainz and the Dom. It is open from mid-March to October. Auf der Maaraue, 55246 Mainz-Kostheim, ☎ 06134-4383, www.krkg.de.

◆ Rheingau

Rheingau is one of the most famous wine-producing areas in Germany with some of the oldest and best-respected vineyards in the country. The southern slopes of the low hills of Rheingau facing the Rhine are covered with vineyards, mostly Riesling.

Information Sources

Tourist Office: In contrast to other parts of the Rhine Valley, Rheingau is in the federal state of Hesse. Information is available from Hessen Touristik Service, Postfach 3165, 65021 Wiesbaden, ☎ 0611-778800, www.hessen-tourismus.de.

Transportation

Rail service is available from Frankfurt via Wiesbaden and/or Mainz to most parts of the Rheingau region. Buses are available to outlying areas. Boats on the Rhine also connect most towns at a more leisurely pace.

Sightseeing

Eltville

In 1136, in a remote valley above Eltville-Kiedrich, Cistercian monks founded **Kloster Eberbach** (Eberbach Monastery), 65343 Eltville, ☎ 06723-4228, www.kloster-eberbach.de. On a large estate, the monks not only built one of the best-preserved monasteries in the region, but also excelled in farming. Strict vegetarians, they concentrated on agriculture and were particularly suc-

Kloster Eberbach

cessful in viniculture. At one stage, the monks even owned their own fleet of ships for transporting the produce down the Rhine. The monastery was secularized in 1803, but most of it has been preserved as a museum. The Romanesque church was stripped of its art in earlier wars and remains bare, which emphasizes the stark, straight lines of the style. The Gothic monks' dormitory, 240 feet long, is one of the largest halls of the period. The monastery is surrounded by a 16-ft-high wall, over half a mile long, which has been preserved from the 13th century.

Eberbach is, at 560 acres, the largest single wine estate in Germany and belongs to the state of Hesse. A wine academy is housed in the estate. Kloster Eberbach wines are highly rated and on sale at the premises. The Monastery is open daily from April to September, 10 am until 6 pm and from October to March, weekdays, 10 am to 4 pm, and weekends, 11 am to 4 pm). Admission to see the inside of the buildings is €3.50.

Where to Stay & Eat

The **Kloster Eberbach Guesthouse** offers the chance to experience some of the peace and tranquility at night that the monks must have valued centuries ago. This small hotel has 20 well-appointed double rooms with simple stark lines and a grayish color scheme in accord with the Cistercian ideals of simplicity.

The hotel is in a 16th-century building formerly used as a mill. The establishment is a comfortable three-star, deluxe hotel. The monks never had it this good. Gastronomiebetriebe, Kloster Eberbach, 65346 Eltville ☎ 06723-993-0, fax 06723-993-100, www.klostereberbach.com. (€€€, singles €€)

The **Klosterschänke**, ☎ 06723-9930, at Kloster Eberbach, offers regional cuisine in a rustic setting with outdoor seating. Open daily from 11:30 am until 10 pm (longer hours on concert nights). The extensive menu offers mainly regional specialties as well as wine from the award-winning local cellar. (€-€€)

Klosterschänke

Schloss Reinhartshausen Kempinski

Much more luxurious is the **Schloss Reinhartshausen Kempinski Hotel**. It is on the banks of the Rhine in a palace erected in 1801 for a Prussian Princess. Rooms are luxurious – some have Jacuzzis and fireplaces. The **Schlosskeller** (€€-€€€€) serves mostly regional cuisine and is open for dinner only. The Michelin star **Marcobrunn** (€€€€) serves classical cuisine with French and Austrian influences. Hauptstraße 43, 65346 Eltville-Erbach, ☎ 06123-6760, fax 06123-676-400, www. kempinski.de. (€€€€€)

Johannisberg

Closer to Rüdesheim, in Geisenheim, is one of Germany's best-known wine estates. **Schloss Johannisberg's** winemaking tradition goes back to the 12th century, when Benedictine monks planted vines here on the south facing slopes.

> ### NOBLE ROT
>
> The most famous moment for the Schloss came in 1775. The messenger bringing permission to harvest from the owner, the prince-abbot of Fulda, was delayed for unknown reasons and the grapes rotted on the vines. The grapes were harvested nonetheless and "noble rot" was discovered. The resulting sweet wine, *Spätlese*, or Late Harvest, has been popular ever since. The estate was also the first to produce *Eiswein* (Ice Wine), where grapes are harvested after they have frozen on the vine.

The estate was given to Austrian Chancellor Fürst von Metternich for his services at the Congress of Vienna (1815). The *Sekt* produced here bears his name and his family still owns part of the estate. A vinothek on the estate allows sampling and purchasing. The Baroque palace, which was damaged during the war but rebuilt, is not open to the public but much of the grounds and the church are.

Where to Eat

The **Gutausschank Schloss Johannisberg**, ☎ 06722-96-090, www.schloss-johannisberg.de, is a pleasant restaurant with marvelous views of the Rhine Valley. It serves mainly regional cuisine. The atmosphere is generally relaxed and unpretentious, despite the noble name of the estate. (€-€€€)

Rüdesheim

Rüdesheim is the most popular tourist town in the Rheingau and caters well for the estimated three million visitors that come here from early spring to late autumn. Up to the middle of the 19th century, the fast and treacherous rapids of the Bingen Gorge made the Rhine unnavigable between Bingen and Lorch. As a result, cargo was carted overland between Rüdesheim and Lorch. Rüdesheim did well out of this and, since much of the cargo involved wine, soon established itself as the center of the wine trade. By the time the rapids were blasted to submission in the mid-19th century, tourists, mainly led by the British, had discovered the Romantic Rhine and Rüdesheim swiftly established itself as the premier tourist town in the area.

Information Sources

Tourist Office: Information is available from Tourist-Information Rüdesheim and Assmannshausen, Geisenheimerstraße 22, 65385 Rüdesheim, ☎ 06722-19433, fax 06722-3485, www.ruedesheim.de.

Transportation

Although walking is generally the best way to get around Rüdesheim, and walks up the vineyard-covered hills above the town are especially rewarding, a motorized mini-train is available for tours of the hills and through the nearby vineyards. The **Winzerexpress**, www.winzerexpress.de, departs from Oberstraße in front of the Musikkabinett. Adults €4.30, children €2.

Parking on the Rhine Promenade is expensive. The parking lots a few blocks inland are much cheaper and a better place to park, especially if planning to take a Rhine cruise from here.

Sightseeing

Eating, drinking, and having a good time is the essential Rüdesheim experience. The most famous street is the 470-ft-long **Drosselgasse** leading from the Rhine promenade uphill. On both sides, this narrow alley is lined with bars and restaurants. Live music is expected on weekends from noon until around midnight and sometimes during the week as well. Weekends, and especially Sunday afternoons, can be very crowded. German guidebooks often snigger that the garish mixture of faux Gothic and Rhine Romantic style in the buildings here is what Japanese and American tourists demand, but more German than English is heard as you walk the streets.

Rüdesheim has several cultural sights to offer apart from the festivities. The **Rheingauer Weinmuseum Brömserburg** (Rheingau Wine Museum), Rheinstraße 2, ☎ 06722-2348, www.rheingauer-weinmuseum. de, is inside the **Brömserburg**, one of the oldest castles along the Rhine, dating from the ninth century. Apart from information on wine making, the museum has a collection of more than 2,000 wine glasses, ranging from Roman times up to the present. The museum is open daily from mid-March until end October, 9 am to 6 pm. Admission is €3.

Siegfried's Mechanisches Musikkabinett, Im Brömserhof, Oberstraße 27-29, ☎ 06722-49217, www.siegfrieds-musik-

Brömserburg

kabinett.de, has one of the largest collections in the world of self-playing musical instruments from the past three centuries. Some of the more than 350 instruments are played during the 45-minute tours. The museum is open daily from March to December from 10 am to 6 pm. Admission is €5.

The **Mittelalterliches Foltermuseum** (Medieval Torture Museum) Oberstraße 49-51, ☎ 06722-47510, www. foltermuseum.com, demonstrates the judicial history of medieval Germany with special emphasis on witch-hunts. The museum is open daily from April to November from 10 am to 6 pm. Admission is €5 for adults.

High on the hills above Rüdesheim is the **Niederwald-denkmal**. This 124-ft monument, featuring a huge bronze statue of Germania, was completed in 1883. It is dedicated to the soldiers who died in the struggle for German unity in the latter half of the 19th century. More rewarding than the monument are the views from here across the Rhine Valley. Walking from here through the vineyards down to Rüdesheim can be done in 30 minutes via the straightest route, but there are many options and making a detour via the ruins of Ehrenfels Castle is popular as well. From here, there is a lovely view of the **Mäuseturm**, a little fortress on a small island near the opposite bank of the Rhine.

Shortly after Rüdesheim, the Rhine makes a 90-degree turn, enters the Bingen Gorge and the valley gradually gets narrower and the hills steeper. The first town is **Assmannshausen**, which administratively is part of Rüdesheim and can also be reached by walking or taking the cable cars over the hill via the Niederwalddenkmal. It is a pretty town with lovely houses but without any major sights. It is famous as the only area along the Rhine that produces red rather than white wines. The Spätburgunder produced here is one of the best-known German red wines.

A PLEASANT HALF-DAY TRIP

A half-open, two-seater Seilbahn (gondola cable car), Oberstraße 37, ☎ 06722-2402, www.seilbahn-ruedesheim.de, operates between Rüdesheim and the Niederwalddenkmal. From there a chair lift goes down to Assmannshausen. For adults, the cost is €4 one-way, €6 round-trip or combination ticket with the chair-lift, children (five-18) and big dogs half-price.

Take the cable car from Rüdesheim to Niederwald-denkmal, and then have a stroll along the Rhine for the views and to see the castle ruins at Ehrnefels. Then take the chairlift down to Assmannshausen. From here, return to Rüdesheim by boat via Mäuseturm and Bingen. Combination tickets, including cable car, chairlift and boat trip are €9 for adults, half-price for children.

Where to Stay & Eat

Rüdesheim: Breuer's Rüdesheimer Schloss Hotel is in a building dating to 1729 . However, the rooms are modern and comfortable, with designer furniture. The restaurant (€-€€) is typical Drosselgasse in design but the food is good and the wine selec-

HOTEL PRICES	
€	. . . . Up to €50 per night
€€	. . . . €50 to €100
€€€	. . . . . €101 to €150
€€€€	. . . . . . Over €150

RESTAURANT PRICES	
€	. . . . Less than €10
€€	. . . . €10 to €20
€€€	. . . . €21 to €35
€€€€	. . . . Over €35

tion excellent. Steingasse 10, 65385 Rüdesheim, ☎ 06722-90-500, fax 06722-47-960, www.ruedesheimerschloss.de. (€€€)

The **Hotel Trapp** is in the center of the Old Town. Rooms are comfortable, with rustic or lightwood furniture. The **Entenstube Restaurant** (€€) serves classical dishes and regional specialties. Kirchstaße 7, 65385 Rüdesheim, ☎ 06722-91-140, fax 06722-47-715, www.ruedesheim-trapp.de. (€€-€€€)

The fourth-generation, family-owned **Winzerkeller Restaurant**, Oberstraße 33, ☎ 06722-2324, is in a half-timbered house dating back to 1609 at the top end of the Drosselgasse. It serves both local and international cuisine. A play corner for smaller children provides peace for parents and grandparents. (€-€€)

Niederwald: High above Rüdesheim is the **Jagdschloss Niederwald**, a comfortable hotel in the former hunting lodge of the princes of Nassau. Rooms are stylishly furnished. The **restau-**

Jagdschloss Niederwald

rant (€€-€€€) with terrace serves fish and game as well as other local specialties. Auf dem Niederwald, 65385 Rüdesheim, ☎ 06722-71-060, fax 06722-710-6666, www. niederwald.de. (€€€)

Assmannshausen: Assmannshausen has several good hotels and restaurants and is generally a more pleasant part of town to stay.

Hotel Krone Assmannshausen

The **Hotel Krone Assmannshausen** is in a 16th-century, half-timbered building with interesting towers and other architectural features. Rooms are luxurious, with antique furniture. The **Restaurant Krone** (€€€-€€€€) serves international and regional cuisine. Rheinuferstraße 10, 65385 Rüdesheim-Assmannshausen, ☎ 06722-4030, fax 06722-3049, www.hotel-krone.com. (€€€-€€€€)

Even older is the **Alte Bauernschänke Nassauer Hof**. The hotel is spread over five buildings, with the oldest dating from 1408. Rooms are furnished in rustic or modern style. The rustic **restaurant** (€-€€) has a pleasant terrace and serves mostly regional specialties. Niederwaldstraße 18-23, 65385 Rüdesheim-Assmannshausen, ☎ 06722-49-990, fax 06722-47-912, www.altebauernschänke.de. (€€-€€€)

■ Camping

Camping Am Rhein is on the banks of the Rhine, half a mile from the Drosselgasse. It has good facilities and over 200 lots. It is open from May to September. Kastanienallee, 65385 Rüdesheim, ☎ 06722-2528, fax 06722-406-783, www.campingplatz-ruedesheim.de.

Camping Ebentaler Hof is inland, close to the Nierderwalddenkmal. It has reasonably good facilities and is surrounded by a forest and next to a pony farm. There are 100 lots and it's open from March to mid-November. 65385 Rüdesheim, ☎ 06722-2518, fax 06722-3006, www.herrliche-natur.de.

Cultural Events

 The **Rheingau Musik Festival**, Rheinallee 1, 65375 Oestrich-Winkel, ☎ 06723 91770, www. rheingaufestival.de, is an annual music and cultural celebration that takes place during summer in various castles, churches, and monasteries of the Rheingau region.

Kloster Eberbach (Eberbach Monastery), 65343 Eltville, ☎ 06723-4228, www.kloster-eberbach.de, frequently schedules classical concerts.

Wine Tasting

Unfortunately, most wine estates offer wine tasting only for groups. Notable exceptions where individuals are also welcome include the follwing.

In Rüdesheim, **Weingut & Vinothek Georg Breuer**, Grabenstraße 8, ☎ 06722-1027, www.georg-breuer.com, has wine tasting for individuals from March to November daily, 10 am to 6 pm. Out of season, by arrangement. English-speaking personnel are generally available.

Kloster Eberbach's wine tasting is generally for groups only, but on Friday nights during the summer season a two-hour tasting is conducted for individuals (in German only). For details contact Kloster Eberbach, 65346 Eltville im Rheingau, ☎ 06723-91780, www.kloster-eberbach.de.

At **Schloss Johannisberg**, where the original Spätlese and Eiswein came from, individuals are welcome to sample in the Weinshäncke, Schloss Johannisberg, ☎ 06722-96-090, www. schloss-johannisberg.de. The adjacent restaurant is a pleasant place to try the wine with a full meal too.

Adventures in Rheingau

On Foot

 Countryside Hikes: There are many hiking opportunities in the Rheingau region, both along the Rhine as well as through the smaller valleys and hills. The Rieslingpfad (Riesling walkway, marked with a red "R") runs through the vineyards of the region along many places associated with the Riesling grape and wine.

Popular starting points for hikes are from Kloster Eberbach, Schloss Johannisberg, and Rüdesheim – all places with ample parking space and public transportation options that make circular routes unnecessary.

On Wheels

By Bicycle: Radkranz Rent a Bike, Oberstrasse 42-44, 65385 Rüdesheim, ☎ 06722-48336, www. rad-kranz.com, rents out various types of bicycles. It also offers guided tours and luggage transfers.

On Water

Riverboats: Rüdesheim is a popular starting point for Rhine cruises through the Loreley Valley. The most interesting part of the valley, from Rüdesheim to St Goarshausen, takes two hours downstream and three hours return. Going all the way to Koblenz takes four hours, six hours return.

Several companies operate from Rüdesheim, including **KD**, Frankenwerft 35, 50667 Cologne, ☎ 0221-208-8318, www.k-d. com; **Bingen-Rüdesheimer**, Rheinkai 10, 55411 Bingen, ☎ 06721 14140, www.bingen-ruedesheimer.com; and **Rössler-Linie**, ☎ 06722-2353, www.roesslerlinie.de.

Wildlife

The **Adlerwart Niederwald** (Falconry), ☎ 06722-47-339, is located right next to the Niederwalddenkmal. Here eagles and other birds can be observed in large cages, with flight demonstrations depending on weather conditions.

◆ The Loreley Valley

The part of the Rhine Valley from Kaub to Boppard is often referred to as the Loreley Valley. Here the river is at its narrowest,
flows fastest, and the valley is at its steepest. This is the most
beautiful part of the valley, with the most dramatic scenery and
several castles.

Information Sources

Tourist Office: Information is available from the
Tourist Information, Bahnhofstraße 8, 56346 St
Goarhausen, ☎ 06771-9100, www.loreley-
touristik.de, or from Rheintouristik, Heerstraße 86,
56329 St Goar, ☎ 06741-1300, www.talderloreley.de.

*The **Burgenticket** (Castle Ticket), www.burgen-
am-rhein.de, allows for one-time entry into the 10
participating castles. It is valid for 24 months after
purchase and is transferable. The cost is €14 and
it's available from all participating castles.*

Transportation

The B42 connects Rüdesheim and Koblenz on the
left bank of the Rhine and the B9 Bingen and
Koblenz on the right bank. Both roads are in excellent condition and follow the flow of the river
closely. No bridges cross the Rhine between Mainz and
Koblenz but several car ferries are available.

Frequent trains run on both sides of the Rhine. Riverboats connect virtually all towns as well.

Kaub (Right Bank)

The small town of Kaub is most famous for **Pfalzgrafenstein**, a
small fortress that was built on an island in the Rhine in 1327 by
Ludwig of Bavaria. Ludwig's spectacularly successful entry into
the Rhine toll extortion business through this venture enraged
even the Pope. Most of what is seen today dates from 1607
when the fortifications were strengthened. Visits to the castle,
which is sparsely furnished, are possible but frankly not worth

Pfalzgrafenstein

the effort. It is best seen from the distance of the riverbank. Open daily from 9 am to 12 pm and 2 to 5 pm, except closed on Monday and in December.

Along the main road through Kaub is a statue of Prussian Field Marshall Blücher, built to commemorate the crossing of the Rhine via pontoon bridge of the Prussian and Russian armies on New Year's Eve 1813-14. Napoleon, who was in Mainz at that stage, was caught off-guard and soon after departed for Elba. The small **Blüchermuseum**, Hotel Stadt Mannheim, Metzgergasse 6, ☎ 06774-222, is in the former headquarters of Blücher. It has mainly 19th-century military memorabilia and information on the historic crossing. It is open Monday to Sunday from April to October, 11 am to 4 pm, and from November to March, 2 to 5 pm. Admission is €2. Other buildings along the Metzgerstraße are also beautifully preserved.

Where to Stay & Eat

Hotel Zum Turm is in a 300-year-old building next to a medieval tower. It is primarily known for its excellent, rustic **restaurant** (€€-€€€), which serves nouvelle cuisine with French and Swiss influences, as well as local specialties. It has only six bedrooms, which are large and comfortably furnished. Zollstraße 50, 56349 Kaub,

☎ 06774-92-200, fax 06774-922-011, www.rhein-hotel-turm. de. (€€)

Bacharach (Left Bank)

Bacharach played an important role in the Rhine wine trade but somehow managed to remain a small town. During the Thirty Years' War, Bacharach changed hands no less than eight times. It withstood the occupations and plundering but in 1689, the French destroyed most of the town.

St Peter's Church is a beautiful example of Late Rhine Romanesque. Although the nave is only 33 ft long, it has a height of 55 ft. However, the more interesting site is the skeletal remains of the Gothic **Wernerkapelle** right behind and about 100 steps above the church.

WERNERKAPELLE

The history of this chapel goes back to 1287 when a young man, Werner, was found murdered at this spot. His death was blamed on a ritual killing by the local Jews and a pogrom followed. The chapel was built to house Werner's bones and became a pilgrimage site. About a century after the event, it

The Wernerkapelle

was acknowledged that the evidence was faked and Werner was scrapped from the church calendar.

High on the hill is **Burg Stahleck**. When the French blew up the castle in 1689, falling rock destroyed the Wernerkapelle, which was never restored. The castle was rebuilt in the 1920s and currently houses what must be one of the most beautifully located youth hostels in Germany. It is worth climbing the steep stairs from the Wernerkapelle to the castle for the view. It is also possible to drive up to the castle – drive through the town towards Rheinböllen and then follow the signposting.

Where to Stay & Eat

The **Hotel Altkölnischer Hof** is in a half-timbered building near the Markt. Rooms are attractively furnished with natural wood. Some rooms have balconies. The wood-paneled restaurant (€€-€€€) serves local spe-

Hotel Altkölnischer Hof

cialties. Blücherstraße 2, 55422 Bacharach, ☎ 06743-1339, fax 06743-2793, altkoelnischer-hof@t-online.de. (€€)

An interesting alternative is the **Landhaus Delle Hotel**, in the hills above the town with excellent views. It is a modern, designer-type hotel with only seven rooms. Rooms are comfortable, with elegant furniture and marble baths. The gourmet restaurant (€€€€) is only open to houseguests. The wine list has around a thousand labels. Gutenfeldsstraße 16, Bacharach-Henschhausen, ☎ 06743-1765, fax 06743-1011, www.landhaus-delle-hotel.com. (€€€€€)

Camping

Camping Sonnenstrand is a quarter-mile from Bacharach. It is on the banks of the Rhine. Facilities are limited and not the most modern, but the location is convenient. 55422 Bacharach, ☎ 06743-1752, fax 06743-3192, www.camping-sonnenstrand.de.

Oberwesel (Left Bank)

Oberwesel maintained 16 medieval towers and large sections of the original town walls. The two Gothic churches at the opposite ends of town are worth seeing. The early 14th-century Gothic **Liebfrauenkirche** (Church of Our Dear Lady) has a characteristic red exterior. There are some interesting art works, including a Baroque organ and an early 14th-century wing altar. The **St Martinkirche** (St Martin's Church) is on a small hill. It is light in color and has some interesting painted vaulting.

St Goarhausen & the Loreley (Right Bank)

Shortly before reaching St Goarhausen, the Rhine turns sharply to the left and narrows to 370 ft, a third of its normal width. Here, a mighty rock, the 432-ft Loreley, blocks the flow of the river creating dangerous rapids that caused the demise of many a shipper and boat.

RHINE LEGEND – THE LORELEY

In the most common form of the story, the Loreley is a maiden who threw herself into the Rhine in despair over a faithless lover, and became a water spirit whose voice lured fishermen to destruction on the rocks. Heinrich Heine, one of Germany's favorite romantic poets, wrote a poem about the Loreley, which was set to music by Friedrich Silchers and became one of the best-known, if slowest, of German folksongs. It is particularly popular in Japan, but known in many languages. Souvenir shops in the region sell postcards with the English translations – most badly done!

Just past the rock are a small parking lot and a winter harbor. At the far end of this land finger protruding into the Rhine is a small mermaid statue of no artistic or historic significance. It was erected in the 1960s as a commercial exercise. It is possible to climb up via steep stairs to the top of the **Loreley rock**, but the less energetic can drive up via a well-marked road in St Goarhausen. The view from the top is splendid and highly recommended. The top of the rock is in private hands, but open freely for visitors, with a pleasant café-hotel available. The €1 parking fee is waived for patrons.

BURG MAUS

Mäuseturm

According to legend, a particularly unpopular archbishop of Mainz, Hatto, hoarded wheat in a tower on a small Rhine island during a famine, hoping to increase the price. Hungry mice were drawn to the bountiful tower and devoured everything in sight, including the despised Hatto. The tower thus became known as **Mäuseturm**, which translates to Mouse Tower. However, the name is most likely a corruption of Maut (meaning toll), which accords better with the tower's role in enforcing toll collection on the Rhine, and the rather inconvenient fact that it was built more than 300 years after the death of Hatto.

Originally, St Goarhausen was just a couple of houses for the fishermen who caught mainly salmon for the market in St Goar. However, at the end of the 13th century, the area came through marriage into the hands of the mighty Katzenelnbogen family. In 1371, they constructed Burg Neu-Katzenelnbogen, better known as **Burg Katz** (Cat Castle) – the twin towers actually resemble the ears of a cat. The main purpose of this castle was to counter the newly constructed Burg Peterseck, built downriver by the

Burg Katz

archbishop of Trier. The mighty Burg Katz showed up the power relationship between the mighty and rich Katzenelnbogens and the rather weak archbishop, whose castle became known as Burg Maus (Mouse Castle). Burg Katz was destroyed by Napoleon in 1806, but rebuilt in the late 19th century. It is in private hands and currently a very exclusive hotel, ☎ 06771-1870.

Although the privately owned **Burg Maus**, ☎ 06771-7669, seems like a ruin, the interior is restored, furnished and well worth a visit. In addition, a falconry is located in the castle.

From the **Drei Bürgenblick** (Three Castles View) on the hill above St Goarhausen, it is possible to see Burg Maus, Burg Katz, and Burg Rheinfels, as well as, of course, the Rhine Valley. It is a 15-minute walk from the station. You can also possibly drive up to the viewing point.

St Goar & Burg Rheinfels (Left Bank)

St Goar is a small town that suffers from Rhine mass tourism. Many restaurants are overpriced, with questionable quality food and most souvenir shops sell the same kind of junk. The largest free hanging cuckoo clock in the world, 10 ft high and 6½ ft wide, hangs in the

Burg Rheinfels

main street of St Goar. Dating from 1973, it has two faces, with cuckoos popping out on both sides every 30 minutes.

High above St Goar are the castle ruins of **Burg Rheinfels**, Schlossberg Straße, ☎ 06741-383, the mightiest fortress ever constructed on the banks of the Rhine. The original was built by Graf Dieter V von Katzenelnbogen in 1245. On completion, he did the obvious thing and increased toll charges. In response, 26 Rhine towns raised an army of 8,000 men and 1,000 knights, then encircled the fortress for a year and 14 weeks, before retreating in defeat. When the Katzenelnbogen family died out in 1479, the castle came into the hands of the Hessen family, who continued building work and constructed the mine tun-

Burg Rheinfels in 1495

nels, which allowed enemies to be surprised from below ground. These tunnels can still be visited, but they require a flashlight. The French failed to conquer the castle in 1692 when a force of 18,000, with 10,000 backups, faced a garrison of 3,000. Despite 10 days of artillery bombardments, the French had to retreat, with 4,000 dead and 6,500 wounded – eight times more than the Germans. A century later, in 1794, the cowardly commander fled before the advancing French army and the castle fell without a shot being fired. It was systematically blown up in following years, but reconstruction started in 1818.

Today the castle is still mostly in ruins, but is well worth a visit. It houses an interesting museum, with a large scale model of the original castle. The view from the castle over the Rhine Valley is breathtaking. The small restaurant at the castle serves good food but, for dining with a view, try the upmarket restaurant in the adjacent castle hotel. The castle is open daily from April to end October, 9 am to 6 pm. Admission is €3.

The parking lot at the castle is very small and the hill very steep, making the motorized train, Burg-Express, well worth the expense. It travels up the hill about four times per hour. While waiting for the train in St Goar, you can look for the houses that mark the high-water levels of various Rhine floods.

Where to Stay & Eat

Schlosshotel & Villa Rheinfels is high above the town, attached to the ruins of the castle. The views of the Rhine Valley are incredible from both the bedrooms and restaurant. The rooms are individually furnished to a very high standard. The **restaurant** (€€-€€€) serves international and regional cuisine – reservations are recommended for a window seat. Schlossberg 47, 56329

St Goar, ☎ 06741-8020, fax 06741-802-802, www.
schlosshotel-rheinfels.de. (€€€)

Camping

Camping Loreleyblick is on the banks of the
Rhine, a half-mile south of the town, with views of
the Loreley rock. It is a bit old fashioned, with limited facilities. There are 200 lots and it's open all
year. 56329 St Goar, ☎ 06741-2066, fax 06741-7233, www.
camping-loreleyblick.de.

Kamp-Bornhofen & the Castles (Right Bank)

Burg Liebenstein (left) & Sterrenberg

Shortly before Kamp
Bornhofen are two
castles: **Burg Lieb-
enstein**, ☎ 06773-
308, and **Burg Ster-
renberg**, ☎ 06773-
323. These are com-
monly known as the
Enemy Brothers'
Castles (Feindlichen
Brüder Schlösser). A
wall was built be-
tween the two castles to improve defenses. However, legend
soon had it that the two brothers had a fight and built the wall,
as they could not bear seeing each other. According to one version, one brother betrayed their sister, but more popular is the
tale involving a beautiful lady and an inevitable love-triangle.
Both castles have cafés and excellent views.

The Marksburg (Right Bank)

The Marksburg castle is an impressive sight. Perched on a
small, steep hill, it can be seen from afar. The defense possibili-
ties are obvious even to the untrained eye. This is the only castle along the Middle Rhine that was never conquered or
destroyed. If you have time to visit only one castle on the Rhine,
make it this one.

Marksburg Castle

The Marksburg, 56338 Braubach, ☎ 02627-206, was erected mainly between the 12th and 14th century. It was intended as a refuge in times of war and was seldom occupied during peacetime. The building is generally in very good, and well-preserved, condition. When entering, note how the main gate was made smaller so no man on a horse could enter. The view from the battery is phenomenal. The large herb garden has 170 different species, including poisonous ones. The impressive armory collection has items from 500 BC to the 15th century. A small 1450 breech-loader is one of the oldest cannons in Germany.

The interior can only be seen on a guided tour – ask for an English brochure when buying tickets. Opening hours are daily from Easter to October, 10 am to 5 pm, and November to Easter, 11 am to 4 pm. Admission is €4.50.

It is a rewarding walk from Braubach up to the Marksburg. Driving up is easier, but from the parking lot it is still quite a climb – either stairs or a steep access road – to reach the castle itself.

Cultural Events

■ Concert Series

The **Mittelrhein Musik Momente** (Middle Rhine Music Moments), www.musikmomente.de, is a series of concerts held during summer in the Loreley Valley. Many events are staged in open-air venues. Information and reservations are available from most tourist information offices in the valley.

The **Loreley Freilichtbühne** (Open Air Theater), www.loreley-klassik.de, Tickethotline, ☎ 0180-500-0511, is one of the best-known in Germany. It offers a wide range of events ranging from rock concerts to opera.

■ Knights' Tournament

Many of the castles of the Rhine were occupied by knights during the Middle Ages and served as dens for robber barons. A special knights' tournament (Rittertournier) and market is held at **Burg Rheinfels** at the end of May and beginning of June.

■ Fireworks – Rhein in Flammen

Each year, huge fireworks displays are held along the Rhine during events known as "Rhine in flames." Reservations for seats on the flotilla of up to 70 boats must be made months in advance and thousands of spectators line the banks of the river. The schedule is as follows:

Rhein in Flammen

- *First Saturday in May: Linz to Bonn – Night of the Bengal Lights.*
- *First Saturday in July: Bingen and Rüdesheim for Magic Fire-Lit Night.*
- *Second Saturday in August: Spay/Braubach to Koblenz – The Mega-night – eight fireworks displays in 90 minutes stretched over 10 miles.*
- *Second Saturday in September: Oberwesel – Night of a Thousand Fires. Music accompanies the fireworks display.*
- *Third Saturday in September: St Goar and St Goarhausen – Loreley Night.*

Adventures in the Loreley Valley

On Foot

Countryside Hikes: Hiking paths abound on both sides of the Rhine and in the surrounding hills and valleys. A special pedestrian and cycling way runs practically the full length of the Rhine from Bingen to Koblenz. The right bank also has long stretches of walkways and cycling routes but these are not totally continuous.

The **Rhein-Wein-Wanderpfad** (Rhine-Wine walking route marked with "RP") extends 31 miles from Kaub to Bornhofen on the edges of the Rhine Valley hills.

On Wheels

By Bicycle: Like walking, cycling has been popular in the Rhine valley for decades and are bikers are well catered for. Many hotels participate in a scheme where luggage is forward to your next destination for a nominal fee.

On the left bank of the Rhine, a cycling route runs the full distance from Bingen to Koblenz, with only a minimal part on public roads. Cycling distances are as follows:

From Bingen, on the left bank, to:

Bacharach - 9 miles
Oberwesel - 4.2 miles
St Goar - 6.6 miles
Bad Salzig - 3 miles
Boppard - 11.4 miles
Koblenz - 11.4 miles

From Rüdesheim, on the right bank, to:

Lorch - 4.2 miles
Kaub - 5.4 miles
St Goarhausen - 6.6 miles
Kamp-Bornhofen - 7.2 miles
Braubach - 8.4 miles
Lahnstein - 2.4 miles

Much of the right bank cycling is on public roads, with the stretch immediately from Rüdesheim particularly dangerous.

Bicycle renting: *Bicycles can be rented in most towns, often from the train station or from many hotels. In Rhineland-Palatinate, bicycles can be taken at no charge on local trains after 9 am on weekdays and all day on weekends and on most boats. The KD lines offer two tickets for the price of one on Tuesdays for one-way tickets if both travelers have bicycles with them.*

On Water

 Fishing: Fishing is allowed along some stretches of the Rhine, but requires a license. Currently, 63 species are recorded in the Rhine and, as water quality improves, the number is increasing. In St Goarhausen, contact **Opticus Schmidt** at Marktplatz 3, ☎ 06771-7577. In St Goar, **Nagelschmidt**, An der Loreley 9, ☎ 06741-7737. In other areas, inquire with the local tourist office.

STRANGE EMPLOYMENT CONTRACTS

Up to the 18th century, St Goarhausen, where the Rhine was once 94 ft deep, was considered one of the best places to catch fresh-water salmon, a species that only recently returned to the Rhine. The fish was so plentiful and cheap that household servants made it an employment condition that they would not have to eat salmon more than three times a week.

Wildlife

 Falconries: Although some of the castles along the Rhine were bought by Prussian nobles in the 19th century as hunting lodges, wildlife is limited despite the heavily forested areas. However, **Burg Maus** in St Goarhausen-Wellmich, ☎ 06771 7669, www.burg-maus.de, has an interesting falconry. From mid-March until early October, one-hour demonstrations are held of sea and stone eagles, kites, and falcons flying freely over the Rhine Valley. Flying demonstrations take place daily at 11 am and 2:

30 pm as well as 4:30 pm on Sundays and holidays. Entry is €6.50. It is a 20-minute walk from the parking lot to the castle.

◆ Cologne (Köln)

Cologne (Köln) is a popular destination for foreign tourists and Germans alike. It is a city known for its easy attitude to life and its relaxed atmosphere. Cologne has the largest Gothic cathedral in the world, 12 surviving Romanesque churches, and some excellent museums.

The city was founded in AD 50 by the Romans. After they left, it came under the control of the Franks. More than 150 churches were built here during the Middle Ages – the most famous, the magnificent Gothic Dom that took 600 years to complete. After Emperor Friedrich Barbarossa had confiscated the relics of the Magi in Milan, he donated them to Cologne in 1164. This started Cologne's role as pilgrimage center, second only to Rome during much of the Middle Ages. In terms of population, it was the largest city in Germany for more than a millennium until Berlin surpassed it in the late 19th century.

During World War II, 90% of the Old Town and 70% of the surrounding area were destroyed by air raids. Like St Paul's in London, the Dom somehow survived with relatively minor damage. The city's population dwindled from more than 800,000 at the outset of war to only 45,000 at the end, since most residents had fled the city.

Information Sources

Tourist Office: Tourist Information is available from Köln Tourismus, Unter Fettenhennen 19, 50667 Köln, ☎ 0221-221-30400, www.stadt-koeln.de.

Transportation

The Old Town area of Cologne is best explored on foot. The Hauptbahnhof is to the north of the Old Town, right next to the Dom and the River Rhine.

Cologne (Köln)

1. Hauptbahnhof
2. Dom (Cathedral)
3. Museum Ludwig
4. Römisch-Germanisches Museum
5. Groß St. Martin, Fischmarkt
6. Rathaus, Altermarkt
7. Wallraf-Richartz Museum
8. St Maria im Kapitol
9. Imhoff-Stollwerck Museum, Deutsches Olympia & Sport Stadium
10. Museum für Angewandtekunst
11. Kölnische Stadtmuseum
12. St Gereon Church
13. 4711 Eau de Cologne
14. Käthe Kollwitz Museum
15. St Aposteln

© 2007 HUNTER PUBLISHING, INC.

250 METERS

Rhein

Kennedy Ufer

Hohenzollernbrücke

Konrad Adenauer Ufer

Deutzerbrücke

Severinsbrücke

Rheinauhofen

Frankenwerft

Am Leystapel

Holzmarkt

Breslauerplatz

Am Hof

Kleine Budeng

Augustinerstraße

Pipinstraße

Filzengraben

Georgstraße

An den Dominikan

Hohe Straße

Brückenstraße

Gürzenichstr

Severinstraße

An der Rechtshule

Tunisstraße

Mohrenstraße

Gereonstraße

Kyotostraße

Breite Straße

Glockengaße

Schildergasse

Cäcilienstraße

Neuköllner Straße

Mühlenbach

Blaubach

Christopherstraße

Gereonshof

Friesenstraße

Magnusstraße

Ehrenstraße

Richmodstraße

Mittelstraße

Hahnestraße

Schaafenstraße

Bayaardsgaße

Hohenzollernring

Neue Weyerstraße

Jahnstraße

Hohenstaufenring

N

HUNTER PUBLISHING

Sightseeing

The most popular tourist sights in Cologne are all concentrated in the Old Town area and easily reached on foot. The principle one is the Dom, with most other attractions in the immediate vicinity. The Rathaus and many museums are slightly to the south, while St Gereon church to the west is worth the few minutes walk. If time is limited, give priority to the Dom and the Wallraf-Richartz Museum, or the Ludwig Museum if you prefer modern art.

The Dom

Inside the Dom

The most important site in Cologne is the magnificent High Gothic **Dom St Peter und Marien** (Cathedral of St Peter and Mary) that dominates the skyline from virtually any place in town. The Dom is right next to the Rhine and Hauptbahnhof, making it an easy destination for travelers even on the briefest of stopovers. It is a UNESCO World Cultural Heritage site that attracts six million visitors annually – by far the highest number for any monitored sight in Germany.

Construction of the High Gothic cathedral started in 1248, to replace a Romanesque predecessor. The chancel was completed by 1300, but the rest followed slowly, with only parts of the south wall and tower completed by 1560 when construction was suspended. For the next three centuries, an enormous wooden crane on the uncompleted Dom tower would be the symbol of Cologne. Construction resumed in 1842 when German Romantics considered Gothic a pure German style – ironically the original commission for the Dom clearly called for a church in the French style – and completion of the Dom became a matter of national honor. In 1880, the Dom was finally consecrated. The presence of the egocentric Protestant Emperor Wilhelm I led to accusations that God had to occupy second place during the ceremony and the archbishop stayed away in protest.

Petersglocke

The cathedral's twin-towered western façade is the largest in the world and it follows the original 13th-century plan. The exterior is decorated with statues, gables, and buttresses. The twin towers are 515 ft high – on completion, it was the tallest building in the world, as was the intention in the 13th century. In the south tower, 509 steps lead to a viewing platform at 318 ft. On the way up, note the bells, including the 24-ton **Petersglocke** (St Peter's Bell), the world's largest swinging bell, which rings only on major religious holidays. Admission to the south tower is €2. Combination tickets with the Treasury are €5.

Dom stained glass windows

The church's interior is the third-largest in the world. The nave is 472 ft long, 148 ft wide, and 143 ft high. More than a hundred pillars and columns keep it all together. During a papal visit in 1980, 8,500 visitors were

Main aisle of the Dom

packed into the interior but normally just under 4,000 are allowed in on special occasions. The huge stained glass windows – altogether larger than a football field – let in ample light. The oldest were installed in 1265 in the **Achskapelle** (also known as the Three Kings' Chapel). This chapel is painted, as the complete cathedral would have been in the Middle Ages.

The most important artwork is the **Dreikönigenschrein** (Shrine of the Three Magi) in the choir behind the high altar. This bejeweled, golden shrine is a masterpiece of medieval goldsmithing. It is in the form of a 7.2-ft-long basilica. In the Marienkapelle (St Mary's Chapel) is the **Altar der Stadtpatrone** (Altar of the City's Patrons), painted in 1440 by Stephan Lochner. It illustrates the adoration of the Magi and has such detail that many

herbs and other plants, as well as a stag beetle, can be recognized in the grass. The left wing shows St Ursula and the right St Gereon – the two patron saints of Cologne. In the Kreuzkapelle (Cross Chapel) is the AD 980 **Gerokreuz** (Gero Crucifixion) – a rare example of Ottonian art. The choir, only open to guided tours, has 104 seats, the largest in Germany.

Dreikönigenschrein

Opening hours are daily from 6 am to 7:30 pm. Sightseeing is not allowed during the frequent services – the daily schedule is posted at the door. Guided tours in English are available daily at 11 am and 2:30 pm (Sundays in the afternoon only). Information on the Dom and tours are available from the Domforum, Domkloster 3, ☎ 0221-9258-4720, www.domforum.de.

The **Schatzkamer** (Treasury), ☎ 0221-1794-0530, is at the north of the church. It houses a large collection of religious paraphernalia, shrines, and reliquaries. Opening hours are daily from 10 am to 6 pm. Admission is €4. A combination ticket with tower access costs €5.

Dom Area

Hauptbahnhof

Immediately to the north of the Dom is the **Hauptbahnhof** (Main Station). It has an impressive glass roof and houses a large number of shops not subject to normal closing hours. The **Hohenzollern-brücke** is a very busy rail and pedestrian bridge across the Rhine – some of the best vistas of the Dom and the Old Town can be had from here. Between the bridge and the Dom is a square named after 1972 Nobel Prize for Literature laureate **Heinrich Böll** (1917-85).

The **Museum Ludwig,** Bischofsgartenstraße 1, ☎ 0221-2212-6165, www.museum-ludwig.de, opened after Peter and Irene Ludwig donated the largest pop art collection outside the USA to the Wallraf Richartz Museum. In addition to the original 350 pop art paintings, the museum also has a major collection of Russian avant-garde works, and a very large collection of works by Picasso. The museum continuously adds new artworks and some are only months old. On the ground floor is the **Agfa Photo-Historama** – a major collection of photos and photographic equipment from the 1840s to the present. Opening hours are Tuesday to Sunday, 10 am to 6 pm, Friday, 11 am to 6. First Friday of the month, 11 am to 11 pm. Admission €7.50.

The **Römisch-Germanisches Museum** (Roman-Germanic Museum), Roncalliplatz 4, ☎ 0221-2212-4438, www.museenkoeln.de, houses articles from the Roman and early Frankish periods. The magnificent glass and jewelry collections show that these "barbarians" knew how to produce first-class artistic pieces. The museum is built on the foundations of a former Roman villa that was discovered in 1941 during the construction of an air-raid shelter. The pride of the museum is the second-century **Dionysius Mosaic**, made up of more than 1.5 million pieces. It is very well preserved and can actually be seen from outside the museum through a huge window. The museum is best visited in the afternoon, or on weekends, to avoid ever-present school parties. Opening hours are Tuesday to Sunday from 10 am to 5 pm. Admission is €4.30.

Bust of Agrippa

The **Museum für Angewandte Kunst** (Museum of Applied Arts), An der Rechtschule, ☎ 0221-2212-6714, www. museenkoeln.de, is one of the principle collections of items from the Gothic to the present in Germany. Articles range from furniture and clothes to jewelry and tableware. German, European and Asian articles are on display. Opening hours are Tuesday to Sunday from 11 am to 5 pm, closing at 8 pm on Wednesday. Admission is €4.20.

Southern Altstadt

Until the completion of the Dom, **Groß St Martin**, An Groß St Martin, ☎ 0221-1642-5650, was the largest church in Cologne. Originally built between 1150 and 1250, this Romanesque church, with its fortress-like square tower and four octagonal turrets, still is a major feature of the Cologne skyline. It was originally a Benedictine monastery church built on what was then an island in the Rhine. The church was virtually destroyed during World War II and the reconstruction has a stark, almost naked interior. Opening hours are Tuesday to Friday from 10:15 am to 6 pm, Saturday from 10 am to 12:30 pm and 1:30 to 6 pm, Sunday from 2 to 4 pm.

Groß St Martin

The **Historisches Rathaus** (Historic Town Hall) was severely damaged during World War II, but rebuilt soon after. It has a lovely Renaissance pavilion and a 197-ft Gothic tower, erected in 1407, with a carillon playing at noon and 5 pm. The impressive Gothic Hansesaal and the rest of the interior can only be seen in conjunction with a guided tour. The area was part of a Jewish ghetto stormed in 1349. A **Mikwe** (Jewish Bath) from around 1170 can be seen under a glass pyramid in front of the Rathaus.

The **Wallraf-Richartz-Museum – Foundation Corboud,** Martinstraße 39, ☎ 0221-2212-1119, www.museenkoeln.de, is the oldest museum in Cologne. Its start was with a major art collection donated by Wallraf Richartz in 1824. It has since grown to one of the largest collections of classical paintings in Germany. Highlights include an impressive medieval painting collection, paintings by Rubens, Rembrandt and others of the Baroque period, as well as works by Romantic, Realist, and Impressionist artists of the 19th century. If time is limited in Cologne, make this gallery a priority. Opening hours are Tuesday to Friday from 10 am to 6 pm, closing at 8 pm on Tuesday, and weekends from 11 am to 7 pm. Admission is €5.80.

Behind the museum is the **Gürzenich, a** 15th-century Gothic hall used for festivities. The annual *Karneval* celebrations start from here.

A few block farther south is the **St Maria Im Kapitol**, Kasinostraße, ☎ 0221-214-615. It was constructed in 1040-65 as an excellent example of Ottonian-Romanesque architecture. This triple nave basilica was the first to use a trefoil chancel – this cloverleaf-like feature is typical of Cologne Romanesque. The crypt runs almost the full length of the nave and is the second-largest in Germany after Speyer. The interior is richly decorated – particularly note the original 1060 wooden doors at the west end of the south aisle and the 1523 Renaissance choir screen. Opening hours are daily from 9 am to 6 pm.

St Maria Im Kapitol

Nearby, on a peninsula in the Rhine, is the **Imhoff-Stollwerck-Museum**, Rheinauhafen 1a, ☎ 0221-9318-880, www.schokoladenmuseum.de, a hugely popular museum of chocolate. In addition to an interesting display on chocolate and its role in society, it has a scaled-down, operational chocolate manufacturing plant with demonstrations. Free sampling opportunities, however, are very limited. Opening hours are Tuesday to Friday from 10 am to 6 pm and weekends from 11 am to 7 pm. Admission is €6.

Western Altstadt

Local history museums can be a bore, but the **Kölnische Stadtmuseum** (Cologne City Museum), Zeughausstraße 1-3, ☎ 0221-2212-5789, www.museenkoeln.de, is everything but. It has an eclectic collection of items related to Cologne's history from the Middle Ages to the present. Items include armor, scale models and paintings, religious objects, and cars – Ford has a major factory in Cologne. The museum is housed in the Renaissance Zeughaus, with red and white window shutters. Large windows allow some displays to be seen from the street and they draw many in. Opening hours are Tuesday to Friday from 10 am to 6 pm, closing at 8 pm on Tuesday, and weekends from 11 am to 7 pm. Admission is €4.20.

A few blocks farther west is the very interesting **St Gereon Church**, Geronsdriesch (entrance in Christopherstraße), ☎ 0221-124-922. It combines Late Roman, fourth-century oval building style elements, with a Late Romanesque, 13th-century decagon cupola. The monumental cupola was the largest built between the construction of Hagia Sophia in Istanbul and the Renaissance Duomo in Florence. The 13th-century baptismal chapel has some original wall paintings of St Gereon. Opening hours are

St Gereon

daily from 9 am to 12:30 and 1:30 to 6 pm, Sunday open in the afternoon only.

Cultural Events & Festivals

Cologne has a very full cultural calendar, with many music halls and theaters in addition to the more than 150 museums, galleries, and art spaces. On offer is everything from old classics to contemporary music, theater, and art. The tourist information has details on events – prior reservations are generally advisable.

Karneval (Carneval) is known as the "fifth season" in Cologne and much of the Rhinelands. It starts at 11:11 am on the 11th

The Rhine Valley

day of the 11th month and continues until Lent. Apart from the first day, a highlight is the parade on Rosenmontag (Rose Monday). It is an interesting and high-spirited parade, but many consider the event as a poor excuse to get drunk. Many shops and even museums close down completely during Karneval.

Shopping

Cologne entered the English language as a term for perfumed water thanks to the "Miracle Water" produced here. The French put a stop to drinking Eau de Cologne and, from the early 19th century, it was appreciated for its smell rather than its supposedly medicinal qualities. Products of 4711, the Original Eau de Cologne, can be bought all over Cologne, and Germany for that matter, but the **Traditionshaus 4711**, Glockengasse, ☎ 0221-925-0450, www.4711.com, once housed the factory. The shop is not particularly attractive, but it stocks a wide range of 4711 products. The Carillon outside plays the Marseillaise hourly from 9 am to 8 pm.

Adventures

On Foot

Town Walks: More than 120 guided tours are available of Cologne, its museums, and other sights. The tourist office has information on schedules.

Guided tours of the various churches and on religious themes are frequently scheduled. Contact the **Domforum**, Domkloster 3, ☎ 0221-9258-4720, www.domforum.de, for schedules.

Jogging: Jogging is popular in Cologne along the Rhine and in the parks. **Good Friends Jog Together**, ☎ 0700-1231-2322, www.laufeninkoeln.de, lists groups that regularly jog, with open invitations for visitors to join in.

On Wheels

By Bicycle: The Cologne area is relatively flat and easily explored by bicycle. **Fahrrad-Verleihservice**, Markmannsgasse/Altstadt, ☎ 0171-629-8796, www.koelnerfahrradverleih.de, rents out bicycles and from April to October conducts three-hour cycling tours daily at 1:30 pm.

On Water

Riverboats: One of the largest riverboat operators in Gemany has its home in Cologne. **Köln-Düsseldorfer** (usually abbreviated simply to KD), Frankenwerft 35, ☎ 0221-208-8319, www.k-d.com, has several hour-long cruises daily as well as services to other towns along the Rhine. Lunch, dinner, and thematic cruises are also available.

Where to Stay & Eat

For well over a century, the **Excelsior Hotel Ernst** has been the leading grand hotel in the region. This luxury hotel is close to the Dom and the Hauptbahnhof. The elegant **Hanse Stube Restaurant** (€€€-€€€€€) serves international cuisine and is one of the best restaurants in the region. The modern **Taku Restaurant** (€€€-€€€€€) serves Asian food. Domplatz, 50667 Köln, ☎ 0221-2701, fax 0221-135-150, www. excelsiorhotel.de. (€€€€)

Excelsior Hotel Ernst

The **Hyatt Regency Hotel** is on the opposite bank of the Rhine, giving many rooms a splendid view of the Cologne Dom and Old Town skyline. The **Graugans Restaurant** (€€€-€€€€) serves Euro-Asian food. Kennedy-Ufer 2a, 50679 Köln-deutz, ☎ 0221-8281-1771, fax 0221-828-1370, www.hyatt.de. (€€€€)

Dom Hotel

The **Dom Hotel** is another grand hotel, with a tradition going back more than a century. It has a perfect location on the square in front of the Dom and within minutes of most of the Old Town attractions. Some rooms have antique furniture and the better ones have views of the Dom. The **Le Merou Restaurant** (€€€€) serves international cuisine and has a terrace with views of the Dom. Domkloster 2a, 50667 Köln, ☎ 0221-20-240, fax 0221-202-4444, www.dom-hotel.com. (€€€€)

The luxury **Maritim Hotel** is on the banks of the Rhine at the south of the Old Town near the Stolwerck-Imhoff Museum. Rooms are comfortable and large but the 328-ft-long glass-roof lobby attracts the most attention. The **Bellevue Restaurant** (€€€)

Maritim Hotel

serves international cuisine and offers views of the Old Town and region. Heumarkt 20, 50667 Köln, ☎ 0221-20-270, fax 0221-202-7826, www.maritin.de. (€€€-€€€€)

The **Hilton Cologne** opened in 2002 close to the Dom and Hauptbahnhof. It is a modern building with straight lines throughout. Rooms have wooden floors and are well-equipped. The hotel aims mostly at business travelers, allowing for good deals on non-conference weekends. The **Ice Bar** has a bar top of ice. Marzellenstraße 13-17, 50668 Köln, ☎ 0221-130-710, fax 0221-130-720, www.hilton.com. (€€€-€€€€)

The **Classic Hotel Harmonie** is in a former monastery a few minutes walk from the Hauptbahnhof. Its peaceful past continues with harmonious warm Mediterranean colors and a relaxed atmosphere. Ursulaplatz 13-19, 50668 Köln, ☎ 0221-

Classic Hotel Harmonie

16-570, fax 0221-165-7200, www.classic-hotels.com. (€€-€€€)

The **CityClass Hotel Caprice** is a new hotel in the middle of the Old Town just south of Groß St Martin. It has modern rooms furnished to high standards. Auf dem Rothenberg 7, 50667 Köln, ☎ 0221-920-540, fax 0221-9205-4100, www.cityclass. de. (€€-€€€)

The **Hotel Ibis am Dom** is typical of this chain – not much personality but decent, clean, and reasonably furnished rooms. It is perfectly located right next to the station. Bahnhofvorplatz, 50667 Köln, ☎ 0221-912-8580, fax 0221-912-858-199, www. ibishotel.de. (€€)

TYPICAL KÖLSCH

The refreshing local beer, *Kölsch*, can be enjoyed everywhere, but doing so in one of the traditional breweries is especially pleasing. **Früh am Dom**, Am Hof 12, ☎ 0221-261-3211, recently celebrated its centenary at this location just south of the Dom. It is spread over three floors, each with slightly different menus – it gets grander and more expensive as you move up in the building. Traditional brewery fare is on offer in the vaulted cellars and the ground floor, while the upper floor offers more elaborate food, including game. On the street-side terrace, only beer and small snacks are served. (€-€€)

Nearby is another famous brewery, **Brauhaus Sion**, Unter Taschenmacher 5, ☎ 0221-257-8540. Traditional food is served in the former brewery, decorated with paraphernalia used in the beer-making process in years gone by. The brewery has its own bowling course. (€-€€)

Alt Köln am Dom, Trankgasse 7, ☎ 0221-137-471, is a large restaurant between the Dom and the Hauptbahnhof. It is spread over three floors and offers cheap food in a traditional locale. (€-€€)

Camping

Camping Berger is south of Cologne on the banks of the Rhine. It has good facilities and 125 lots each for tourists and long-term campers. It is open year-round. Uferstraße 53a, 50996 Köln-Rodenkirchen, ☎ 0221-935-5240, fax 0221-935-5246, www.camping-berger-koeln.de.

Bonn

Bonn is a pleasant day-trip from Cologne. It can be reached in 30 minutes by either road or very frequent trains.

After World War II, Bonn suddenly found itself catapulted from a provincial backwater to the capital of what was soon to be one of the richest democracies in the world. It was never a natural capital and, although the status came with huge spending on public works, Bonn would always be considered a sleepy, provincial town. In Germany, it was often referred to as the *Bundeshauptdorf* (federal capital town), rather than the *Bundeshauptstadt* (federal capital city).

Shortly after the reunification of Germany in 1990, the decision was made to move the capital back to Berlin and, by 2006, only six government departments remained in Bonn. For tourists, the main attractions remain the excellent museums set up during the federal capital years.

Information Sources

Tourist Office: The Tourist Information Office, Windeckstraße 1, 53103 Bonn, ☎ 0228-775-000, www.bonn.de, is at the Münsterplatz near the Hauptbahnhof.

Transportation

The Old Town is best explored on foot but to reach the Museum Mile it is best to take the U-Bahn. Although the U-Bahn continues all the way to Cologne, regular trains are much faster.

Sightseeing

Sightseeing in Bonn can be divided into two main areas: the Old Town with several interesting buildings and the Museum Mile a few miles to the south, with a number of excellent museums.

■ Old Town

A top priority for many visitors is the **Beethoven-haus** (Beethoven's birthplace), Bonngasse 20, ☎ 0228-981-7525, www.beethoven-haus-bonn.de. Ludwig van Beethoven (1770-1827) was born here. He spent his early years in Bonn until he left for Vienna in 1792. The museum covers Beethoven's entire life, with exhibitions of original manuscripts and items

Beethovenhaus

used by Beethoven, including some hearing pipes and his last grand piano. Opening hours are Monday to Saturday from 10 am to 5 pm, closing at 6 pm from April to October, and year-round on Sunday from 11 am to 4 pm. Admission is €4.

The Rococo **Rathaus** (Town Hall), Markt, was completed in its current form in 1737. It is a pretty pink and grey-blue building, with elaborate decorations. During Bonn's time as federal capital, most state visitors passed by. Several, including John F Kennedy (1963) and Michael Gorbachev (1989), received a warm welcome when addressing the public from the external double-flighted staircase. The inside, which is still in daily use, can only be seen between May and October on the first Saturday of the month from noon to 4 pm. Admission is free.

Münsterbasilika

The **Münsterbasilika** (Minster Basilica), Münsterplatz, ☎ 0228-985-880, is a lovely example of Rhineland Romanesque, with some Gothic additions blending in harmoniously. It was built mostly in the 11th century, although much of the interior is Baroque or 19th century. The mid-11th-century Romanesque cloister is one of the best-preserved examples in Germany from this period. Opening hours are daily for the church from 7 am to 7 pm and for the cloister from 9:30 am to 5:50 pm.

At the north end of the Münsterplatz is the **Beethoven Memorial** – it was erected in 1845 as the first one to honor the composer. In its base is the original score of the 9th Symphony.

The Baroque **Poppelsdorfer Schloss** (Palace), Meckenheimer Allee 171, is about half a mile down the lovely chestnut tree-lined Poppelsdorf Allee. It was built as a summer residence by the archbishop of Cologne, but has been part of the university since 1818. The palace is generally not open to the public, but the surrounding botanical gardens are.

■ **Museum Mile**

The Museum Mile is about 1.8 miles south of the Bonn Old Town in the federal government buildings area. It is best reached by U-Bahn or Buses 16, 63, or 66. Heussallee/Museummeile stop is the most convenient to all three museums listed below.

The **Haus der Geschichte der Bundesrepublik Deutschland (H**ouse of History of the Federal Republic of Germany),

Willy-Brandt-Allee 14, ☎ 0228-91-650, www.hdg.de, is a fascinating exhibition on post-World War II German history. It has around 7,000 items ranging from Konrad Adenauer' official Mercedes to the original arrest warrant for Erich Honecker. It uses modern technology to make displays interesting and to illustrate the background to items and events. Opening hours are Tuesday to Sunday from 9 am to 7 pm. Admission is free.

Bonn was fortunate that an impressive exhibition space was already under construction when the decision came to move the capital back to Berlin. The **Kunst- und Ausstellungshalle der Bundesrepublik Deutschland** (Art and Exhibition Hall of the Federal Republic of Germany), Friedrich Ebeert Allee 4, ☎ 0228-9171-200, www.bundeskunsthalle.de, which for obvious reasons is usually shortened to just **Bundeskunsthalle** (Federal Art Space), is a huge modern exhibition space that can be used simultaneously for up to five temporary exhibitions. The institution has no permanent collection, but hosts rotating world-class exhibitions. Admission fees depend on the specific exhibition, but can be less than 50% of the price for the same show in London! Furthermore, two adults with a child qualify for a family ticket that costs less than for two adults alone. Opening hours are Tuesday and Wednesday from 10 am to 9 pm and Thursday to Sunday from 10 am to 7 pm. Admission is €7 per day, €9.50 for two consecutive days, and €10.50 for a family ticket. A combination ticket with the Kunstmuseum is available for €10.50.

The adjacent **Kunstmuseum Bonn** (Museum of Art), Friedrich-Ebert-Allee 2, ☎ 0228-776-260, www.bonn.de/kunsthalle, is in an equally impressive, specially designed building. It shows 20th-century art, with a special emphasis on post-World War II German artists. Temporary exhibitions are usually of international artists and used to place the German works in context. Opening hours are Tuesday to Sunday from 10 am to 6 pm, closing at 9 pm on Wednesday. Admission is €5, or €10.50 when combined with the Kunsthalle.

Where to Stay & Eat

Right next to the Rathaus is a very pleasant traditional restaurant, **Em Höttche,** Markt 4, ☎ 0228-690-009. It serves local cuisine, with some international dishes in a building with a history going back to 1389. Inscriptions on the wooden beams remind you of historic dates and events: in 1628, Elizabeth Kurzrock was burned here as a witch! A young Ludwig von Beethoven also danced here with his sweetheart. (€-€€)

A hotel with superb views of the Rhine Valley is the **Steigenberger Gästehaus Petersberg**. It is 12 miles from Bonn on the right bank of the Rhine. This building was used as the official guesthouse of the government until the capital moved back to Berlin. Rooms are luxurious and stylishly furnished. The **Rheinterrassen Restaurant** (€€€-€€€€) serves international cuisine. It is open for dinner only and reservations are recommended. In summer, a bistro (€€) serves lighter meals on the terrace, with grand views. It is a favorite stopover on several hiking trails. Auf dem Petersberg, 53639 Königswinter, ☎ 02223-740, fax 02223-74-443, www. steigenberger.de. (€€€€)

The Mosel Valley

The 327-mile Mosel River (the French Moselle is sometimes used in English) is one of the longest tributaries of the Rhine. The direct air-distance is only 167 miles, but it is a meandering river with a steep valley, often more dramatic than that of the wider Rhine. Like the Rhine, the valleys are planted with vines and castles lurk at every twist and turn. Driving through the valley is slow, due to all the river curves, but very rewarding. The natural beauty of the valley is awesome and many picture-perfect villages are strewn along the way.

Close to the confluence of the Mosel and the Rhine in Koblenz is **Burg Eltz**, the loveliest castle in Germany. **Cochem** is a famous town with an impressive Historicist castle. **Trier** is at the far end of the Mosel, where the river enters Germany from France and forms part of the German-Luxemburg border. It is 115 river miles from Koblenz. The city was founded by the Romans and has the largest collection of Roman monuments in Germany.

The Mosel Valley

◆ Information Sources

Tourist Office: Information on the Mosel is available from **Mosellandtouristik**, Postfach 1310, 54463 Bernkastel-Kues, ☎ 06531-2091, www.mosellandtouristik.de.

◆ Transportation

In the Mosel Valley, at least hourly trains run from Koblenz to Trier. The faster trains take 90 minutes and the local trains two hours. All trains stop in Cochem, but only the Regional Bahn (RB) trains stop at Moselkern (Burg Eltz) and other smaller towns. The trains follow the flow of the river from Koblenz to Cochem but, after that, Trier is the next Mosel town on the main line. Buses are available to smaller towns.

Driving is a very pleasant option – keep following the main route as it crosses the river several times. The meandering of the Mosel and the wide curves make for slow progress. If in a hurry, use the Autobahn A48 between Koblenz and Trier, but do not expect any river views en route.

Boat excursions are popular and are the best way to enjoy the valley. Progress is slow, however, and boats are used for excursions rather than actual transportation.

◆ The Lower Mosel Valley

Burg Eltz

The most beautiful medieval castle in all of Germany is **Burg Eltz**, 56204 Burg Eltz, Münstermaifeld, ☎ 02672-950-500, www.burg-eltz.de. It is in a small side-valley near Moselkern. Parts of the castle date back to 1160 but building work continues to the present day. Three branches of the Eltz family built their dwellings in the castle complex, but the whole castle has been owned by the Golden Lion branch of the family since 1815. In the courtyard, the three buildings in different architectural styles can easily be distinguished.

The castle is full of period furniture and decorations. In contrast to other castles, Burg Eltz has 20 flushable toilets that date back to the 15th century. (The splendid Palace of Versailles, for

Burg Eltz (Olga Shelego)

example, has none.) Parts of the building are Gothic, with original ornamentation. The late-medieval kitchen also survived. The interior can only be seen on a guided tour (usually in German only, but an excellent English brochure is available). The treasury has some family heirlooms and can be seen without a tour. Opening hours are daily from April to October, 9:30 am to 5:30 pm. Admission is €6 and €2.50 for the treasury.

Getting to the castle can be challenging. The easiest way is by car. If approaching from the Autobahn A48, take the Mayen off-ramp towards Münstermaifeld. From the Mosel Road B416, turn off at Hatzneport. From Münstermaifeld, follow the signs to the Schloss – a parking lot is available at the Antoniuskapelle past Wald Wierschem. From here, it is a half-mile walk. A shuttle bus is available for part of the journey. Although the inclines are very steep, the route is paved.

A more interesting approach is from the small town of Moselkern on the Mosel River. Use the parking lot Ringelsteiner Mühle and hike through the lovely Eltzbachtal (Eltz Stream Valley) – an easy 35-minute hike. This is the standard approach when arriving by train or boat.

Cochem

Cochem seen from the Reichsburg

Cochem is a picture-perfect Mosel town. It has lovely half-timbered houses, a few surviving medieval defense towers and city gates, as well as a giant castle. It is hugely popular with tourists and can get very busy during the summer and Advent.

The main sight is the **Reichsburg Cochem**, Schlossstraße 36, ☎ 02671-255, www.reichsburg-cochem.de, which towers over the Old Town. Its history dates back to around AD 1000, but only a small part of the original keep survived. The French destroyed it in 1689 and the current Neo-Gothic building with ample towers and turrets was constructed in the late 19th century. Opening hours are mid-March to mid-October daily, 9 am to 5 pm. The 40-minute guided tour in German is the only way to see the interior. Admission is €4.

Where to Stay & Eat

The **Hotel Alte Thorschenke** is at the start of the pedestrian zone in an interesting building dating from 1332. Rooms are comfortable and use period furniture, including some four-poster beds. The wood-paneled **restaurant** (€€-€€€€) serves international and regional cuisine. Brückenstraße 3, 56812 Cochem,

Hotel Alte Thorschenke

☎ 02671-7059, fax 02671-4202, www.castle-thornschenke.de. (€€-€€€)

The **Moselromantik-Hotel Thul** is in the vineyards above the town. It is a modern hotel with comfortable rooms, some with balconies and views of the Reichsburg. The rustic **restaurant** (€€) serves classical and local dishes. Brauselaystraße 27, 56812 Cochem-Cond, ☎ 02671-914-150, fax 02671-9141-5144, www.hotel-thul.de. (€€-€€€)

Moselromantik-Hotel Thul

In town, a great place to dine is the **Lohspeicher – L'Auberge du Vin**. This restaurant (€€€) serves nouvelle cuisine with strong Mediterranean influences. It also has nine comfortable, modern rooms. Obergasse 1, 56812 Cochem, ☎ 02671-3976, fax 08671-1772, www.lohspeicher.de. (€€-€€€)

Camping

Camping am Freizeitzentrum is a pleasantly located campsite just over half a mile upstream from Cochem. It is open from April to October and has around 300 lots. 56812 Cochem-Cond, ☎ 02671-4409, fax 02671-910-719, www.campingplatz-cochem.de.

Adventures

On Foot

Countryside Hikes: The Mosel is a popular hiking area. The **Moselhöhenweg** (Mosel Heights Trail) goes the full length of the German Mosel on both banks, through the hills rather than the valley. The views are breathtaking.

Multi-day trips including accommodations and luggage transfers can be arranged by **Mosellandtouristik**, Gestade 18a, Bernkastel-Kues, ☎ 06531-3075, www.mosellandtoursitik.de.

On Wheels

By Bicycle: Many long-distance cycling routes are in the direct vicinity of the Mosel. Very popular is the route in the valley itself. The 165-mile

Moselradweg (Mosel Cycling Route) is from Thonville in France to Koblenz. It is mostly on dedicated, level cycling routes. Public transportation connections make cycling short parts of the route easy. Full seven-day cycling trips on this route can be arranged by **Mosellandtouristik**, Gestade 18a, Bernkastel-Kues, ☎ 06531-3075, www.mosellandtoursitik.de.

Many hotels have bicycles available for guests, but rentals are also available from **Fahrradshop Kreutz**, Ravenéstraße 42, Cochem, ☎ 02671-91-131, and **Fun Bike Team**, Schanzstraße 22, Bernkastel-Kues, ☎ 06531-94-024.

On Water

Riverboats: Several companies arrange riverboat excursions on the Mosel. The season is generally from May to October. Most operate only on certain parts of the river. Due to the meandering of the river and several locks, a complete cruise from Koblenz to Trier would take 16 hours and no company currently provides a complete one-day trip.

From Bernkastel-Kues, **Hans Michels & Mosel-Schiffstoursitik**, Goldbachstraße 52, ☎ 06531-6897, www.mosel-schiffstouristik.de, has up to five daily cruises to Traben-Trarbach. The journey takes two hours each way with several stops en route.

Gebr. Kolb, 56820 Briedern, ☎ 06673-1515, has up to six daily excursions between Bernkastel-Kues and Traben-Trarbach. It also has frequent services from Traben-Trarbach to Cochem – around four hours. Services to Trier are also available.

Köln-Düsseldorfer (KD), ☎ 02671-980-023 (Cochem) or ☎ 0261-31-030 (Koblenz), www.k-d.com, has one daily excursion between Koblenz and Cochem, taking five hours each way. Mosselkern (Burg Eltz) is three hours from Koblenz.

◆ Trier

Trier is Germany's oldest city. Archeological finds of Celtic settlements show residential activity as early as 2000 BC. Even taking written history as the criterion, Trier was founded in 16 BC as the Roman city of Augusta Treverorum, which makes it the oldest town in Germany.

Trier was originally a residential city and was overrun in 274 AD by invading Germanic tribes. It was re-conquered by the Romans, rebuilt in an even grander style, leading to its description as a Second Rome. It became an imperial residential city under Constantine (306-337) and functioned as the capital of Germany, Gaul, Spain, and Britain. Continued waves of attacks by Germanic tribes forced the Imperial family to return to Italy and the city itself finally succumbed to the Franks by the end of the fifth century.

Constantine made Trier the first See in Germany (314) and about 500 years later Charlemagne upgraded it to a full archbishopric. The Archbishop of Trier was a prince elector and therefore an important religious and political figure in the Holy Roman Empire.

The most impressive sights in Trier are still the Roman ruins, with the most extensive collection north of the Alps, but there are some architectural treasures from later periods as well. The town's most famous son is the economist and philosopher **Karl Marx**.

Modern Trier is a city of 100,000 inhabitants on the banks of the Mosel River. It is close to the border with the Grand Duchy of Luxemburg. The proximity to France also influenced local cuisine, style, and language. Trier is a major exporter of wine, but the tourist-oriented wine trade here is much less in your face compared to other Mosel Valley towns.

Information Sources

Tourist Office: Tourist Information Trier, An der Porta Nigra, 54290 Trier, ☎ 0651-978-080, www. trier.de.

Transportation

Trier is a bit off the beaten track but not difficult to get to. By car, it can be reached via Autobahn from Koblenz, but the local roads on the banks of the Mosel are much more pleasant, if slow. Trains usually require a changeover at Koblenz or Saarbrücken. If arriving by air, it is only 30 minutes to Luxemburg's airport or an hour by car from Frankfurt-Hahn.

The Mosel Valley

Trier has a good public transportation network using both trains and buses. Although all the main sights are within walking distance, buses are useful to get to the outlying sights. From Easter to October, the **Trier Tour** runs half-hourly buses to 16 of the main sights. It costs €5.60.

Sightseeing

The four story **Porta Nigra** (Black Gate) is the largest Roman building in Germany and one of the best preserved. It dates back to 180 AD and is a UNESCO World Cultural Heritage site. As part of the city's defenses,

Porta Nigra aerial view

it has a set of double gates with an inner courtyard, leaving potential attackers exposed to attacks from above and from all sides. The building is constructed out of sandstone blocks,

Porta Nigra

weighing up to six tons each, colored black from centuries of pollution. It was built without mortar and some of the original iron clamps attached with lead to the stone can still be seen. Note the holes in the stones where clamps were dug out during the Middle Ages when people recycled the lead.

The Porta Nigra owes its survival to a Greek monk, Simeon, who lived as a hermit in the gate. After he was declared a saint, two churches were constructed in the gate in the 11th century, thereby preventing locals from recycling the building material as had happened at many other ruins. Both churches were torn down and the gate restored on the orders of Napoleon, but traces of the church decorations can still be seen on the upper floors. A spiral staircase leads all the way to the fourth floor, which has fine views of the city and surrounding hills.

Next to the Porta Nigra is the **Städtisches Museum Simeonstift** (Municipal Museum in Simeon's College), Simeonstiftplatz, ☎ 0651-718-1450, www.museum-trier.de. Parts of the building date back to the 11th century with the original oak floor of 1060 still being used in the cloisters. The museum has mainly exhibits relating to Trier from the Middle Ages to the present. It also has more than 300 Coptic textiles dating from the third to the ninth century. The museum is open daily from April to October, 9 am to 5 pm. From November to March, it is open Tuesday to Friday, 9 am to 5 pm and to 3 pm on weekends. Admission is €2.60.

From here, stroll down Simeonstraße, a major shopping street, to the **Hauptmarkt**. En route, note the Early Gothic **Dreikönigenhaus** (around 1230), now a café. The cross in the center of Hauptmarkt dates from 958, when the town obtained the right to hold a market. The magnificent gables of buildings

Hauptmarkt

facing the market are from all ages. On the corner with Dietrichstraße are two medieval-looking buildings rebuilt in 1970 after being destroyed during World War II. The older building with arcades is the **Steipe**, a former town hall, and adjacent is the **Rotes Haus** (Red House) still bearing its 17th-century inscription: ANTE ROMAM TREVIRIS STETIT ANNIS MILLE TRECENTIS (There was life in Trier 1,300 years before Rome even existed). Also on Hauptmarkt is the early-15th-century **St Gangolf** church. Its 200-ft tower was once the highest in town, until one of the towers of the nearby cathedral was raised by one story to regain that status. The **Löwen-Apotheke** has a Baroque façade, but founded in 1241, it is the oldest pharmacy in Germany.

The fortress-like **Dom**, Domfreihof, ☎ 0651-979-0790, www.trierer-dom.de, was built on the site of the former Constantinian Palace. The palace was destroyed in 330 after the Emperor's last visit and replaced by the largest Christian church in antiquity, which was about four times the size of the current Cathedral. Note the large pillar, the Domstein, at the main entrance, which was part of the Ro-

Dom & Liebfrauenkirche

man church. The Roman church was destroyed in the fifth and ninth centuries, but the central sections can still be seen, with some parts of the original Roman walls, up to 85 ft high, incorporated into the 11th-century Romanesque building. Although most of the current structure is Romanesque, the cathedral incorporates, not always smoothly, 1,650 years of architectural styles. Most of the somewhat restrained interior decorations are Baroque, with interesting altarpieces. The cathedral has a small treasury with gold and silver works and ivory carvings. The prize relic is "Christ's seamless robe." The Dom is open daily from 6:30 am to 6 pm (5:30 pm from November to March). Admission is free, except €1.50 to see the treasury.

In contrast to the dark interior of the cathedral, the adjacent **Liebfrauenkirche** (Church of Our Lady), ☎ 0651-979-0790, www.trierer-dom.de, shows the advances Gothic church architecture made to allow natural light into the building. It was built between 1235 and 1260 on the original southern part of the Roman church as one of the first fully Gothic churches in Germany. Its floor plan is a Greek cross with two smaller chapels between each of the larger apsidal ones. It gives the impression of a round shape, sometimes described as a rose with 12 petals. Opening hours are daily from 8 am to noon and 2 to 6 pm. Admission is free.

To the north of the Dom is the **Bischöflichen Museum** (Bishop's Museum), Windstraße 6-8, ☎ 0651-710-5255, www.museum.bistum-trier.de. The main treasures here are archeological finds from the Roman church and other sites in the region. Highlights include a 60,000-stone mosaic found 10 ft under the crossing of the church and presumed to have been part of Constantine's Palace. Opening hours are Monday to Saturday, 9 am to 5 pm, Sundays and holidays, 1 pm to 5 pm, and closed on Mondays from November to March. Admission is €2.

A few minutes stroll down Liebfraustraße is the second-largest single-room structure from Roman times, the **Basilika** or **Römische Palastaula**, which currently houses the Protestant church **Zum Erloeser** (Our Savior), Konstantinplatz, ☎ 0651-42-570. This was the pillarless throne room of Emperor Constantine and is an impressive 90 ft wide, 108 ft high, and 220 ft long. The windows narrow progressively toward the cen-

The Römische Palastaula

ter of the building to create the optical illusion of the hall being even bigger. Since the mid-19th century, after Trier became part of Prussia, it became the first Protestant church in this predominantly Catholic city. Decorations are very limited, but note the organ pipes in the front window and the beautifully coffered wooden ceiling. From April to October, opening hours are daily from 10 am to 6 pm, except Sunday from noon to 6 pm. Visiting the church from November to March is more of a challenge when it is open Tuesday to Saturday, 11 am to noon and 3 to 4 pm, and Sundays from noon to 1 pm. Admission is free.

Adjacent is the magnificent Rococo **Kurfürsteliche Palais** (Electoral Palace), ☎ 0651-9494-202. The north and east wings are the older parts and date from 1615, but the Baroque south wing is the main draw. Unfortunately, the Palace is used for administrative offices and not generally open to the public. The exterior of the south wing can be admired from the lovely Baroque palace gardens. Admission is free.

The **Rheinische Landesmuseum** (Archeological Museum), Weimarer Allee 1, ☎ 0651-97-740, www.landesmuseum-trier. de, has the largest collection of Roman artifacts in Germany and perfectly complements a tour of the larger ruins in the town. Highlights include several Roman burial monuments and mosaics. One of the mosaics is still displayed and used as a floor, allowing visitors to walk on and admire it up-close. A reconstruction of the 75-ft **Iglerer Säule**, a grave monument near Trier, confirms that the Roman color taste was rather kitsch. Some non-Roman finds, including Stone Age, Celtic and Merovingian, and a few Renaissance and Baroque rooms, round out the display. The museum is open weekdays from 9:

30 to 5 pm (but closed on Mondays from November to April) and 10:30 am to 5 pm on weekends. Admission is €5.50.

The Kaiserthermen

The Mosel Valley

At the edge of the Baroque garden is the **Kaiserthermen** (Imperial baths), which were constructed 1,600 years ago as one of the largest such complexes in the then civilized world. Now mostly in ruins, it is possible to descend into the subterranean labyrinth of the engineering feat that provided the hot water for one of the major social rituals of Roman life. The original hot water bath was large enough for its remains to be used for opera and theater performances, with seats for 650 spectators. Cold water was heated in six boiler rooms, of which four are still distinguishable, to around 104°F. A hollow floor system was used to heat the entire complex.

A good 10 minutes walk uphill is the Roman **Amphitheatre**, originally located just outside the city with the town walls actually running along the highest level of the west

Amphitheatre

pavilion. It was used for popular entertainment such as gladiator fights and executions by wild animals. During the Middle Ages, it was used as a quarry, but much of the original remained. It had a seating capacity of 20,000 and is still sometimes used for open-air concerts. You can climb up to the highest levels for fine views, or descend to the subterranean level in the center of the stadium where prisoners and animals were held.

Near the Mosel River, the **Barbarathermen** (Barbara Baths) were built in the second century and was largest Roman-bathing complex at the time. Its ruins were used as a castle in the Middle Ages, but torn down in the 17th century and the materials were recycled to build a college. Only the foundations and subterranean service tunnels survived to the present day. To date, only about a third of the complex has been excavated.

The **Römerbrücke** (Roman Bridge) is the oldest bridge in Germany (AD 144-152) and, amazingly, five of the seven foundations and pilings are the originals from Roman times. The arches and roadway are 18th-century – the Romans used a flat wooden roadbed without arches. The

Römerbrücke

black stones are local basalt and not blackened sandstone like the Porta Negra. The bridge was due to be demolished at the end of World War II, but General Patton's troops captured the bridge on March 2, 1945 before the charges were set. The empty charge chambers can still be seen from the upriver side. The bridge is still in daily use.

From the bridge, follow Karl-Marx-Straße until it changes to Brückenstraße. The first part of this road was not renamed in order to preserve the historic address of the place of birth of Karl Marx. The **Karl-Marx-Haus**, Brückenstrasse 10, ☎ 0651-970-680, www.fes.de/marx, is a lovely 18th-century patrician house. It is best described as a documentation center and its prized possessions are first editions of *Das Kapital* and the *Communist Manifesto*. The museum is open November to March, Tuesday to Sunday, 10 am to 1 pm and 2 to 5 pm; Monday, 2 to 5 pm. From April to October, it is open Tuesday to Sunday, 10 am to 6 pm, and on Monday, 1 to 6 pm. Admission is €2.

The **Thermen am Viehmarkt** (Forum Baths) were rediscovered in 1987 during excavation work for an underground parking garage. The baths were covered by a modern glass and steel box allowing passersby a peak at most of the ruins. The ruins cover a surprisingly large area, with many remaining arches and tunnels. Descriptions are in German only and rather vague.

Cultural Events & Festivals

Trier has a busy cultural and festival program – from Karneval in March to the Christmas market in December, they do not seem to miss any available event. Wine, good food, and culture are never far apart at these events. Information on events is available from www.trier-today.de or from the tourist office.

Highlights include the **Wine and Gourmet Festival**, www.wein-gourmetfestival.de, in May, and several shorter wine-related events usually scheduled over weekends.

The amphitheater is sometimes used for major dramas and operas, while other Roman monuments serve as backdrops to concerts ranging from classics to jazz.

Adventures

On Foot

Town Walks: The tourist office conducts two-hour guided walking tours of the old city for April to October. The English tour is daily at 2 pm and in German at 10:30 am and 2:30 pm.

On Wheels

By Bicycle: Bicycle rentals are available from **Fahrrad-Service-Station** in the Hauptbahnhof, ☎ 0651-148-856, from April to October and year-round from **Zweiradwerkstatt TINA**, Hornstraße 32, ☎ 0651-89-555.

On Water

Riverboats: Several boat trips on the Mosel start from Trier. **Personenschifffahrt Kolb**, 56820 Briedern, ☎ 02673-1515, departs from Tier-Zurlauben. From April to October, daily trips depart at 10 am for Trier-Pfalzel – a two-hour round-trip. From early May to mid-October, cruises to Bernkastel-Kues depart from Tuesday to Sunday at 9:15 am.

Where to Stay & Eat

The **Mercure Hotel Trier Porta Nigra** is directly behind the Porta Nigra. It is a

HOTEL PRICES	
€	. . . . Up to €50 per night
€€	. . . . €50 to €100
€€€	. . . . . €101 to €150
€€€€	. . . . . . Over €150

modern city hotel with comfort-able rooms. The local Spielbank (Casino) is in the hotel – it opens daily at 7 pm. Porta-Nigra-Platz 1, 54292 Trier, ☎ 0651-27-010, fax 0651-270-1170, www.accorhotels.com. (€€€)

The **Hotel Aulmann** is in the heart of the Old Town at the Kornmarkt. It is partly in an old building, but mostly in one erected in the late 1990s. Rooms are comfortable and spa-cious. Fleischstraße 47, 54290 Trier, ☎ 0651-97-670, fax 0651-976-7102, www.hotel-aulmann.de. (€€-€€€)

The **Hotel Paulin** is close to the Porta Nigra. Rooms in the old building have rustic oak furniture, while the newer wing is better equipped and uses modern natural wood furniture. Paulinstraße 13, 54292 Trier, ☎ 0651-147-400, fax 0651-147-4010, hotelpaulin@aol.com. (€€)

A very pleasant small hotel with an excellent restaurant is the **Hotel Klosterschenke** in Trier-Pfalzel. It is 4.2 miles down-stream and on the opposite bank of the Mosel in what was a fourth-century monastery. Each of the 11 rooms is individually furnished in widely different styles. The **restaurant** (€€-€€€) serves Mediterranean and local dishes in a room with vaulted ceilings. Reservations are recommended. The hotel can be reached most easily by car, but it is also a stop on the riverboats from Trier, and the Mosel Cycling path passes right in front of the hotel. Klosterstraße 10, 54293 Trier, ☎ 0651-968-440, fax 0651-968-4430, www.hotel-klosterschenke.de. (€€)

Where to Eat

Trier has its fair share of cheap eateries catering to the tourist trade, with many options in Simeonstraße and the roads leading from the

RESTAURANT PRICES	
€	Less than €10
€€	€10 to €20
€€€	€21 to €35
€€€€	Over €35

Hauptmarkt. The McDonalds signs at Hauptmarkt are so low-key, it is easy to miss the entrance. However, more rewarding options are also easy to find.

The restaurant complex **Zum Domstein**, Hauptmarkt 5, ☎ 0651-74-490, has entrances from both the Hauptmarkt and the Domfreihof. Food and wine are served in several separate areas, including a restaurant, wine cellars, and a courtyard if the weather cooperates. Most interesting is the **Römischer Weinkellar**, a cellar built around 326 AD and restored in the 1970s. Dishes are local cuisine with some recipes dating from Roman times. Reservations are recommended. (€€-€€€)

Across the road from the Liebfraukirche is the upscale **Palais Kesselstatt**, Liebfrauenstraße 10, ☎ 0651-40-204, www.restaurant-kesselstatt.de. Located in a former Baroque palace, this smart, but unpretentious, restaurant serves upscale regional dishes with a French touch. Simpler food and wine tasting are available in the Weinstube. (€€€)

Another fine option in the Dom area is **Schlemmereule**, Domfreihof 1 b, ☎ 0651-73-616, www.schlemmereule.de, which serves light regional and French cuisine in a modern setting. Reservations are essential. (€€€-€€€€)

Right next to the Porta Nigra in the City Museum is **Brunnenhof**, Simeonstr 60, ☎ 0651-700-295, which serves mainly hearty German food. (€-€€)

An interesting option is the **Historischer Keller,** Simeonstraße 46, ☎ 0651-469-496. It is in a Gothic cellar dating from 1200, beneath the Karstadt department store. International and local food is served. (€-€€)

Camping

Camping Trier City is 2.4 miles from the center of Trier on the banks of the Mosel. It has some shade, reasonable facilities, and 140 lots. It is open from April to October. 54294 Trier, ☎ 0651-86-921, fax 0651-83-072.

The Mosel Valley

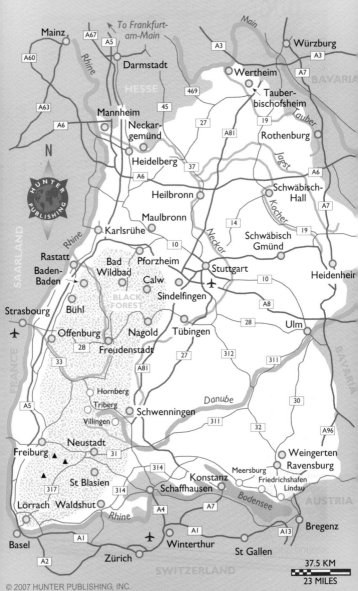

Baden-Württemberg

Baden-Württemberg

Baden-Württemberg is Germany's favorite getaway destination after Bavaria. It offers a combination of culture and nature that is hard to find elsewhere. In addition, Baden is famous for its good food – the French influence from across the Rhine certainly rubbed off – and parts of the state are among the sunniest in Germany.

Heidelberg, long the capital of the Palatinate, is one of Germany's most popular destinations with foreign visitors. It is a romantic university town with the marvelous ruins of a large castle towering over the town and the Neckar Valley.

The **Black Forest** is a popular year-round tourist destination. It has incredibly beautiful areas and is a haven for outdoor enthusiasts. The spa town **Baden-Baden** is one of the most refined and wealthy towns in Germany. **Freiburg** has the loveliest church spire in Christianity.

◆ Getting Here & Around

By Rail: The major cities of Baden-Württemberg are easily reached by rail from other centers in Germany. At least three trains per hour connect Frankfurt and Heidelberg in less than an hour. Hourly trains run between Frankfurt and Basel, stopping in Karlsruhe after an hour, and an hour later in Freiburg.

By Road: Although most parts of Baden-Württemberg can be reached by train, it is easier to see the beautiful countryside by car. Major Autobahnen cross the state, allowing you to get around quickly. The A5 runs parallel to the Rhine from Switzerland past Freiburg, Baden-Baden, Karlsruhe, Heidelberg, Frankfurt, and beyond. The A8 runs from Karlsruhe to Munich via Stuttgart and Ulm.

In rural areas, roads are much more scenic and, although generally in very good condition, the going can be much slower. Do not expect to do much more than 36 mph on most Black Forest roads, even during the quiet season.

 By Air: Baden-Württemberg has several airports, but often **Frankfurt International** (see Frankfurt chapter) is still the most convenient. Most destinations in Baden-Württemberg can easily be reached by train, either directly from the airport or via Frankfurt or Mannheim. **Stuttgart Airport**, ☎ 0711/-9480, www.stuttgart-airport.de, is the largest one in the state. It has connections to domestic and European destinations. S-Bahn lines S2 and S3 connect every 10 to 20 minutes to the Hauptbahnhof in under 30 minutes. **A Lufthansa Airport Bus** (☎ 0180-583-8426), open to all travelers, runs between Frankfurt International Airport's Terminal 1 (Halle B) and the Crowne Plaza Hotel in Heidelberg. The journey takes 75 minutes. Fares are €19 one-way or €35 round-trip. (It is possible to check luggage at Heidelberg for most Lufthansa and SAS flights; ☎ 06221-653-256 for specific details.) **TLS**, ☎ 06221-770-077, www.tls-heidelberg.de, has an airport-to-door shuttle service between Heidelberg and the airport. Fares are around €30 one-way.

◆ Information Sources

 Information on the whole state is available from Info und Prospektservice Baden-Württemberg, Yorckstraße 23, 79110 Freiburg, ☎ 0761-8979-7979, www.tourismus-baden-wuerttemberg.de.

◆ Heidelberg

Heidelberg is very popular with tourists and during July and August can be uncomfortably crowded. However, during the quieter months, it is a pleasant town, which can be enjoyed without having to wander into any of the formal museums.

For five centuries, Heidelberg was the principal residence of the prince electors of the Kurpfalz (Palatinate). It was therefore an important political center and its position was enhanced by the foundation of the first German university here in 1386. The castle was damaged in 1537 by a thunderbolt but soon after rebuilt as one of the most beautiful Renaissance palaces north of the Alps.

In 1618, Prince Friedrich V was elected king of Bohemia, although a family member of the emperor was already appointed. The defenestration of an imperial delegation in Prague by supporters of Friedrich was a direct cause of the Thirty Years' War and made Heidelberg an immediate target of the Imperial Army. In the 1620s, both Heidelberg and its castle were destroyed. The region lost three-quarters of its population during the war but both town and castle were rebuilt soon afterwards.

During the War of the Palatinate Succession, French troops of King Louis XIV occupied and eventually destroyed the town and castle in 1688, 1689, and 1693. As a result, Heidelberg's Old Town has no buildings from the Middle Ages. Most of the restored parts of the castle date from the 19th century when Heidelberg castle became the focus of several Romanticism movements.

Information Sources

Tourist Office: The Tourist Information Office, Willy-Brandt-Platz 1, ☎ 06221-19-433, www.cvb-heidelberg.de, is located at the main train station.

Transportation

The main train station is in the newer part of town, about a 20-minute walk from the Old Town. It is more convenient to use public transportation departing in front of the station.

Heidelberg has several parking garages and an electronic display system showing the number of unoccupied parking spaces. Street parking is very limited, with severe restrictions.

HEIDELBERG CARD

The Heidelberg Card gives unlimited access to all public transportation in Heidelberg including the funicular to the Castle and Königstuhl. It also allows free or reduced entry into many sights. It costs 12 for two days and 20 for four days. The card comes with a city map and guide.

Sightseeing
Schloss

The Heidelberg skyline is dominated by the ruins of the Schloss. It was for five centuries the principle residence of the prince electors of the Kurpfalz. However, since its destruction by the French in the late

Schloss Heidelberg

17th century, it has been Germany's most famous ruin. Parts have been restored but most are still in ruins.

Most of the remaining castle follows a Renaissance style, but older parts are Gothic and a small section is in an English style built by the ill-fated Friedrich V. He also laid out the large garden behind the castle.

To the left of the main entrance is the Old Battery with great views of the roofs of the Old Town. A closer inspection of the Dicker Turm (Fat Tower), 1533, is possible before passing through the Elisabeth Gate – a gate erected overnight by Friedrich V as a surprise birthday present to his wife.

Access to the inner courtyard and buildings is via the mighty Torturm. A small museum with paintings and models is housed in the former library. However, the main draw is the **Großes Fass** (Great Vat). This huge cask, which could hold 58,000 gallons, was installed in 1751 and connected to the banqueting

hall via pipes and a hand pump. It is possible to climb to the small dance and wine-tasting platform on top of the cask. A statue of Perkeo, a famous court jester, guards the cask. According to legend, tiny Perkeo could consume astonishing amounts of liquor but died when he drank a glass of water by mistake.

Across the courtyard is the surprisingly interesting **Deutsches Apothekenmuseum** (German Pharmacy Museum). On display is mainly pharmaceutical equipment from the 18th and 19th centuries including complete pharmaceutical shops.

Grosses Fass

The rest of the castle interior can only be seen on a guided tour.

The gardens offer good views of the castle and the Neckar Valley. The gardens are free of charge and especially pleasant in the late afternoon. Little of the original splendor remains, but a few statues, grottos, and fountains survive.

The Schloss, ☎ 062 21-538-422, is open daily from 8 am to 5:30 pm (the Apothekenmuseum from 10 am to 5 pm). Admission is €2.50. Guided tours, ☎ 06221-538-421, sometimes available in English, are an additional €3.50. The Schloss is about 15 minutes walk, mostly stairs, or a few minutes funicular ride, from the Old Town.

Old Town

Most of Heidelberg's Old Town consists of Baroque buildings, often erected on top of Gothic foundations that remained after the demolition efforts by the French. Most sights are in a narrow strip on either side of the pedestrian-only Hauptstraße.

The **Kornmarkt** (Wheat Market), at the east end of town, is an open square with a statue of the Madonna dating back to 1718. The main reason to visit the square is for the clear view it affords of the Schloss towering above.

Adjacent to this square is the larger and more impressive **Marktplatz** (Market Square). The **Heiliggeistkirche** (Holy Ghost Church), 1398-1441, is 197 ft long and, rare for a Gothic

Baden-Württemberg

church, consistently 66 ft wide although architectural techniques create the optical illusion that it gets wider towards the choir. It once housed the largest single library in the world, the *Bibliotheka Palatina*, until it was carted off to the Vatican, never to return, during the Thirty Years' War. The church, with the tombs of the prince electors, was destroyed by the French at the end of the 17th century, but rebuilt shortly after. It was used by both the Lutheran and Roman Catholic congregations and a dividing wall remained in place until 1936.

On the Hauptstraße side of the square is the famous **Hotel Haus zum Ritter**. It is the only Renaissance building in Heidelberg to have escaped the wrath of the French. Ironically, it was erected in 1592 by a French Huguenot who fled prosecution in France. It has been a guesthouse since 1703 and is still a popular place to sleep and eat.

On the northern side of the Heiliggeistkirche is the **Fischmarkt** (Fish Market) with fountain. Note the small stalls built into the walls of the church, as was common since at least medieval times. From here, Steingasse leads to the Neckar River and the **Alte Brücke** (Old Bridge), which is guarded by the **Brückentor** (Bridge Gate). Prince Carl Theodor had the stone bridge erected in 1788 to replace earlier wooden ones – high-water levels are indicated on the second arch. Several statues adorn the bridge, including one of Carl Theodor surrounded by the water gods of the Rhine, Danube, Neckar, and Mosel. The

Alte Brücke & Brückentor

bridge is a good place to view and photograph the castle and Old Town. For even better views, cross the bridge and follow the steep Schlangenweg to **Philosophenweg** (Philosophers'

Way), which is halfway up Heiligenberg and runs parallel to the Neckar River.

The Baroque **Alte Universität** (Old University), Universitätsplatz 1, was erected in 1711 to bring all the different parts of the university together in a central location. Nowadays the university has around 30,000 students but, apart from the humanities, all faculties have relocated to the newer parts of town. The 19th-century aula (auditorium) is decorated in grand, Historicist style typical for the period.

Studentenkarzer

Most popular with tourists, however, is the graffiti-filled **Studentenkarzer** (Students' Prison), Augustinergasse 2, ☎ 06221-543-554. From 1778 until 1914, it was used to imprison students, mostly on minor offenses such as public drunkenness, for terms of up to two weeks. The first couple of days the prisoners had to survive on bread and water but, after that, visits and better food were possible. The cells are open from April to September from Tuesday to Sunday, 10 am to 6 pm, in October, 10 am to 4 pm, and from November to March, Tuesday to Saturday, 10 am to 4 pm. Admission is €2.50.

The eclectic collection of the **Kurpfälzisches Museum** (Electoral Palatinate Museum), Haupstraße 97, ☎ 06221-583-402, is well worth seeing. A cast of the jaw of Homo Heidelbergensis, who roamed the region 600,000 years ago, is a star attraction. Opening hours are Tuesday to Sunday from 10 am to 6 pm. Admission is €2.50.

Excursions from Heidelberg

Königstuhl

Königstuhl is a 1,864-ft peak three miles to the southeast of Heidelberg. It can be reached by car, bus, or most easily with the Bergbahn (funicular) that runs from Heidelberg Old Town via the castle and Molkenkur. **Molkenku**r was the site of a castle that was destroyed by lightning in the early 16th century and never rebuilt. It currently has a restaurant with great views.

TRAVELING WITH CHILDREN

At the top of Königstuhl is **Märchenparadies** (Fairy Tale Paradise), ☎ 06221-23-416, www.maerchenparadies.de. It is a theme park, very much aimed at children, illustrating famous fairy tales. Some rides are also available. It is open daily from March to November, 10 am to 6 pm (7 pm on Sundays as well as in July and August). Admission is €3 for adults, €2 for children between two and 12 – some rides and activities require additional charges.

At the top of **Königstuhl** are several restaurants, a television tower, and a fairy tale theme park. It is also the start of at least 12 marked hiking trails – see *Adventures* below. The funicular, which runs every 10 minutes in summer and every 20 minutes in winter, takes just over 15 minutes and costs €4 one way or €6 round-trip.

Burgenstraße (Castles Road)

The Burgenstraße, www.burgenstrasse.de, connects Mannheim and Prague but en route passes through Heidelberg, the Neckar Valley, Rothenburg ob der Tauber, and Nürnberg among others. The total route is almost 600 miles long and passes castles, fortified towns, and exciting landscapes. The Neckar Valley upriver from Heidelberg is particularly interesting, with many castles and natural beauty.

Deutsche Touring, Am Römerhof 17, 60486 Frankfurt am Main, ☎ 069-790-350, www.deutsche-touring.de, has a daily bus from May to September on the stretch between Mannheim and Rothenburg.

Cultural Events & Festivals

Heidelberg has several cultural festivals – contact the tourist office for specific dates and details. The **Spring Festival** stretches over three weeks in March and April. It features mainly classical music.

More famous, and running more than two months in summer, is the **Schlossfestpiele** (Castle Festival). Many events ranging from operettas to theater are stage in the castle grounds. Sigmund Romberg's *The Student Prince*, performed in English, is a perennial favorite.

Three times a year, huge fireworks shows are staged with the Schloss as backdrop.

Adventures

On Foot

Town Walks: Guided walking tours of the Old Town take place daily from April to October at 10:30 am. On Friday and Saturday, the tour is available in English. From November to March, the tour is only on Saturday and in German only. Meeting point is the information board at Universitätsplatz and the tour lasts around 90 minutes.

A very pleasant walk, with wonderful views of the Old Town and the castle, is along Philosophenweg, halfway up the hill on the opposite bank of the river.

Countryside Hikes: Hiking opportunities abound in the immediate vicinity of Heidelberg. The Neckar Valley is best explored by bicycle or boat and the highlands on foot. Take the Bergbahn from the Old Town to **Königstuhl** from where 12 clearly marked hiking routes are available. The easiest walk, accessible to wheelchairs as well, is a 1½-mile circular route along the highest points of the mountain. Routes back to the Old Town average about three miles and to the other side of the mountain close to five miles. They always end at bus stops, allowing easy returns to Heidelberg.

On Wheels

By Bicycle: The Neckar Valley and the Odenwald areas around Heidelberg are ideal cycling territory. In Heidelberg, bicycles can be rented from **Fahrrad-Verleih Per Bike**, Bergheimer Str. 144, ☎ 06221-161-108, www.perbike.de.

Near Heidelberg, **Rudi's Radladen**, Mühlgasse 2, 69151 Neckargemünd, ☎ 06223-71-295, www.rudis-radladen.de, rents out quality bicycles of all types.

Inline Skating: From April to September, on the third Monday of the month, **TSG78**, ☎ 06221-160-563, www.tsg78-hd.de, organizes an inline skating parade through the streets of Heidelberg. Start is at 7:30 pm from Tiergartenstraße 9. From 500 to 2,000 skaters participate.

Inline skating is also possible on the Hockenheim Formula 1 racing circuit. During summer, four-hour events, attracting up to 4,000 participants, are scheduled in the evenings. Rental equipment is available. Schedules and information are available from **Inline Skating am Hockenheimring**, ☎ 06205-104-820, www.skate-hockenheimring.de.

By Car: Hockenheim auto racing circuit, ☎ 06205-152, www.hockenheim.de, just south of Heidelberg, hosts the annual German Formula 1 Grand Prix. On most Thursday nights from April to October, 5 to 8 pm, it welcomes anyone interested in racing their own cars. Admission is €4 per person and €12 per 15 minutes on the circuit. "Racing" is done in groups of up to 40 cars and safety regulations must be followed. Double-check insurance policies *prior* to participating!

In the Air

Hot Air Ballooning: Heidelberg Ballon, Hauptstr. 24, 69253 Heiligkreuzsteinach, ☎ 06220-922-227, www.heidelberg-ballon.de, starts from various locations around Heidelberg.

On Water

Canoeing & Kayaking: The Neckar Valley, especially upriver from Heidelberg, is a great area for cycling and canoeing. For tours ranging from a few hours to several days, **100% Kanu+Bike**, Holderstraße 2, 74196 Neuenstadt-Kochertürn, ☎ 07139-934-900, www.kanu-bike.de, can arrange cycling and canoe combinations on the Neckar as well as its Kocher and Jagst tributaries.

Riverboats: From Easter to October, **Rhein-Neckar-Fahrgastschifffahrt,** ☎ 06221- 20181, www.rnf-schifffahrt.

de, offers cruises on the Neckar River from Heidelberg. Round-trips to Neckarsteinach take three hours and cost €10. Shorter 40-minute trips of the Heidelberg riverfront cost €3.50.

Wildlife

The **Deutsche Greifenwarte** (German Birds of Prey Station), Burg Guttenberg, 74855 Haßmersheim-Neckarmühlbach, ☎ 06266-388, www.burg-guttenberg.de, is an interesting place to visit about 36 miles up the Neckar Valley from Heidelberg. This historic castle hosts around a hundred eagles, falcons, and owls. It is open from April to October, from 9 am to 6 pm with flights at 11 am and 3 pm. In March and November it is open from noon to 5 pm with flights at 3 pm. Admission is €8.

The fortress itself was built around 1200 during the Staufen era. It has been the residence of the Gemmingen family for the past 550 years and the current owner, the 17th generation, often conducts guided tours of the castle himself. The castle museum is open April

Burg Guttenberg

to October from 10 am to 6 pm and admission is €4. The **Burgschäncke Restaurant** (€-€€) offers a wide range of regional specialties at very reasonable prices.

Golf

One of Germany's highest-rated golf courses is just south of Heidelberg at the **Golf Club St Leon & Rot**, Opelstraße 30, 68789 St. Leon-Rot, ☎ 06227-86-080, www.golfclub-stleon-rot.de. Tourists who are registered members of other golf clubs are allowed to play on one of the two 18-hole courses if they have a handicap of 36 and on the nine-hole course with a handicap of 54.

Where to Stay & Eat

The best hotel in Heidelberg is **Der Europäische Hof** on the edge of the Old Town. This hotel has individually furnished luxurious rooms. The restaurant **Kurfürstenstube** (€€€-

Der Europäische Hof

€€€€) is highly regarded and serves classical and local cuisine. The style is rustic, with wood paneling that partly dates from the 18th century. Friederich-Ebert-Anlage 1, 69117 Heidelberg, ☎ 06221-5150, fax 06221-515-506, www. europaeischerhof.com. (€€€€)

Marriott Heidelberg

The **Marriott** is a new, modern hotel on the banks of the Neckar River, close to the station. Rooms are modern and comfortable. The best rooms, as well as the **Globetrotter Restaurant** (€€), have views of the river. Vangerowstraße 16, 69115 Heidelberg, ☎ 06221-9080, fax 06221-908-698, www.marriott. com. (€€€-€€€€)

The **Crowne Plaza** is a modern hotel at the edge of the Old Town. Rooms are spacious and comfortable. The restaurant, **Westcoast** (€€-€€€€), serves California cuisine, while the more cozy beer and wine bar **Gaudiamus** (€€-€€€) has hearty regional dishes to complement the wine and beer. Kurfürstenanlage 1, 69115 Heidelberg, ☎ 06221-9170, fax 06221-21-007, www.ichotels.com. (€€€-€€€€)

The **Hirschgasse Hotel** is on the opposite bank of the Neckar River from the Old Town and dates to 1472. Rooms are very comfortable and furnished in Laura Ashley style. The restaurant, **Le Gourmet** (€€€), serves international and nouvelle cuisine. The **Mensurstube** (€€-€€€) serves nouvelle cuisine and local specialties. It has a 200-year tradition and can

Hirschgasse Hotel

count Otto von Bismarck as a previous patron. Both restaurants are open for dinner only. Hirschgasse 3, 69120 Heidelberg-Neuenhaim, ☎ 06221-4540, fax 06221-454-111, www.hirschgasse.de. (€€€€)

Romantik Hotel Zum Ritter

Arguably, one of the most popular hotels with foreign tourists in Germany is the **Romantik Hotel Zum Ritter St. Georg**. It is in the center of the Old Town in a beautifully preserved building dating from 1592. A large statue of St George slaying the dragon stands guard over the façade. It is the only Renaissance building in Heidelberg that survived the three demolition sprees of

the French armies of Louis XIV in the 17th century. Rooms are comfortable, although the cheaper ones are a bit small. It is a very romantic place to stay. The **restaurants** (€€-€€€) serve international cuisine as well as local specialties. Hauptstraße 178, 69117 Heidelberg, ☎ 06221-1350, fax 06221-135-230, www.ritter-heidelberg.de. (€€€-€€€€)

Also in the Old Town is the **Hotel Weisser Bock**. The half-timbered building has a simple, yet comfortable interior with wooden floors but modern amenities. The **restaurant** (€€-€€€) maintains the feeling of a student's inn. Regional specialties as well as Italian food are served. Große Mantelgasse 24, 69117 Heidelberg, ☎ 06221-90-000, fax 06221-90-099, www.weisserbock.de. (€€-€€€)

The **Hotel Acor** is in a small Neo-Classical building at the edge of the Old Town. The rooms are functional and clean with some offering views of the castle. Friederich-Ebert-Anlage 55, 69117 Heidelberg, ☎ 06221-654-070, fax 06221-654-0717, www.hotel-acor.de. (€€-€€€)

The elegant **Simplicissimus Restaurant**, Ingimstraße 16, ☎ 06221-183-336, serves nouvelle cuisine in the heart of the Old Town. The restaurant has an Art Nouveau décor and a very pleasant courtyard. Reservations are recommended. (€€€)

Schönmehls Schlossweinstube, Im Schlosshof, ☎ 06221-97-970, is located inside the Heidelberg castle. It has five rooms, with styles ranging from medieval to luxurious. Food is classic regional dishes and the wine list is extensive. The restaurant is open for dinner only and reservations are recommended. (€€€-€€€€)

A very pleasant and informal café in the Old Town is **Café Journal**, Hauptstraße 162, ☎ 06221-161-712. It serves international dishes but is also very popular for coffee and cake. Newspapers and magazines from all over the world are available for reading and front covers decorate the walls. It is popular with tourists and locals alike. (€-€€)

The oldest coffee shop in town is **Café Knoesel**, Haspelgasse 20, ☎ 06221-22-345. The Heidelberger Students' Kiss was invented here – when physical contact between sexes was still taboo, students would present chocolates instead. (€-€€)

Café Knoesel

Zum Roten Ochsen, Hauptstraße 217, ☎ 06221-20-977, is a traditional students' pub, which has been run by the Family Spengel for six generations. Although students are now few and far between, it is still atmospheric and the bare oak tables are full of carved initials. Mark Twain and Marilyn Monroe, among others, left their marks here. Food is simple home-style dishes. Reservations are recommended. (€-€€)

Camping

Camping Heidelberg is open from April to mid-October. Tents and bicycles can be rented on-site and cheap sleeps are available in rental RVs. Heidelberg Old Town is five minutes away by bus. Schlierbacher Landstraße 151,69118 Heidelberg, ☎ 06221-802-506, www.camping-heidelberg.de.

◆ The Black Forest

This is one of Germany's most popular vacation areas. It is the largest forested area in the country and the pleasant weather makes it a popular year round destination. The area is mountainous with lovely valleys and areas of outstanding beauty. It also has wonderful hot springs and spas. Despite claims by the Swiss, the area actually had both downhill skiing and cuckoo clocks first.

Tourism is a major industry and the region continuously develops new activities to lure in travelers with diverse interests. It has culture in the form of numerous museums, ruins of monasteries, Baroque palaces, and frequent musical festivals. Much is done to keep the traditional Black Forest experience alive. *Trachten* (national dress) is often worn at numerous festivals. Hotels and vacation homes are in traditional style, using lots of wood and covering balconies with blooming geraniums. Many small towns are simply picture-perfect. It is almost impossible

Baden-Württemberg

to pick a road here that is not scenic. The area is popular with hikers and cyclists, the numerous rivers and small lakes offer water sports, and the reliable snow makes it a popular winter sports destination.

The Black Forest is famous for its cuisine and the extraordinary range of award-winning restaurants. France is just a river crossing away and its influence shows especially in the higher-end restaurants. In the more rustic deeper valleys, the food is heartier. Black Forest ham, cured by cold smoke over a series of months, is always popular. It is carved very thin so as to bring out the full flavor.

The wines from Baden are famous and the vineyards facing the Rhine are an integral part of the landscape. Local beers also appeal and some, such as the Alpinsbacher Klosterbräu, are beloved throughout Germany. Stronger liquors, liqueurs, or *Schnapps*, are also local specialties.

THE BLACK FOREST CAKE

The most famous food from the region is probably the **Schwarzwälder Kirschtorte** (Black Forest cherry cake) made of chocolate, cream, cherries, and Black Forest *Kirschwasser* (cherry liqueur). It is what the Germans call a *Kalorienbombe* – a calory bomb. It is popular and available all over Germany, but having at least one piece in the Black Forest is almost compulsory. No one in the region will volunteer this information, and very few would even admit it, but this cake does not originate here. The first one was baked in the late 19th century in a café in Bad Godesberg, a sleepy town near Bonn. It was called Black Forest cake because of the Black Forest liqueur used to flavor the cream. Many foreign visitors, used to the lavishly decorated Black Forest cakes available back home, may find the local version a bit bland.

Information Sources

Tourist Information: The tourism information offices generally divide the Black Forest into three major areas, and then again into smaller units. It is best to contact one of the big three first, and then narrow things down to a specific region or town.

For the northern area: **Touristik Nördlicher Schwarzwald**, Am Waisenhausplatz 26, 75172 Pforzheim, ☎ 07231-147-380, www.noerdlicher-schwarzwald.de.

The middle: **Mittlere Schwarzwald Tourismus**, Gerberstraße 8, 77652 Offenburg, ☎ 0781-923-7777, www.schwarzwald-tourismus.de.

The south: **Tourismus Südlicher Schwarzwald**, Stadtstraße 2, 79104 Freiburg, ☎ 0761-218-7304, www.schwarzwald-sued.de.

THE SCHWARZWALD CARD

The Schwarzwald Card (Black Forest Card), www.schwarzwaldcard.info, is an electronic chip card designed by the tourism industry to give access to around 130 attractions in the region. In the summer season, it is valid on three freely selected days and in the winter season on four days. It costs €42 for those over 12 and €34 for children aged four to 11. It is transferable but not on the same day. The card can pay for itself with three visits to some of the spas. Available from most tourist offices and many hotels.

Adventures in the Black Forest

The beautiful hills and forests, combined with generally fine weather and good infrastructure, despite the relatively sparse population, makes for excellent adventures here. Hiking and cycling are particularly favored during all seasons. In winter, cross-country skiing is the main draw but downhill skiing and snow hiking are also options. Adventures are listed under the nearest town below, but some hiking and cycling routes run the full stretch of the forest and are listed here.

Baden-Württemberg

Long-Distance Hikes

Three long-distance hiking routes run the full length of the Black Forest from Pforzheim in the north. The **Westweg** (West Route) leads to Basel and at 168 miles is the longest. It is usually split into 12 stages. Claimed to be the most popular long distance walking route in Germany, it has been in use since 1900. The **Mittelweg** (Middle Route) to Waldshut is 138 miles. It is split into nine stages and passes down the beautiful Nagold Valley. The **Ostweg** (East Route) leads to Schaffhausen on the Rhine, is 146 miles, and is divided into 12 stages.

Long-Distance Cycling Routes

The Black Forest has 17 major multi-day cycling routes. Some routes are easy one way, but have extremely challenging returns. Often it is possible to catch up on lost time by using trains for part of the route. Hotels usually rent bicycles to patrons, but for longer tours it is often better to rent equipment from specialists. Most tourism offices can supply information and cycling maps are available from bookstores all over Germany and tourism providers in the region.

The **Mountainbikeweg Schwarzwald** is a 212-mile route along the crest of the Black Forest. It is divided into six challenging stages. Information is available from the **Schwarzwaldverein**, ☎ 0761-380-530, www.schwarzwaldverein.de.

Part of the Bodensee to Heidelberg route runs for 30 miles, called the **Nagoldweg**, through this beautiful valley. This part of the route is not particularly challenging, allowing for full enjoyment of the beautiful surroundings.

Fishing

Fishing opportunities abound in the rivers and lakes of the Black Forest. A permit is always required – German residents must also present their annual fishing license, but that requirement is usually waved for non-residents. For more information and rental equipment, contact the applicable tourism office. Fishing without a permit is a serious criminal offence.

Baden-Baden

Internationally, Baden-Baden is the most famous of all Black Forest towns. Its hot springs attracted visitors from Celtic times to the present and are the source of the town's fame, although the casino and excellent wines are also major contributing factors to its wealth.

Baden-Baden has more millionaires per capita than any other German city. There is a stylish quality about this town, from the high-class shopping streets to the manicured lawns of the public parks. It is an expensive town – hotel rooms above €300 per night are easy to find – but can also easily be enjoyed without spending a cent.

THE RUSSIAN CONNECTION

Baden-Baden in 1870

Baden-Baden became fashionable with Russian nobles during the 19th century and even the Czar himself visited frequently. The Russian author Dostoevsky, who made a fortune gambling in Wiesbaden, lost most of it, including his wife's wedding ring and the shirt off his back, in Baden-Baden and wrote several novels about his experience and misery. For most of the 20th century, Baden-Baden was off-limits to the Russians but they are back. In recent years, the Russian nouveaux riches rediscovered the joys of Baden-Baden and they visit in droves. Although the largest foreign market is still the USA, the Russians are the fastest-growing sector.

Baden-Württemberg

Information Sources

Tourist Office: Tourist information is available from Kur & Tourismus, Schloss Solms, Solmsstraße 1, 76530 Baden-Baden, ☎ 07221-275-266, www.baden-baden.com.

Transportation

The main station is in the Oos district, about 1.2 miles east of the center.

When driving, note that two tunnels lead traffic on the main roads past the center of town. Pedestrian zones and other restrictions make it impossible to cross through the Old Town by car for most of the day.

Sightseeing

Humans settled in Baden-Baden at least 10,000 years ago, but the area's written history started around 70 AD after the Romans evicted the Celts and took to the waters themselves.

Baden-Baden served as a residence of the dukes of Baden until the French destroyed the city during 1689 and the dukes moved to Rastatt. Although the city is a mixture of architectural styles from all periods, the Neo-Classical and *Gründerzeit* villas from the 19th century are particularly attractive.

Baden-Baden has been a magnet for artists, especially during the Romantic period of the 19th century. Several writers such as Dostoevsky, Goethe, Mark Twain, and musicians such as Johannes Brahms, Clara Schumann, and Franz Liszt were frequent guests.

It is easy to enjoy Baden-Baden by just strolling through the magnificent parks and streets. None of the museums or galleries is an absolute must-see – water and gambling remain the main sources of revenue and the stylish ambiance comes for free.

■ Left Bank of the Oos

The **Lichtentaler Allee** along the River Oos was the meeting point of the European nobles and diplomats during the 19th century. Originally just an oak-lined street, it was changed into a large English landscape

Lichtentaler Allee

park in 1850 by the owner of the casino. It currently has more than 300 types of trees and plants. The most popular part of the park is between Goetheplatz and Kleingolfplatz but it is worth continuing to the more formal park at Gönneranlage, on the opposite bank of the River Oos, which has 300 different types of roses.

The **Staatliche Kunsthalle** (National Art Hall), Lichtentaler Allee 8a, ☎ 07221-300-763, www.kunstahlle-baden-baden.de, houses temporary exhibitions of 19th- and 20th-century art. Opening hours are Tuesday to Sunday from 11 am to 6 pm (8 pm on Wednesday). Admission is €5.

Kurhaus

The magnificent Neo-Classical **Kurhaus**, by Friedrich Weinbrenner, opened in 1824 as a "Conversation House." The name was not far off the mark – while Baden-Baden was the summer capital of Europe, it was here that nobles came to be seen, and gossip was created and spread. The four halls were decorated during the 1850s in the Neo-Baroque of the Belle Époque and have lost none of their over-the-top styling since then. It now houses the **Spielbank** (Casino), Kaiserallee 1, ☎ 07221-21-060, www.casino-baden-baden.de, Germany's oldest and largest casino. Admission is €3, the minimum bet is €5 and the maximum is €10,000. The Casino operates daily from 2 pm, for suitably dressed adults only – at least a jacket and tie for men. In the morning, you can wear whatever you want if you're part of a guided tour, sometimes in English, of the building. Opening hours for tours are daily from April to September from 9:30 am to noon and from October to March, 10 am to noon. Tours are €4.

North of the Kurhaus in the Kurgarten is the Neo-Classical **Trinkhalle**, Kaiserallee 3. The Trinkhalle opened in 1842 and has a 2,952-ft-long arcade with Corinthian columns and 14 frescos depicting local tales. It has a free drinking fountain with water from the source that fills the Caracalla and Friedrichsbad spas. Apart from a small bistro-café, it also has a tourist information office, open Monday to Sunday, 10 am to 5 pm, and Sunday and holidays, 2 to 5 pm.

■ Right Bank

The **Neues Schloss** (New Palace), Schlossstraße 22, constructed in 1479, was the former residence of the margrave of Baden. It was recently sold by his heirs and is being converted into a luxury hotel. The terrace offers lovely views of

Neues Schloss

the Old Town, including, in the foreground, the mainly Gothic **Stiftkirche** (Collegiate Church), Marktplatz, which has the tombs of the margraves of Baden from the 14th to 18th centuries. The monument of Ludwig the Turk (1753) is particularly opulent.

In contrast to many other German towns, the Marktplatz in Baden-Baden is rather dull. The **Rathausplatz**, in front of the Rathaus (Town Hall) is much livelier, with several outdoor restaurants. It also has an oversized statue of Bismarck, creator of the German Empire in the 19th century and a frequent spa guest. A plaque thanks him for his services in ensuring a long period of peace.

The **Römischen Badruinen** (Ruins of the Roman Baths), Römerplatz 1, ☎ 07221-275-934, www.badruinen.de, are underneath the current Friedrichsbad. The floor and wall heating systems of this soldiers' bath are in excellent preserved condition and an exhibition explains the Roman bath culture. Opening hours are daily from 11 am to 5 pm. Admission is €2.

Both the historic Friederichsbad and the adjacent modern Caracalla Therme are open to the public. See Adventures *below.*

The **Russische Kirche** (Russian Church), Lichtentaler Straße 76, ☎ 07221-390-634, was erected in the Byzantine style in the 1880s to serve as place of prayer for the visiting Russian nobles. It is open daily from February to November, 10 am to 6 pm. Admission is 70 cents.

Excursions

■ Rastatt

After the French destroyed Baden-Baden, Ludwig the Turk moved his residence six miles downhill and turned Rastatt into a stronghold. His new palace, Schloss Rastatt, was Baroque and with a garden front of 750 ft, the first such large Baroque structure in Germany. It was inspired by Versailles and was completed in 1707, around the time Ludwig died.

Schloss Rastatt

The main sights at **Schloss Rastatt**, Herrenstraße 18, Rastatt, ☎ 07222-978-385, www.schloesser-und-gaerten.de, are the royal apartments and the Ahnensaal used for balls. The interior can only be seen on guided tours. Opening hours are Tuesday to Sunday from April to October, 10 am to 5 pm, and from November to March, 10 am to 4 pm. Admission is €4.

A few miles away, in Rastatt-Niederbühl/Förch, is the Romantic pleasure palace **Schloss Favorite**, ☎ 07222-41-207, www. schloesser-und-gaerten.de, built in 1710-12 for Sibylla Augusta, widow of Ludwig the Turk. This small, but opulent Baroque palace served as her summer residence and a place to house her magnificent porcelain collection. Much of this collection of tableware, vases, and figures is still on display. Opening hours are Tues-

Schloss Favorite

day to Sunday from mid-March to September, 10 am to 5 pm; from October to mid-November, 10 am to 4 pm. Admission is €4.50 and includes the compulsory guided tour.

Cultural Events

Festspielhaus

The **Festspielhaus,** Beim Alten Bahnhof 2, ☎ 07221-301-3101, www.festspielhaus.de, opened in 1998, incorporating part of the Neo-Renaissance old station in its design. It was more than a century in the making and finally offered Baden-Baden a concert venue in keeping with its strong cultural tradition. It has two galleries and seats 2,500 people – the second-largest opera house in Europe.

Adventures

■ On Foot

Town Walks: The **fountains' walk** leads past more than 50 fountains scattered through the parks and streets of Baden-Baden, constantly reminding the visitor of the importance of water to this town. A map is available from the tourism office.

■ On Wheels

By Bicycle: Baden-Baden has 180 miles of marked cycling paths. Challenges range from simply avoiding the well-heeled on the flat, but oh-so-grand shopping streets, to professional endurance training up the Schwarzwald-Hochstraße. The routes in the Rhine plains are easier but the higher ones offer better views. On weekends, from May to October, the **VeloBus** transports cyclists with equipment from Baden-Baden to Sand and the Mummelsee in the Black Forest hills.

Bicycles can be rented at most hotels, usually for guests only, or from the **parking garages of the Kurhaus**, ☎ 07221-277-201; **Vincenti**, ☎ 07221-277-203; and **Festspielhaus**, ☎ 07221-277-298.

By Car: Two major touring routes from Baden-Baden are best explored by car. The **Badische Weinstraße** (Wine Route) runs from Baden-Baden through the local vineyards along the Rhine plains to Offenburg and back into the Black Forest. Several vineyards, cellars, and wine shops can be visited en route.

The **Schwarzwald-Hochstraße** (Crest Road) runs from Baden-Baden along the B500 to Freudenstadt. It follows the crest of the mountains and offers stunning views. It is a busy road, with both commercial and tourist traffic. The 36-mile route takes about three hours if sights en route are visited (see below).

■ In the Air

Hot-Air Ballooning: Europe's largest balloon fleet is stationed in Baden-Baden. **Ballooning 2000 Baden-Baden**, Dr Rudeolf-Eberle-Straße 5, ☎ 07223-60-002, www.ballooning2000.de, flies up to 25 balloons per day in the region. Surprisingly, wheelchair users can also join some of the flights.

■ On Horseback

Baden-Baden has 90 miles of marked trails for horseback riding. For riding opportunities enquire from the **Reitclub Baden-Baden**, Buchenweg 42, ☎ 07221-64-666, www.reitclub-baden-baden.de.

In fine weather, a horse-drawn carriage is available for hour-long rides from the Theater along Licthentaler Allee and through the center of Baden-Baden.

Twice yearly, the **International Club**, Lichtentaler Allee 8, ☎ 07221-21-120, www.baden-galopp.de, stages major horse-racing events at Iffezheim. The Spring Meet is held late May and the *Großen Woche* (Grand Week) late August or early September. Both attract international competition and spectators. For those not interested in racing itself, these weeks are also a good opportunity to see the gathering of the largest and grandest chauffeur-driven cars and high-end fashion. The use of pantsuits became socially acceptable after they were worn here in 1907.

■ On Water

Spas: For a brief period during the mid-19th century, Baden-Baden was more famous for its casino and as a gathering place for the European nobles, than for its spas. However, as soon as the prudish Prussians had gambling banned in all of Germany in 1872, the balance of attention swung back to the waters that already drew the Celts and Romans to the region. Daily, around 53,000 gallons of water bubbles from 23 springs at temperatures up to 155°F. Many hotels have their own spas, and several exclusive clinics offer medical water treatments, but two of the best spas are open to all and well worth the splurge.

The **Friedrichsbad**, Römerplatz 1, ☎ 07221-275-920, www.roemisch-irisches-bad.de, is by far the classiest. The 125-year-old Friederichsbad combines the Roman bathing tradition of steam and thermal baths at different temperatures with Irish spa traditions. Visitors go through 16 basic steps and can add additional treatments and massages. The spa is open Monday to Saturday, 9 am to 10 pm, and Sunday, noon to 8 pm. Sometimes the sexes are split in some of the facilities but they still use the same main pools. The whole spa is textile free. A basic three-hour stay costs €21. The minimum age for admission is 14.

Friedrichsbad

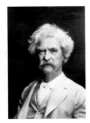

Mark Twain, who did not particularly like Baden-Baden, wrote, "At Friedrichsbad you lose track of time within 10 minutes and track of the world within 20..." He also observed that he lost his rheumatism in Baden-Baden and that the town was welcome to it.

The nearby **Caracalla-Therme**, Römerplatz 1, ☎ 07221-275-940, www.caracalla.de, is a far less highbrow, more accessible, and clothes-on facility located in one of the loveliest spas in Germany. It has seemingly endless water facilities, including indoor and outdoor pools, whirlpools, and hot and cold-water grottos. Seven different saunas and a range of massages, mudpacks, and other treatments are available. Childcare facilities for children 18 months and older are available – children under three are not allowed in the pool area. Opening hours are daily from 8 am to 10 pm. Admission is €12 for two hours and €16 for four.

■ **On Snow & Ice**

Many winter sports opportunities are available along the Schwarzwald-Hochstraße, which leads from Baden-Baden to Freudenstadt in the heart of the Black Forest. More information is available from the tourist office for activities listed below without specific contact details.

Skiing: Although the Feldberg region claims to be the original home of downhill skiing, cross-country skiing (*Langlauf*) is more popular in the Black Forest. The Northern Black Forest has over 600 miles of marked trails and groomed tracks (*Loipen*).

The longest downhill (*Alpinski*) run is at **Mehliskopf** just outside Baden-Baden. The course is open daily from 9 am to 10 pm. It is floodlit from around 5 pm. Snow machines assure skiing most of the winter. Around 20 more runs are available along the Schwarzwald-Hochstraße toward Freudenstadt.

 For snow conditions: ☎ *07231-147-380 or www.noerdlicher-schwarzwald.de.*

Tobogganing: On weekends, if the snow conditions are right, "snow buses" run from Baden-Baden to Scherrhof at Lichtenthal. From here, a 1.8-mile tobogganing run goes through the forests to the bottom of the valley, from where the buses provide transportation back to the top. Children of all ages are welcome.

Ice Skating: From mid-December to late February, an outdoor skating-rink at **Freiluft-Kunsteisbahn Wiedenfelsen**, ☎ 07226-722-6282, www.eisbahn-wiedenfelsen.de, is open daily from 10 am to 10 pm. Equipment can be rented on-site.

Summer Bobsledding: Around nine miles along the Schwarzwald-Hochstraße is the **Mehliskopf Bobbahn**, ☎ 07226-1300, www.mehliskopf.de. Tandem bobsleds use gravity to reach speeds up to 24 mph down the hillside, navigating 11 curves and several jumps en route. The facilities are open May to March and rides cost €3.

■ Archery

Archery can be practiced on the grounds of the **Heimbachtäler Schützen Club**, ☎ 07221-681-686, from April to October. Equipment can be rented and instructions are available at a minimal charge.

■ Golf

The Baden-Baden area has some of Germany's best golf courses. The tourism office has a special bilingual brochure explaining the fares and availability to non-members. Proof of membership in some golf club is usually required to play on the better courses. Most have equipment for rent.

Where to Stay & Eat

If money is no object, the **Brenner's Park Hotel** is the natural choice. It is one of Germany's best hotels – a luxury hotel in the grand tradition with service and décor to match. It has a spa and beauty farm in addition to a

Brenner's Park Hotel

large private, fenced-off park along the River Oos. The **restaurant** (€€€€), with views of the Kurpark and the River Oos, serves international cuisine with strong Mediterranean influences. Schillerstraße 4, 76530 Baden-Baden, ☎ 07221-9000, fax 07221-38-772, www.brenners.com. (€€€€)

Schlosshotel Bühlerhöhe

The **Schlosshotel Bühlerhöhe** is about nine miles outside Baden-Baden, but from its location 2,624 ft higher, it offers a view of the Rhine plains second to none. The service is outstanding too and many rate this Grande Époque hotel dating from the Wilhelmian era as the best in the region. Its spa and beauty centers rank among the most beautiful in Europe. The **Restaurant Imperial** (€€€€) serves excellent French cuisine, a reminder that the French border is but a few minutes drive away. On weekdays, it is only open for dinner and reservations are recommended. The **Schlossrestaurant** (€€€) offers international and regional cuisine. Schwarzwald-Hochstraße 1, 77815 Bühl, ☎ 07226-550, fax 07226-55-777, www.buehlerhoehe.de. (€€€€)

The **Steigenberger Europäischer Hof** is another top hotel with an extravagant tradition and history. It was the hotel of choice of Queen Victoria, Russian nobles, and heads of state during the 19th century. The interior

Steigenberger Europäischer Hof

and rooms are very luxurious. The **restaurant** (€€-€€€€) with bar and terrace offers international cuisine with seasonal regional specialties. Kaiserallee 2, 76530 Baden-Baden, ☎ 07221-9330, fax 07221-28831, www.steigenberger.com. (€€€€)

Dorint-Sofitel Maison Messmer

For 40 years, the **Dorint-Sofitel Maison Messmer** was the summer residence of Kaiser Wilhelm I. In 2001, the hotel reopened with a new wing to complement the two historic buildings. It is a popular, luxury alternative to the other grand hotels in town and the closest to the Kurhaus. The restaurant, **J.B. Messmer** (€€€-€€€€), serves international and nouvelle cuisine. The **Theaterkeller** (€€-€€€) is a more rustic wine cellar serving regional specialties. Both restaurants are open for dinner only. Werdestraße 1, 76530 Baden-Baden, ☎ 07221-30-120, fax 07221-301-2100, www.accorhotels.com. (€€€€)

Although located in a former monastery, the **Steigenberger Badischer Hof** is luxurious and comfortable. It is located at the

Dorint-Sofitel Maison Messmer

northern edge of the pedestrian zone. The elegant **Park Restaurant** (€€-€€€) offers regional and nouvelle cuisine. Lange Straße 47, 76530 Baden-Baden, ☎ 07221-9340, fax 07221-934-470, www.steigenberger.com. (€€€€)

The third Steigenberger property in town, the **Bad-Hotel Zum Hirsch**, is in a building dating back to 1689. Rooms are comfortable and stylishly furnished. Hirschstraße 1, 76530 Baden-Baden, ☎ 07221-9390, fax 07221-38-148, www.steigenberger.com. (€€€)

Bad-Hotel Zum Hirsch

Despite, or perhaps because of, all its style, class, and pomp, central Baden-Baden has only one Michelin star restaurant and it is not in one of the top hotels. **Le Jardin de France**, Lichtentaler Straße 13, ☎ 07221-300-7860, not surprisingly, serves French cuisine. The restaurant is refined, with the terrace in the courtyard particularly popular. Reservations are recommended. (€€€-€€€€)Despite its name, **Medici**, Augustuaplatz 8, ☎ 07221-2006, serves not only Italian food but also a wide range of international dishes, including sushi. Bill Clinton dined in this opulent fin de siècle building. It is open only for dinner and reservations are recommended. (€€-€€€€)

The **Kurhaus Baden-Baden**, ☎ 07221-9070, www.kurhausrestaurant.de, has a restaurant café with a pleasant terrace ideal for people-watching. International cuisine is served. The selection of cakes and ice creams is vast. (€-€€€)

■ Camping

Free parking is available for motor homes at the Aumatt Stadium, about 1.2 miles east of the town center. Contact the tourism office for details.

The Schwarzwald-Hochstraße (Black Forest Crest Route)

One of the most popular drives in the Black Forest is along the Schwarzwald-Hochstraße (Crest Road) between Baden-Baden and Freudenstadt. The route mostly follows the B500, a major route from the Black Forest to the highways in the Rhine plains, and is usually busy with both commercial and holiday traffic. However, ample stopping points are available to safely enjoy the views. Driving the 36 miles takes about an hour, but plan on more than three hours if stopping en route at the listed sights and to take in the views.

Mummelsee

The Mummelsee is a very small lake at the **Hornisgrinde**, the highest peak of the Northern Black Forest. The small lake is a reminder of the time when most of the Black Forest was covered by an enormous lake. The Mummelsee itself is at

The Mummelsee

3,375 ft, allowing an ascent of the 3,818-ft Hornisgrinde in a less than 30 minutes. The area has a large restaurant, an even larger souvenir shop, and a huge parking lot somewhat out of proportion to the actual beauty of the lake itself.

Statistically, it rains here every second day but, otherwise, the lake is filled with vacationers. Paddleboats are available from April to October, 8 am to 9 pm, from **Tretbootfahrt Mummelsee**, ☎ 07842-99-286. Cost is €4 per person.

Allerheiligen

At Ruhestein, it is worth turning off the B500, heading toward Oppenau – but avoid this route during snowfall or heavy rain. A very narrow, winding road leads downhill to the ruins

Kloster Allerheiligen

of **Kloster Allerheiligen**. This monastery operated from the late 12th century up to 1803. It was destroyed by lightning weeks after the last monk left. Parts of the Gothic chapels and a vaulted porch are still standing. The monastery and a restaurant are five minutes walk from the parking area.

Allerheiligen Wasserfälle

More impressive than the actual ruins is the surrounding area. The top destination is the **Allerheiligen Wasserfälle** (Waterfalls), which can be reached in a 15-minute walk from the monastery. Since the late 19th century, a series of stairs have been built adjacent to the falls, making them accessible to the public. A circular route leads down the 232 steps next to the waterfall and then uphill again along a gentler slope. It is also possible to drive 1.2 miles down the road and approach the waterfalls from the bottom. From here, it is less than 10 minutes walk to the bottom of the falls. The falls are not particularly big, but are lovely, dropping more than 270 ft in several places.

Return to the B500, as several viewing points follow directly after the turn-off at Ruhestein.

Baden-Württemberg

Freudenstadt

Information Sources: The tourist information office is at Marktplatz 1, 72250 Freudenstadt, ☎ 07441-8900, www.freudenstadt.de.

■ Sightseeing

In 1599, the Duke of Württemberg founded Freudenstadt in order to have a town on the crest of his Black Forest lands. He gave the town Germany's largest market square – 708 by 718 ft. The town center was extensively damaged during World War II, but rebuilt, mostly according to the historic example, immediately afterwards. Freudenstadt has excellent transportation links and its central location at the meeting point of several valleys makes it a major tourist town.

Freudenstadt Marktplatz

The main sight is still the huge **Marktplatz**, although the major roads that intersect inside the square itself somewhat reduced the visible impact of its size. At the center of the square is the Post-World War II town hall, with the **Heimat Museum** (Local History), ☎ 07441-864-718.

Opening hours are Sunday from 10 am to noon. The modern statue of Venus reminds the visitor of the destruction of the town in 1945 and the reconstruction between 1949 and 1954.

The **Evangelische Stadtkirche** (Protestant Church), Marktplatz, ☎ 07441-81469, dates from the early 17th century, but was mostly destroyed in the war. Of note is its odd shape: it has two naves at a right angle allowing half of the church congregation to attend the same services without seeing the other half. The carved lectern (1140) came from the monastery in Alpirsbach and the Romanesque baptismal font is from the same era. It is open daily from 10 am to 5 pm. Free guided tours in German are held on Friday at 2 pm. Admission is free.

■ Cultural Events

The **Schwarzwald Musikfestival** (Music Festival), Lauterbachstraße 5, 72250 Freudenstadt, ☎ 07441-864-732, www.schwarzwald-musikfestival.de, is held annually for about six weeks in May. Most events involve classical music and are staged at different venues in the region.

■ Adventures

Town Walks: The neighboring town of Dornstetten-Hallwagen has a rather unusual hiking route. In the **Barfusspark** (Bare Feet Park), www.barfusspark.de, visitors have to kick off their shoes and experience the therapeutic effects of different surfaces on the soles of their bare feet. Two circular routes are available: .8 mile (25 minutes) for beginners and 1½ miles (around an hour) for experienced barefoot walkers. It is open daily in summer from 9 am to 6 pm. Admission is free and shoe lockers are available.

Baiersbronn

Baiersbronn has no specific sights worthy of a detour, but it is a very pleasant area to stay and dine in. Baiersbronn is actually 12 small villages spread through the district to form the most popular winter sports area in the Northern Black Forest. It has many hotels, holiday homes, and some of the best restaurants in Germany. It's a convenient place to stay with easy access to all the attractions of the Northern Black Forest.

■ Information Sources

Tourist information is available from Baiersbronn Touristik, Rosenplatz 3, 72270 Baiersbronn, ☎ 0744284140, www.baiersbronn.de.

■ Adventures

Town Walks: Seven walking paths are scattered through the towns that make up Baiersbronn. These walks range in length from 1.2 to six miles; many are paved and accessible to wheelchairs and strollers. Although in town, Baiersbronn is so green that many paths could equally qualify as country hikes. The tourism office has brochures on these walks.

Nordic Walking: Nordic walking – a hiking style from Finland using two sticks like ski poles – is currently very fashionable in Germany. Baiersbronn took up the cause in a big way and has two dedicated Nordic Fitness Parks in addition to the normal hiking trails. The Tourist

Baiersbronn

Office as well as **Sport Klumpp**, Bildstöckleweg 27, ☎ 07442-84-250, www.sport-klumpp.de, rent out equipment. Guided Nordic walking tours are available on Thursday at 10 am and Wednesday at 6 pm.

By Bicycle: Bicycles can be rented from **Sport-Frey**, Klosterreichenbach, ☎ 07442-6468, www.sport-frey.de.

On Snow & Ice: Baiersbronn is the center of winter sports activities in the Northern Black Forest and has many options for participants of all development levels. Horse-drawn sleighs are popular and operate as long as snow conditions permit.

For activities without specific contact details, contact the tourism office. Equipment can be rented from **Sport-Frey**, Klosterreichenbach, ☎ 07442-6468, www.sport-frey.de; **Sport Klumpp**, Bildstöckleweg 27, ☎ 07442-84-250, www.sport-klumpp.de; or **Sport Faißt**, Ruhensteinstraße 289, ☎ 07442-50-416, www.sport-faisst.de.

Cross-Country Skiing: Baiersbronn has 10 cross-country skiing tracks, ranging from 1.2 to 4.2 miles. Most are relatively easy and some are floodlit. More tracks are available in nearby Freudenstadt and the Schwarzwald-Hochstraße.

Downhill Skiing: Eight ski lifts operate in Baiersbronn, ranging from 720 to 2,247 ft. Seven of the slopes are floodlit. Another 18 lifts operate along the Schwarzwald-Hochstraße, with the four at Mehliskopf (up to 2,952 ft) particularly popular (see *Baden-Baden*).

Ice Skating: Skating is often possible on some ponds, but from mid-November until early April, the **Eislaufhalle** (Indoor Ice Skating Rink), ☎ 07442-7702, is in operation. It is open on weekdays from 2 to 9 pm, and weekends from 10 am to 7 pm.

Tobogganing: Baiersbronn has two short, 492-ft courses. Nearby Freudenstadt has three, including a 1,312-ft course.

Where to Stay & Eat

The **Traube Tonbach Hotel** is one of the most famous in Germany. This luxury hotel is quietly located at the end of the road leading up the Tonbach Valley. Rooms are large and comfortable with stylish furniture. A large spa area adds to the appeal. In summer, red geraniums lavishly color the balconies. The hotel has four restaurants on-site. Chef Harald Wohlfard, has kept the **Schwarzwaldstube** (€€€€) at the top of the league and has

been awarded with a Michelin three-star rating for several decades. French food and his own creations are served in luxurious surroundings. The **Köhlerstube**

Traube Tonbach Hotel

(€€€-€€€€) has a more country-house style and serves international dishes and nouvelle cuisine.

Compiling a list of Germany's best restaurants by combining the ratings of seven gourmet guides, the Schwarzwaldstube here came out on top and the Köhlerstube ranked a creditable 69th.

The ambiance in the rustic **Bauernstube** (€€-€€€€) is more relaxed. Regional specialties are served. All these restaurants have excellent wine lists and service. Reservations are advisable. Tonbachstraße 237, 72270 Baiersbronn-Tonbach, ☎ 07442-4920, fax 07442-492-692, www.traube-tonbach.de. (€€€€)

Things are equally refined at the modern **Hotel Bareiss**. This luxury hotel has large rooms with balconies and perfect views of the Black Forest.

Hotel Bareiss

The huge spa area has an array of indoor and outdoor pools. The **Restaurant Bareiss** (€€€€) has two Michelin stars, although other gourmets rate it higher than the Schwarzwaldstube. It serves French and Mediterranean cuisine in an elegant atmosphere. The **Kaminstube** (€€€-€€€€) has a fine country house-style décor and serves international cuisine. The **Dorfstube** (€€-€€€) is more rustic, with solid wood furniture. It serves regional specialties and is very popular. All restaurants here have excellent service and superb wine lists. Reservations are recommended. Gärtenbuhlweg 14, 72270 Baiersbronn-Mitteltal, ☎ 07442-470, fax 07442-47-320, www.bareiss.com. (€€€€)

Romantik Hotel Sackmann

The **Romantik Hotel Sackmann** is beautifully located in a building typical of the region with many balconies and flowerpots. Rooms are comfortable and service excellent. The **Schlossberg Restaurant** (€€€-€€€€) has a Michelin star and serves nouvelle cuisine but with strong Euro-Asian influences. It seats only 24 so reservations are advisable. Murgtalstraße 602, 72270

Baiersbronn-Schwarzenberg, ☎ 07447-2890, fax 07447-298-400, www.hotel-sackmann.de. (€€-€€€)

The **Hotel Forsthaus Auerhahn** is beautifully located in a quiet, somewhat isolated valley inside a former forester's house. Rooms are comfortable and well equipped. The spa area is worthy of a much more expensive establishment. Fam Zepf, 72270 Baiersbronn-Hinterlangenbach, ☎ 07447-9340, fax 07447-934-199, www.forsthaus-auerhahn.de. (€€-€€€)

Hotel Forsthaus Auerhahn

■ Camping

Camping Langenwald has excellent facilities and space for 100 campers. Bicycles can be rented on-site. It is open from Easter to October. Strassburger Straße 167, 72250 Freudenstadt, ☎ 07441-2862, www.camping-langenwald.de.

Königskanzel Hallwangen, in the nearby town of Dornstetten, is an equally excellent camping site. It has 150 lots and very good facilities. Bicycles can be rented on-site. The swimming pool is not particularly large, but is solar-heated. It is open year-round. Fam Eiermann, 72280 Dornstetten, ☎ 07443-6730, fax 07443-4574, www.camping-koenigskanzel.de.

Kinzig Valley

The Kinzig Valley forms the natural division between the south and northern Black Forest regions. The upper parts of the valley are the most frequented, especially by travelers en route from the Freudenstadt area to Triberg and Titisee in the south. Highlights include the Alpirsbach Monastery and the open-air museum near Hausach in the Gutach Valley.

■ Information Sources

Tourist Information: Werbegemeinschaft Kinzigtal, Hauptstraße 41, 77709 Wolfach, ☎ 07834-835-353, www.kinzigtal.de, has information on all towns in the valley.

Kloster Alpirsbach

Alpirsbach

The Benedictine **Kloster Alpirsbach** (Monastery), Klosterplatz, ☎ 0744-951-6281, www.alpirsbach.de, was founded in 1095. The first church was consecrated in 1099 and the Torturm (Gate Tower) survived from this structure. The Romanesque parts of the St Nicolas Church date from 1130, while the Gothic parts are mainly late 15th century. The wall paintings in the middle altar niche of the east apses are original 13th-century (the light switch is on the left of the niche). The sacristy is from the first part of the 13th century and one of the oldest Gothic works in Germany. The richly decorated Late Gothic cloisters south of the church are surrounded by late-15th-century structures. The introduction of the Reformation spelled the end for the Benedictine order here, but it was used as a Protestant institution up to 1807. Opening hours are mid-March to October daily, 9:30 am to 5 pm (Sundays only from 11 am), and from November to mid-March, Sunday to Monday, 1 to 3 pm. Admission is €2.50.

Alpirsbach Klosterbräu beer is famous not only in town but across the region and beyond. The **Brauerei-Museum** (Brewery Museum), ☎ 07444-67-146, is a block from the Monastery and guided tours of the facilities are available on weekends at 3 pm.

■ Cultural Events

Alpirsbacher Kreuzgangkonzerte (Cloister Concerts), ☎ 07444-951-6281, www.kreuzgang-konzerte.de, are held during summer. They attract orchestras from all over Europe and the focus is classical music. Other concerts are also held throughout the year, mostly in the church.

Schiltach

Schiltach

Schiltach is a small village at the confluence of the Kinzig and Schiltach rivers. It has a beautiful town panorama with many half-timbered buildings in an outstanding state of preservation. The main road passes it by – turn off at either end of the tunnels.

The most beautiful area is the **Marktplatz** (Market Square), which is unusual in that it slopes steeply. It is surrounded by mostly half-timbered buildings as well as the painted, **Early Renaissance Rathaus** (1593). The market fountain is from 1751 and the **Gasthof Adler** dates from 1604. The **Museum am Markt**, Marktplatz 13, ☎ 07836-5875, explains the history of the town. It is open daily from April to October, 11 am to 4 pm. Admission is free.

The **Gerberviertel** (Tanners' Quarter), often flooded in the past, is currently in a good state of repair. The traditional industries were tanning and rafting. Trees were cut and bound together in rafts and then the local young men would float them down to the Rhine and often all the way to Amsterdam. It was a well-paid profession but risky. The **Schüttesägemuseum**, Haupstraße 1, ☎ 07836-5850, is housed in a former water-driven sawmill and recalls the industries from the past. The waterwheel is 23.6 ft in diameter. It is open from Easter to October, Tuesday to Sunday, 11 am to 5 pm. Machines are demonstrated Friday afternoons from 3 pm. Admission is free.

■ Where to Eat

Café Kaffeebohne, Marktplatz, ☎ 07836-1200, is on the Market Square itself. It serves exquisite cakes and smaller meals. (€-€€)

Hausach

Near Hausach, in the Gutach Valley is the **Schwarzwälder Freilichtmuseum Vogtsbauernhof** (Black Forest Open Air Museum), on the B33, 77793 Gutach, ☎ 07831-93-560, www.vogtbauernhof.org. It is one of the most popular destinations in the region. At its center is the large, original farmhouse of the Vogt farm, dating from 1570. It is surrounded by some 25 other buildings, mostly farmhouses moved here from other parts of the Black Forest. The traditional life of the region is demonstrated in the museums with different themes covered in each building. Opening hours are daily from end of March to early November, 9 am to 6 pm. Admission is €4.50.

Haslach

Bollenhut

Haslach has a beautifully preserved, mainly 18th-century town center. However, the sight most visitors come to see is the **Schwarzwälder Trachtenmuseum** (Black Forest National Dress Museum), Im Alten Kapuzinerkloster, ☎ 07832-706-172. The museum exhibits the different *Trachten* (traditional clothes) worn in the various regions of the Black Forest. The most famous is the Bollenhut, the hat with red or black balls, worn by women in the Gutach area. It is open April to mid-October, from Tuesday to Saturday, 9 am to 5 pm, and Sundays, 10 am to 5 pm; mid-October to March, Tuesday to Friday, 10 am to noon and 1 to 5 pm. Admission is €2.

Triberg Area

Triberg is Black Forest tourism central. It is full of souvenir shops and restaurants willing to dish out the authentic Black Forest experience. For independent travelers it is generally best to eat and stay elsewhere.

■ Information Sources

Tourist Office: The tourist information office is in the Kurhaus, Luisenstraße 10, 78098 Triberg, ☎ 07722-953-230, www.triberg.de.

■ Transportation

Although Triberg is a stop on the Intercity train line connecting Offenburg and Konstanz, trains are infrequent. The local bus network is better developed but it is generally easier to use a car in this area. A large number of visitors are on organized bus trips.

■ Sightseeing

Germany's highest **waterfall** is in Triberg. Three well-marked paths, usually crowded, lead from the town center to the falls, where the Gutach River tumbles 534 ft in seven cascades. The shortest route takes about half an hour from the bottom gate to the top of the falls and back. The falls attract a half-million visitors annually. From April to October the waterfalls are lit until midnight. During winter, two routes are lit up to 10 pm. Admission to the falls is €1.50.

Also in the heart of town is the **Schwarzwaldmuseum** (Black Forest Museum), Wallfahrtstraße 4, ☎ 07722-4434, www.schwarzwaldmuseum.de, with exhibitions of typical items such as cuckoo clocks, mechanical instruments, and traditional dress. It is open from 10 am to 5 pm, daily from April to mid-November, and Tuesday to Sunday from mid-December to March. Admission is €3.

Maria in der Tanne, ☎ 07722-9532-3031, is a lovely Baroque pilgrimage church built around 1700. The high altar and pulpit are especially worth seeing. The church is on the edge of town on the road to Furtwangen. It can also easily be reached on one of the walks from the waterfalls.

Shopping

Triberg is a good area to buy cuckoo clocks, and any other Black Forest kitsch. **Haus der 1000 Uhren**, An der B33, 78098 Triberg, ☎ 07722-96-300, www.houseof1000clocks.com, is one of the largest sellers of Black Forest clocks. It sells the complete range from items for around €15 to grandfather clocks costing thousands of euros. Worldwide shipping can be arranged and the prices quoted to include all handling, customs, and delivery charges. The main shop is on the B33 near Triberg en route to Hornberg. A smaller shop is in Triberg itself at the crossing below the entrance to the waterfalls. Opening hours are Monday to Saturday from 9 am to 5 pm.

THE ORIGINS OF THE CUCKOO CLOCK

Through the centuries, the watchmakers of the Black Forest produced many types of clocks, but none more famous or more often associated with the area than the cuckoo clock. The first clocks using the two-tone sound of the cuckoo were produced around 1730 – argument still rages about whether it happened in Schönwald or Neukirch. The cuckoo clock in the form known today is more recent – it was first produced in 1850 after a competition to find a design that would be more popular.

An alternative is **Eble Uhren-Park**, Schonachbach 27, ☎ 07722-96-220, www.uhren-park.de, an enormous souvenir and clock sales center. Opening hours are daily from 9 am to 6 pm (from 10 am on Sunday).

Adventures

■ On Wheels

By Train: The **Schwarzwaldbahn** (Black Forest Train) runs from Offenburg to Konstanz on the Bodensee. The whole journey is beautiful but nowhere more so than the 15.6-mile stretch between Hornberg and St Georgen. This stretch has an altitude difference of 2,198 ft, a maximum gradient of up to 20%, and 39 tunnels. Normal trains use this line and cover the stretch from Hornberg to St Georgen via Triberg in 20 minutes. If you're planning a short round-trip, bear in mind that both Hornberg and Triberg stations are completely lifeless, with nothing to do, if the return connection is missed.

Where to Stay & Eat

■ Triberg

The **Romantik Parkhotel Wehrle** is a refined establishment with its own private park. Rooms are individually furnished with modern or antique furniture. The **Ochsenstube Restaurant** (€€-€€€€) serves international and regional cuisine in a stylish, wood-paneled setting. The rustic **Alte Schmiede Restaurant** (€€) serves mainly local dishes. Gartenstraße 24, 78098 Triberg, ☎ 07722-86-020, fax 07722-860-290, www.parkhotel-wehrle.de (€€€-€€€€)

Best Western Schwarzwald Residenz uses light-colored, natural wood in the functional, yet comfortable rooms. All have balconies. The **restaurant** (€€-€€€) serves international and regional cuisine, but is open only for dinner. Bürgermeiseter-De-Pellegrine-Straße 20, 78098 Triberg, ☎ 07722-96-230, fax 07722-962-365, www.bestwestern.de. (€€)

Best Western Schwarzwald Residenz

■ Hornberg

Schloss Hornberg is in a former palace and is an interesting alternative to the traditional Black Forest-style hotels in the region. Rooms are comfortable and stylish; most have excellent views. Auf dem Schlossberg 1, 78132 Hornberg,

Schloss Hornberg

☎ 07833-6841, fax 07833-7231, www.schloss-hornberg.de. (€€)

Furtwangen

Furtwangen is a mainly industrial town but it is well worth stopping here to see the excellent **Deutsches Uhrenmuseum** (German Clock Museum), Robert-Gerwig-Platz 1, 78120 Furtwangen, ☎ 07723-920-117, www.deutsches-uhrenmuseum.de. It is one of the largest clock and watch collections in the world and is easy for even non-enthusiasts to enjoy. It also has an impressive collection of early self-playing musical instruments. Opening hours are daily from April to October, 9 am to 6 pm, and from November to March, 10 am to 5 pm. Admission is €3.

Shopping

Furtwangen is not a particularly good place to buy watches. However, at the end of August each year, Europe's largest **antique watch and clock exchange**, www.antik-uhrenboerse.info, takes place in the school at the Clock Museum. Priority is given to Black Forest clocks, but all kinds of watches and clocks are exhibited and sold as long as they are not new.

Adventures

■ On Foot

About 3.6 miles north of Furtwangen is the **Bregquelle** (Breg Springs), the source of the mighty 1,733-mile Danube River (*Donau* in German). The start of the Danube proper is in

Donaueschingen, about 18 miles southeast. The Bregquelle and the small adjacent **St Martinskapelle** (St Martin's Chapel) are popular stops on hiking routes that crisscross the area.

Freiburg im Breisgau

Freiburg is a beautiful city in the southern Black Forest. It has a population of around 200,000 but somehow manages to maintain the unhurried charm of a small town. Its location between the Rhine plains and the western edge of the Black Forest assures a mild climate. Spring comes early; autumn comes late and drags. It claims the sunniest climate in Germany (although since reunification that honor actually belongs to the island of Rügen).

lthough the Old Town suffered severe damage during World War II, it has been lovingly restored. The magnificent Gothic cathedral is the main sight but the entire Old Town invites to wander and explore. Rather unusually for a city of this size, many of the Old Town's streets still have "Bächle," little channels with water. In summer, children of all ages cool off in the water. According to legend, if you step in a Bächle by mistake you shall return to Freiburg.

Information Sources

Tourist Office: Information is available from Freiburg Wirtschaft und Touristik, Rotteckring 14, 79098 Freiburg, ☎ 0761-3881-880, www.freiburg.de.

Sightseeing

■ Münsterplatz

Freiburg's best-known sight is the magnificent **Münster**, Münsterplatz. Small parts of the Romanesque church built around 1200 survived, but most of the building is Gothic. Construction of the Gothic structure started in 1354, but it was only consecrated in 1513. The belfry is housed in a delicately crafted openwork spire of stone. It has been described as the most beautiful tower in Christianity. The abundant use of gargoyles is a constant source of amusement – look out for the one showing his rear, confirming that the medieval church was not as prudish as commonly thought. The interior is bright with several important art works. Some of the windows in the south transept date from the 13th century. The 380-ft tower can be ascended, via 328 steps, for wonderful views of Breisgau and the Vosges Mountains in France. The church is open Monday to Saturday from 10 am to 5 pm, and Sunday from 1 to 7:30 pm. The tower can be ascended up until 5 pm.

Several restaurants are housed in the buildings facing the church. The most beautiful

Münster (Florian K)

of these is the arcaded, red **Historisches Kaufhaus** (Historic Department Store), erected in 1522-32. It was used by foreign traders in the city. The statues adorning the front of the building are Habsburg emperors.

Historisches Kaufhaus (Dieter Salomon)

The 18th-century, Baroque **Wetzingerhaus** houses the **Museum für Stadtgeschichte** (Local History). The magnificent Baroque staircase is especially worth seeing. Opening hours are Tuesday to Sunday from 10 am to 5 pm. Admission is free.

Nearby is the 1733 **Alte Wache** (Old Guard House). It currently houses a wine shop with tasting opportunities for Baden wines.

At the south end of the square is the Baroque archbishop's palace and next to it the **Mittelalterliches Foltermuseum** (Medieval Torture Museum), Münsterplatz 12, ☎ 0761-292-1900, www.foltermuseum-freiburg.de, which takes a serious look at justice in the Middle Ages. Popular exhibits include chastity belts, a guillotine, and instruments of shame. Opening hours are daily from 11 am to 6 pm (opening at 10 am from June to August). Admission is €4.10.

■ Augustinerplatz

A former Augustinian monastery houses the **Augustiner-museum**, Augustinerplatz 1, ☎ 0761-201-2531, www.augustinermuseum.de. The museum has a significant collection of regional art from the ninth century to the present. The High Gothic cloisters are also worth seeing. Opening hours are Tuesday to Sunday, 10 am to 5 pm. Admission is free.

Nearby is the romantic **Schwabentor** (Swabian Gate) dating from the mid-13th century but restored in 1954. The statue above the arch reminded travelers that they were leaving Freiburg's jurisdiction. Upper floors house the small **Zinnfigurenklause** (Tin Figures Collection), ☎ 0761-383-315, www.zinnfigurenklause.de. It has over 6,000 figures displayed in 17 dioramas with 24 castles from the region. It is open May to October from Tuesday to Friday, 2:30 to 5 pm, and weekends, noon to 2 pm. Admission is €1.20.

■ Rathausplatz

Rathausplatz

The Rathausplatz (Town Hall Square) is a lovely area of the Old Town with chestnut tress, outdoor cafés and, of course, the Rathaus itself. The **Neues Rathaus** (New Town Hall) was constructed in 1901 by connecting two 16th-century buildings. The small Glockenspiel (carillon) plays daily at 12:03. The red, Late Gothic **Altes Rathaus** was destroyed in World War II but reconstructed to resemble its original mid-16th-century form.

Just north of the St Martin Church is the **Haus zum Walfisch** (Whale House). Most of this 1516 building, where the humanist Erasmus once lived, was destroyed in the war, but the oriel and the richly ornamented Gothic doors are original.

■ Schauinsland

Although not within the Freiburg city limits, the locals consider the 4,211-ft Schauinsland peak as their own. The **Bergwelt Schauinslandbahn** (cable car), Im Bohrer 63, 79289 Horben bei Freiburg, ☎ 0761-292-930, www.bergwelt-schauinsland. com, takes visitors up to near the peak. At 2.1 miles, it is the longest Umlaufbahn cable car in Germany and lifts visitors up 2,446 ft in 15 minutes. From the mountain station at 4,000 ft, it is a short walk to the peak. Lovely views are available from the top. Many walks, scooter rides, and other adventures start from here.

The cable car operates daily from May to June, 9 am to 5 pm (6 pm on weekends), from June to September, 9 am to 6 pm, and from October to April, 9:30 am to 5 pm. Round-trips cost €10.20 for adults, €5.60 for children, bicycles, and dogs. Combination tickets with adventures are available.

By public transportation, it can be reached from Freiburg on S-Bahn 4; change at Günterstal to Bus 21.

Shopping

Most of the Old Town is filled with shops of all kinds and sizes. The heart of the shopping area is the intersection of Kaiser Joseph and Bertoldstraße. The Markthalle (Market Hall) is in Kaiser Josephstraße just before the Martinstor – this area has many restaurants and specialty stores.

Next to the Minster in the Alten Wache is the **Haus der Badischen Weine**, Münsterplatz. It sells wine from the Baden region and tasting is available.

Adventures

■ On Foot

Town Walks: The tourist information office offers a wide range of guided city walks. Tours are generally two hours and are often available in English.

The more energetic can join a free guided jog through the city. The **Morgenlauf-Treff** (morning-run meeting), ☎ 0761-202-3426, www.morgenlauf-treff.de, meets on Monday, Wednesday, and Friday at 6:45 am at the main station for a three- or six-mile guided jog through the city.

■ On Wheels

By Scooter (Roller): From the peak of Schauinsland, a 4.8-mile downhill run can be done on 26-inch-wheel scooters – the minimum age is 12 years. It requires precious little effort, except for the hand-operated brakes. Combination tickets, including the scooter, safety equipment, and cable car ride up, are available from the bottom station of the cable car. For information, contact **Bikers Paradise KG**, Im Bohrer 63, 79289 Horben, ☎ 07602-920-313, www.downhillrollerstrecke.de. Opening hours are from May to October on Friday and weekends, 10 am to 6 pm, and from June to early September daily at the same hours. The course is closed during heavy rain.

■ In the Air

Flugschule Dreyeckland, Freiburger Straße 5, 79199 Kirchzarten, ☎ 07661-627-140, www.flugschule-dreyeckland.de, arranges hang-gliding and paragliding jumps in the region.

■ On Snow

Tobogganing: The preferred site for tobogganing is on top of Schauinsland. From the top station of the cable car, it is about a 120-yard walk to the **Rodellift**, ☎ 07602-920-313, www.rodellift.de, which pulls sleds up to the start of the 700-ft-long slope. Combination tickets including the cable car and rental equipment are available. If snow permits, it is open Tuesday to Friday from 3 to 5 pm and weekends from 10 am to 5 pm.

Where to Stay & Eat

The top temporary address in Freiburg is the luxury **Colombi-Hotel**, halfway between the station and Münster. It is family-run and offers excellent service. Rooms

Colombi-Hotel

are stylish and very comfortable. The Michelin star **Colombi Restaurant** (€€€€) serves international cuisine in a luxurious setting. Reservations are recommended. The **Hans Thomas-Stube** (€€-€€€) serves nouvelle cuisine and regional specialties in an original 18th-century wood-paneled setting. Rotteckring 16, 79098 Freiburg, ☎ 0761-21-060, fax 0761-31-410, www.colombi.de. (€€€€)

The **Ringhotel zum Roten Bären** claims to be the oldest guesthouse in Germany with the building dating back to 1120 and the guesthouse tradition to 1311. It is in the Old Town between the Münster and the Schwabentor. The

Ringhotel zum Roten Bären

rooms are comfortable and adapted to the needs of the modern traveler. The **restaurant** (€€-€€€) serves local specialties. Oberlinden 12, 79098 Freiburg, ☎ 0761-387-870, fax 0761-387-8717, www.rote-baeren.de. (€€€)

Oberkirchs Weinstuben

The **Oberkirchs Weinstuben** is next to the Münster and many rooms have views of the church and square. Rooms are comfortably furnished with either modern or country-style furniture. The popular, rustic **restaurant** (€€) serves hearty, regional cuisine. Münsterplatz 22, 79098 Freiburg, ☎ 0761-202-6969, fax 0761-202-6869, www.hotel-oberkirch.de. (€€€)

The **Intercity Hotel** is at the main train station. Like others in this group, the focus is on the business traveler, with well-equipped, modern rooms. The room key gives access to free public transportation.

Bismarckallee 3, 79098 Freiburg, ☎ 0761-38-000, fax 0761-380-0999, www.intercityhotel.com. (€€€)

The **Schwarzwälder Hof** is a simple hotel and a good budget choice in the Old Town area. Rooms are mostly furnished in light wood. Herrenstraße 34, 79098 Freiburg, ☎ 0761-30-030, fax 0761-380-3135. (€€)

The best choice for food near the Münster is the Michelin star **Zur Traube**, Schusterstraße 17, ☎ 0761-32-190. The restaurant is rustic, yet elegant. Food is mainly light regional and Italian dishes. (€€€€)

Near the Colombi is the fashionably modern **Basho-An**, Am Predigertor 1, ☎ 0761-285-3405, serving sushi and other Japanese dishes. (€€)

The **Ganter Brauereiausschank**, Münsterplatz 18, ☎ 0761-34-367, is an informal restaurant in front of the Münster. It has rich wood paneling and serves local specialties. (€-€€)

Hoch Schwarzwald

The southern Black Forest is sparsely populated and very popular, especially with German families for longer holidays. Vacation homes are the main accommodations. For the foreign traveler, the area is of less interest and most sights can easily be seen on a driving day-trip from Freiburg. An interesting circular drive could include Titisee, Schluchsee, St Blasien, and the views from either Feldberg or Mt Belchen.

Titisee-Neustadt

■ Information Sources

Tourist Office: Tourist Information Titisee-Neustadt, 79815 Titisee-Neustadt, ☎ 07651-98-040, www.titsee.de.

■ Sightseeing

The **Titisee** is a small, beautiful lake. It is at the crossing of many tourist routes and is very popular. Serenity is not easily found here, even in the off-season. In the high season, it can become unpleasantly crowded. It is best avoided on summer weekends when no bus passes through the Black Forest without spewing its passengers out here for a while.

The Titisee was formed by a moraine barrier in the Ice Age. It is 130 ft deep, but only 1.2 miles long and 820 ft wide – leading to the observation (almost true) that the car park in summer is slightly bigger than the lake.

■ Adventures

 Countryside Hikes: One of the most beautiful hikes in all of the Black Forest is in the **Wutachschlucht** (Wutach Gorge). This gorge near Titisee has somehow managed to remain untamed and, as a nature conservation area since the 1930s, may succeed in remaining that way. The gorge itself is only accessible on foot, although crossroads make access by car and bus easy at various points along the route. The path is 19 miles long, and generally divided into three equally long sections requiring about three hours of hiking each.

 By Bicycle: An interesting, circular 58-mile cycling route, taking five hours, starts from Titisee. It passes the Schluchsee, St Blasien, Boll, and Lenzkirchen at the edges of the unspoiled Wutach Gorge, before returning to Titisee via Neustadt.

Bicycles can be rented from **Ski-Hirt**, Wilhelm-Stahl-Straße 6, Neustadt, ☎ 07651-92280, www.ski-hirt.de; or in Titisee from **Bootsvermietung Drubba**, Seestraße 37, ☎ 07651-981-200, www.drubba.com.

 By Train: About 24 miles east of Titisee is one of Germany's most interesting train journeys. The **Wutachbahn**, also known as the Sauschwänzle, covers 15 miles from Blumberg-Zollhaus to Weizen (nine miles by road) making four 180° turns and one 360° turn (mostly inside a tunnel), to cross the mountains. This strange track, of no economic value, was constructed at the end of the 19th century to allow the easier east-west movement of troops in southern Germany, without crossing the Swiss cantons north of the Rhine, in case of war with France. Although the track was used during both World Wars, in neither case did it contribute to troop movements as originally envisioned.

From May to October, steam and diesel engines pull museum trains along this track on a journey of just over an hour. Trains run at 10 am on Wednesday, Saturday, and Sunday. On most Sundays, afternoon trains run also at 2 pm. During the high season afternoon trains run on Saturday and Wednesday as well, and occasionally on Thursday too. The round-trip takes 90 minutes (€13, or €10 one-way). For reservations contact Stadt Blumberg, Postfach 120, 78170 Blumberg, ☎ 07702-51-200, www.sauschwaenzlebahn.de. Information is also available from the Wutachbahn Supporters' Club, www.ig-wtb.de.

Boating: Rowboats, pedal boats, and electrical boats can be rented from **Fa. Drubba**, Seestraße 37, ☎ 07651-981-200, www.drubba.com; or from **Firma Schweizer**, Seerundweg 1, ☎ 07651-8214, www.bootsbetrieb-schweizer-titisee.de.

■ Where to Stay & Eat

Treschers Schwarzwaldhotel am See is perfectly located right next to the Titisee. The large, comfortable rooms are furnished in country house style furniture. The **restaurant** (€€-€€€) serves a wide range of inter-

Treschers Schwarzwaldhotel am See

national and regional dishes and offers a good view of the lake. Seestraße 10, 79822 Titisee, ☎ 07651-8050, fax 07651-8116, www.schwarzwaldhotel-trescher.de. (€€€-€€€€)

Maritim Titiseehotel

The **Maritim Titiseehotel** is another first-class hotel next to the lake. Rooms are comfortably furnished. The **Viertaler Restaurant** (€€-€€€) has international cuisine and local specialties, with a marvelous panoramic view of the lake.

Baden-Württemberg

Seestraße 16, 79822 Titisee, ☎ 07651-8080, fax 07651-808-603, www.maritim.de. (€€€)

The **Ringhotel Parkhotel Waldeck** is across the road from the Kurpark, about a hundred yards inland. It is a large, typical Black Forest building and has various categories of rooms. All are comfortable and service is friendly. The **restaurant** (€€-€€€) serves regional and Mediterranean cuisine.

Ringhotel Parkhotel Waldeck

Parkstraße 4, 79822 Titisee, ☎ 07651-8090, fax 07651-80-999, www.parkhotelwaldeck.de. (€€-€€€)

■ Camping

Camping Bankenhof is on the banks of the Seebach stream, about 1,300 ft from the banks of the lake. It has 190 lots and is open year-round. There is a special section for young campers about 1,000 ft from the main site. Bicycle rental is available on-site. Camping Bankenhof, Bruderhalde 31, 79822 Titisee, ☎ 07652-1351, fax 07652-5907, www.bankenhof.de.

Feldberg

Feldbergbahn

The highest peak in the Schwarzwald is the 4,897-ft Feldberg. With a million and a half annual visitors, it is one of the most popular sites in the region and reasonably easy to reach. This is a nature conservation area and strict rules forbid wandering off the marked paths – it was the first nature conservation area in Germany with its own ranger.

The **Feldbergbahn** (cable car/chair lift), ☎ 07655-8019, operates from Feldberg town to the 4,749-ft Seebuck, where there is a monument to Bismarck and a TV tower. A further easy 45-minute walk leads to the peak itself. From the top of Feldberg, the views are fantastic. On a clear day the Alps, as well as the Vosges Mountains and Schwäbische Alb, can be seen.

The Feldbergbahn operates daily from 9 am to 5 pm. In winter, it is a *Sesselbahn*, with six seats for skiers, and in summer a *Kabinenbahn*, with a cabin for eight persons. In summer, bicycles, wheelchairs, and strollers can use the cable car as well. Even in summer, it is usually cool and windy at the top. Round-trips cost €7.

Schluchsee

Sightseeing

 The Schluchsee (lake) was originally a glacial lake but was dammed in the 1930s to become the largest single body of water in the Black Forest. It has a health resort on its shores, but most popular are activities on the water.

The lake is only 4.2 miles long, nine miles wide, and 200 ft deep, but the height difference from here to the Rhine is 2,034 ft. As a result, several hydro-electrical plants are between the lake and the Rhine. The villages on the northeastern bank of the lake are typical getaway towns with hotels, health clinics, and outdoor sports activities.

Adventures

■ On Water

 Boating: Boats of all kinds can be rented from several companies along the shores of the lake, including: **A Schlachter**, Wolfsgrundbucht and Strandbad Schluchsee, ☎ 07656-512; **G Müller**, Staumauer Blasiwald, ☎ 07656-850; and **E Pohl**, Segelschule Aha, ☎ 07656-366. The latter also offers sailing courses and rents out windsurfing boards.

Fishing: Already in the 19th century, the Schluchtsee was known for its good fishing and attracted anglers from as far away as England to this rather forgotten corner of Germany.

Fishing is still allowed, but it requires a permit (*Angelkarte*) – available from the tourist office, the kiosk at the dam wall, and several boat rental companies.

Where to Stay & Eat

The **Hotel Vier Jahreszeiten** is a first-class hotel with modern, comfortable rooms. The spa and beauty treatment area is large and indoor golf is available too. The rustic **Am Kachelofen Restaurant** (€-€€) serves regional specialties and the **Bella Vista** (€€), Mediterranean and especially Italian cuisine. Am Reisenbühl 13, 79859 Schluchsee, ☎ 07656-700, fax 07656-70-323, www.vjz.de. (€€€€)

■ Camping

Wolfsgrund has 300 lots and is right on the lake, with a beach in front of the site. It has good facilities and is open year-round. Campingplatz Wolfsgrund, Im Wolfsgrund, 79853 Schluchsee, ☎ 07656-7732, fax 07656-7759, www.schluchsee.de. Mobile homes can park free for one night in the parking lot at Aqua Fun.

St Blasien

Information Sources

Tourist Information: Tourist Information St Blasien-Menzenschwand, Postfach 1140, 79829 St Blasien, ☎ 07672-41-460, www.st-blasien.de.

Sightseeing

The main reason to visit St Blasien is to see the third-largest dome in Europe. The **Dom Zu St Blasien** (Cathedral), ☎ 076272-678, was consecrated in 1781. Back then, as now, it was the largest dome in Germany and totally out of context with its surroundings. It overpowers the town.

The cathedral was erected in a Classical style to replace the Benedictine monastery's previous church that burned down in 1768. The prior at the time had visited Rome and Paris and wanted the new church to be a Pantheon north of the Alps, with some elements from Les Invalides.

Dom Zu St St Blasien

Most of the church is under the enormous 118-ft diameter dome. The rectangular choir is the same length but seems smaller. The weight of the cupola rests on 20 Corinthian columns rather than on the outside walls. The interior is mostly white with a few light Baroque decorations.

Following secularization in 1806, the church was nearly razed for budgetary reasons. A fire in 1874 destroyed most of it but it was rebuilt and restored in 1977 to its present form.

Kolleg St Blasien, ☎ 07672-270, the school next to the cathedral, has massive proportions – around 300 by 600 ft. It houses one of Germany's top private schools and is only open for a guided tour on Tuesday afternoons.

Cultural Events

The **St Blasien Klosterkonzerte** (Monastery Concerts), ☎ 07672-270, www.kloster-konzerte.de, are held, mostly on Thursday evenings, in the Festival Hall of the former monastery. Tickets are available from the monastery as well as from many tourism offices in neighboring towns.

Adventures

■ On Wheels

By Bicycle: A lovely circular 54-mile, five-hour, cycling route runs through St Blasien, to the Rhine River and then back via the Wehr Valley, Todmoos and Bernau. It passes through Bad Säckingen, which has the longest wooden bridge in Europe.

■ Dogsled Races

Near St Blasien, in the small town of Todtmoos, international **husky sled dog races** are held each year, usually in February. Details on this Jack London experience in the middle of Europe are available from Todtmoos Tourist Information,

Wehratalstraße 19, 79682 Todtmoos, ☎ 07674-90-600, www. todtmoss.net.

Where to Eat

 Several restaurants face the cathedral, but for small meals and excellent cakes it is worth crossing the stream to **Café Ell**, Hauptstraße 15, ☎ 07672-2023. Although its interior is thoroughly modern, it has been in business for more than a century. (€-€€)

Mt Belchen

Mt Belchen, at 4,637 ft, is the third-highest peak in the Black Forest, but for many it is the most beautiful. The views from the stop can't be beat, even by the higher Feldberg. It has been a nature conservation area since the 1940s and some of the flora are usually found only in the Alps.

Prior to December 2001, it was possible to drive up to the top of the mountain. However, since then the road has been closed to private vehicles and the only ways up are on foot (about two hours) or, much easier, cable car.

The more than half-mile-long **Belchen-Seilbahn**, ☎ 07673-888-280, www.belchen-seilbahn.de, lifts visitors up 859 ft from the *Talstation* (Valley Station) to the *Bergstation* (Mountain Station) at 4,448 ft. The Bergasthaus (restaurant) is the highest in Baden-Württemberg. From here, it is a 15-minute stroll to the peak. The views are magnificent – on a clear day, even Mt Blanc can be seen.

Belchen-Seilbahn

The cable car operates daily from 9 am to 5 pm. The gondola takes eight passengers – wheelchairs, bicycles, and strollers are allowed. Round-trip tickets are €5.50.

By public transportation, the *Talstation* (Valley Station) can be reached by bus from Münstertal, with rail connections to Freiburg.

Bavaria

Bavaria is Germany's largest state and the favored vacation destination of both domestic and foreign tourists. No part of the country offers more to visitors than Bavaria. It has a rich cultural heritage, natural beauty, and is a haven for outdoor enthusiasts. For many foreigners this is what Germany is all about – rolling green meadows set off against an Alpine backdrop, small villages with half-timbered houses, Baroque churches with onion-shaped domes, beer, sausages, women in traditional dresses and men in *Lederhosen*. Bavaria is all of that and a lot more....

Munich, the state capital, offers the most to visitors of any city, except Berlin. It has a rich heritage and, despite war damage, many historic buildings, including churches and palaces that testify to its glorious past. It has the largest technology museum in the world and some of the best art galleries in Germany. The English Garden is the largest urban park in Europe. The beer gardens open as soon as the weather is sunny. The historic center is surrounded by a modern city and interesting modern architectural features such as the 1972 Olympic arena with its tent-like glass roof and the BMW headquarters. The wealth of modern Munich is built on high-technology industries and no other German city has a higher concentration of electronic and computer firms.

Franken, the northern part of Bavaria, has an equally impressive cultural heritage. Bamberg, one of the best-preserved historic cities in Germany, and Würzburg used to be centers of

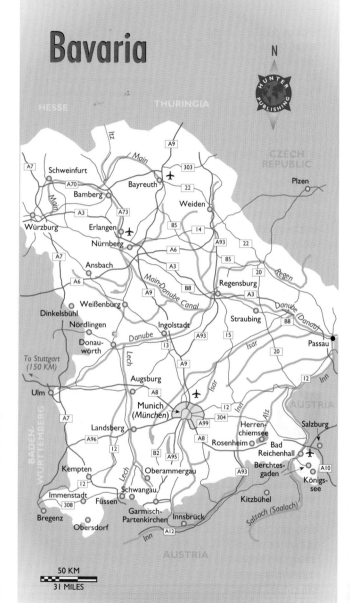

Bavaria

N

HESSE   THURINGIA   CZECH REPUBLIC

Schweinfurt
Bayreuth
Bamberg
Weiden
Plzen
Würzburg
Erlangen
Nürnberg
Ansbach
Regensburg
Weißenburg
Straubing
Dinkelsbühl
Nördlingen
Ingolstadt
Donau-wörth
Passau
To Stuttgart (150 KM)
Augsburg
Ulm
Munich (München)
Landsberg
Herren-chiemsee
Salzburg
Rosenheim
Bad Reichenhall
Kempten
Oberammergau
Berchtes-gaden
Immenstadt
Schwangau
Königs-see
Bregenz
Füssen
Kitzbühel
Garmisch-Partenkirchen
Innsbrück
Obersdorf

BADEN-WÜRTTEMBERG   AUSTRIA

50 KM
31 MILES

© 2007 HUNTER PUBLISHING, INC.

religious power, while Nürnberg was a very important political center long before the Nazis ruined the city's reputation. The Eastern Bavarian Danubian cities of **Regensburg** and **Passau** are often overlooked by the hurried foreign traveler. That's a mistake as both suffered very limited war damage and both have natural beauty in addition to their magnificent historic old towns.

The **Romantic Road**, one of Germany's most popular touring routes, links several romantic sights in the western part of Bavaria. The most famous stop is the completely walled-in medieval town of Rothenburg ob der Tauber, one of the country's most popular sights. At the south end of the route is the fantasy castle Schloss Neuschwanstein that inspired Disney.

Nearby is **Garmisch-Partenkirchen**, which hosted the 1936 Winter Olympics, the Rococo masterpieces at the Ettal Monastery and the Wieskirche, the Schloss Linderhof folly, as well as Zugspitze – Germany's highest mountain.

The **German Alpine Route** runs through the south of Bavaria and passes by some of the most spectacular natural scenery in Germany. It ends at **Berchtesgaden**, which, in addition to the beauty of the mountains and countryside, is also closely associated with Hitler's Berghof mountain retreat.

◆ History

Much of current Bavaria south of the Danube was occupied by the Romans from 15 BC to around 500 AD as the province of Raetia. Following their departure, the Bavarian tribe from Bohemia settled in the eastern parts of the region making Bavaria the oldest continuous political entity in Germany. Christianization followed from the mid-eighth century and Bavaria would be a bastion of the Roman Catholic Church during the Middle Ages. The church is still very influential up to the present day.

Participation in several wars saw Bavaria grow and decline in size, but the trend was mostly upwards. Through opportunistic coalition-forming and side-swapping during the Napoleonic wars, Bavaria doubled in size between 1800 and 1815 and upgraded to a kingdom in 1806. During this period, the areas of Franken and Allgäu were added as well as many Free Imperial Cities.

The Wittelsbach family ruled Bavaria from 1180 to the abolition of the monarchy in 1918. The dukes of the 17th and 18th century generally had good taste in architecture and art and erected many buildings that are now major tourist attractions. The kings of the 19th century were enlightened rulers who continued the art and building tradition of their forebears.

Architectural Tastes (1806-1918)

King Maximilian I (1806-25) favored the Classical style, while his son **Ludwig I** (1825-48) admired classical antiquity. Ludwig built the Pinakothek, Glyptothek, and university in Munich. He also cut the elegant Ludwigstraße through the Old Town. He had a gallery in Schloss Nymphenburg filled with paintings of beautiful women who caught his roving eye. One of them, Lola Montez, a Spanish dancer and opportunist, eventually cost him his throne when her involvement in politics led to a rebel movement. **Maximilian II** (1848-1864) continued the building and generally showed above average good taste.

His son, **Ludwig II** (1864-86), also known as Mad Ludwig, is probably the most famous of all Bavarian kings. He became king at age 18. His follies included Schloss Neuschwanstein, which served as inspiration for the Disney castles, Linderhof, and Herrenchiemsee, which was inspired by Versailles. He died in mysterious circumstances days after being deposed in 1886. He was succeeded by another son of Ludwig I, **Prince Luitpold** (1886-1912), who built the Deutsches Museum and the monumental Prinzregentenstraße. His son, **Ludwig III** (1912-18) was forced to abdicate at the end of World War I.

In the chaotic aftermath of World War I, Bavaria briefly became a Soviet republic before right-wingers took over power. Hitler unsuccessfully attempted a putsch in 1923. As the Nazi party was founded in Bavaria, it was a favorite of many of the top leaders. Hitler had his vacation home in Berchtesgaden and

Munich was declared the Capital of the Movement. Annually huge party rallies were held in Nürnberg.

Following World War II, Bavaria was occupied by American forces. Although an economic powerhouse, the state is relatively conservative, with strong traditional values.

◆ Getting Here & Around

 By Rail: Munich has good high-speed rail connections to other parts of Germany. Most towns in Bavaria can be reached on regional trains, although transfers are often required in Munich.

From **Munich Hauptbahnhof**, at least two trains per hour run to Nürnberg (1h40), Augsburg (40 minutes), Stuttgart (2h20), Frankfurt (less than four hours, but not always direct), and Salzburg (90 minutes to two hours). At least hourly trains are available to Berlin (six to seven hours, mostly not direct) and Hamburg (six hours, mostly direct). Connections to Berlin and other East German cities will improve drastically in coming years as new high-speed rails are added to the network.

Nürnberg is a major railway junction. At least every two hours, an ICE or IC train connects Frankfurt, Würzburg, Nürnberg, Regensburg, and Passau, with the traveling time around an hour in each case. The train continues to Vienna. Bamberg is an hour by train from Würzburg.

 By Road: The Bavarians love their cars – this is the home of both BMW and Audi – and roads are generally in excellent condition. The state has many Autobahnen with large sections having no speed limits. That allows for blistering-fast traveling times between major centers. Driving is probably the easiest and most pleasurable way to enjoy Bavaria.

A quick glance at a Bavarian map confirms that all highways lead to Munich. This allows *Münchner* to get away easily for weekends and daytrips in the countryside. The A8 connects Salzburg and the Berchtesgaden area with Stuttgart, passing Munich and Augsburg en route. The A9 connects Munich and Berlin via Nürnberg. The A95 allows fast access to the excellent skiing area at Garmisch-Partenkirchen. In the north of Bavaria, the A3 from Cologne and Frankfurt passes through

Würzburg, Nürnberg, Regensburg, and Passau before continuing into Austria. Off the Autobahnen, the going is much slower but generally more interesting.

 By Air: Munich International Airport, 85356 Flughafen München, ☎ 089-97-500, www.munich-airport, has established itself as the second-largest airport in the country. It currently serves more European destinations than chronically overcrowded Frankfurt Airport. The airport is easiest to reach by S-Bahn lines S1 and S8, each of which connects to the Hauptbahnhof every 20 minutes. The journey takes 40 minutes and cost €8. Transfer services are available from the airport to all major towns in Bavaria and nearby parts of Austria. A list of the different service providers – most serve only one town – is available from the airport's website. **Frankfurt Airport** (see Frankfurt am Main chapter) is generally the most convenient airport for travelers to Franken, with fast road and rail connections to the main towns in Franken. The Bavarian border is a 30-minute drive from the airport. **Nürnberg Airport**, Flughafenstraße 100, 90411 Nürnberg, ☎ 0911-93-700, www.airport-nuernberg.de, is a small airport but serving a growing number of European destinations. It is reached within 12 minutes by U-Bahn U2 from the Hauptbahnhof, or in 15 minutes by taxi (around €15).

 By Boat: Two major European rivers, the Main and the Danube, flow through Bavaria. A channel connecting the two had been in the pipeline for centuries but was ultimately completed in the 1990s. River cruises on both rivers, usually a week long, are increasingly popular. Passau is a favorite starting and finishing port for cruises into Austria and Hungary.

◆ Information Sources

 Tourist information on the whole of Bavaria is available from Bayern Tourismus Marketing, Postfach 662228, 8121 München, ☎ 0180-585-5050, www.bayern.info.

◆ Munich

Munich (*München* in German) is Germany's third-largest city, with 1.3 million inhabitants, but it is by far the city most Germans claim they would prefer to live in. It is relatively rich with a very high quality of life.

Munich is perhaps most famous for its Oktoberfest and beer in general, but it also has fine museums and a wide range of cultural offerings. The three Pinakotheken form one of the largest art collections in Europe and the Deutsches Museum is one of the largest science and technology museums in the world. Munich has been a royal residence for around seven centuries and has some of the most splendid Baroque palaces in Europe – the Residenz, Schloss Nymphenburg, and Schloss Schließheim. It has a wide variety of architecture, from the old Gothic churches to the modern glass, tent-like roof of the 1972 Olympic Arena and the BMW headquarters.

 Most museums in Munich are free on Sunday!

Information Sources

Tourist Office

 The tourist information office has two branches for casual callers in the Hauptbahnhof and at the Marienplatz. For written or telephone inquiries, contact the Fremdenverkehrsamt München, Sendlinger Straße 1, 80331 München, ☎ 089-2339-6500, www.muenchen.de.

Bavaria

MÜNCHEN WELCOME CARD

The München Welcome Card allows unlimited public transportation in central Munich and reduced admission fees to most museums and many attractions. It costs €6.50 for one day or €16 for three days. A partner ticket, for up to five traveling together, is available for €11 and €23.50 respectively. The card is available from the tourist office and many hotels.

NOT TO SCALE

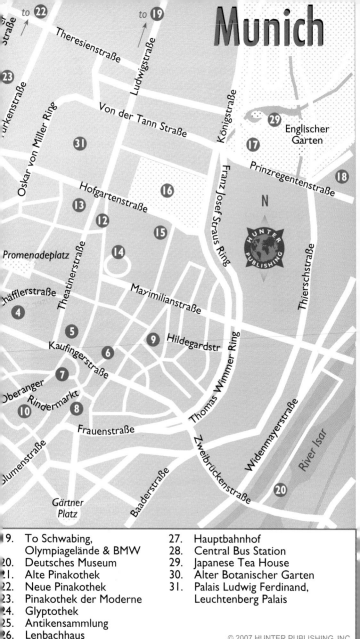

Munich

Transportation

Munich has an excellent public transportation system that combines S-Bahn, U-Bahn, trams, and buses in a single network. Tickets must be validated on the tram or bus and before entering the platform of the S- and U-Bahn. Single and strip tickets are available but day-tickets are more economical if more than two journeys are planned. A day ticket is €4.50 or €7.50 for up to five traveling together. The three-day version costs €11 and €17. 50 respectively.

Sightseeing

Old Town Pedestrian Zone

■ Karlsplatz to Frauenkirche

Approaching the Old Town and pedestrian zone from the main station, the first sights that deliver some impression of what is to follow, are the monumental buildings at **Karlsplatz**. The square is locally known as

Karlstor

Stachus, named after a long-gone inn. The Old Town area is entered via the 14th-century **Karlstor** (Karl's Gate).

The **Bürgersaal** (Citizens' Hall), Neuhauserstraße 14, ☎ 089-219-9720, has a plain exterior but a richly decorated interior. This church was erected on a citizens' initiative as a prayer hall in the early 18th century. The almost crypt-like lower church area has the tomb of Priest Rupert Mayer, a fierce critic of the Nazis who spent many years in Dachau and died shortly after the war. He was declared a saint in 1987. Artistically, the Baroque Oberkirche (Upper Church) is more interesting. It has many Rococo features, although the main decorations were not restored after World War II. This part of the church is open only from 3 to 5 pm. The rest of the church is open daily from around 6:30 am to 7 pm.

Across the road is the **Augustinerbräu** beer cellars – it is the oldest of Munich's famous brewing houses and now houses a popular restaurant and beer garden.

The Jesuit **Michaelskirche** (St Michael's Church), Neuhauserstraße 52, ☎ 089-231-7060, was one of the first and is still the largest Renaissance church north of the Alps. It was erected by Duke Wilhelm V between 1583 and 1597. The impressive three-story gabled façade shows 15 of his forebears, going back to the Agilolfingers. All are overshadowed though by the bronze statue of the Archangel Gabriel, a masterpiece by Hubert Gerhard

Michaelskirche

(1588). The single-nave interior, with a 66-ft-wide cradle vault ceiling, is mostly white and inspired many of the Baroque churches that would soon follow in southern Germany. The crypt has the graves of 41 Wittelsbach rulers. Opening hours are daily from 8 am to 7 pm.

The **Deutsches Jagd- und Fischereimuseum** (German Hunting and Fishing Museum), Neuhauser Straße 2, ☎ 089-220-522, www.jagd-fischerei-museum.de, is in an impressive Gothic former church building. The museum is very popular and displays include stuffed animals, hunting weapons, and the world's largest collection of fishing hooks. Despite the name, many items are of non-German origin. Opening hours are daily from 9:30 am to 5 pm, closing at 9 pm on Thursday. Admission is €3.50.

The two 321-ft copper onion-domed towers of the **Frauenkirche** are the symbols of Munich. The official name Domkirche zu Unserer Lieben Frau (Cathedral of Our Dear Lady), Frauenplatz, ☎ 089-290-0820, never really caught on. The Late Gothic church was erected in 1468-88 and has a simple red brick exterior. Inside, it is bright, with mostly white walls. The church is over 328 ft long and 134 ft wide. Although damaged in World War II, many parts, including the towers, are orig-

Bavaria

inal. The rose windows in the choir of the Annunciation date from 1392. From April to October, Monday to Saturday, 10 am to 5 pm, the south tower elevator (€2) will take you to a viewing platform. Do note that it is 86 steps to the elevator and that the views from St Peter (see below) are better. The church is a popular venue for concerts. Opening hours are from around 8 am to 7 pm.

Frauenkirche from Town Hall

■ **Marienplatz**

Marienplatz

Marienplatz (Mary's Square) is the heart of Munich and the center of most festivals and protest rallies. In 1638, Prince-Elector Maximilian erected the Mariensäule (Mary's Column) to give thanks for the relief of the city from the Swedish threat during the Thirty Years' War. It has a statue of the Virgin made in 1590 by Hubert Gerhard on top of a 36-ft Corinthian column.

The north of the square is occupied by the **Neues Rathaus** (New Town Hall). This Neo-Gothic (1867-1908) monumental building looks a bit out of place in Baroque and Rococo Munich but people got used to it. An elevator (€1.50) to the top of the 262-ft tower is available on weekdays from 9 am to 4 pm, closing at 1 pm on Friday. Particularly popular is the famous **carillon**, with 43 bells the fourth-largest in Europe. At 11 am and noon, and summer at 5 pm as well, it plays a knight's tourna-

Altes Rathaus

ment and local dance with 32 lifesize figures. At 9 pm, the night watchman and *Münchner Kindl* are blessed by an angel.

At the east is the **Altes Rathaus** (Old Town Hall), a Gothic building from 1474. The Rathaus was severely damaged during World War II but restored in simplified form. The Rathaus incorporated a former defense tower that now houses the **Spielzeugmuseum** (Toy Museum), Marienplatz, ☎ 089-294-001, which shows toys from the past two centuries. It is open daily from 10 am to 5:30 pm. Admission is €3.

Close by is the **Alter Hof** (Old Castle), Burgstraße 8, which was the castle of the Wittelsbach rulers from 1253 to 1474. It is currently used for local government offices but it is worth strolling into the courtyard to see the medieval oriel.

The **Peterskirche** (St Peter's Church), Rindermarkt, ☎ 089-260-4828, is the oldest church in Munich. It dates to the 11th century but has style elements of almost every period since. Its main structure is a triple-nave, 13th-

Peterskirche

century Gothic basilica but the interior is mostly Baroque. It is 306 steps to the top of the tower for the best views of Munich and the Alps if the skies are clear (€1.50). Opening hours are Monday to Saturday from 9 am to 6 pm and Sunday from 10 am to 7 pm.

The nearby **Viktualienmarkt** (Victuals Market) has been in operation since 1807. It is a popular spot, with all kinds of people from businessmen to blue color workers grabbing a quick bite to eat or buying fresh produce. The market women are famous for both quick wit and zero tolerance – no self-service here. Do not fret if your school German doesn't work – most non-locals won't understand what they are saying either.

The nearby **Hofbräuhaus** is a legend too. See *Where to Eat* below.

ENTARTETE KUNST (DEGENERATE ART)

In the summer of 1937, while Nazi kitsch went on display in the Haus der Kunst, a separate exhibition of *Entartete Kunst* (Degenerate Art) opened in the Hofgarten. This exhibition included 300 paintings, 25 sculptures, and 400 graphics that the Nazis considered un-German. The exhibition toured Germany and drew huge crowds – two million in Munich alone. Another 16,000 works were then added to the list and many were destroyed, but some were saved by being sold secretly to private and international collectors to earn foreign exchange. The artists themselves were banned from exhibiting, fired from academic posts, and many ended up in concentration camps or fled abroad.

Three blocks southwest of the Marienplatz is the **Münchner Stadtmuseum** (Municipal Museum), St.-Jakobs-Platz 1, ☎ 089-2332-2370, www.stadtmuseum-online.de. It has an eclectic collection ranging from musical instruments and rare movies to puppet theaters and home décor. A star exhibit is the collection of 10 wood-carved, painted and gilded Moriskentänzer (Moorish Dancers) made by Erasmus Grasser in 1480. Opening hours are Tuesday to Sunday from 10 am to 6 pm. Admission is €2.50, free on Sunday.

Nearby, close to the Sendlinger Tor, is the **Asamkirche** (Asam Church), Sendlinger Straße 32. The official name is St Johannes Nepomuk Church but everybody calls it the Asamkirche, named for the two talented Baroque master-builder Asam brothers. Both were multitalented, but Cosmas Damian (1686-1739) specialized in frescoes and his brother

The Asamkirche

Egid Quirin (1692-1750) specialized in sculpture and stucco work. They decorated many Baroque churches in Munich and central Europe. They financed and designed the Asamkirche themselves, which helps to explain the harmony of the interior. It is over-the-top Baroque with no square inch left undecorated and all beautifully integrated. Described as a combination of a fanciful grotto and a court theater, it shows off the absolute skill of the two brothers and serves as a remarkable example of Bavarian Late Baroque. There are only 12 rows of pews but enough art to fill a cathedral. Opening hours are daily from 9 am to 5:30 pm.

■ Odeonsplatz

The roads on either side of the Neues Rathaus eventually lead to the Odeonsplatz. At the east side is the huge Residenz complex – see below. At the south is the **Feldherrnhalle** (Field Marshalls' Portico), erected in the 1840s as a copy of the Loggia dei Lanzi in Florence. It has statues of General Tilly (Thirty Years' War) and General Wrede (Napoleonic Wars) guarded by Bavarian lions.

HITLER'S BEER HALL PUTSCH

In 1923, Adolf Hitler, the leader of a minor right-wing political party, decided to take over power in Munich. After a spirited speech in a beer hall – contrary to popular belief it was the Bürgerbräukeller and *not* the Hofbräuhaus – he and his followers marched through the old city in what was supposed to have been the start of a Fascist march on Berlin similar to Mussolini's earlier successful march on Rome. When troops opened fire on the marchers in Odeonsplatz, Hitler threw himself into the gutter with such force that he dislocated his shoulder and was unable to flee.

Unfortunately, Hitler learned from this experience that grabbing power illegally was not a good idea – a decade later he would still employ illegal means but became dictator legally, i.e., with parliamentary approval. As the Feldherrnhalle bore testimony to the 1923 event, a guard of honor was installed here in the Residenzstraße after the Nazis took power. Passersby, who wanted to avoid the obligatory Nazi salute, took a slight detour through the Viscardigasse to pass on the guard-free Theatinerstraße side of the monument.

The **Theatinerkirche** (Theatine Church, or officially, St Kajetan), Theatinerstraße 22, is an excellent example of Late Baroque architecture. It was built in 1663-88, with the Rococo façade added a century later by Cuveliés. The interior is mostly white and well lit, with a 233-ft cupola. The stuccowork is particularly fine. The crypt contains the graves of 25 members of the Wittelsbach dynasty.

North of the Odeonsplatz is the monumental **Ludwigstraße**, commissioned by King Ludwig I in the early 19th century when he made Munich a major European cultural center. The huge Neo-Renaissance and Neo-Byzantine buildings are interesting but add no life to the area. Once past the Siegestor (Triumphal Arch), the street comes alive as **Leopoldstraße**, lined with cafés and the good life of Bohemian Schwabing.

Residenz

The Wittelsbach family, who ruled Bavaria for 700 years, built the massive Residenz (Residence) complex from 1385 onwards. It has examples of all building styles, with large sections in the Renaissance and Classical styles. The interior, inevitably, also has many Baroque and Rococo rooms. The palace is one of the most important in Germany and, although severely damaged during World War II, it has been restored to its original condition. The complex houses several museums – if time is limited give preference to the Treasury.

The Residenz

The **Schatzkammer der Residenz** (Treasury in the Residence) contains the treasures of the Wittelsbach family collected over a period of 300 years. It comprises eight rooms and is one of the most important collections of its kind in Europe. Included are the crown (1280) of Heinrich II, a bejeweled small statue of St George Slaying the Dragon (1597), and the royal insignia produced in 1807 after Napoleon had elevated Bavaria to a kingdom. Opening hours are daily from April to mid-October, 9 am to 6 pm, and from mid-October to March, 10 am to 4 pm. Admission is €6 and includes an excellent English audio guide. A combination ticket with the Residenzmuseum is €9.

The enormous **Residenzmuseum**, Max-Joseph-Platz 3, ☎ 089-290-671, www.schloesser.bayern.de, comprises around 120 rooms of the former palace. The main attraction is the wall and ceiling decorations of the many rooms, as most are without furniture. The museum also has a large porcelain and silverware collection. Highlights include the Antiquarium (1570), which is the largest secular Renaissance hall north of the Alps. It is filled with Roman and Greek busts. Also popular are the Reichen Zimmer (Rich Rooms) in Rococo that were the state rooms during the 18th century, and the Royal Apartments constructed for King Ludwig I in the mid-19th century. The museum has no English signs, making an audio guide or guidebook essential. Opening hours are daily from April to mid-October, 9 am to 6 pm, and from mid-October to March, 10 am to 4 pm. Admission is €6. A combination ticket with the Treasury is €9.

The **Cuvilliés-Theater** (Altes Residenztheater/Old Residence Theater), Residenzstraße1, ☎ 089-290-671, is a magnificent Rococo theater built in 1751-3 by Francois Cuvilliés. It has four rows of boxes using different designs and decorations. The theater is still in frequent use. Opening hours are daily from April to mid-October, 9 am to 6 pm, and from mid-October to March, 10 am to 4 pm. Admission is €2.

Englischer Garten & Schwabing

The **Hofgarten** (Royal Garden) is a Renaissance garden to the north of the Residenz complex. It is flanked by 19th-century arcades and the modern Staatskanzlei (State Chancellery). The octago-

The Hofgarten (Oliver Kurmis)

nal temple in the middle of the garden is crowned by Huberd Gerhard's 1594 *Diana*.

In the south end of the Englischer Garten is the **Haus der Kunst** (House of Art), Prinzregentenstraße 1, ☎ 089-211-270, www.hausderkunst.de. It was commissioned by the Nazis to exhibit their ideas of real German art. Hitler opened the building in person (and broke the hammer with the first blow!). It currently has no permanent collection but houses varying temporary exhibitions and events.

Southeast of the Englischer Garten is the **Bayerisches Nationalmuseum** (Bavarian National Museum), Prinzregentenstraße 3, ☎ 089-211-2401, www.bayerisches-nationalmuseum.de. It focuses on local art and cultural items but many are world-renowned. A highlight is European sculpture from the Middle Ages to the Art Nouveau, including works by Tilman Riemenschneider. Opening hours are Tuesday to Sunday, 10 am to 5 pm, closing at 8 pm on Thursday. Admission is €5, free on Sunday.

Nearby is the **Schack-Galerie**, Prinzregentenstraße 9, ☎ 089-2380-5224. It has a collection of 270 German 19th-century paintings. Opening hours are Tuesday to Sunday from 10 am to 5 pm. Admission is €2.50.

The **Englischer Garten** (English Garden) is Europe's largest city park. It was laid out as an English landscape park in the early 19th century and is a favored place to relax. In the south of the park is a Japanese Tea House (1972). Towards the middle of the park is a 52-ft-high classical round temple, the Monopteros (1838). It is supposed to have great views of the Old Town skyline but the number of drug users and undesirables that frequent

Chinesischer Turm (Nico Kaiser)

the place leads many to remain on the rolling lawns. The five-story **Chinesischer Turm** (Chinese Pagoda) of 1760 burned down during World War II but was reconstructed in 1952. In its shade is a 6,000-seat beer garden. Nude sunbathing is still practiced in many parts of the park, although students strolling around naked are much less common nowadays than they were in the 1970s and 1980s.

West of the Englischer Garten is the neighborhood of **Schwabing** – a mythical, nostalgic place for many Germans, a bit like Paris's Left Bank. It saw its golden age at the turn of the 19th century and early 20th century when the neighborhood was crowded with artists of all kinds. Although present Schwabing is not even a shadow of its former self, it is still the liveliest neighborhood with the most popular nightspots and small shops. It tries to cling to its Bohemian tradition but is very much bourgeois, with the trendiest cafés and "in" places. It is most easily reached by U-Bahn (station: Münchener Freiheit).

Deutsches Museum

The Deutsches Museum (German Museum), Museumsinsel 1, ☎ 089-21-791, www.deutsches-museum.de, is one of the largest technology museums in the world. It is located on an island in the River Isar and is a vast collection, with around 18,000 scientific and technology items on permanent display. Many working models and frequent demonstrations add further interest. Seeing it all will require a nearly 10-mile hike. Particularly popular are the various transportation departments that include the first Benz automobile, the first German submarine, early trains and planes, boats, and missiles. Large sections are also devoted to pure science, with physical laws and chemical reactions explained. Further exhibitions include paper and porcelain making, photography, weather prediction, electronics, agriculture, and astronomy. Opening hours are daily from 9 am to 5 pm; on Wednesday, selected collections are open until 9 pm. Admission is €7.50.

Pinakotheken Viertel & Königsplatz

The **Pinakotheken Viertel** (Art Gallery Quarter) is an informal name for the area a few blocks northeast of the Hauptbahnhof that houses several major art galleries. The most impressive are the three Pinakotheken that together present art from the Middle Ages to the present. The individual collections are among the best in Germany, with the Alte Pinakothek one of the best in the world.

 Tickets: *Day tickets for all three Pinakotheken are €12 – a bargain for those visiting the Pinakothek der Moderne. All are free on Sunday.*

Virgin & Child (Leonardo da Vinci, 1473)

The **Alte Pinakothek** (Old Masters' Gallery), Barer Straße 27, ☎ 089-238-052, www.alte-pinakothek.de, is one of the world's greatest collections of European paintings from the Middle Ages to the early 19th century. It is housed in a large early 19th-century Neo-Renaissance building reconstructed after World War II. The catalogue reads like a Who's Who of European painters, with excellent works by all the great masters. German, Dutch, and Flemish artists are particularly well represented. The Rubens collection is one of the largest in the world. Opening hours are Tuesday to Sunday from 10 am to 5 pm, closing at 8 pm on Tuesday. Admission is €5, free on Sunday.

Across the road is the **Neue Pinakothek** (New Art Gallery), Barer Straße 29, ☎ 089-2380-5195, www.neue-pinakothek.org. The post-modern building was completed in 1981 to house the mainly 19th-century art collection. The sculptures and paintings cover all periods from Rococo to Art Nouveau. It has works by all the famous Impressionist artists but it is really the German works that come to the fore.

Peasant Woman & Children (Ferdinand Georg Waldmüller, 1840)

Opening hours are Tuesday to Sunday from 10 am to 5 pm, closing at 8 pm on Wednesday. Admission is €5, free on Sunday.

Adjacent, the **Pinakothek der Moderne** (Modern Art Gallery), Barer Straße 40, ☎ 089-2380-5118, www.pinakothek-der-moderne.de, opened in 2002. This glass and steel building houses four collections that together represent the largest modern art gallery in Germany. The exhibition comprises sections on modern art, industrial and graphic design, graphic art, and an architectural museum. Opening hours are Tuesday to Sunday from 10 am to 5 pm, closing at 8 pm on Thursday and Friday. Admission is €9, free on Sunday.

The area around **Königsplatz** was destined to become the *Acropolis Germaniae* under the Nazis, but clever redesigning after the war left it with a less bombastic and still Classical appearance. Few visitors would associate the buildings here with the Nazi era, in stark contrast to what happened with the Party Rallying grounds in Nürnberg. The area houses several impressive museums to complement the nearby Pinakotheken.

At the north of the square is the Greek temple-like **Glyptothek**, Königsplatz 3, ☎ 089-286-100. This Ionic-columned building was erected in 1816-30 to house one of Europe's largest collections of sculpture from antiquity. Opening hours are Tuesday to

Sunday from 10 am to 5 pm, closing at 8 pm on Tuesday and Thursday. Admission is €3, free on Sunday.

On the south side of the square with a Corinthian colonnade is the **Antikensammlungen** (Antiquities Collection), Königsplatz 1, ☎ 089-598-359, www.antikensammlungen.de. It has an impressive collection of Greek ceramics, Etruscan art, small sculptures, bronzes, and jewelry. Opening hours are Tuesday to Sunday, 10 am to 5 pm, closing at 8 pm on Wednesday. Admission is €3, free on Sunday.

The **Städtische Galerie im Lenbachhaus und Kunstbau** (Municipal Gallery), Luisenstraße 33, ☎ 089-2333-2000, www.lenbachhaus.de, is in a Florentine-style villa constructed in the late-19th century for the artist Lenbach. A large part of the collection is by local painters or of regional objects. However, of international fame is the Avant Garde Blaue Reiter collection, which includes works by Kandinsky, Marc, Kubin, Klee, and Jawlensky. The attached Kunstbau is actually a former subway platform and is used to house temporary exhibitions. Opening hours are Tuesday to Sunday from 10 am to 6 pm. Admission is €6.

Olympiagelände & BMW

In the northern suburbs of Munich are the **Olympiagelände** (sites of the 1972 Summer Olympic Games). The 80,000-seat Olympic Stadium and the 14,000-seat multipurpose Olympiahalle are frequently used for sports and cultural events, while the Olympic swimming pool is open to the general public.

Of particular architectural note is the enormous glass tent that was constructed to cover the main stadiums and large public areas. It was fabulously expensive and over-budget but is now much loved. Twelve 265-ft pylons and 36 smaller ones keep the massive glass roof in the air. The 197-ft Olympiaberg (Olympic Mountain) was created by rubble carted out of Munich after World War II. Most of the Olympiagelände is unfenced and freely accessible. It is a fa-

The Olympiaturm

vored place for jogging, cycling, and inline skating.

The 950-ft **Olympiaturm** (Olympic Tower, 1968) is one of the highest television towers in Germany. At 623 ft is a revolving restaurant and a viewing platform that attracts up to 700,000 annual visitors. The views of Munich are fine – it really is too high to see much detail – but the views of the Bavarian Alps are fantastic when the weather is clear. The elevator costs €3 and operates from 9 am to midnight.

Adjacent to the Olympiagelände are the headquarters and a factory of Bayerischen Motoren Werken, better known by the acronym BMW. The headquarters are in a futuristic-looking silver building from the early 1970s. It looks as if four cylinders of 19 stories each are hanging from the support structure at the top. The **BMW-Museum**, Petuelring 130, ☎ 089-3822-3307, www.bmw.com, has an interesting exhibition of BMW cars, aircraft engines, and motorcycles, ranging from the 1928 Dixi to design studies. (The museum will be closed until early 2007.) Factory tours are also possible – book well in advance for the limited number of English-language tours. Opening hours are daily from 9 am to 5 pm. Admission is €3.

The area is easily reached from the Old Town on U-Bahn U3, station Olympia-Zentrum.

Schloss Nymphenburg

Schloss Nymphenburg

Schloss Nymphenburg (Palace) was erected originally in 1664-74 as a small summer palace west of the city for the ruling family. However, Prince Elector Max Emmanuel altered it to a lavish Baroque palace. For most of the 18th century, his successors added more features and structures until Nymphenburg became the largest Baroque palace in Germany. The large garden was developed from 1700 onwards and eventually combined formal Italian and French elements with English landscape garden areas.

Bavaria

Schloss Nymphenburg is over half a mile long and can be visited without a tour. It is mostly Baroque and has a splendid interior. The huge banqueting hall has rich stucco work and frescoes by Johann Baptist Zimmermann. Several royal apartments are on display including the Geburtzimmer (Birth Room) of mad King Ludwig II. Of special note is the Schönheitengalerie (Gallery of Beauties) – a huge collection of painting by Joseph Stieler of beautiful women that caught the roving eye of King Ludwig. Especially of note is the painting of Lola Montez, the woman who cost him his throne.

The **Marstallmuseum mit Museum Nymphenburger Porzellan** (Carriage Museum with Porcelain Collection) is in the south wing of the palace. It includes the collection of lavish carriages of the Wittelsbach family. On the second floor is the porcelain collection of around 1,200 items of the Alt Nymphenburg production, from Rococo to Art Nouveau.

Of the number of structures in the garden, **Amalienburg** is the most interesting. Originally conceived as a simple hunting lodge, Cuvilliés created a simple exterior but a magnificent Rococo interior (1739). This pleasure pavilion served as inspiration for many others that were created all over Europe during the 18th century. It has lavish kennels for the royal hunting dogs, a hall of mirrors rotunda, and a kitchen tiled in blue-and-white Delft.

Amalienburg

Three further early-18th-century structures in the garden are open to the public. The **Badenburg** contained the first heated swimming pool since Roman times. The **Pagodenburg** has an elegant French exterior but the interior is an exotic Asian teahouse. The **Magdalenenklause** is a folly of artificial ruins. It contains a chapel dedicated to Mary Magdalene.

VISITOR'S INFORMATION

Schloss Nymphenburg, Amalienburg, and the Marstallmuseum with Porcelain Collection are open daily from April to mid-October, 9 am to 6 pm, and from mid-October to March, 10 am to 4 pm. The three Parkburgen (Badenburg, Pagodenburg, and Magdalenenklause) are only open during the summer season. Admission to the Schloss and Museum is €5 each and to the Parkburgen €2 each. A combination ticket for the Parkburgen and Amalienburg is €4 and to all buildings in the complex €10 in summer and €8 in winter.

Admission to the park itself is free and daily opening hours are long, if complex. From March to October, it opens at 6 am but closes at 6:30 pm in March, 7 pm in October, 8:30 pm in April and September, and 9:30 pm from May to August. From November to February, it opens at 6:30 am and closes at 6 pm, but 5:30 pm in December.

The contact details for all are Schloss Nymphenburg, Eingang 1, ☎ 089-179-080, www.schloesser.bayern.de. The area is now firmly within the city boundaries and around 3½ miles west of the Old Town. It is easily reached by tram 17 in 12 minutes from the Hauptbahnhof.

Farther Afield

■ Dachau

Dachau liberated

In 1933, on orders from Heinrich Himmler, the Nazis' first concentration camp was created at Dachau near Munich. Those incarcerated here were mostly political prisoners. Although gas chambers were built, they were not used and the camp remained primarily a slave labor camp. Up to liberation in

1945, 31,591 of the 206,000 prisoners died, mostly of malnutrition and disease. At liberation, the camp had just under 70,000 prisoners of which about a third were Jews. A local priest, Rupert Mayer, who was interned here, was later declared a saint – see *Bürgersaal* for details.

The whole camp area is now a memorial site to those who died here as well as to those who suffered under the Nazi regime elsewhere. Many parts of the camp has been restored or rebuilt. In the main building is the **KZ-Gedenkstätte Dachau Museum** (Concentration Camp Memorial), Alte Römerstraße 75, 85221 Dachau, ℅ 08131-669-970. It has photos and information about the tragic and disturbing events. An English-language information video is shown at 11:30 am and 3:30 pm. Opening hours are Tuesday to Sunday from 9 am to 5 pm. Admission is free. It is worth investing in the audio guide (€2.50) as signposting is limited.

To reach the camp from the Hauptbahnhof, take S-Bahn S2 in the direction of Petershausen to Dachau Station. From here, it is a 10-minute walk, or take Bus 724 or 726. The train ride takes just over 20 minutes, but waiting for the bus can easily increase the total journey time to 50 minutes.

■ Schleißheim

Prince Elector Max Emmanuel, who built large parts of Schloss Nymphenburg, erected another magnificent Baroque palace to the north of Munich. **Neues Schloss Schleißheim** (New Palace) Max-Emanuel-Platz 1, ☎ 089-315-8720, www.schloesser.bayern.de, was to have been his Versailles. Debt and exile ruined his plans but one of the four planned wings of monumental proportions was eventually completed in 1719. The 1,100-ft-long building has a Late Baroque and Rococo interior, which is partly the work of Johann

Schleißheim

Baptist Zimmermann and Cosmas Damian Asam. The art gallery has a remarkable collection of European Baroque paintings including three works by Rubens. Around 50 rooms on two floors are open to the public. Opening hours are Tuesday to Sunday from April to September, 9 am to 6 pm, and October to March, 10 am to 4 pm. Admission is €4. Combination tickets with Schloss Lustheim are €5.

The **Hofgarten** (Royal Garden) at Neues Schloss Schleißheim is one of only two Baroque gardens in Germany that survived in an unaltered form. It is in a French style with formal geometric design. The basic structures were already designed in 1684 and most of it completed early in the 18th century. A center canal leads to the end of the garden where a Baroque folly, the late-17th-century hunting palace, Lustheim, is encircled by smaller canals. Side-canals run the full length of the garden at the width of the main building and come together in a half circle behind Lustheim. The fountains are operational daily from April to mid-September, 10 am to 4 pm. The gardens are freely accessible year-round.

Schloss Lustheim currently houses the most important early-Meissen porcelain collection outside Saxony. Opening hours are the same as the main palace. Admission is €3 or €5 when combined with the main palace.

The **Flugwerft Schleißheim** (Airport), Effnerstraße 18, ☎ 089-315-7140, is a branch of the Deutsches Museum in the north of Munich. It has historic aircraft and missiles on display. Opening hours are daily from 9 am to 5 pm. Admission is €3.50 or €10 when combined with the main museum.

Schleißheim is best reached by private car or S-Bahn line S1 to Oberschleißheim. It is a 15-minute walk to the palaces and the Flugwerft.

Cultural Events

Munich has a very busy cultural calendar and offers everything from classical music to the latest pop stars. It is famous for its 50 theaters that perform works in all genres but, unfortunately for most foreign visitors, usually in German only.

Munich has three symphony orchestras and two opera houses. The **Bayerische Staatsoper** (Bavarian National Opera House) and **Bayerisches Staatsorchester** (Bavarian National Orchestra), www.staatsoper.de, are two of the oldest companies in Germany, with the orchestra founded in 1523. Mozart raved over their talent. The orchestra first performed several Wagner operas in Munich and Bayreuth. The **Münchner Philharmoniker**, www.muenchnerphilharmoniker.de, is just over a century old. With 16,000 subscribers, tickets are seldom available to outsiders. The symphony orchestra of the **Bayerischer Rundfunk** (Bavarian Radio), www.br-klassik.de, was founded in 1949 and has an international reputation for excellence.

A good source for tickets to all kinds of events is **München Ticket**, *www.muenchen-ticket.de,* ☎ *089-5481-8181. It has offices in the Rathaus next to the tourist information, in the Gasteig, and in the Olympiapark at the Info-Pavillion. For the Bayerischen Staatsoper, reservations must be made at the Staatsoper, Max-Joseph-Platz 2,* ☎ *089-2185-1920, www.staatsoper.de.*

Festivals

Munich has a very busy festival calendar that includes many originally Catholic holidays as well as purely secular merriments. The two largest festivals are described in more detail below.

Fasching (in other areas called Karneval or Fastnacht) starts early January and last about two months. Particularly popular is the dancing of the market women at the Viktualienmarkt. After two weeks of fasting, usually end of March, comes the **Starkbierzeit** (Strong Beer Period) during which all local breweries brew a particularly strong variety.

This is followed by the first **Dult** (see below), and in June the city's **Foundation Day**. In summer, several festivals are held including film and open-air music festivals. Two further Dults are held at each end of Okotberfest, which is mostly in September. The year ends with the **Christkindlmarkt** (Christmas Market) held during Advent at several locations throughout the city.

■ Oktoberfest

Munich is world famous for the largest festival in the world – the annual 16-day Oktoberfest. It is actually held mostly in September and ends the first Sunday in October. It all started as a celebration of the wedding of Crown Prince Ludwig and Princess Therese of Saxony-Hildburghausen in 1810. It became an annual event and is now a firm part of Munich's cultural program. It is combined with an agricultural show every three years, but the main attractions to the millions of visitors are the beer tents, rides, and other entertainment.

Annually, Oktoberfest attracts over six million visitors, who each consume at least a a quart of beer plus wine and non-alcoholic beverages. Half a million chickens and a hundred oxen are slaughtered and consumed, together with 110,000 lbs of fish and 200,000 pairs of pork sausages. Oktoberfest's contribution to Munich's economy is estimated at around a billion euros.

The festival is held at a special terrain, known as the Theresienwiese, about a 10-minute walk south of the Hauptbahnhof. The show grounds are usually open from around 10 am to midnight, with most drinking stopping at 10:30 pm. Beer tents close for new arrivals when full – on weekends that can be before noon! It is generally a good idea to leave before 10 pm for both safety reasons and to avoid the crowds on public transportation. Finding accommodation in Munich during Oktoberfest is problematic – expect to pay top dollar for even the simplest hotel.

■ Auer Dult Festivals

Auer Dult, www.auerdult.de, is a traditional Munich folk festival dating back to 1310. It is a combination market, flea market, and entertainment festival that lasts for nine days. Almost everything is sold at the market but it is particularly famous as the largest market in Europe for tableware, pots, and pans, although more people are drawn by the food, drink, and entertainment. Three *Dulten* are organized annually – end of April, end of July, and mid-October. The market stalls are generally open from 9 am to 8 pm. The market is held at Mariahilfplatz – there is no parking in the area but Bus 52 connects to Marienplatz and Tram 27 to Karlsplatz.

Shopping

Munich is a pleasant city for shopping. The haute couture shops are in very stylish Maximilianstraße as well as in streets near the Residenz. The pedestrian zone, especially Neuhauser and Kaufingerstraße, has the larger department stores. The largest and most famous store in Munich is the Herties department store, which spreads over several blocks between Karlsplatz and the Hauptbahnhof.

Probably the most desired souvenir to take home from Munich is a BMW car. Residents of the USA (other areas need not apply), who are buying a BMW made in Germany can save, depending on the model, between $2,000 and $8,000 by taking personal delivery in Germany, rather than in the USA. The car may be driven up to six months in Europe before being shipped to the USA. The insurance for the first 30 days is included. The car can be dropped off at several cities in Europe at the end of the vacation and then shipped by BMW and delivered in the USA through the normal channels. There is no catch, paperwork, or hidden costs, but do note that some options, often including radios, are only fitted once the car arrives in the USA. Contact any BMW dealer in the USA, or www.bmwusa.com, for details on the European Delivery Program. (Other German car companies have similar schemes, but presently none with such huge savings.)

Adventures

On Foot

Town Walks: Munich Walking Tours, Discover Bavaria, Hochbrückenstraße, ☎ 089-2554-3987, www.mikesbiketours.com, conducts guided tours daily at 3:30 pm from mid-April to August. Participation is €9 for this three-hour walking tour that ends at the Hofbräuhaus, where Mike has a *Stammtisch*. Further tours, including to Schloss Neuschwanstein and Dachau, are also available.

Munich Walks/Radius Bikes, Arnulfstraße 3, ☎ 089-5502-9374, www.radius-munich.com, has several guided tours of Munich and Dachau. A fascinating two-hour tour is on Hitler and the Nazi-period sights in Munich. It departs daily between April and October at 3 pm from the office at the Hauptbahnhof (near tracks 32-33).

On Wheels

By Bicycle: Munich is a relatively flat city with around 420 miles of dedicated cycling routes, making for easy and safe cycling.

Mike's Bike Tours, Discover Bavaria, Hochbrückenstraße, ☎ 089-2554-3987, www.mikesbiketours. com, is a pleasant way to discover Munich. From March to mid-November, one to four tours are available daily. The standard four-hour tour costs €22 and the extended seven-hour tour (in June and July only) costs €33 – both prices include bicycle rental. Bicycle rental without a tour is also available.

Bicycles can be rented in the Hauptbahnhof from Radius **Tour and Bikes**, Arnulfstr. 3, ☎ 089-596-113.

By Inline Skating: Inline skating is very popular in Munich with many parks and the Isar River banks open to skaters. On Monday nights from May to August, **Münchner Bladenights** allow skaters to skate through the streets of Munich. It claims to be the biggest skating event in Europe. Information on routes is available from **Green City**, Klenzestraße 54, ☎ 089-8906-6833, www.muenchner-bladenight.de. The party starts at 7 pm, but the actual skating is from 9 to 10:30 pm.

By Tour Bus: Several companies operate traditional bus sightseeing tours of Munich and surrounding areas. Prices are from around €10 for one-hour tours.

Major operators include **Münchner Stadtrundfahrten**, Arnulfstrasse 8, ☎ 089-5502-8995 and **Yellow Cab**, Sendlinger-Tor-Platz 5, ☎ 089-2602-5183.

AutobusOberbayern, Heidemannstraße 220, ☎ 089-323-040, www.autobusoberbayern.de, operates city tours as well as daytrips to several destinations near Munich, including Rothenburg, Herrenchiemsee, Berchtesgaden, Salzburg, and Innsbruck. A particularly popular tour that departs daily at 8:30 am is to Schloss Neuschwanstein and Schloss Linderhof – using public transportation, it is virtually impossible to do both on the same day.

By Taxi: Taxi Guide München, Ganghoferstraße 63a, ☎ 089-3537-9808, www.taxi-guide-muenchen.de, uses taxis with drivers qualified as tour-guides. The price is around €70 for the first hour and €20 for each additional hour. A full-day tour for up to eight persons covering 180 miles, e.g. to Schloss Neuschwanstein or Berchtesgaden, costs just over €400.

Where to Stay & Eat

Luxury Hotels & Restaurants

The **Hotel Bayerischer Hof** is a privately managed luxury grand hotel close to the Old Town and the Pinakotheken Museums. Rooms are rustic, nostalgic, or modern but all are very luxurious. The **Garden-Restaurant** (€€-€€€€) with terrace serves Mediterranean cuisine. **Trader Vic's** (€€-€€€€) serves Polynesian

HOTEL PRICES	
€	. . . . Up to €50 per night
€€	. . . . €50 to €100
€€€	. . . . . €101 to €150
€€€€	. . . . . . Over €150

RESTAURANT PRICES	
€	. . . . Less than €10
€€	. . . . €10 to €20
€€€	. . . . €21 to €35
€€€€	. . . . Over €35

Room in the Bayerischer Hof

and Caribbean food. The very pleasant **Palais Keller** (€€-€€€) is a traditional Bavarian beer cellar and serves local specialties. Promenadeplatz 2-6, 80333 München, ☎ 089-21-200, fax 089-212.0906, www.bayerischerhof.de. (€€€€)

The **Mandarin Oriental Hotel** is close to the Hofbräuhaus, just minutes from the Marienplatz. The hotel is very luxurious with large rooms. The 19th-century building was originally a ballroom but successfully converted to a hotel in 1989. The manager recently reportedly told a

Mandarin Oriental room

very famous British pop star, who demanded a discount, to stay elsewhere. The pool is on the roof and has fantastic views of the Old Town and Alps when weather allows. The dinner restaurant **Mark's** (€€€-€€€€) serves international and nouvelle cuisine. **Mark's Corner** (€€-€€€) is open for lunch only. Neuturmstraße 1, 80331 München, ☎ 089-290-980, fax 089-222-539, www.mandarinoriental.com. (€€€€)

The **Königshof Hotel** is between the Old Town and the Hauptbahnhof at the Stachus intersection. It is an establishment in the grand hotel tradition with luxurious, individually furnished rooms. The **Königshof Restaurant** (€€€-€€€€) is one of the best in Munich and serves nouvelle cuisine in opulent surroundings. Karlsplatz 25,

Room 5 at Königshof Hotel

80335 München, ☎ 089-551-360, fax 089-5513-6113, www. koenigshof-muenchen.de. (€€€€)

Hotel Vier Jahreszeiten

The **Kempinski Hotel Vier Jahreszeiten** is on the Maximilianstraße close to the Opera. It is a grand hotel with a history dating back to the mid-19th century. Rooms combine traditional elements with modern comforts. The **Bistro Restaurant** (€€-€€€€) has views of the shoppers. It serves international and nouvelle cuisine. Maximilianstraße 17, 80331 München, 089-21-250, fax 089-2125-2000, www. kempinski.com. (€€€€)

Old Town Area

The **Platzl Hotel**, close to the Hofbräuhaus, has very comfortable, individually furnished rooms. The ones facing the courtyard are particularly pleasant. The **Pfistermühle Restaurant** (€€-€€€€) serves Bavarian specialties in a vaulted setting with old-Munich atmosphere, though without the beer hall

Platzl Hotel

effects. Pfisterstraße 4, 80331 München, ℅ 089-237-030, fax 089-2370-3800, www.platzl.de. (€€€-€€€€)

Hotel Torbräu

The **Hotel Torbräu** is close to the Hofbräuhaus and within easy walking distance of the Deutsches Museum. The building dates back to the 15th century and claims to be the oldest hotel in Munich. Rooms are very comfortably furnished and spacious. Tal 41, 80331 München, ☎ 089-242-430, fax 089-2423-4235, www.torbraeu.de. (€€€-€€€€)

The nearby **Concorde Hotel** is a modern, family-run establishment with comfortable, individually furnished rooms. The ones facing the courtyard are very quiet. Herrnstraße 38, 80539 München, ☎ 089-224-515, fax 089-228-3282, www.concorde-muenchen.de. (€€€)

The **Hotel Acanthus** is a small hotel at the Sendlinger Tor. Rooms are either in English country-house style with some antiques or modern. All are comfortable and furnished to high standards. An der Hauptfeuerwache 14, 80331 München, ☎ 089-231-880, fax 089-260-7364, www.achanthushotel.de. (€€-€€€)

Hauptbahnhof Area

As with most other major cities in Germany, the area around the Hauptbahnhof is not particularly inviting. The red light district, sex shops, and video booths are all close by. The first three hotels listed here are all next to or directly across the road from the station and not in bad areas. The others are also close by and in safe areas but a sex shop or two may be passed en route from the station.

Hotel Le Méridien

Hotel Le Méridien opened in 2002 across the road from the Hauptbahnhof. It is unashamedly modern with well-equipped, stylish rooms. The **Le Potager Restaurant** (€€€) serves international cuisine with strong French influences. Bayerstraße 41, 80335 München, ☎ 089-24-220, fax 089-2422-1111, www.lemeridien.de. (€€€-€€€€)

The **Excelsior Hotel** is a very comfortable hotel with a rustic-elegant décor. Rooms are very comfortable with country-style furniture.

The **Geisel's Vinothek** (€-€€€) serves German and Italian food to complement the wine list of 400 labels. Schützenstraße 11, 80335 München, ☎ 089-551-370, fax 089-5513-7121, www. excelsior-muenchen.de. (€€€-€€€€)

Excelsior Hotel

The **Intercity Hotel** is part of the station building and has been in operation since the early 1950s. Rooms are modern, very well equipped, and quiet. The room key gives free access to local transportation. Bayerstraße 10, 80335 München, ☎ 089-545-560, fax 089-5455-6610, www.intercity-hotel.de. (€€€-€€€€)

Hotel Drei Löwen is a block from the station. It is a modern hotel with individually furnished rooms using currently fashionable wood furniture. A pleasant option at the price. Schillerstraße 8, 80336 München, ☎ 089-551-040, fax 089-5510-4905, www. hotel3loewen.de. (€€-€€€)

The **King's Hotel First Class** and the **King's Hotel Center** are two comfortable, modern hotels that use ample wood in the interior. All rooms have four-poster beds. The hotels are two blocks north of the Hauptbahnhof and close to the Glyptothek. King's Hotel First Class, Dachauer Straße 13, 80335 München, ☎ 089-551-870, fax 089-5518-7300, www.kingshotels.de. (€€€-€€€€). King's Hotel Center, Marsstraße 15, 80335 München, ☎ 089-515-530, fax 089-5155-3300, www. kingshotels.de. (€€-€€€€)

The **Apollo Hotel** is in a side-street close to the station. Rooms are and comfortable, with mahogany furniture. The rooms in the back of the building are quieter. Mitterstraße 7, 80336 München, ☎ 089-539-531, fax 089-534-033, www.apollohotel. de. (€€-€€€)

Where to Eat

 The luxurious **Schuhbeck's in den Südtiroler Stuben**, Platzl 6-8, ☎ 089-216-6900, is a refined restaurant with partly wood-paneled walls and a Baroque ceiling. The food is first-class, classical dishes and South Tyrolean specialties. (€€€-€€€€)

The nearby **Boettner's**, Pfisterstraße 9, ☎ 089-221-210, serves mostly classical dishes and nouvelle cuisine. It uses ample dark wood in its décor. Reservations are advisable. (€€€-€€€€)

The **Halali**, Schönfeldstraße 22, ☎ 089-285-909, is an refined-rustic spot suited to the hunting tradition that its name recalls. It is located in between the Hofgarten and Englischer Garten. Food is classical international and regional dishes. Reservations are advisable. (€€€)

Hunsinger's Pacific, Maximiliansplatz 5 (enter from Max-Joseph-Straße), ☎ 089-5502-9741, is arguably the best-known fish restaurant in Munich. It serves a wide selection ranging from the standard to the exotic. The food is mostly international but with an Asian touch. Meat is also served. (€€-€€€)

The **Dallmayr Restaurant**, Dienerstraße 14, ☎ 089-213-5100, in the famous Delicatessen Shop Dallmayr, is at the heart of the Old Town at the Marienplatz. The prices reflect the quality of the food rather than a tourist markup for the location. The restaurant is opulent and has a wide selection ranging from international cuisine to local specialties. (€€€)

Lenbach, Ottostraße 6, ☎ 089-549-1300, is between Stachus and Maximiliansplatz. It is an enormous restaurant designed by British architect Sir Terrance Conran and with a modern, stylish interior. The food is mostly international and Asian, with a separate sushi bar. (€€-€€€)

The **Weinhaus Neuner** is a block from the Stachus in a mid-19th-century building, claiming to be the oldest wine bar in Munich. It has cross-vaulting and wall paintings. Food is regional cuisine and hearty local dishes. (€-€€)

Zum Alten Markt, Dreifaltigkeitsplatz 3, ☎ 089-299-995, is a restaurant with wood paneling in a 400-year-old building at the Viktualienmarkt. It serves regional cuisine. (€-€€)

The **Ratskeller**, Marienplatz 8, ☎ 089-219-9890, is an enormous restaurant in the cellars of the historic Town Hall. It has many rooms, niches, and hidden corners in a romantic, rustic style. Food is local, with Franconian specialties. Reservations are essential. (€-€€)

Close to the Asmankirche is the very pleasant **Prinz Myshkin Restaurant**, Hackenstraße 2, ☎ 089-265-596, www.prinz-myshkin.com. It is the best vegetarian restaurant in town, though, granted, competition is limited. It is a modern restaurant in a large building with a vaulted ceiling. (€€-€€€)

Another vegetarian option is the self-service **Buxs Restaurant**, Frauenstraße 9, ☎ 089-291-9550. It has published seven cookbooks thusfar and is a good place to stop for a quick bite in the Marienplatz vicinity. (€-€€)

Beer Halls & Beer Gardens

BEER GARDEN ETIQUETTE

Munich is inevitably associated with beer and has several beer gardens and beer halls popular with locals and visitors alike.

Beer is usually served by *Mass* (one liter) or, if requested, by *Halb* (half-liter). Ordering anything smaller will raise eyebrows. Colas are available in some beer

Bavaria

gardens, but non-drinkers will not be sniggered at when asking for an *Apfelschaftschorle* – apple juice and soda water mix. It is much healthier and more refreshing than cola. A *Radler* (literally "cyclist") is half-beer, half-lemonade.

The typical food in beer gardens is large, soft pretzels and sausages in all forms, served with potatoes and sauerkraut. A Munich favorite is Weißwurst (white sausage). It is traditionally only served in the morning and correct etiquette is not to eat the skin and to eat it by hand. It goes well with sweet Bavarian mustard, and, of course, beer. Payment is usually due at delivery. In most beer gardens, it is permissable to bring your own food, but never your own drink.

It is common to share tables with strangers in busy restaurants; beer gardens with their long tables and bench seats are no exception. Simply ask if there is free space – *Platz frei?* However, never sit down at a *Stammtisch* even if it is completely empty. This is a table reserved for members of a society or group and sitting there is by membership or invitation only.

The best-known building in Munich is the **Hofbräuhaus**, Platzl 6, ☎ 089-290-1360, www.hofbraeuhaus.de. Its best features are also the worst – its international fame and popularity. It can be packed at night with international visitors, who think getting hopelessly drunk and singing out of tune is the German idea of having a good

Hofbräuhaus

time. It can also be packed with locals and visitors having a good time – it is often simply a case of good or bad luck on the day. You may prefer reserving a table at the more formal restaurants on the upper levels, or visit for lunch. An oompah band usually plays at all hours. (€-€€€)

The **Augustiner Gaststätten**, Neuhauser Straße 27, ☎ 089-2318-3257, is probably the most famous beer hall in Munich after the Hofbräuhaus. Augustiner beer was brewed here up to 1885. Parts of the building are Art Nouveau, and the beer garden is particularly pleasant. (€-€€)

The **Paulaner im Tal**, Tal 12, ☎ 089-219-9400, is a nostalgic restaurant with terrace and beer garden serving local cuisine with a reasonable vegetarian selection and some Austrian dishes. (€-€€)

The **Löwenbräukeller**, Nymphenburger Straße 2, ☎ 089-526-021, is close to the Hauptbahnhof and next to the brewery itself. It has a rustic locale and pleasant beer garden. The food is unapologetically Bavarian. It tends to draw fewer foreign tourists than the breweries in the Old Town area. (€-€€)

The **Bratwurstherzl**, Dreifältigkeitsplatz 1, ☎ 089-295-113, is a traditional bratwurst restaurant at the Viktualienmarkt with self-made sausages grilled over beech-wood fires. (€-€€)

A very pleasant similar establishment is the **Nürnberger Bratwurst Glöckl am Dom**, Frauenplatz 9, ☎ 089-295-264. It serves Nürnberger Bratwurst (finger-sized grilled sausages) and Bavarian cuisine. Ask for cola and you will receive the server's assurance, with a pained face, that no cola has ever fouled this fine establishment. (€-€€)

The second-largest beer garden in Munich is at the **Chinesischer Turm** (Chinese Pagoda) in the Englischer Garten. It seats about 6,000 people! You can bring your own food, but not drinks! Several other smaller beer gardens are scattered through the park.

Camping

München Thalkirchen Campingplatz is conveniently located only 2.4 miles from the Old Town in the Isar Valley. It can be reached in 15 minutes by public transportation. There is space for 300 tents and 250 RVs or mobile homes. It is open from mid-March to October. Zentralländstrasse 49, 81379 München, ☎ 089-723-1707, fax 089-724-3177.

Campingplatz Nord-West is 1.2 miles from the Olympiagelände and convenient to both public transportation and Autobahnen. There are many shady spots and three lakes for swimming within half a mile. It is open year-round. Auf den Schrederwiesen 3, 80995 München, ☎ 089-150-6936, fax 089-1582-0463, www.campingplatz-nord-west.de.

Kapuzinerhölzl - The Tent has been in operation for 30 years. It is a camping site for tents only but is best known for its large communal tent for backpackers and youth groups. The location is in a park near Schloss Nymphenburg, but the Hauptbahnhof can be reached in 15 minutes by tram. Sleeping space in the big tent goes for around €10. It is open from June to August. In den Kirschen 30, 80992 München, ☎ 089-141-4300, fax 089-175-090, www.the-tent.com.

◆ Franken

Franken is in the northwestern part of Bavaria. The name derives from the Franks that lived in the area and eventually ruled most of Central Europe during the time of Charlemagne. Franconia is the correct English term for Franken, but in contrast to Bavaria (*Bayern* in German) it is very seldom used in Germany.

Information Sources

Tourismusverband Franken, Postfach 440453, 90209 Nürnberg, ☎ 0911-941-510, www. frankentourismus.de.

Würzburg

Würzburg is a city of 130,000 on the banks of the River Main. It is famous for both its Baroque buildings and for being at the heart of the Franken wine region, which still uses flat, oval-shaped *Bocksbeutel* wine bottles.

Much of Würzburg's history was determined by religion. In 689, the Irish missionary St Kilian was murdered here and in 742, the bishopric of Würzburg was founded. In the 12th century, Emperor Friedrich Barbarossa elevated the bishops to prince-bishops, who would rule the Duchy of Franken up to secularization in 1802. Würzburg became part of Bavaria in 1814. In

1945, around 90% of Würzburg was destroyed by air raids. Large parts of the Old Town were rebuilt true to the original.

Several important artists are closely associated with Würzburg, although none of them is native: the medieval poet Walther von der Vogelweide, sculptor and woodcarver Tilman Riemenschneider, Baroque master builder Balthasar Neuman, and the painter Giovanni Battista Tiepolo. Wilhelm Röntgen discovered X-rays here in 1895.

Information Sources

Tourist Office: Tourist information is available from Tourist Information, Falkenhaus am Markt, 97070 Würzburg, ☎ 0931-372-398, www.wuerzburg.de.

Transportation

Trams 1, 2, 3, and 5 connect the Hauptbahnhof with the Old Town, although the distance is only a few minutes walk. Of more use is Bus 9, which connects the Residenz and Festung Marienburg at least once per hour – it halts at Juliuspromenade, near the Hauptbahnhof.

Sightseeing

■ Residenz

The Residenz, Residenzplatz 2, ☎ 0931-355-170, www.bsv.bayern.de, was constructed between 1720 and 1744 by Balthasar Neumann for the bishops of Würzburg. It is one of the finest Baroque palaces in Europe and is a UNESCO World Cultural Heritage Site. Large parts of the Residenz were destroyed in 1945 but reconstructed. Original parts include the magnificent monumental Treppenhaus (staircase) with the vaulted ceiling containing the 6,400-sq-ft fresco by Tiepolo; the Weißer Saal (White Hall) with stuccos by Bossi; the Kaisersaal (Imperial Hall) with more frescoes by Tiepolo; and the Gartensaal (Garden Hall) with frescoes by Johann Zick. The rich Rococo Paradezimmer (Parade Room) was reconstructed. Opening hours are daily from April to October, 9 am to 6 pm, and from November to March, 10 am to 4:30 pm. Admission is €4.50 and includes a 45-minute guided tour – daily in English at 11 am and 3 pm, more frequent

The Residenz

in German. (Although the tour is not compulsory, it is the only way to see the south wing and mirrors cabinet.)

The **Hofkirche** (Court Chapel) is in the south wing of the Residenz, but visitors use a separate entrance. It was the private chapel of the bishop and is a superb example of Baroque architecture. Neumann had to adapt to the existing building and used hidden windows and mirrors to draw in light. The gilding here uses real gold, although the marble is fake. The frescoes are by Rudolf Byss, but the two paintings above the side altars are by Tiepolo. Opening hours are April to mid-October, daily from 9 am to 6 pm, closing at 8 pm on Thursday. From mid-October to March, it is open daily, 10 am to 4 pm. Admission is free.

The **Hofgarten** (Court Garden) is a formal Baroque garden with Italian and French sections. The eastern part of the garden offers great views of the palace façade. The

The Hofkirche (Christian Horvat)

garden is open until dark. Admission is free.

The **Martin von Wagner Museum**, ☎ 0931-312-288, in the south wing of the Residenz, has a fine gallery with European paintings and statues from the 14th to 19th century. It also has

The Hofgarten (Christian Horvat)

an interesting antiquities collection with Egyptian jewelry, Roman pottery, and Greek vases. To see the whole collection requires at least two visits since opening hours are complicated. The museum is open Tuesday to Saturday, with the art gallery open from 9:30 am to 12:30 pm and the antiquities collection from 2 to 5 pm. The two sections are open in turn on Sunday from 9:30 am to 12:30 pm. Admission is free.

Guided tours of the **Staatlicher Hofkeller** (National Wine Cellar), Residenzplatz 2, ☎ 0931-305-0931, www.hofkeller.de, are available on weekends from March to November and end with a glass of locally produced wine.

■ East Bank & Old Town

The **Dom St Kilian**, Domerpfarrgasse 10, ☎ 0931-321-1830, retained its original 1188 exterior and, at 344 ft long, is the fourth-largest Romanesque church in Germany. The church burned out during 1945 and the nave collapsed a year later, but was restored to its original condition. The Baroque

The Dom St Kilian

Bavaria

Schönbornkapelle (Schönborn Chapel) was constructed in 1721-36 by Balthasar Neumann. The interior of the Dom has several noteworthy artworks, including sandstone statues by Tilman Riemenschneider and 12th- to 17th-century funerary monuments for the bishops. Opening hours are Monday to Saturday from 10 am to 5 pm, but it's closed between noon and 2 pm from November to Easter. On Sunday, it's open from 1 to 6 pm. The Schönbornkapelle can only be seen on the guided tour of the Dom, which takes place daily from Easter to October at 12:05 (Sunday at 12:30).

Neumünster Church

The oldest part of the **Neumünster Church**, Kürschnerhof, is a triple-aisle Romanesque basilica built in the 11th century over the place where the Irish missionary St Kilian was murdered in 689 AD. However, later Baroque additions now dominate, with the impressive western façade attributed to Johann Dientzenhofer. The structural components survived the bombing of 1945, but much of the interior was destroyed. Some noteworthy artworks survived, including a *Madonna and Christ* by Tilman Riemenschneider. Behind the church, in the Lusamgärtlein, is the tomb of medieval troubadour Walther von der Vogelweide (1170-1230), who died in Würzburg.

The **Falkenhaus** on the Markt has the loveliest mid-18th-century Rococo façade with stuccowork in Würzburg. It currently houses the municipal library and information office.

The Falkenhaus

Adjacent is the **Marienkapelle** (St Mary's Chapel), a Gothic hall church erected by the town between 1377 and 1440. The Neo-Gothic steeple has a double gilded 18th-century *Madonna*. The interior has noteworthy works by Tilman Riemenschneider, including the 1502 tombstone of Konrad von Schaumberg, and copies of the statues of Adam and Eve in the portal. (The originals are in the Mainfränkisches Museum). The church contains the tomb of the master Baroque architect Balthasar Neumann (1687-1753).

Parts of the **Rathaus** (Town Hall) date to the 13th century, while the Renaissance façade is from 1660. The tower is 180 ft high. Ironically, the oldest parts of the building survived the bombing of 1945, while most of the

The Rathaus

newer additions were destroyed and subsequently rebuilt.

■ West Bank & Marienberg

The **Alte Mainbrücke** (Old Main Bridge) was constructed between 1473 and 1543 to replace a previous Romanesque bridge destroyed by floods. Twelve huge Baroque statues of saints, including Charlemagne, were added in the early 18th century.

Festung Marienberg (Fortress), ☎ 0931-355-1750, www.schloesser.bayern.de, served as primary residence of the bishops from 1253 to 1719. Its history, however, is much older. Celts first built a fort here around 1000 BC. In 706 AD, the first Marienkapelle (St Mary's Chapel) was erected. Construction of the fortress started around 1200. In the 17th century, it was altered to a Renaissance palace but, after the Thirty Years' War, it was converted into a Baroque fortress. Opening hours are from April to October, Tuesday to Sunday, 9 am to 6 pm. Admission is €2. (The two museums in the fortress have separate opening hours and admission fees.)

Alte Mainbrücke & Festung Marienberg above it (Christian Horvat)

The former Baroque Zeughaus (Arsenal) now houses the **Mainfränkisches Museum** (Main Franconian), ☎ 0931-205-940, www.mainfraenkisches-museum.de. It has the largest collection of Tilman Riemenschneider works in the world, including the originals removed from the Dom. It also has exhibitions on local history as well as the role of wine in the regional economy and way of life. Opening hours are Tuesday to Sunday from 10 am to 7 pm. Admission is €3 or €5 with the Fürstenbaumuseum.

In the east wing is the **Fürstenbaumuseum**, ☎ 0931-43-838. It includes the former bishops' apartments, treasury, and a section on the town's history. Opening hours are Tuesday to Sunday from 10 am to 5 pm. Admission is €4 or €5 with the Mainfränkische Museum.

The fortress is a good 20-minute walk from the bottom of the hill or take Bus Line 9, which runs from the Residenz via the Juliuspromenade near the Hauptbahnhof to the top of the hill. Limited parking is available.

The finest views of Würzburg are from the terrace of the **Käppele**, Nikolausberg/Leutfresserweg, on a hill slightly farther upstream from the Marienfestung. This pilgrim's chapel is the last work by the Baroque master architect Balthasar Neumann. The stuccos are by Johann Feuchtmayer and Materno Bossi and the frescos by Matthäus Günther. A miracle passage leads to the adjacent chapel of mercy. The Käppele is reached on foot via a steep walkway with many stairs and the Stations of the Cross.

Cultural Events

Contact the tourist office for information and reservations on the following festivals.

The **Mozartfest** (Mozart Festival) is the best-known musical event in Würzburg and attracts internationally renowned orchestras and conductors. It is held mainly during June, using several venues, including the Residenz.

The **Bachtage** (Bach Days) are held the last week of November. They involve several Bach performances, including a 100-voice choir.

The **Barockfeste** (Baroque Festival) is held end of May, with music and fine dining in the Residenz.

The **Africa-Festival** held end May, early June claims to be the largest African music festival in Europe.

Wine Festivals

Würzburg is at the heart of the Franconian wine lands and sees eight major wine-related festivals annually. Most are held in May or June, but a highlight is the **Wine Parade** at the Dom held the last week of July. For exact details contact the tourism office and for wine festivals in the whole area inquire from **Fränkischer Weinbauverband**, Haus des Frankenweins, Kranenkai 1, 97070 Würzburg, ☎ 0931-390-1111, www.weinland-franken.de.

Adventures

■ On Foot

Town Walks: The tourist office conducts 90-minute walking tours of the Old Town daily from April to October at 10:30 am. The tour departs from the tourist office at the Markt. Once a month, tours of 17th-century witch-hunt sights are available.

Night tours conducted by a **night watchman**, Wolfgang Mainka, ☎ 0931-409-356, start from the Vierröhrenbrunnen at the Rathaus. The 60-minute tour is available at 8 and 9 pm on

Friday and Saturday from mid-January to March, and Wednesday to Saturday from April to shortly before Christmas.

■ On Wheels

By Bicycle: Cycling is popular in the Würzburg area, with a cycling route running the full length of the River Main. **Der Rad-Touren-Teufel**, Erthalterstraße 18, 97074 Würzburg, ☎ 0931-882-830, www. radtourenteufel.de, arranges multi-days cycling tours with luggage transfers, rental bicycle, accommodations, and maps.

Bicycle rentals are available from **Fahrradstation**, Am Hauptbahnhof, ☎ 0931-57-445; **Radsport Schuster**, Raiffeisenstraße 3, ☎ 0931-12-338; or **Velo-Momber**, Landwehrstraße 13, ☎ 0931-12-627.

■ In the Air

Hot-Air Ballooning: Bernhardt Ballonfahrten, Am Feller 8, 97234 Reichenberg, ☎ 09366-99-211, www.bernhardt-ballonfahrten.de, starts balloon flights from several sites in Franken including Würzburg.

■ On Water

Riverboats: From April to October, several companies operate boat cruises on the River Main. Boats depart from the Alter Kranen near the Congress Centrum. A popular excursion is the 40-minute trip to Veitshöchheim run by **Kurth und Schiebe**, Alter Kranen, Roter Kiosk, ☎ 0931-58-573, or **Veitshöchheimer Personenschifffahrt**, Alter Kranen, Weißer Kiosk, ☎ 0931-55-631.

Where to Stay & Eat

■ Old Town Center

The **Maritim Hotel** is beautifully located on the banks of the Main close to both the main station and the Old Town. Rooms are luxurious and spacious with some having views of the Marienberg. The **Viaggo Restaurant** (€€€) is open for dinner only and serves international cuisine with a strong Mediterranean selection. Pleichertorstraße 5, 97070 Würzburg, ☎ 931-30-530, fax 0931-305-3900, www.maritim.de. (€€€-€€€€)

The **Best Western Hotel Rebstock**, in the center of the town, has an early 18th-century Rococo façade and an refined interior. The **restaurant** (€€€-€€€€) serves classical dishes and has an excellent wine list. Neubaustraße 7, 97070 Würzburg, ☎ 0931-30-930, fax 0931-309-3100, www.rebstock.com. (€€€€)

The **Dorint Novotel Hotel** is a modern, comfortable hotel with a very convenient location be-

Dorint Novotel

tween the station and the Residenz. The rustic **Frankenstube** (€€-€€€) serves mostly local specialties. Ludwigstraße/Ecke Eichstraße, 97070 Würzburg, ☎ 0931-30-540, fax 0931-305-4423, www.accorhotels.de. (€€€)

Zur Stadt Mainz is located behind an original colorfully painted façade dating from 1430. The 15 rooms are comfortably furnished with country-style furniture. The rustic **restaurant** (€€-€€€) has an old-Franconian atmosphere and serves regional dishes; reservations are recommended. Semmelstraße 39, 97070 Würzburg, ☎ 0931-53-155, fax 0931-58-510, www.hotel-stadtmainz.de. (€€).

Zur Stadt Mainz

■ Camping

Camping Kalte Quelle is on the banks of the River Main to the south of Würzburg. It has rather basic facilities with 170 lots for tourists and 130 for long-term rental. It is open from mid-March to late No-

Bavaria

vember. 97084 Würzburg-Heidingsfeld, ☎ 0931-65-598, fax 0931-612-611.

Bamberg

Bamberg is one of Germany's most beautiful towns. It has a long history, with architectural gems spanning a millennium. Its main attractions are the 2,300 protected buildings that led to the town being listed on the UNESCO World Cultural Heritage List.

Bamberg has a written history going back to 902, but its moment came in 1007 when Emperor Heinrich II founded a bishopric and erected an Imperial Palace in the town. As with other Episcopal towns in the region, the clergy chose the high ground and frequently came into conflict with the citizens who settled in the valley. The most impressive buildings in Bamberg are mostly Baroque and are found in the former bishop's town.

Following secularization, Bamberg became part of Bavaria. After World War I, it briefly served as capital of Bavaria while Munich was in the hands of revolutionaries. World War II left Bamberg virtually unscathed.

Tilman Riemenschneider (1460-1531), one of the most famous German sculptors, was born in Bamberg. His most famous work in town is the tomb for Heinrich II and his wife in the Dom. The talented **Dientzenhofer family**, who designed and built many a Baroque palace in Germany, also hailed from here. The Bamberg Neues Residenz is one of their masterpieces.

Information Sources

Tourist Office: Tourist Information, Geyerswörthstraße 3, 96047 Bamberg, ☎ 0951-297-6200, www.bamberg.de.

Transportation

The train station is about 10 minutes walk from the Old Town. Follow Luitpoldstraße, turn right into Obere Königsstraße and then cross the Main-Danube-Canal on Kettenbrücke into the Old Town. Alternatively, several bus lines run from the station to the ZOB (Central Bus Station) near the Maximiliansplatz.

Most rail travel to Bamberg requires changeovers at Würzburg, an hour away on the hourly train.

Sightseeing

 The major sights in Bamberg can be grouped into three distinct sections – all within the UNESCO World Cultural Heritage listed area. The **Bürgerstadt** is the area between the Main-Danube Canal and the River Regnitz. It is here that the civilians lived. The Episcopal area is the higher ground to the west of the Regnitz. This is often referred to as the **Bischofsstadt** (Bishop's City) and has the largest and most impressive buildings in town. The **Michaelsberg** is higher than the Dom area and offers marvelous views of the Old Town.

■ Bürgerstadt

The citizens' Old Town area is dominated by two large squares. The **Maximiliansplatz** is surrounded by Baroque buildings – the large former priests' seminary is now used as the **Rathaus** (Town Hall). The long, narrow **Grüner Markt** (Green Market) is also lined by Baroque buildings, including the **St Martins-Kirche** (St Martin's Church), another work by the talented Johann Dietzenhofer.

The **Altes Rathaus** (Old Town Hall) is, with the Dom, the most famous sight in Bamberg. It is on a small island between the civilian and religious towns. The core of the building is 15th-century Gothic, but it received a Baroque exterior during the mid-18th century. Note the angel's leg

Altes Rathaus

Bavaria

sticking out at the bottom of the wall in an attempt to add some 3-D! On the south side is the Rottmeisterhaus, a half-timbered house that seems to piggyback on the main building. This 1688 building was erected on the pontoon of the bridge but from many angles seem to float in the air. The Altes Rathaus now houses the **Sammlung Ludwig** (Ludwig Collection), Obere Brücke 1a, ☎ 0951-871-871, a mostly Baroque porcelain collection donated by the Ludwigs (see *Cologne* for more on this art loving couple). Opening hours are Tuesday to Sunday from 9:30 am to 4:30 pm. Admission is €3.10.

The best views of the Altes Rathaus are upstream from the bridge leading to the Geyerswörth Castle. The Unteres Brücke, on the opposite side of the Rathaus, has good views of the former fishermen's houses that are often referred to as **Klein Venedig** (Small Venice).

■ Bischofsstadt

The four-tower **Dom**, Domplatz, was consecrated in 1237. It replaced the original church, erected on the orders of Heinrich II in 1012, which burned down twice. The newer church is mainly Gothic but with strong Romanesque influences – the plan was altered around

Dom (Immanuel Giel)

20 times during its construction as traditionalists argued with progressives over the suitability of the new *French* style. The result is one of the most impressive medieval buildings in Germany. The **Fürstenportal** (Princes' Portal), facing the Domplatz, has 10 recessed arches and an interesting sculpture of the Last Judgment. The **Adamspforte** (Adam's Door), on the south side, is the main entrance.

Most of the interior walls are bare, as Bavarian King Ludwig I stripped off the medieval paintwork in the 19th century, but some early reliefs can still be seen in the choir. The most famous artwork in the church is the **Bamberger Reiter** (Bamberg Knight). This 13th-century equestrian statue of a king is an idealized view of the medieval world, but mystery surrounds its creator, or indeed who it is suppose to represent. It is generally assumed that it is King Stephan of Hungary, but many other theories exist. The Nazis misused it as a symbol of Aryan perfection. No less impressive is **St Heinrichs-Grab** (St Henry's Tomb) in the east choir. It was carved between 1499 and 1513 by Tilman Riemenschneider as a suitable memorial to Heinrich II, founder of the cathedral and later declared a saint. Opening hours are daily from 8 am to 5 pm. The choir performs during the 8:45 am services on Sunday.

Bamberger Reiter

Figure from the Dom tympanum

The **Diözesanmuseum** (Diocesan Museum), Domkapitelhaus, Domplatz 5, ☎ 0951-502-325, is entered through the cathedral. It has the usual collection of lapidary remains and vestments. Of special note is Heinrich II's Blue Coat of Stars and the original statues of Adam and Eve from the Adamspforte – these were the first nudes in German art. Opening hours are Tuesday to Sunday from 10 am to 5 pm. Admission is €2.

The **Alte Hofhaltung** (Old Residence) was erected mostly in the 16th century as residence for the bishop. It was built on the site of the 11th-century Kaiserspfalz (Imperial Palace) but most of the visible façades are Renaissance. The doorway has a

Bavaria

statue of Heinrich II and his wife Kunigunde with a model of the cathedral. The Innenhof (Inner Courtyard) has Gothic half-timbered buildings.

The **Neue Residenz** (New Residence), Domplatz 8, ☎ 0951-519-390, is the largest building in Bamberg. It was erected by Johann Dientzenhofer in 1695-1704 for the Prince Elector of Mainz and Bishop of Bamberg. The interior has historic rooms and a painting gallery with old

Kaisersaal in the Neue Residenz

German masters and Baroque paintings. The Kaisersaal (Emperor's Hall) is where Napoleon signed the declaration of war with Prussia on October 6, 1806. The Rosengarten (Rose Garden), behind the Residenz, offers good views of the town. Opening hours are daily from April to September, 9 am to 6 pm, and from October to March, 10 am to 4 pm. Admission is €4.

■ The Michaelsberg

The Michaelsberg is higher than the Dom and has good views of the Old Town. It housed a Benedictine monastery from 1015 until 1803. A fire destroyed much of the original monastery and it was rebuilt in 1610 in a Gothic style.

Most of the former monastery is now a home for the aged but a small part is used for the **Fränkisches Brauereimuseum** (Franconian Brewery Museum), Michaelsberg 10f, ☎ 0951-53-016, www.bierstadt.de/museum. It has a small exhibition on the history of beer-making in the region as well as models and a display of traditional equipment. Opening hours are from April to October, Wednesday to Sunday, 1 to 5 pm. Admission is €2. No free sampling, but a beer garden is at hand.

The **Michaelskirche** (St Michael's Church) erected between the 12th and 15th centuries, has a ceiling decorated with 578 flowers and medicinal herbs. It is open daily from 9 am to 5 pm.

To get to the Michealsberg from the Domplatz, either follow the road between the two residences via Jakobsplatz, or take the walkway through the park across from the Rosengarten. Alternatively, use Bus line 10 from the Domplatz to the top.

Cultural Events

Concerts are frequently scheduled in the Dom, www.bamberger-dommusik.de. From May to October, short organ concerts are held in the Dom on Saturday at noon.

Shopping

■ Antiques

There are about 30 antique dealers in the narrow alleys between the Altes Rathaus and the Domberg. This allows for variety and fair prices, but bargains are hard to find. The **Bamberger Antiquitätenwochen** (Antiques Weeks) are held annually from end July to end August and they attract many dealers and buyers. Exact dates are available from the tourism office.

Adventures

■ On Foot

Town Walks: Two-hour guided walking tours of the Old Town sights are arranged by the tourist office from April to October from Monday to Saturday at 10:30 am and 2 pm, and on Sunday at 11 am.

The self-guided **Bierschmeckertour** (Beer Lover's Tour) is available for €20 from the tourist office. The fee includes a backpack, a color guide to the best beer sights, and five vouchers for a pint of beer in several restaurants.

Where to Stay & Eat

The **Hotel Residenzschloss Bamberg** is at the edge of the Old Town in a former hospital and the bishop elector's residence, combined with a modern wing. Rooms are

Hotel Residenzschloss

luxurious and very comfortable. The **restaurants** (€€-€€€) serve mainly international cuisine. Untere Sandstraße 32, 96049 Bamberg, ☎ 0951-60-910, fax 0951-609-1701, www. residenzschloss.com. (€€€€)

The **Bamberger Hof Bellevue** is a first class hotel in the heart of the Old Town – the best rooms have views of the Kaiserdom. Although rooms range in style from turn-of-the-19th century to thoroughly modern, all are very comfortable and well equipped. The **restaurant** (€€-€€€) serves French cuisine. Schönleinsplatz 4, 96047 Bamberg, ☎ 98-550, fax 0931-985-862, www.bambergerhof.de. (€€€)

A very pleasant place to stay is the **Romantik Hotel Weinhaus Messerschmitt**. It's in a building dating partly from 1422 and the hotel itself has a 170-year tradition. The exterior is white

Romantik Hotel Weinhaus Messerschmitt

and yellow, while the interior makes ample use of wood. Rooms are furnished using either antique or modern furniture. The highly rated **restaurant** (€€-€€€) serves international and

nouvelle cuisine. Lange Straße 41, 96047 Bamberg, ☎ 0951-297-800, fax 0951-297-8029, www.ho-tel-messerschmitt.de. (€€€)

The **Barock-Hotel am Dom** is next to the cathedral. Behind its beautiful façade are 20 comfortable rooms. The stairways are Baroque; the breakfast room is Gothic. Vorderer Bach 4, 96049 Bamberg, ☎ 0951-54-031, fax 0951-54-021. (€€)

Barock-Hotel am Dom

■ Camping

Campingplatz Insel is on the banks of the River Regnitz. It has 170 lots, good facilities and is open year-round. Am Campingplatz 1, 96049 Bamberg-Bug, ☎ 0951-56-320, fax 0951-56-321, www. campinginsel.de.

Nuremberg (Nürnberg)

Nürnberg is a city of around half a million people. The second-largest city in Bavaria, it's a major industrial center. It is a popular destination with German and continental tourists, but receives far fewer English-speaking visitors than it should. Many English-speakers associate Nürnberg with the events before and directly after World War II, rather than the vast political and cultural role the town played over a period of 800 years.

The oldest reference to Nürnberg goes back to 1050 and eight centuries of glorious history followed. Two towns on either side of the River Pegnitz, Lorenz and Sebald, developed separately until united in the 14th century. Emperor Konrad II built a palace in Lorenz and Emperor Heinrich III started the castle in Sebald.

The Golden Bull, forced on Emperor Karl IV in 1356, among others, stipulated that all new emperors had to hold their first Reichstag (Imperial Parliament) in Nürnberg – a tradition that continued until 1543. The imperial jewels were kept in Nürnberg from 1424 to 1796, and again briefly during the Nazi period.

Nürnberg's golden age was in the late 15th and early 16th centuries. During this period, it was at the peak of its economic and cultural development. Several artists and scientist were based here. Albrecht Dürer (1471-1528), the man who brought the Renaissance to Germany, was born and spent most of his life in Nürnberg. The poet Hans Sachs (1494-1576); the sculptor Veit Stoß (1445-1533); Peter Henlein (1480-1542), the builder of the first pocket watch; and Martin Behaim (1459-1506), the cosmographer and creator of the first globe – all worked here during the period.

Ironically, it was the maps created in Nürnberg that helped with the discovery of sea routes to the east. This altered trade patterns and spelled the end of wealth in the area for centuries. Additionally, Nürnberg backed the Reformation early on and thus upset the staunchly Catholic Emperors. They refused to hold future parliaments in the town and, worse, favored Augsburg in southern Bavaria, which increasingly took away trade and culture. The decline continued until the area industrialized in the 19th century. The town became part of Bavaria in 1806.

THE NAZI PARTY RALLIES

The Nazi Party held rallies in Nürnberg in 1927 and 1929, mostly due to the city's central location and easy access from all parts of Germany. This, along with the symbolism of Nürnberg's links to the old empire, led to the town being selected as the permanent seat for the party rallies. From 1933 to 1938, six party rallies were held here.

As the distinction between party and state became increasingly vague, the rallies increasingly served as a showpiece of military might. The 1938 rally was attended by 1.6 million people over a period of a week. The rallies involved endless speeches, military parades, and sporting events.

The Nazis picked Nürnberg to host the annual party rallies that attracted up to 1.6 million participants. At the 1935 rally, anti-Semitic laws, often referred to as the Nuremberg Laws, were adopted that legalized the segregation of Jews, which had been common practice since the Nazis came to power in 1933.

On January 2, 1945, an air raid destroyed 90% of the Old Town. Most of the buildings are therefore reconstructions, but are generally faithful to the original plans. The town walls largely escaped undamaged.

For many, Nürnberg will always be associated primarily with the Nazi rallies, the Nuremberg Laws, and the Nuremberg Trials. In contrast to Berlin and Munich, which have managed to hide their Nazi heritage somewhat, sites associated with the Nazis are large and easily accessible in Nürnberg. They are well worth seeing.

Information Sources

Tourist Office: Information is available from the Verkehrsverein, Postfach 4248, 90022 Nürnberg, ☎ 0911-23-360, www.tourismus-nuernberg.de.

Information offices for personal callers are across from the Hauptbahnhof in the Künstlerhaus, Königstraße 93, ☎ 0911-233-6131, and at the Hauptmarkt, ☎ 0911-233-6135.

Transportation

Nürnberg has an excellent public transportation system, combining, S-Bahn and U-Bahn trains, trams, and buses. The Hauptbahnhof, directly south of the Old Town, is the hub for all modes of transportation.

Walking is by far the best option, as many parts of the Old Town are for pedestrians only and one-way streets make for difficult navigation by car. To reach the Nazi sites, public transportation is more convenient.

Sightseeing

Virtually all tourist sights are within the three-mile-long medieval town wall. It is possible to cross the Old Town on foot from the Hauptbahnhof to the Kaiserburg in about half an hour – however, few would want to rush through that fast.

If time is limited, give preference to the German National Museum, the Kaiserburg, the town fortifications, and the Reichsparteigelände. The St Lorenz, St Sebald, and Frauenkirche are also interesting.

■ St Lorenzkirche Area

The modern Hauptbahnhof is just outside the town walls. From here, the main entrance into the Old Town is via the **Königstor** (King's Gate), one of four remaining fat, round towers. Around 2.3 miles of the original three miles of up to 26-ft town walls and 71 of the original 130 defensive towers survived. Fine parts of the wall can be seen at Frauengrabe, but the sections at the

Bavaria

west of the town and below the Kaiserburg are even better. Behind the gate is the **Handwerkerhof**, Am Königstor, ☎ 01805-860-700-590, a restored medieval-looking area selling mainly arts and crafts – see *Shopping* below for details.

Nürnberg panorama from the Spittlertor

Königstraße leads up to the **St. Lorenzkirche** (St Laurent's Church), Lorenzer Platz, ☎ 0911-244-6990, www.lorenzkirche.de. This High Gothic church was erected over a century, starting in 1260, and further enhanced in 1477 with Late Gothic elements. It was severely damaged in 1945, with only the towers left standing, but rebuilt with much of the art original. Of special

note is the *Englischer Gruß* (*Annunciation*, 1517-18) by Veit Stoß, and the tabernacle (1493) by Adam Krafft, adorned with a crucifix by Stoß. The rose window in the west façade is 29 ft across. Opening hours are Monday to Saturday from 9 am to 5 pm and Sunday from 1 to 4 pm.

At the west of the church is the **Nassauer Haus**, Karolinenstraße 2, the oldest private home in Nürnberg. The lower two

Nassauer Haus (S. Kormann)

floors are from the 13th century while the choir and towers are 15th century.

The **Tugendbrunnen** (Virtues Fountain) was completed in 1589 as a symbol of Nürnberg's independence as Free Imperial City. The figures symbolize good virtues, with justice towering over them on the third level of the fountain.

The **Museumsbrücke** (Museum Bridge) crosses the River Pegnitz to the Sebald part of town. There are actually no museums near the bridge, but it affords the best views of the **Heilig-Geist-Spital** (Holy Ghost Hospice), Spitalgasse/Hans-

Heilig-Geist-Spital (Keichwa)

Sachs-Platz. It is partly 14th-century, but the most famous parts that span the River Pegnitz are 16th century. It now houses an old age home.

■ Hauptmarkt Area

The **Hauptmarkt** (Main Market) is the center of all markets and festivals in Nürnberg. Its beginnings were anything but celebratory. In 1349, Emperor Karl IV, who was constitutionally responsible for the protection of Jews in the city, was dependent on Nürnberg for financing and secretly made it known that he would not oppose the town's plans to rid themselves of debts owed to Jewish moneylenders. Following the example of Swiss and French towns, the Jews were blamed for the nearing plague. The local Jews were forced into their houses, the doors cemented shut, and the whole ghetto set on fire. With the Jews dead and debts cleared, the former ghetto area was used to create the new market square.

Probably to atone for this sin, Karl IV donated the **Frauenkirche** (Church of Our Lady), Hauptmarkt, ☎ 0911-206-560. This 14th-century Gothic church was the first hall church in the area. More interesting than the church or the art is the carillon. The **Männleinlaufen** is a set of seven small metal men, representing the seven Prince Electors, who come out daily at noon to pay homage to the Emperor. It reflects the constitutional decree determined by the Golden Bull of 1356, which determined the seven electors, who could elect the emperor and in return sworn allegiance. The symbolism is more interesting than the actual show. Opening hours are Monday to Saturday from 9 am to 6 pm and Sunday from 12:30 to 6 pm.

Männleinlaufen

The Schöner Brunnen

The **Schöner Brunnen** (Beautiful Fountain) is a century-old copy of the original late-14th-century Gothic marvel. It stands 62 ft high and has 40 colorfully painted figures representing biblical figures, philosophy, liberal arts, and political figures. Note the Golden Ring, a seamless copper ring inside the fencing. Tourists turn it three times for good luck – locals know one turn is quite sufficient! (Parts of the original fountain are in the German National Museum.)

The **Altes Rathaus** (Old Town Hall) was completed in 1622 in a mixture of High Renaissance and Early Baroque. It also incorporated parts of a building from 1340, such as the large reception hall. This is the largest secular building in historic Nürnberg. It has copies of the imperial jewels in the foyer. The building was severely damaged in the war and much of the interior, including Albrecht Dürer's wall paintings, has not been restored

The **St. Sebaldkirche**, Albrecht-Dürer-Platz 1, ☎ 0911-214-2500, is the largest church in town. It was initially a Late Ro-

manesque triple-nave church, erected in 1230-40, but altered up to the 14th century with Gothic additions. The interior is far more harmonious than the somewhat odd-looking exterior. The church was severely damaged in 1945 but restored – photos with peace messages show some of the damage. The church is filled with art. A highlight is the Gothic St Sebald's tomb – a

St. Sebaldkirche (Keichwa)

1519 bronze by Peter Vischer. In the chancel and ambulatory are several works by Veit Stoß. The church opens daily at 9:30 am and closes at 4 pm from January to March and November, at 6 pm in October, December, April, and May, and at 8 pm from June to September.

Nürnberg has long been important in toy production and still hosts a large annual toy trade fair. Admission to this fair is strictly limited to bona fide traders and manufacturers, but open to all is the **Spielzeugmuseum** (Toy Museum), Karlstraße 13-15, ☎ 0911-231-3164, www.museen.nuernberg.de. It has displays of toys over the centuries, with historic wooden toys, dolls, mechanical toys, tin toys, and model trains. The upper floor has post-World War II toys, including Lego and Barbies. It is very much a look-but-do-not-touch museum, but a special room on the top floor has toys for children to play with while parents look at the historic ones. Opening hours are Tuesday to Friday from 10 am to 5 pm and weekends from 10 am to 6 pm. Admission is €5.

Adjacent to St Sebald is the triangular **Albrecht Dürer Platz**, with an 1840 bronze statue of the great artist. Behind the statue is the entrance to the **Nürnberger Felsengänge** (Nuremberg Rock-Cut Cellars), Bergstraße 19, 0911-227-066. These are huge cellars cut out of sandstone to provide cold storage for beer. The first ones were cut before 1380 and were used up to 1900. Four levels of cellars were cut and, during the air raids of World War II, up to 25,000 people hid here. As with the Art Bunker, there is not much to see other than the bare walls. Note that even in summer, the temperature stays below 46°F. Guided tours meet daily at the Albrecht-Dürer-Platz, behind the memorial, at 11 am, 1, 3, and 5 pm. Admission is €4.

The **Stadtmuseum Fembohaus** (Fembo House City Museum), Burgstraße 15, ☎ 0911-231-2595, www.museen.nuernberg.de, is ensconced in the best-preserved patrician house in town from the 16th century. Note the large sundial when walking uphill from the Hauptmarkt – Nürnberg still has 32 of the original 73 in working condition. Nürnberg's position at the heart of Germany and the wealth of the artists who lived here during the Middle Ages insure interesting displays. Opening

Fembohaus

hours are Tuesday to Sunday from 10 am to 5 pm, closing at 8 pm on Thursday. Admission is €5.

■ Kaiserburg

The **Kaiserburg** is a highlight of any visit to Nürnberg. It is in this mighty fortress that the Emperor stayed while in town. Construction of the castle started in 1167. The Holy Roman Empire of the German Nation had no permanent capital and the emperor had to move around with his entourage from palace to palace. Between 1050 and 1571, every emperor visited

The Kaiserburg

Nürnberg. In total around 300 imperial visits took place and several imperial parliaments met here.

It is a steep walk up from the Old Town to the Castle. The ticket office recently moved to the deepest inner courtyard next to the **Kaiserburgmuseum** (Imperial Castle and Kaiserburg Museum, Auf der Burg 13, ☎ 0911-244-6590, www.schloesser. bayern.de. This branch of the German National Museum is a good place to spend time while waiting for the guided tour of the Castle. The museum focuses on military history and practices during the Middle Ages and has a fine collection of armor and weapons.

The interior of the Castle can only be seen on a guided tour – sometimes available in English. During the tour, the palace is seen, with the double chapel, the imperial reception rooms, and apartments. The tour ends with a demonstration of the **Tiefer Brunnen** (deep well) – a 173-ft-deep well cut out of solid rock. It is worth climbing the mighty, round **Sinwell Tower** for fantastic views of the Old Town. Opening hours of the buildings are daily from April to September from 9 am to 6 pm, and October to March from 10 am to 4 pm. Some parts of the Castle grounds remain open until dark. Admission to the whole complex, including a guided tour, is €6.

■ **Dürer-Museum Area**

The **Tiergärtnerplatz**, directly below the Castle, is one of the loveliest medieval squares in Nürnberg. It is framed by several half-timbered houses and the former town defenses. The lower, smaller gate is from the 13th century, but the wider gate had to be added in the 16th century in order to allow the increasingly

The Albrecht Dürer-Haus

larger carts to pass through. It is possible to walk from here to Neutor on the sentries' walk.

The **Albrecht-Dürer-Haus**, Albrecht-Dürer-Straße 39, ☎ 0911-231-2568, www.museen.nuernberg.de, is a museum dedicated to the great Early Renaissance artist who lived and worked here from 1509 up to his death in 1528. The house miraculously survived the carnage of 1945. The museum is furnished mostly as it was in the time of Dürer and demonstrations of some of the printing techniques Dürer introduced are held in the upper floor studio. Some Dürer drawings are on display but, for his greatest works, visit the German National Museum. Opening hours for the Albrecht-Dürer-Haus are Tuesday to Sunday from 10 am to 5 pm, closing at 8 pm on Thursday. In July and August, as well as during the Christmas market, the museum is also open on Monday. Admission is €5 and includes an English-language audio guide.

Looking down on the Albrecht Dürer-Haus

The **Historischer Kunstbunker im Burgberg** (World War II Art Bunker), Obere Schmiedgasse 52, ☎ 0911-227-066, is where much of Nürnberg's art was stored during World War II. In these medieval cellars cut out of rock 79 ft underneath the Kaiserburg Castle, the art was safe from air raids and fires. The bunker can only be seen on the daily guided tour at 3 pm. Frankly, there is not much to see here except the bare bunker, some photographs, and the ingeniously simple air circulation system. Admission is €5.

The most impressive parts of the town defenses are the section from the Kaiserburg Castle to **Spittlertor**. The defenses over the River Pegnitz are impressive and can be seen from **Hallertorbrücke** outside the Old Town, or more interestingly from a hanging bridge on the inside of the walls. The area at Maxbrücke and the Henkersteg that leads to a small island in the river is especially picturesque.

■ German National Museum

The **Germanisches Nationalmusem** (National Museum of German Art and Culture), Kartäusergasse 1, ☎ 0911-13-310, www.gnm.de, was founded in 1852 to collect art, cultural objects, and ocuments related to the German-speaking world. Currently it has about 1.2 million pieces, of which some 20,000 are on display, making it the largest cultural history museum in Germany. The core of the museum complex is a medieval monastery, whose church and cloisters are used to exhibit religious artworks. The rest of the museum is more mod-

Albrecht Dürer, Portrait of Elsbeth Tucher, 1499

Bavaria

ern. The layout is somewhat confusing, but free floor plans are available.

The Picture Gallery has a large number of works by Dürer, Cranach, Rembrandt, and Holbein, while the sculpture section has excellent works by Veit Stoß and Tilman Riemenschneider. The applied and decorative arts sections are very impressive and include the oldest globes in the world, early clocks, pianos, other musical instruments, and even a 17th-century dollhouse. The early and pre-history sections have jewelry from the Germanic tribes and the oldest item, a 35-inch-high golden cone dating from around 1200 BC. Opening hours are Tuesday to Sunday from 10 am to 6 pm, closing at 9 pm on Wednesday. Admission is €5.

■ Nazi Sights

The sights associated with the Nazis are not within walking distance from the Old Town but can be reached easily with public transportation. The parade ground of the Nazi Rallies is southeast of the Old Town and the Court of the Nürnberg trials is to the west.

Reichsparteigelände (Nazi Party Rallying Grounds): It is best to start a visit to the Nazi Party Rallying grounds at the documentation center. That will help to explain the background and the lay of the land. Three major structures survived to the present: the Congress Hall, the Great Road, and the Zeppelin Tribune. The area is easiest to reach by Tramlines 6 and 9 (stop Dokumentations-Zentrum), or S-Bahn S2 (station Dutzenteich).

The massive **Kongreß-halle** (Congress Hall) was designed to accommodate 50,000 delegates. It was never completed but what was done was built "to last a thousand years." Nürnberg has been stuck with the building, since

Kongreßhalle

demolishing it would be expensive and the whole area is now

under protection order. Most of the building is now a storage warehouse, but it also houses the very interesting **Dokumentationszentrum Reichsparteitagsgelände** (Documentation Center Nazi Party Rallying Grounds), Bayernstraße 110, ☎ 0911-231-5666, www.museen.nuernberg.de. The center has an excellent permanent exhibition entitled *Fascination and Terror*, which uses photos, models, audio, and video to explain the Nazi regime, with special emphasis on the events surrounding the Party Rallies. Opening hours are weekdays from 9 am to 6 pm and weekends from 10 am to 6 pm. Admission is €5.

The area and buildings are surprisingly large and it takes a good 15 minutes to walk around the Kongreßhalle to the **Große Straße** (Great Road). This 1.2-mile-long and 196-ft-wide road was to have been the central axis of the monumental area. It is paved with 60,000 slabs of granite. Immediately after the war, the American forces used it as a landing strip and currently most of it serves as a very good-looking parking lot for the nearby conference center and soccer field.

Walk down the Great Road and turn left once across the Dutzenteich pond to reach the 1,000-ft-long **Zeppelin Tribune**. Although the columns along the top of the main tribune were destroyed for safety reasons in 1967, the tribune is still instantly recognizable as the place from where Hitler addressed the party faithful. The main and side tribunes provided seating for 60,000, while the field could hold another 100,000. The field is fenced off but the tribune is open and freely accessible.

■ The Nuremberg Trials

The Nuremberg Trials took place from November 20, 1945 and continued for 218 days. In the dock were 21 top Nazi officials – 12 received the death sentence and were executed on October 16, 1946. Hermann Göring cheated the hangman by committing suicide hours before. Proceedings took place in the **Schwurgerichtssaal 600 - Nürnberger Prozesse** (International Military Tribunal - Nuremberg Trial), Landgericht Nürnberg-Fürth/Schwurgerichtssaal, Fürther Straße 110, ☎ 0911-231-5421, www.museen.nuernberg.de. The court is still in use and is open weekends only and only on guided tours that depart on the hour between 1 and 4 pm. Reservations are not possible. Inquire about the availability of English tours. Admission is €2.50. (It is usually possible to peak into the court on weekdays but sightseeing is not allowed when the court is in use.) The court is easiest to reach by U-Bahn U1 or U11 (station Bärenschanze).

Cultural Events

Nürnberg has a busy cultural schedule with a wide range of performances and styles. In addition to the special events, regular concerts are held in the Meistersingerhalle and inside the Kaiserburg. Information is available from the tourist office or www.tourismus.nuernberg.de if no other details are given.

The **Rock im Park**, www.rock-im-park.de, is an open-air rock festival that attracts international stars. It is held on Pentecost weekend at the Zeppelinfield.

Klassik Open Air is an open-air classical music festival held in the Luitpoldhein Park at the end of July, beginning of August. Admission is free and picnic baskets are welcomed.

The **Internationale Orgelwoche** (International Organ Week), ☎ 0911-214-4466, www.ion.nuernberg.de, is held end of June, beginning of August and is the oldest and largest religious musical festival in the world.

The **Tucher Ritterspiele** is a knight tournament held in August at the Kaiserburg. It features typical medieval tournament sport and a medieval market.

The **St Lorenzkirche**, ☎ 0911-2446-9937, www.kirchenmusik-st-lorenz.de, is a frequent venue for religious music. On weekdays in May, half-hour organ recitals follow the Männleinlauf at around 12:15 pm. Most 10 am church services on Sunday are accompanied by choral or orchestral music.

The **St Sebaldkirche**, ☎ 0911-214-2525, www.kirchenmusik-st-sebald-nbg.de, is also a popular venue for frequent concerts. About once a month, the church has a musical guided night tour of the church and its history.

Festivals

Nürnberg enjoys a couple of good annual festivals. Although the town is in beer-drinking Franken, it does have a wine festival. The **Fränkische**

Weinfest is held annually over two weeks at the end of June, beginning of July. The **Spargelmarkt** (Asparagus Market) is held the last week of May to welcome the start of the asparagus season. The **Altstadtfest** (Old Town Festival) is held at the end of September and claims to be the largest in Germany.

The **Nürnberger Christkindlemarkt** (Christmas Market) has a 400-year tradition and is world-famous. It is one of the best in Germany and is held annually from end of November to Christmas. It is best to arrive on a Sunday or Monday to avoid the crowds. The month is also a cultural highlight with musical concerts staged in many churches.

Shopping

 A good place to buy arts and crafts is the **Handwerkerhof**, Am Königstor, ☎ 01805-860-700-590. It is a large courtyard with medieval-style small half-timbered houses selling mostly locally made items. Even if you don't want to buy anything, it is interesting to see how much of Nürnberg must have looked prior to 1945. Opening hours are weekdays from 10 am to 6:30 pm and Saturday from 10 am to 4 pm.

Nürnberg is famous for two edible products: the finger-size Nürnberger Bratwurst sausages and Lebkuchen. **Lebkuchen** are gingerbread delicacies, especially associated with Christmas but available throughout the year. The best ones are baked without the use of flour. They are usually available in colorful tins that make good souvenirs. One of the most famous producers is **Lebkuchen Schmidt**, Zollhausstraße 30, ☎ 0911-896-631, www.leckuchen-schmidt.com. It has stores at Plobenhof 6 (at the Hauptmarkt), in the Handwerkerhof, and at the Christmas Market.

The **Trempelmarkt** is Germany's largest open-air flea market and is held twice annually in the Old Town in May and September.

Adventures

■ On Foot

 Town Walks: Nürnberg has an astonishing number of competing guided walking tours. The tourist office conducts a two-hour guided walking tour in English of the Old Town daily from May to October at 1 pm, departing from the tourist office at Hauptmarkt. Audio guides in English can also be rented from the tourist office for self-guided tours.

Die **Stadtführer**, www.nuernberg.de, conducts a wide range of tours emphasizing history and art. The **Institute for Regional History**, Wiesentalstraße 32, ☎ 0911-307-360, www. geschichte-fuer-alle.de, has frequent tours in the city and region focusing on history

■ On Wheels

By Bicycle: Bicycle rentals are available from **Fahrradkiste**, Knauerstraße 9, ☎ 0911-287-9064; **Ride a Rainbow**, Adam-Kraft-Straße 55, ☎ 0911-397-337; or **Play it Again Sports**, Rennweg 7-9, ☎ 0911-538-580.

■ In the Air

Hot-Air Ballooning: Ballonfahren macht Spaß, Richard-Wagner-Straße 11, 91207 Lauf/Pegnitz, ☎ 09123-99-393, www.ballonfahren.de, flies in the Nürnberg region but also offers longer flights, including crossing the Alps.

Where to Stay & Eat

■ Station Area

The modern **ArabellaSheraton Hotel Carlton** is a very comfortable luxury hotel a block from the station. Rooms are spacious and modern, with straight lines and light colors. Eilgutstraße 15, 90443

ArabellaSheraton Hotel Carlton

Nürnberg, ☎ 0911-20-030, fax 0911-200-3111, www.carlton-nuernberg.de. (€€€-€€€€)

The **Le Méridien Grand Hotel** combines a hundred-year tradition with modern comforts. Rooms have Art Nouveau influences and marble baths. The **Brasserie** (€€-€€€€) serves

Le Méridien Grand Hotel

international and regional dishes in upscale surrounding with ample use of marble, mirrors, and carved glass. Bahnhofstraße 1, 90443 Nürnberg, ☎ 0911-23-220, fax 0911-232-2444, www.grand-hotel.de. (€€€€)

The **InterCity Hotel** offers good value in the same area close to the station. Rooms are comfortably furnished and well equipped. The room key gives free access to public transportation. Eilgutstraße 8, 90443 Nürnberg, ☎ 0911-24-780, fax 0911-247-8999, www.steigenberger.de. (€€-€€€)

The best value is offered by the two Ibis hotels close to the station. Rooms are clean, bright, and equipped with the necessities. The **Ibis Marientor** is just outside the city walls behind the Grand Hotel. Königstorgraben 9, 90402 Nürnberg, ☎ 0911-24-090, fax 0911-240-9413, www.ibishotel.com. (€) The new **Ibis Königstor** is just inside the Old Town, close to the Handwerkerhof. Königstraße 74, 90402 Nürnberg, ☎ 0911-232-000, fax 0911-209-684, www.ibishotel.com (€€).

■ Old Town

Although the top hotels are near the Hauptbahnhof, some pleasant hotels can also be found inside the Altstadt itself.

Two small hotels with modern rooms and facilities are near the Dürer House. The **Hotel Agneshof** is pleasantly located in the heart of the Old Town. Rooms are modern and stylish. Most look out on the courtyard but some have balconies facing the Kaisersburg. Agnessgasse 10, 90403 Nürnberg, ☎ 0911-214-

Hotel Agneshof

Bavaria

440, fax 0911-2144-4140, www.agneshof-nuernberg.de. (€€€-€€€€)

The **Dürer Hotel** is thoroughly modern and close to its namesake's museum. Rooms are comfortable and furnished mostly with light wood. Neutormauer 32, 90403 Nürnberg, ☎ 0911-214-6650, fax 0911-2146-6555, www.altstadthotels-nuernberg.de. (€€€)

Several pleasant, informal restaurants with terraces enliven the scene at the picturesque Tiergärtenplatz in between the Dürer Haus and the Kaisersburg. However, some nearby restaurants offer a more upscale experience.

Leading the way, with a Michelin star, is **Essigbrätlein**, Weinmarkt 3, ☎ 0911-225-131, close to the Sebaldkirche. This comfortable, refined restaurant is located in the oldest guesthouse in town; the building dates from 1550. Nouvelle cuisine and the chef's own creations are offered. (€€€-€€€€)

Nearby is **Goldenes Posthorn**, Glöckleingasse 2, ☎ 0911-225-153, dating back to 1498. It claims to be Germany's oldest wine cellar. Local specialties feature prominently on the menu that also includes international cuisine. (€-€€€)

The **Nassauer Keller**, Karolinenstraße 2, ☎ 0911-225-967, inside Nuremberg's oldest private house, serves mainly regional specialties. The entrance door is low and the stairway down is steep, as is to be expected from such an old building. (€€-€€€)

■ Bratwurt Restaurants

Bratwurst is available all over town but the three restaurants listed below are the most famous and they still grill over beech wood fires.

NÜRNBERGER BRATWÜRSTCHEN

Nürnberg's famous contribution to German cuisine is the small finger-size sausages served all over town and in other German cities too. By law, they must be seven to nine cm (2.7-3.5 inches) long and weigh between 20 and 25 grams (.7-.88 oz). They may only contain pork meat – no innards – encased in sheep entrails. Of course, they need to be produced inside the city limits in order to add "Nürnberg" to the name.

Historische Bratwurstküche Zum Golden Stern, Zirkelschmiedsgasse 26, ☎ 0911-205-9288, dates from 1419 and claims to be the oldest bratwurst restaurant in town. It is close to Färbertor. (€-€€)

Das Bratwurstglöcklein, Im Handwerkerhof, ☎ 0911-227-625, is inside the picturesque Handwerkershof at Königstor. The sausages are served on bell-shaped plates by waitresses in traditional costumes. (€-€€)

A personal favorite is the **Bratwursthäusle**, Rathausplatz 1, ☎ 0911-227-695, located in the morning shade of St Sebaldkirche. It has a small, rustic room, where smaller parties have to share tables, and a pleasant terrace with views of the passersby. (€-€€)

■ Camping

Knaus Campingpark is at the Dutzenteich near the Nazi Party Rallying grounds around 2.4 miles south of central Nürnberg. It has excellent facilities, with 150 often shady lots and it's open year-round. Hans-Kalb-Straße 56, 90471 Nürnberg, ☎ 0911-981-2717, fax 0911-981-2718, www.knauscamping.de.

◆ Eastern Bavaria

In contrast to Franken, the areas of Eastern Bavaria have been in Bavaria from the start. Regensburg served as ducal seat from the sixth to the 13th century. Passau was an Episcopal city with a superb location on the confluence of the Danube and the Inn Rivers.

Information Sources

For information on Eastern Bavaria, contact the Tourismusverband Ostbayern, Luitpoldstraße 20, 93047 Regensburg, ☎ 0941-585-390, www. otsbayern-toursimus.de.

Regensburg

Regensburg, at the northernmost point of the Danube and with 140,000 inhabitants, is the fourth-largest city in Bavaria. As World War II left little damage, it has one of the most beautiful medieval city centers in Germany. It is very popular with European travelers but somehow English speakers tend to pass it by.

In the High Middle Ages, Regensburg, with 10,000 inhabitants, was the largest and richest city in the region. In 1245, it became a Free Imperial City. Its decline was gradual. By the 16th century, trade routes had gradually shifted and talent moved to the new upcoming cities of Augsburg and Nürnberg. As a result, much of the core of Regensburg that survived is older than that of those two cities.

From 1663 to 1806, Regensburg had the prestige of housing the Reichstag – the first Permanent Diet or Parliament in Germany. But the Napoleonic wars ended the Holy Roman Empire and in 1810 Regensburg lost its independence to become a provincial backwater in an enlarged Kingdom of Bavaria.

Information Sources

Tourist Office: Tourist Information, Altes Rathaus, 93047 Regensburg, ☎ 0941-507-4410, www.regensburg.de.

Transportation

Regensburg has a well-developed bus system. However, tourists generally need only the Altstadtbus (Old Town Bus). It runs from the main station via the most important sights in the Old Town. It departs every six minutes or so and costs €0.60.

Sightseeing

All the sights in Regensburg are in the Old Town, on the south bank of the River Danube. Most of the Old Town is a pedestrian zone. The area is 15 minutes walk from the main station along roads lined with shops. The Altstadtbus is a convenient alternative.

■ Dom Area

Construction of the **Dom St Peter** (Cathedral), Domplatz 5, ☎ 0941-586-5500, www.bistum-regensburg.de, started around 1260 shortly after Regensburg became a Free Imperial City. It was a prestige project to show off the wealth of the city and it is still the most important Gothic structure in Bavaria. The new cathedral replaced its Romanesque predecessor, of which

Dom St Peter

the Eselturm (Donkey Tower) above the north transept is the only remaining part. The city overestimated the size of its purse as well as the skill of the architect. His planned 524-ft single tower could never have been constructed. In addition to the laws of physics, a shortage of funds meant that the building was not completed until 1525, sans tower. The current spires, making the west towers 344 ft high, were only added in the 19th century and it was a shoddy job – they had to be replaced a century later. The western façade is richly decorated.

Inside, the church has three naves and a non-projecting transept. It is 269 ft long and 105 ft wide. Most of the stained glass windows, as well as the sculptures of Mary and the Archangel Gabriel on the west transept pillars, are from the 13th century. Note the plaque on the south wall for Pastor Johann Maier. He was hanged on April 24, 1945 for demanding that the city should surrender to the advancing American army rather than waste life and property on a lost battle. Opening hours are daily from 6:30 am to 6 pm, closing at 5 pm from November to March. The cloisters, the Romanesque Allerheiligenkapelle, and the Carolingian Stephanskapelle can only be seen on the guided tour of the cathedral.

The **Domschatzmuseum** (Cathedral Treasury), ☎ 0941-57-645, shows the wealth of the cathedral in goldsmith work and vestments from the 11th to the 19th centuries. Plans of the single tower for the cathedral can be seen at the entrance to the museum. Opening hours are April to October from Tuesday to Sunday, 10 am to 5 pm; only from noon on Sunday. From November to March, it is open only on Friday and Saturday, 10 am to 4 pm, and Sunday from noon to 4 pm. Admission is €1.50.

Bavaria

The **Diözesanmuseum St Ulrich** (Diocesan Museum), Domplatz 2, ☎ 0941-51-688, has a rich collection of sculpture, paintings, and goldsmith work from the 11th century to the present. The museum is housed in the Early Gothic former church of St Ulrich. Opening hours are April to October from Tuesday to Sunday, 10 am to 5 pm. Admission is €1.50.

The Alte Kapelle

The **Alte Kapelle** (Old Chapel), Alter Kornmarkt, was originally a Carolingian Pfalzkapelle, but after two centuries of neglect was rebuilt as a Romanesque structure in 1002. However, in the 18th century it was transformed into a Rococo masterpiece. Its rich gilded interior decorations can be seen through the gates at the rear of the church during the same hours as the cathedral.

The **Historisches Museum** (City History Museum), Dachauplatz 2, ☎ 0941-507-2448, is in a former Minorite monastery. It has displays on local history from the Stone Age to the present. Highlights include the Act of Foundation – a 26-ft-long stone with an inscription referring to the foundation of the Roman garrison here in AD 179. Opening hours are Tuesday to Sunday from 10 am to 4 pm. Admission is €2.20.

The **Porta Praetoria**, Unter den Schwibbögen, is part of a gate that remained from the Roman garrison, Castra Regina, established here in the second century. It is part of a more modern building and was covered by plaster for centuries, but is now again uncovered. Apart from the

Steinerne Brücke

huge monuments in Trier, this is the largest surviving Roman structure in Germany.

■ Danube Banks

With 16 arches, the 1,016-ft-long **Steinerne Brücke** (Stone Bridge) was built between 1135 and 1146. Its construction greatly facilitated trading with northern areas and for eight centuries it was the only permanent crossing point of the Danube in the region. Fine views of the Old Town can be enjoyed from halfway across.

Brückturm-Museum

The 14th-century **Brückturm-Museum** (Bridge Tower Museum), Weiße-Lamm-Gasse 1, ☎ 0941-567-6015, has some displays of objects and photos on the history of the Stone Bridge and shipping on the Danube. However, the main reason to visit is to enjoy the view of the Old Town from the top of the tower. Opening hours are April to October from Tuesday to Sunday, 10 am to 5 pm. Admission is €2.

The adjacent 1620 **Salzstadel**, with its enormous five-floor roof, was used as a salt warehouse. It currently houses a restaurant. The small, old building next to it on the banks of the Danube is the **Historische Wurstkuchl** (Historic Sausage Kitchen). It dates from the 12th century and claims to be the oldest sausage restaurant in Germany.

A few blocks upstream is the **Kepler-Gedächtnishaus** (Kepler Memorial Center), Keplerstraße 5, ☎ 0941-507-3442. The mathemati-

Johannes Kepler

Bavaria

cian and astronomer Johannes Kepler (1571-1630) lived and died in this house. It is now a museum with period furniture, instruments used by him, and some functioning models. Opening hours are Tuesday to Sunday, 10 am to noon and 2 to 4 pm. From November to March, it is closed on Sunday afternoons. Admission is €2.20.

■ Rathaus Area

The **Altes Rathaus** (Old Town Hall) was built as a prestige project to celebrate Regensburg's status as a Free Imperial City. The oldest parts date from the mid-13th century, while the large Gothic additions are a century younger.

Altes Rathaus

The building currently houses the information office as well as the **Reichstagmuseum** (Imperial Diet Museum), which can only be seen on a guided tour. From 1663 until the dissolution of the Holy Roman Empire of the German Nation in 1806, a permanent Imperial Diet sat in Regensburg. The tour includes four sections. The **Beratungszimmer**, a discussion room for the prince electors, is in the oldest part of the building. Most impressive though is the **Reichsaal** (Imperial Hall), where the actual diet congregated according to a strict protocol, which kept the different estates apart. (Commoners were not represented.) The **Fragstatt**, literally questioning place, is in the cellars and includes the original torture equipment and dark cells that were used in the disbursement of justice and injustice. The tour ends

Hinter der Grieb

with some cannons and a huge official city scale that astonishingly can distinguish weight differences of 5 grams or .17 ounce. It is open daily with German tours at various times from around 10 am to 4 pm. Tours in English are available from May to September, Monday to Saturday, at 3:30 pm. Admission is €3 and tickets are sold only inside the tourism office.

Nearby **Haidplatz** is a particularly picturesque square surrounded by historic buildings. The Neue Waage held the official scales. The 13th-century **Zum Goldenen Kreuz**, at Number 7, was a guesthouse and for centuries the choice of visiting emperors and kings. The **Justiabrunnen** (Fountain of Justice) is mid-17th century. **Hinter der Grieb** is a narrow alley with medieval houses leading from the square.

■ Schloss Thurn und Taxis

THURN UND TAXIS

From the mid-15th century up to the 19th century, the Thurn und Taxis family held a postal monopoly in much of Europe. The horn used by many European countries as symbol of the postal service originates from the family emblem. From 1748, the head of the family was also the emperor's principal representative (Prinzipalkommissäre) at the Permanent Diet. The former Benedictine monastery of St Emmeram was converted into one of Europe's most modern and lavish palaces for their use. It is still the principal seat of the family. Inheritance taxes eventually forced the family to open parts of the palace to the public.

St Emmeramkirche (St Emmerammus' Church), Emmeramsplatz 3, ☎ 0941-510-30, is a basilica dating back to the late seventh century, when the region was converted to Christianity. Most of the exterior is Romanesque and Gothic. The statues at the main entrance of Jesus Christ, St Emmerammus, and St Dionysius are 11th-century and among the oldest in Germany. The interior is a bit of a surprise – the Asam brothers altered the original Romanesque into Baroque with frescos and stuccowork. Despite their efforts, the highest art here is still the tombstone of Queen Hemma, dating to about 1280. The crypt dates from 740 AD. The church is open daily, 10 am to 4:30 pm but opens at 1 pm on Friday and at noon on Sunday. Admission is free.

Fürsterliches Schloss Thurn und Taxis (Thurn und Taxis Palace), Emmeramsplatz 5, ☎ 0941-5048-133, www.thurnundtaxis.de, is still the principal residence of the noble family. Three sections are open to visitors but only on compulsory guided tours. The tour of the **Schlossmuseum** (Palace Museum) includes the state apartments, the ball and throne rooms, and other rooms converted by the family in the 19th century into the Historicist style. The **Kreuzgang** (Cloisters) of the former monastery can be seen as part of the palace tour, or separately. The cloisters are a Romanesque-Gothic combination erected between the 11th and 14th centuries. From April to October, tours of the Palace Museum and Cloisters are available daily at 11 am and 2, 3, and 4 pm (on weekends also at 10 am). From November to March, tours are on weekends only at 10 and 11 am as well as 2 and 3 pm.

The **Marstall Museum** houses more than 70 coaches that were used by the Thurn und Taxis postal service. It is open from April to October on weekdays, 11 am to 5 pm, and weekends, 10 am to 5 pm. From November to March, it can only be seen on guided tours on weekends at 11:30 am and 2 pm. Admission is €4.50 – in winter that includes the compulsory guided tour and in summer, it includes admission to the Thurn und Taxis Museum.

The **Thurn und Taxis Museum**, Emmeramsplatz 5, ☎ 0941-504-8133, houses artwork from the family and the Bavarian National Museum. Highlights include goldsmith work, clocks, porcelain, glass, and furniture, mainly from the 17th to 19th centuries. Opening hours are April to October on weekdays, 11 am to 5 pm, and weekends, 10 am to 5 pm, and from November to March only on weekends, 10 am to 6 pm. Admission in summer is €4.50 and includes admission to the Marstall Museum. In winter, admission is €3.50 for this museum only.

Excursions

■ Walhalla

A popular excursion from Regensburg is downstream to **Walhalla**, Donaustauf bei Regensburg, ☎ 09403-961-680. According to Nordic mythology, the Valkyries carried the souls of fallen heroes to Walhalla to meet the god

Walhalla (© David Barison & Daniel Ross)

Odin. In the 19th century, King Ludwig I of Bavaria constructed a huge marble monument inspired by the Parthenon in Athens to house the hall of fame of Germany. Here 121 busts and 64 plaques commemorate the great and good from German history – mostly statesmen, scientists, and artists. A committee evaluates every six years who should be added or removed.

The monument is easiest to reach by car – follow the road on the northern bank of the Danube for 4.8 miles towards Donaustauf and park at the top of the hill behind the monument. A more interesting way is by boat – see *Adventures* below for details. Arriving by river requires climbing 358 marble steps to get to the top. Opening hours are daily from April to September, 9 am to 5:45 pm, in October, 9 am to 4:45 pm, and from November to March, 10 to 11:45 am and 1 to 3:45 pm. Admission is €2.50.

■ Weltenburg

A popular excursion 18 miles upriver is to Weltenburg. The main sight in Weltenburg is the High Baroque **Stiftskirche Sts George und Martin** (Abbey Church of St George and St Martin) erected in 1720 by the famous Asam brothers. Its interior is lavishly decorated. Opening hours are daily from 9 am to dusk.

Bavaria

The most interesting way of approaching Weltenburg is by boat from Regensburg or Kelkheim – see *Adventures* below for details. Along a three-mile stretch of the river, known as the **Donaudurchbruch** (Danube breakthrough), the Danube carved its way through the Fran-

The Donaudurchbruch

conian Jura mountains. At times stone walls over 300 ft high rise from both banks of the river.

Cultural Events

Regensburg has a very busy cultural calendar. Details of programs are available from the tourist office, which can also make reservations for several events.

Apart from the symphony orchestra and several theaters, many churches schedule concerts. The **Regensburger Kultursommer** (Culture Summer) sees a month of events, both indoors and outdoors, mostly in August.

From June to September, on Wednesday at noon, free 20-minute organ concerts are held in the Dom. When not on tour, the *Domspatzen* (Cathedral Sparrows) boys' choir sings at the 9 am service on Sunday.

Adventures

■ On Foot

Town Walks: The tourist office arranges frequent two-hour town walks for individuals. Tours in English are available from May to September on Wednesday and Saturday at 1:30 pm.

■ On Wheels

By Bicycle: Bicycles can be rented from **Bikehaus**, Bahnhofstraße 17, ☎ 0941-599-8193, www.bikeprojekt.de.

■ In the Air

Hot-Air Ballooning: Balloon flights are offered by **Airsport**, Ockerweg 3, Hinterzhof, 93164 Laaber, ☎ 09498-902-460, www.airpsport.de.

Flugzentrum Bayerwald, Schwarzer Helm 71, 93086 Wörth an der Donau, ☎ 09482-959-525, www.flugzentrum-bayerwald.de, offers balloon flights and tandem paragliding jumps.

■ On Water

Canoeing & Kayaking: A popular day-trip is on the Regen River from Ramspau to its confluence with the Danube in Regensburg.

Kayak rentals are available from **Penk an der Naab**, ☎ 09401-567-777, www.trekking-kanu-laden.de; **Kanuverleih Platzeck**, Embacher Straße 10, Niedertraubling, ☎ 09401-51-295, www.kanu-outdoor.de; or **Regental Kanu**, Am Burghof 16, Nittenau, ☎ 094326-2740, www.bootswandern.de.

Riverboats: Regensburger Personenschifffahrt Klinger, Werftstraße 6, ☎ 0941-55-359, has 50-minute cruises each hour, 10 am to 4 pm, from end March to early October. Very popular are the Regensburg to Walhalla cruises that depart daily at 10:30 am and 2 pm. Cruising time is 45 minutes in each direction and allows just over an hour stop at Walhalla.

Personenschiffahrt im Donau und Altmühltal, Postfach 1641, 93305 Kelkheim, ☎ 09441-5858, www.schiffahrt-kelkheim.de, has daily cruises from the end of March to October on the Danube and the Altmühl. Particularly popular are cruises to the Donaudurchbruch and Kloster Weltenburg.

Where to Stay & Eat

A top choice is the modern **Sorat Insel-Hotel**, located on one of the islands in the River Danube. Rooms are comfortable and stylish and offer lovely views of the Old Town. The **Brandner Restaurant**

(€€-€€€) serves international and regional dishes in a modern, stylish restaurant with views of the Dom. Müllerstraße 7, 93059 Regensburg, ☎ 0941-81-040, fax 0941-810-444, www.sorat-hotels.com. (€€€-€€€€)

The Brandner Restaurant

The **Park Hotel Maximilian** is located halfway between the station and the Old Town in a 19th-century palace with an exquisite Neo-Rococo façade. Rooms are elegant and some are very spacious. The rustic Locanda Botticelli (€€-€€€) serves Italian food and the cellar restaurant **High Fish** (€€-€€€) offers Mediterranean cuisine. Maximiliansraße 28, 93047 Regensburg, ☎ 0941-56-850, fax 0941-52-942, www.maximilian-hotel.de. (€€-€€€€)

A very romantic choice is **Bischofshof am Dom**, located in a former bishop's palace adjacent to the cathedral. Romantic rooms are furnished in country house style. Part of the building

Bischofshof am Dom

includes the Porta Praetoria. The rustic **restaurant** (€-€€) with a beer garden in the romantic courtyard serves hearty local specialties. Kräutermarkt 3, 93047 Regensburg, ☎ 0941-58-460, fax 0941-584-6146, www.hotel-bischofshof.de. (€€€-€€€€)

The Ibis group has two modern, functionally furnished hotels near the station. The **Ibis Castra Regina**, Bahnhofstraße 22, 93047 Regensburg, ☎ 0941-56-930, fax 0941-569-3505, is north of the railway lines. South of the railway lines, across the road from the large shopping complex, is the similar **Ibis Furtmayr**, Furtmayerstraße 1, 93047 Regensburg, ☎ 0941-78-040, fax 0941-780-4509, www.ibishotel.com. (€-€€)

On the banks of the Danube, in the afternoon shadows of the Brückturm and the Salzstadel, is the **Historische Wurstkuchl**, Thundorferstraße 3, ☎ 0941-466-210, www.wurstkuchl.de. It claims to be the oldest sausage kitchen in Germany and looks the part. Sausages with sauerkraut and beer are mostly enjoyed on the Danube terrace but there is also some seating space inside. (€)

■ Camping

 Azur-camping is 1.8 miles from the town center on the south bank of the Danube. It has 200 lots. Bus 6 from the Hauptbahnhof stops in front of the camping terrain. Weinweg 40, 93049 Regensburg, ☎ 0941-270-025, fax 0941-299-432, www.azur-camping.de.

Passau

Passau is a lovely town, beautifully located at the confluence of the Danube, Inn, and Ilz rivers on the border with Austria. A major fire destroyed most of the town in 1662. As a result, most of the Old Town is Baroque, although the narrow alleys confirm that much of the Baroque splendor stands on medieval foundations.

Information Sources

 Tourist Office: Passau has two tourist offices, one at the Hauptbahnhof and a larger one at Rathausplatz 3, Neues Rathaus, 94032 Passau, ☎ 0821-955-980, www.passau.de.

Transportation

 The narrow alleys of Passau are best explored on foot. The Hauptbahnhof is about 10 minutes stroll through a shopping district to the edge of the Old Town and another 15 minutes to the Rathaus. The City Bus makes the same journey for €0.25. From the Rathausplatz, it is a steep, but rewarding, 30 minutes walk up to the Veste Oberhaus. From April to October, a shuttle bus does the journey for €1.50 one-way or €2 round-trip.

Sightseeing

Most of the sights are in the compact Old Town area on the land arm, known as the **Donaustadt**, ending at the confluence of the Danube and Inn Rivers. The **Ilzstadt** is the area between the Danube and the Ilz and was the traditional bastion of the Prince-Bishops. The main sight in the **Innstadt**, south of the Inn River, is the Mariahilf church.

■ Dom Area

The **Dom Sankt Stephan** (Cathedral of St Stephan), Domplatz, is at the highest point of the Old Town. The Late Gothic east chancel and transept are the only parts that survived the 1662 town fire. The new cathedral is Baroque and has a decorated façade facing the Domplatz. The dome was only completed in the 19th century. The delicate Gothic parts can be seen from Residenzplatz.

The huge interior, one of the largest Baroque churches north of the Alps, was designed by Carlo Lurago and he left no surface uncovered. It is overloaded with gilded stuccowork and frescos. However, the true high-

Dom Sankt Stephan

light is the organ – originally built in the 1920s but enlarged in the 1970s. With 17,974 pipes, 233 registers, and four carillons, it is the largest church organ in the world. The cathedral has fantastic acoustics and the organ is put through its paces frequently – see *Cultural Events* below.

The church is open daily from November to April, 6:30 am to 6 pm. From May to October, it is open from 6:30 am to 7 pm, but on weekdays when organ recitals are given it is closed from 10:45 until 12:30 pm. Admission for the noon concerts is from 11:20

and a fine time to see the interior if you're planning to stay for the concert. Admission is free, but €3 at concert time.

The small **Domschatz** (Cathedral Treasure) and the **Diözesan-Museum** (Diocesan Museum), ☎ 0851-393-374, is in the 18th-century bishop's palace. The museum can be entered via a spiral staircase to the right of the choir in the cathedral, or from the Residenzplatz. Enter from the latter if you're planning to see only the Baroque

The Diözesan-Museum

staircase (free). The museum itself has the usual collection of Episcopal paraphernalia as well as a lovely Baroque library. Opening hours are Monday to Saturday from May to October, 10 am to 4 pm. Admission is €1.50.

■ Rathaus Area

The **Altes Rathaus** (Old Town Hall) was erected in 1399 but the tower with clock was only added in the 19th century. Bavaria's largest carillon plays inside daily at 10:30 am, 2, 7:25, and 9 pm, and also at 3:30 pm on Saturdays. High-water levels are marked on the front of the building. The **Großer Rathaussaal** (Large Town Hall), entrance on Schrottgasse, is a Baroque building with large wall and roof paintings depicting the Niebelungenlied and events from local history. Opening hours are daily from April to November, and December, from 10 am to 4 pm. Admission is €1.50.

The **Passauer Glasmuseum** (Glass Museum) is inside the Hotel Wilder Mann, Am Rathausplatz, ☎ 0851-35-071, www. glasmuseumde. Its enormous collection of 30,000 items is the world's largest collection of Bohemian glass. It exhibits works of all periods of Bohemian glasswork from the 17th-century Baroque to the modern, up to 1950. The collection also includes Bavarian and Austrian works. Opening hours are daily from 1 to 5 pm. Admission is €5.

The **Dreiflußeckspaziergang** (Three Rivers' Corner Walk) is a lovely short walk on the banks of the Danube and Inn rivers. The far end of the promontory is the only point from where all three rivers can actually be seen at the same time. Note how long the green water of the Inn and the muddy-brown water of the Danube flow next to each other before eventually mixing deep into Austrian territory. Boat trips, to observe this process up-close are popular – see *Adventures* below.

■ Ilzstadt

The **Veste Oberhaus** was founded in 1219 as the residence of the prince-bishops. It is on the hill between the Danube and the Ilz and offers spectacular views of the Old Town and the valleys, either from the Battery Linden belvedere or from the castle tower (€1).

View from the Veste Oberhaus

The complex houses the impressive **Oberhausmuseum**, ☎ 0851-493-350, www.oberhausmuseum.de. It has exhibitions on local history but, more importantly, impressive special exhibitions on Bavarian-Austrian-Czech cultural history. Opening hours are from April to October, weekdays from 9 am to 5 pm and weekends from 9 am to 6 pm. Admission is €5.

■ Innstadt

The main sight in the Innstadt is the **Wallfahrtskirche Kloster Mariahilf** (Pilgrim's Church of the Monastery Maria Help). The complex can be seen from the Old Town and in return, some of the best views of the Altstadt are from the church. The church is reached via 321 steps along the Pilgrims' Stairs, or by car. The church was erected in 1627, but achieved fame after Emperor Leopold I prayed here in 1683 requesting help to lift the Turkish siege of Vienna.

Cultural Events

Organ concerts are frequently held in the **Dom**. Most popular are the half-hour concerts held at noon on weekdays from May to October. The organist ensures that the program shows off the full range of the organ's many features. Admission is €3. On Thursdays at 7:30 during the same period, longer concerts are arranged. Admission is €5 for organ-only concerts and €8 if choral music is included.

The **Europäische Wochen** (European Weeks), www.ew-passau.de, is a large musical festival held from mid-June to end of July. Towns in Austria, the Czech Republic, and Germany host events but Passau is the center of the festival.

Adventures

■ On Wheels

By Bicycle: Passau is a major crossing point for long-distance cycling routes. The most famous route is the **Donau Radweg** (Danube Cycling Route, traditionally done over a week, from Passau to Vienna with extensions possible to Bratislava and Budapest.

Bicycles can be rented from **Fahrrad-Klinik**, Bräugasse 10, ☎ 0851-33-411, www.fahrradklinik-passau.de, or at the station from **Österreichischer Tourismusradverleih**, Bahnhof, ☎ 0851-490-5872, reisezentrum.passau@t-online.de, which gives 20% discount for travelers arriving by train.

■ On Water

Canoeing & Kayaking: Canoes and kayaks can be rented from **Bichlmoser Oberhofer**, Hochstraße 33, ☎ 0851-966-3603, www.wandern-klettern.de.

Riverboats: With three rivers to pick from, an above average range of boat trips is available from Passau. **Wuem & Köck**, Höllgasse 26, ☎ 0851-929-292, www.donauschiffahrt.de, has several options. From March to October, 45-minute cruises to the three-river confluence depart every 30 minutes. Longer cruises are also available, including a four-hour cruise to Linz in

Austria. Long weekend cruises to Vienna, with overnight stays in hotels, are also arranged in the high season.

Where to Stay & Eat

The **Holiday Inn** is a modern hotel located close to the main station inside a shopping center. Rooms are comfortably furnished and many have views of the Danube. Bahnhofstraße 24, 94032 Passau, ☎ 0851-59-000, fax 0851-590-0529, www.holiday-inn-passau.com. (€€-€€€€)

The **Hotel Weisser Hase**, at the edge of the Old Town, has a tradition going back to the 16th century but the rooms are up-to-date, with marble bathrooms. The **restaurant** (€€) serves international and regional cuisine.

Hotel Weisser Hase

Ludwigstraße 23, 94032 Passau, ☎ 0851-92-110, fax 0851-921-1100, www.weisser-hase.de. (€€€)

Hotel Passauer Wolf (at far right)

The **Hotel Passauer Wolf** is on the banks of the Danube below the Dom. Rooms are comfortably furnished to the standards of a traditional luxury hotel. The **restaurant** (€€-€€€€) is in a vaulted, 16th-century cellar and has views of the Danube. International and regional dishes are available. Rindermarkt 6, 94032 Passau, ☎ 0851-931-5110, fax 0851-931-5150, www.passauerwolf.de. (€€-€€€€).

The **Hotel Wilder Mann** dates back to the 11th century and has seen its share of famous guests from emperors to Neil Armstrong. It is in a large patrician house next to the Rathaus and houses the famed Glass Museum as well. Rooms are opulently furnished with antiques or country house-style furniture. Some cheaper rooms are a bit cramped though. The **restaurant** (€€-€€€) on the fifth floor is in a Baroque room and open for dinner only. Rathausplatz, 94032 Passau, ☎ 0851-35-071, fax 0851-31-712, www.wilder-mann.com. (€€)

A very pleasant restaurant is the **Heilig Geist Stift Schenke**, Heiliggeistgasse 4, ☎ 0851-2607, a rustic, vaulted wine cellar dating from 1358. Both the terrace and wood-paneled interior are popular. Dishes are regional and Austrian specialties. Especially recommended are the Austrian wines. (€-€€€).

◆ The Romantic Road

The Romantische Straße (Romantic Road) is the most popular of Germany's roughly 150 themed vacation routes. It connects several romantic sights along a 210-mile route from Würzburg on the Main to Füssen at the foot of the Bavaria Alps. En route, it passes romantic towns, hamlets, castles, and churches. This section describes some of the stops along the way; some are worth stopping over for a few hours, while others can literally be seen in minutes. **Rothenburg ob der Tauber** and **Schloss Neuschwanstein** are the two most popular sights on the route.

Information Sources

Tourist Office: For information on the Romantic Road, contact Touristik-Arbeitsgemeinschaft Romantische Straße, Waaggässlein1, 91550 Dinkelsbühl, ☎ 09851-90-271, www.romantische-strasse.de, or any tourist information office on the route.

Transportation

The complete route can easily be driven in less than a day, but the time required depends on the number of stopovers made. Mostly back roads are used, but much faster parallel Autobahns are sometimes available to make up time. Tourist offices have free maps of the road, which is handy, as it is not generally marked with signboards.

Bavaria

From April to October, **Deutsche Touring**, Am Römerhof 17, 60486 Frankfurt, ☎ 069-790-350, www.deutsche-touring.com, operates a daily bus departing from Frankfurt at 8 am, running the full route and arriving in Füssen at 8 pm. Stopovers are permitted and a 90-minute break in Rothenburg is included. Reservations (free) are recommended, especially during the high season. Bicycles may be taken on the bus but reservations three days in advance are required.

Rail services are available to some of the towns, but trains do not run along the route itself. Würzburg and Augsburg are major stops on high-speed networks, while Rothenburg, Donauwörth, and Füssen can also be reached by rail.

Rothenburg ob der Tauber

This is one of Germany's best-known little towns. It is a medieval walled town in an excellent state of repair. It has a population of 12,000 but around 2½ million day-trippers visit annually and just under half a million spend the night. It certainly is not the only medieval walled town in Germany but none is as attractive, or as popular. In the high season it is best to arrive in the afternoon, spend the night, and leave before lunch to avoid the crowds.

Rothenburg was founded in the 12th century and became a Free Imperial City in 1274. Around 1400, Rothenburg was at the peak of its power and, with 6,000 inhabitants, one of the largest cities in the empire. Decline started in the 16th century and was hastened when it adopted the Reformation. It was occupied several times during the Thirty Years' War. Thereafter, the town was generally too poor to rebuild in the latest styles, so most of the town remained in a 16th-century time warp. It became part of Bavaria in 1802 and by the end of the 19th century was discovered by tourists. During World War II, artillery fire destroyed about 40% of the town, but most buildings were restored.

Information Sources

Tourist Office: The tourist information office is at Marktplatz 2, 91541 Rothenburg ob der Tauber, ☎ 09861-40-492, www.rothenburg.de.

Transportation

Rothenburg is close to the Autobahn A7 and can be reached on the Europa Bus from Frankfurt. By train it is just over an hour from Würzburg (change at Steinach) or between one and two hours from Nürnberg (change at Ansbach and Steinach). The station is about 10 minutes walk to the east of the Old Town.

Once at Rothenburg, walking is the only option. Street-side parking is scarce and time-restricted. Large, well-marked parking lots are outside the walls. Most of the Old Town is closed to cars on weekdays from 11 am to 4 pm and from 7 pm to 5 am. The whole Old Town is closed to traffic on weekends – drivers with hotel reservations may enter through Galgentor.

Sightseeing

The main attraction of Rothenburg is its medieval atmosphere and the magnificent fortifications. Large sections of the wall may be explored at will. The tourist information office and most hotels have free maps with suggested walking routes to see the town from its most picturesque angles. Apart from St Jakob and the Criminal Museum, indoor attractions are best reserved for very rainy days.

The **Markt** is a large square in the center of the Old Town. The Gothic parts of the **Rathaus** (Town Hall) date from the 14th century and the Renaissance additions are late 16th century. The

Bavaria

197-ft tower offers the best views in town. Opening hours are daily from April to October, 9:30 am to 12:30 pm. From November to March, it is open on weekends only from noon to 3 pm, but daily during December. Admission is €1.

To the north is the former **Ratstrinkstube** (City Councilors' Tavern), formerly open to council members only. It has several clocks, including a carillon that recalls the Meistertrunk legend daily at the full hour between 11 am and 3 pm and between 8 and 10 pm.

Käthe Wohlfahrt's Christmas ornament shops seem to be everywhere in Rothenburg, but a more historic approach is in the **Deutsches Weihnachtsmuseum** (German Christmas Museum), Herrngasse 1, ☎ 09861-409-365, www.weihnachtsmuseum.de. It is in the back of the main Käthe Wohlfahrt shop and has a huge exhibition of historic Christmas ornaments, mostly from the late 19th century. Opening hours are daily from 10 am to 5:30 pm, but closed on Sunday from January to April. Admission is €4.

St Jakobs-Kirche

The **St Jakobs-Kirche** (St James' Church) is a triple-nave Gothic basilica. Construction of the east chancel started in 1311, the nave was completed in 1436, and the west chancel built in 1450-71, with a passageway underneath. The church has several remarkable art treasures from the 15th and 16th centuries. None is more impressive than Tilman Riemenschneider's **Heilig-Blut Altar** (Holy Blood Altar) carved between 1499 and 1505. Its main panel shows the *Last Supper.* Opening hours are daily from April to October from 9: 30 am to 5:30 pm, December from 10 am to 5 pm, November and January to March from 10 am to noon and 2 to 4 pm. Admission is €1.50.

The **Reichsstadtmuseum** (Imperial City Museum), Klosterhof 5, ☎ 09861-939-043, is in a former Dominican monastery. It has mostly exhibits on furniture, weapons, sculpture and the former 14th-century monastery kitchen. Opening hours are daily from April to October, 10 am to 5 pm and from November to March, 1 to 4 pm. Admission is €3.

Many German towns and castles have a torture museum, but the **Mittelalterliches Kriminalmuseum** (Medieval Crime Museum), Burggasse 3-5, ☎ 09861-5359, approaches the subject more seriously and more thoroughly. It is a large display on the development of justice in Europe up to the 19th century. The instruments of torture obviously attract the most attention, but the illustrated law books and explanations of procedures are also interesting. All descriptions are in English. Opening hours are daily from April to October, 9:30 am to 6 pm, November and January to March, 2 to 4 pm, and December from 10 am to 4 pm. Admission is €3.20.

Towards the southern part of the Old Town is the **Plönlein**, a picturesque little square with a fork in the road. The main road leads to the **Spitaltor**, the mightiest of the city gates. Its 16th-century bastions encircle two large inner courtyards. Walking on stretches of the wall from here to Burgtor often affords grand views of both the Old Town and the Tauber Valley.

The Rothenburg Wall (Arthur W. Mohr, Jr).

Cultural Events

The St Jakobskirche and Franziskanerkirche are frequent venues for musical concerts, www. kirchenmusik.rothenburg.de. Reservations can be made at the tourist information office.

Festivals

Rothenburg has three major annual festivals on the Markt – the exact dates are available from the tourist information office. The **Meistertrunk Festpiel** (Master Draught Play) in June recalls the events during the Thirty Years' War. The **Reichsstadt Festtage** (Imperial City Festival) in September is accompanied by theatrical performances, traditional dancing, and fireworks. The **Reiterlesmarkt** in December is a small Christmas market but with arguably the most romantic setting in all of Germany.

THE MEISTERTRUNK LEGEND

Rothenburg's most famous moment came during the Thirty Years' War when General Tilly threatened to destroy the town. According to legend, all pleas were rejected until the general was offered the best local wine. He offered to spare the town if a burgher could drink a hanap (around a gallon and a half) in a single gulp. A certain Nusch, a former Burgomaster came forward and achieved the feat. This event is commemorated annually during the Pentecost weekend with an open-air play on the market square. (Historians generally agree that a bag of cash is what actually changed the general's mind.)

Shopping

Käthe Wohlfahrt has Europe's largest Christmas ornament business. They have several shops in Rothenburg, the main one at Herrngasse 1, ☎ 09861-4090, www.wohlfahrt.com. It is Christmas here all year. Prices are high but so is the quality of the products. A small outlet shop for discontinued and slightly damaged goods is across the road from the St Jakobskirche at the corner of Kirchgasse. Ignore all the shops claiming cheap Christmas decorations in the immediate vicinity – it is the low-key nameless one with just a small "Schnäppchenmarkt/Discount Store" sign. The name Käthe Wohlfahrt is not displayed, except when the goods are finally packed into the normal Wohlfahrt bags.

Adventures

■ On Foot

Town Walks: English guided walking tours of the Old Town area are conducted by the tourist information office daily between April and October at 2 pm and with the night watchman at 8 pm.

Countryside Hikes: The Tauber Valley is a popular hiking area. The tourist information office has details on more than 10 walks starting from the Markt into the nearby countryside, ranging from two to five hours. Hiking maps are available for the tourist office or any bookstore. On Wednesday at 2 pm, a *Wandern & Singen* (Walking and Singing) tour starts from the Markt to the surrounding countryside.

Joggers meet Saturday at 4:30 pm in the Waldparkplatz Aidenau parking area for a cross-country run.

■ On Wheels

By Bicycle: The Tauber Valley is a popular cycling area – the tourist office has maps on cycling routes. Very popular are multi-day cycling tours along the Romantic Road.

Bicycles can be rented from **Rat & Tat**, Bensenstraße 17, ☎ 09861-87-984, or from **Skazel**, Rad und Freizeittouristik, Am Stadtschreiber 27, ☎ 09341-5395.

In the Air

Hot-Air Ballooning: Happy Ballooning, Paradiesgasse 17, ☎ 09861-87-888, www.happy-ballooning.de, has late-afternoon flights starting directly south of Rothenburg.

Where to Stay & Eat

The **Eisenhut Hotel** is the best temporary address in town. It is in four 15th-century patrician houses at the Markt. Rooms are very comfortable and individually furnished to a very high standard. The **restaurant** (€€-€€€), with wall paintings and ample use of wood, serves in-

RESTAURANT PRICES	
€	Less than €10
€€	€10 to €20
€€€	€21 to €35
€€€€	Over €35

HOTEL PRICES	
€	Up to €50 per night
€€	€50 to €100
€€€	€101 to €150
€€€€	Over €150

Eisenhut Hotel

ternational dishes and local specialties. Herrngasse 3, 91541 Rothenburg ob der Tauber, ☎ 09861-7050, fax 09861-70-545, www.eisenhut. com. (€€€-€€€€)

The **Romantik Hotel Markusturm** is in a former customs house with a history going back to 1264. The hotel has been run by the same family for four generations and has large, very comfortable, individually furnished rooms. The **restaurant** (€€-€€€) serves local specialties accompanied by local wine. Rödergasse 1, 91541 Rothenburg ob der Tauber, ☎ 09861-94-280, fax 09861-942-8113, www.markus-turm.de. (€€€-€€€€)

Romantik Hotel Markusturm

The **Burghotel** is in a quiet spot by the town wall near St Jakobs-Kirche. Rooms are well appointed and furnished with good taste and attention to detail. Breakfast can be enjoyed on the town wall itself when weather allows. Klostergasse 1-3, 91541 Rothenburg ob der Tauber, ☎ 09861-94-890, fax 09861-948-940, www.burghotel. rothenburg.de. (€€-€€€)

The **Tilman Riemenschneider Hotel** is in a romantic half-timbered building. Rooms are comfortable, mostly with handpainted country-style furniture. The rustic **restaurants** (€€-€€€) in the complex serve mainly local cuisine. Georgengasse 11-13, 91541 Rothenburg ob der Tauber, ☎ 09861-9790, fax 09861-2979, www. tilman-riemenschneider.de. (€€-€€€€)

Tilman Riemenschneider Hotel

Gerberhaus Hotel

The **Gerberhaus Hotel** is in the southern part of the Old Town close to the Spitaltor. It is a very pleasant place, with bright, comfortable rooms. Spitalgasse 25, 91541 Rothenburg ob der Tauber, ☎ 09861-94-900, fax 09861-86-555, www.romanticroad. com/gerberhaus. (€€)

At the Markt are two lovely restaurants. A pleasant place for coffee and cake, or full meals, is the **Baumeisterhaus Restaurant**, Obere Schmiedgasse 3, ☎ 09861-94-700. It is inside a 1596 Renaissance house with courtyard, wall paintings, and antique decorations. A rustic spot, it serves excellent cakes and local dishes. The adjacent **Zum Greifen Restaurant**, Obere Schmiedgassse 5, ☎ 09861-2281, has hearty local cuisine. (€-€€)

■ Camping

Camping Tauber-Idyll is 1.2 miles outside the walled town. It has very good facilities, but only 40 lots, and is open from early April to early November.

Bavaria

91541 Rothenburg ob der Tauber-Detwang, 09861-3177, fax 09861-92-848.

Camping Tauberromantik is also around 1.2 miles outside Rothenburg in the Tauber valley. It has very good facilities and 120 lots. It is open from mid-March to October. 91541 Rothenburg ob der Tauber-Detwang, ☎ 09861-6191, fax 09861-86-899, www.camping-tauberromantik.de.

Dinkelsbühl

Information Sources

Tourist information is available from Touristik Service Dinkelbühl, Marktplatz, 91550 Dinkelsbühl, ☎ 09851-90-240, www.dinkelsbuehl.de.

Transportation

The town is best reached by car or on the Europa Bus. It is 30 miles southeast of Rothenburg on country roads and six miles from the Autobahn A7. Most of the Old Town is closed to private vehicles – large parking areas are on the edge of the Old Town.

Sightseeing

Dinkelbühl is for many an alternative to over-crowded Rothenburg. Like Rothenburg, it is entirely surrounded by a town wall and most of the Old Town buildings date from before the 16th century. The town was spared the ravages of war and since 1826 had the town defenses under protection order. Currently, 18 watch-towers survived. The town walls are lower and much thinner than those of Rothenburg and, although it is possible to walk around the town, it is not actually possible to walk on the walls.

Dinkelsbühl is best enjoyed by walking the old streets and seeing the interesting architecture. The **Münster St Georg** (Minster of St George) is worth entering, as it is one of the most beautiful hall churches in Germany. The church has a 213-ft Romanesque tower but most of the rest of the building and interior is Gothic. Note the statues of the *Last Supper* on the outside wall of the choir. Inside, the church is filled with art with the

Dinkelsbühl

late-15th-century tabernacle of the sacristy and the high altar especially noteworthy.

The **Weinmarkt** and **Marktplatz** directly in front of the Minster are the most beautiful parts of the town. It has several large, half-timbered houses, including the Deutsches Haus from the 16th century. **Segringer Straße**, leading west from the square, also has particularly beautiful buildings.

Adventures

■ On Foot

Town Walks: Guided tours of the Old Town are conducted by the information office daily from April to October at 2:30 and 8:30 pm. A walk with the night watchman is possibly daily during the same period at 9 pm. All tours start from the Münster St Georg.

■ On Wheels

By Bicycle: The tourism office rents out bicycles and arranges half-day guided cycling tours in the region. Maps are also available for self-guided tours.

By Train: On some weekends, a historic steam train makes three round-trips between Nördlingen and Dinkelsbühl. Occasionally, the journey continues to Harburg and Feuchtwangen.

Bavaria

Details are available from the tourist offices or from the **Bayerisches Eisenbahnmuseum**, Postfach 1316, 86713 Nördlingen im Ries, ☎ 09083-340, www.bayerisches-eisenbahnmuseum.de.

Where to Stay

 Dinkelsbühl has several comfortable hotels and offers a good alternative to staying in Rothenburg. Prices are much lower too.

The **Hotel Deutsches Haus** is in one of the most beautiful half-timbered secular buildings in southern Germany. Rooms are comfortable and romantic, with antique furniture. The **restaurant** (€€) serves re-

Hotel Deutsches Haus

gional cuisine with a good local wine selection. Weinmarkt 3, 91550 Dinkelsbühl, ☎ 09851-6058, fax 09851-7911, www.deutsches-haus-dkb.de. (€€-€€€)

The **Hotel Blauer Hecht** is in a former brewery dating back to 1648. Rooms are comfortable and romantic with all modern comforts. The old German **restaurant** (€€-€€€) serves regional and international dishes. Schweinemarkt 1, 91550 Dinkelsbühl, ☎ 09851-5810, fax 09851-581-170, www.hotel-blauer-hecht.de. (€€)

The **Hotel Goldene Kanne** is in a 17th-century building in the heart of the Old Town. Rooms are fairly modern though, with the two bay-window suites especially nice. The **Angus Restaurant** (€-€€) serves steaks and Mexican dishes. Segringer Straße 8, 91550 Dinkelsbühl, ☎ 09851-572-910, fax 09851-572-929, www.hotel-goldene-kanne.de. (€€)

■ Camping

 Campingplatz Dinkelsbühl, a well-equipped camping site, is just to the north of town. It is on a small lake and offers fishing and pony rides on-site.

It has 475 lots and is open year-round. Kobeltsmühle 2, 91550 Dinkelsbühl, ☎ 09851-7817, fax 09851-7848, www. campingpark-dinkelsbuehl.de.

Nördlingen

The walled city of Nördlingen

Nördlingen is even farther from the highways and attracts visibly fewer tourists than Rothenburg and Dinkelsbühl. It is once again a completely walled-in town but, interestingly, the town is almost completely round. The town's written history started in 898 and it became a Free Imperial City in 1215. The town population was halved in the Thirty Years' War and it never recovered its former important position. It became part of Bavaria in 1803.

Information Sources

 Tourist Office: Information is available from the Verkehrsamt, Marktplatz 2, 86720 Nördlingen im Ries, ☎ 09081-4380, www.noerdlingen.de.

Transportation

 Nördlingen is best reached by car or the Europa Bus. By car, the Old Town can only be entered via one gate – signposting is clear. On quiet days, it is possible to park in the heart of the Old Town; otherwise use the parking lots just outside the town walls.

Bavaria

Sightseeing

The main sights are once again the interesting old houses. Here, in contrast to Rothenburg and Dinkelsbühl, it is fairly easy to see decaying and less well maintained buildings in the back streets.

The 15th-century **St Georgskirche** (St George's Church), Am Obstmarkt, has a 295-ft tower. This tower, virtually in the center of town, gives the best view on the Romantic Road, as the interesting circular Old Town and the concentric development are clearly visible. The interior of the church itself is bright and has intricate vaulting.

St Georgskirche

The nearby **Rathaus** (Town Hall) is the oldest stone building in town. Parts date from the 13th century, but the building was significantly altered around 1500.

The **Stadtmauer** (Town Walls) are the only ones in Germany that are still fully accessible. It is possible to walk around the town, mostly under cover, on the wall and pass 11 watchtowers and five gates in the process.

Adventures

■ On Foot

Town Walks: From Easter to October, the tourist office conducts guided walking tours of the Old Town at 2 pm. More romantic are the walks with the night watchman, daily from mid-May to mid-September at 8:30 pm.

■ On Wheels

By Bicycle: Bicycle rentals are available from **Radsport Böckle**, Reimlinger Straße 19, ☎ 09081-801-040, or from **Zweirad Müller**, Gewerbestraße 16, ☎ 09081-5675.

■ On Horseback

The **Scharlachrennen**, www.scharlachrennen.de, are held annually at the end of July. This is one of the oldest horse racing events in Europe, dating back to at least 1438. It is one of the largest riding events in south Germany and involves races and show jumping.

Where to Stay & Eat

The **Hotel Am Ring** is a comfortable option outside the walled-in area. Rooms are modern and tastefully decorated. The **restaurant** (€€) serves regional dishes with seasonal specialties. Bürgermeister-Reiger-Straße 14, 86720 Nördlingen, ☎ 09081-290-030, fax 09081-23-170, www.hotelamring.de. (€€)

The **Kaiserhof Hotel Sonne** is in the heart of the Old Town. The building dates back to the 15th century and not all walls and floors are straight. Rooms are comfortable and individually furnished. The **Weinstäpfele Restaurant** (€-€€) serves regional cuisine in a rustic setting with vaulted ceilings. Marktplatz 3, 86720 Nördlingen, ☎ 09081-273-8380, fax 09081-23-999, www.kaiserhof-hotel-sonne.de. (€€-€€€)

Kaiserhof Hotel Sonne, at right

A surprisingly pleasant informal restaurant with excellent pizza and pasta is **La Fontana Pizzeria Espresso-Bar**, Bei den Kornschrannen, ☎ 09081-211-021, www.lafontana.ws. It is inside a large, red building with a terrace on the square, next to a fountain recalling the town's history. Prices are low, for both the food and the long wine list. (€)

■ Camping

RVs and mobile homes are allowed to use the parking lot at the Kaiserwiese.

Augsburg

With 265,000 inhabitants, this is the third-largest city in Bavaria, after Munich and Nürnberg. The main attractions are the splendid Renaissance and Rococo buildings that reflect the wealth this town once enjoyed

Augsburg is one of Germany's oldest cities. It was founded in 15 BC by Druses and Tiberius, stepsons of Roman Emperor Augustus. According to Tacitus, it was the most splendid city in the colony. It maintained its importance as a trading center well into the 17th century. It was the first city to introduce the Italian Renaissance to Germany and later also the home of Rococo. During the late Middle Ages, the Fugger family, based in Augsburg, served as banker for popes, kings, and emperors. Much of the wealth and splendor rubbed off on the surviving buildings.

Augsburg, a Free Imperial City since 1276, was forced to become part of Bavaria in 1806. The city was severely damaged during World War II but large parts of the Old Town were restored.

Information Sources

Tourist Office: Regio Augsburg Tourismus, Bahnhostraße 7, 86150 Augsburg, ☎ 0821-502-070, www.regio-augsburg.de.

Transportation

Augsburg is a mere 40 minutes by train from Munich. There are at least four trains per hour – the cheaper local trains (RE and RB) are only minutes slower than the IC and ICE trains. It is a major stop on the route from Munich to Stuttgart and beyond.

By car it is reached equally fast on the Autobahn A8 that connects Munich and Stuttgart. It is also easy to reach all Romantic Road destinations by road from here.

Sightseeing

The main sights of Augsburg are in a long, narrow stretch of the Old Town. To the north of the Rathaus are the Dom and Mozarthaus, and to the south most sights are in or near the Maximilianstraße. A walking tour of the sights described here takes around two hours plus time spent inside the attractions.

■ Northern Old Town Area

The Renaissance **Rathaus** (Town Hall), Rathausplatz, ☎ 0821-502-0724, replaced its Gothic predecessor in 1614. It is the most important work of Elias Holl and arguably one of the loveliest and most important secular Renaissance buildings in Germany. It was severely damaged by an air raid in 1944, but rebuilt true to the

Rathaus (Sven Jansen)

original. The **Goldene Saal** (Golden Hall) is one of the most impressive ceremonial rooms north of the Alps. The Rathaus and Goldene Saal are open daily from 10 am to 6 pm. Admission is €1.50.

The **Perlachturm** (Tower) dates partly from 1060. Its present height of 231 ft was achieved in 1616. For the best views of Augsburg, and on a clear day all the way to the Alps, climb the 258 steps to the viewing platform at the top. It is open daily from May to October from 10 am to

The Goldene Saal (Carina Hessmer)

6 pm, and on Advent weekends from 2 to 7 pm. Admission is €1. Since 2000, a Glockenspiel (Carillon) plays Mozart tunes daily at 11 am, noon, 5 and 6 pm.

Near the Rathausplatz is the **St Annakirche** (St Anne's Church), Anna-Straße. In 1321, a Carmelite monastery built the Gothic church, which was enlarged in the 15th century. Martin Luther stayed in the monastery during his 1518 visit to Augsburg. The church is famous for the **Fuggerkapelle** (Fugger Funeral Chapel), the first religious Italian Renaissance structure erected on German soil. It cost more than the Fuggerei (see below). Most of the church received a Rococo makeover in the 18th century. However, the 15th-century **Goldschmiedekapelle** (Goldsmiths' Chapel), used as Lutheran a church, still has its original Gothic layout and wall paintings. It also has paintings by Lucas Cranach. Opening hours are Tuesday to Sunday from 10 am to 12:30 pm and 3 to 6 pm, Sunday from noon to 6 pm.

The playwright Bertolt Brecht (1898-1956) was born in what is now the **Gedenkstätte für Bertolt Brecht** (Memorial), Auf dem Rain 7, ☎ 0821-324-2779. He spent his youth in Augsburg until moving to Munich in 1917 and during the Nazi period to Scandinavia and the USA, before settling in East Berlin. Opening hours are Tuesday to Sunday from 10 am to 5 pm. Admission is €1.50.

In 1516, Jakob Fugger the Rich (see below) donated the **Fuggerei** as home for the poor. It is the oldest social housing project in the world that is still in use. Even now,

The Fuggerei

Augsburgers, who become poor and destitute through no fault of their own, can find accommodation here. The annual rent is still a symbolic Rhenish guilder (€0.88!)*and* three daily prayers for the founder. The 104 homes currently house around 150 people. The building is a city inside a city, with eight streets and four access gates that are locked at 10 pm. Residents arriving late are fined 25-50 cents. The small **Fuggereimuseum**, Mitelgasse 13, is in an original house in the Fuggerei. It explains the history of the institution and is furnished in the style of the 17th and 18th century. It is open daily from March to December 23, 9 am to 6 pm. Admission is €1. (From the Rathaus follow Barfüßer and Jakoberstraße east and turn right into Herrengasse.)

The **Dom St Maria** (Cathedral of St Mary), Domplatz, is mainly 14th-century Gothic, but the core, including the crypt is from the 10th century and Romanesque. The church has wall paintings from the Romanesque and Gothic periods, but the altar by Hans Holbein receives the most attention. Note the five windows of the prophets on the south side of the nave. This 12th-century painted glass is considered the oldest of its kind in Germany.

The musical Mozart family worked in Augsburg from 1643 onwards. Leopold Mozart, father of Wolfgang Amadeus, was born in Augsburg in 1719. His place of birth is now called the **Mozarthaus**, Frauentorstraße 30, ☎ 0821-324-3894, with a museum dedicated to Mozart and his works. Wolfgang Amadeus visited Augsburg five times – both as tourist and as musician. His music is frequently performed at various venues. The museum is open Tuesday to Sunday from 10 am to 5 pm. Admission is €1.50.

■ Maximilianstraße

Maximilianstraße leads from the Rathaus southward. It is the traditional shopping street, with many fine gabled houses from the Renaissance and Baroque periods.

The Damenhof (Peter Bubenik)

The **Fuggerhäuser** (Fugger Houses), Maximilianstraße 36-38, are a group of existing buildings that were united behind a Renaissance façade in 1515 to serve as city residence and offices of the Fugger family.

Bavaria

The building is mostly in private use, but enter the **Damenhof** (Ladies' Courtyard) to see the colonnaded area reserved for the Fugger women.

THE FUGGER FAMILY OF AUGSBURG

Jacob Fugger (Albrecht Durer, 1519)

At the end of the 15th century, the Fugger family owned a prominent trading firm in Augsburg. Jakob Fugger implemented ideas learned in Italy about double entry bookkeeping and cashless trade into the business practices, but it was cornering the European market for copper that made his fortune. From 1500, Jakob Fugger, by now known as The Rich, acted as banker to the Pope and in 1519 financed the election of Emperor Karl V. Foundations set up by Jakob Fugger still finance the tourist magnets of the Fuggerei and the Fugger Chapel in St Anne's. He also spent lavishly on the arts, bringing the Renaissance to Germany, and he had several paintings and drawings done by Albrecht Dürer, among others.

Despite his nickname, Jakob Fugger was not the richest man in the world. Only his nephew, Anton Fugger, managed that around 1546. By many counts, he was the richest man the world has ever known. The continuous demands for financing from the Habsburg Emperors, who never bothered to repay debts, forced the Fuggers to diversify out of financing into property. By 1658 the financing firm was dissolved.

A block farther is the magnificent Rococo **Schaezler-Palais** (Palace), Maximilianstraße 46, ☎ 0821-324-4117. It was erected in 1765-70 by the Von Liebenhofens, a wealthy banking family. It has a huge **Festsaal** (Banqueting Hall) with Rococo ceiling and wall panels. Marie Antoinette attended a ball here en route to getting married in Paris. The palace houses several galleries. The Baroque Gallery has mostly paintings by German artists. The **Staatsgalerie Alter Kunst** (National Old Masters' Gallery) has work by local painters, including Holbein and Dürer, as well as works by Van Dyck, Veronese, and Tiepolo. Opening hours are Tuesday to Sunday from 10 am to 5 pm. Admission is €3.

St Ulrich and St Afra

At the far end of the Maximilian-straße are the Roman Catholic **St Ulrich and St Afra**, ☎ 0821-345-560, and the Lutheran **St Ulrichskirche**. The Late Gothic church was built on the site where St Afra was martyred in 304 AD. St Ulrich, whose grave is in the crypt, helped in the victory over the Hungarians in the 10th century. A Baroque preaching hall was added in the early 18th century to serve as a Lutheran church.

The **Augsburger Puppenkiste** (Marionettes) are among the most famous in the world. Presentations are held on most Wednesday, Friday, Saturday, and Sunday at 2 and 7:30 pm. Their program is available from the tourism office or at www.augsburger-puppenkiste.de. A small museum, **Die Kiste** (The Box), Spitalgasse 15, ☎ 0821-450-3450, www.diekiste.net, is dedicated to this art form. It is open Tuesday to Sunday from 10 am to 7 pm.

The 16th-century **Rotes Tor** (Red Gate) was remodeled by Elias Holl in the early 17th century. This fortified gate is most popular as a huge open-air stage.

Cultural Events

The **Fugger und die Musik** (The Fuggers and Music) is a concert series arranged by the tourism office annually from May to June. It involves music played in places associated with the Fuggers, including several churches and the Goldene Saal in Augsburg, as well as in Nürnberg and other towns.

The **Freilichtbühne am Roten Tor** (Open-Air Theater), ☎ 0821-324-4900, www.theater-augsburg.de, is the largest open-air theater in southern Germany. Its largest performances are operas and musicals staged usually between June and August.

Adventures

■ On Foot

Town Walks: The tourism office conducts guided walking tours departing from the Rathaus, daily from April to October at 2 pm but only on Saturday at 2 pm from November to March.

Where to Stay & Eat

The **Steigenberger Hotel Drei Mohren** is in the center of town close to the pedestrian zone. It is an exquisite hotel with large, luxurious rooms. The upper floors are more modern. **Maximilian's Restaurant**

Hotel Drei Mohren

(€€-€€€) serves international cuisine with strong Euro-Asian and Mediterranean influences. Maximilianstraße 40, 86150 Augsburg, ☎ 0821-50-360, fax 0821-157-864, www. steigenberger.de. (€€€)

Romantik Hotel Augsburger Hof

The **Romantik Hotel Augsburger Hof** is the oldest hotel in town. It has a historic Renaissance façade but is more modern inside. It is close to the Dom and next to the former city walls. Rooms are comfortable and individually furnished with good taste and attention to detail. The rustic **restaurant** (€€-€€€) serves international cuisine, but the local, Swabian dishes are what regulars come for. Auf dem Kreuz 2, 86152 Augsburg, ☎ 0821-343-050, fax 0821-343-0555, www.augsburger-hof.de. (€€-€€€)

The **Dom Hotel** is a fourth-generation, family-run establishment close to the Dom. Rooms are very pleasant – some have exposed beams and great views. All are comfortable. Frauentorstraße 8, 86152 Augsburg, ☎ 0821-343-930, fax 0821-3439-3200, www.domhotel-augsburg.de. (€€)

The **Ibis Hotel beim Hauptbahnhof** is, as the name implies, right at the main station. Rooms are simply furnished, but clean and modern. Halderstraße 25, 86150 Augsburg, ☎ 0821-50-160, fax 0821-501-6150, www.ibishotel.com. (€-€€)

Schwangau

Near Füssen, this is a small town in an idyllic location that caught the eye of the Bavarian royals during the 19th century. First King Maximilian II built a hunting castle here and then Mad King Ludwig erected the fantasy castle Schloss Neuschwanstein. Visitors come from all over the world to see this magical folly.

Schloss Neuschwanstein attracts 1.3 million visitors annually, making it one of the most popular tourist destinations in Germany. Another sight is **Schloss Hohenschwangau** where Ludwig spent much of his youth. Although much of the small town near the castles is geared to mass tourism, the area has some outstanding natural beauty, making it worth staying for longer than the flood of day-trippers usually do.

Information Sources

Tourist Office: Tourist Information Schwangau, Münchener Straße 2, 87645 Schwangau, ☎ 08362-81-980, www.schwangau.de.

Transportation

At least hourly **trains** connect Munich Hauptbahnhof with Füssen in just over two hours. Some trains require transfers at Buchloe. Hourly trains from Augsburg take just under two hours and often require transfers at Buchloe. From Füssen train station,

Bavaria

take any bus marked Königschlösser to Schwangau. Alternatively, it is a three-mile hike from Füssen to Hohenschwangau or a taxi would cost around €10.

Limited **buses** are available from Füssen and Schwangau to the Wieskirche, Oberammergau, Ettal, and Garmisch-Partenkirchen.

From Munich, a good option would be a guided **bus tour**. It cuts out the hassle of getting tickets in advance and some include both Schloss Neuschwanstein and Schloss Linderhof – something that is impossible to do in one day on public transportation.

AutobusOberbayern, Heidemannstraße 220, ☎ 089-323-040, www.autobusoberbayern.de, offers day-tours that include both castles or just Schloss Neuschwanstein.

A more active tour is offered by **Discover Bavaria**, Hochbrückenstraße, ☎ 089-2554-3987, www.mikesbiketours.com. It includes a hike up the Pöllat Gorge, a visit to Schloss Neuschwanstein, a bike tour, and a swim in the lake if weather allows. The tour is available most days from mid-April to September.

By **car**, Füssen is a just over 60 miles from Munich and a bit more than an hour's drive from Garmisch-Partenkirchen.

TICKETS FOR THE CASTLES

Tickets can be bought in person or online from **Ticketcenter Neuschwanstein–Hohenschwangau**, Alpseestr. 12, 87645 Hohenschwangau, ☎ 08362-930-830, fax 08362-930-8320, www.ticket-center-hohenschwangau.de. Reserved tickets cost €1.60 extra but are worth it. The tickets need to be picked up at the ticket center but a special counter is set apart for reserved tickets.

Sightseeing

 Both Schloss Neuschwanstein and Schloss Hohenschwangau are open daily from April to September, 9 am to 5 pm, and from October to March, 10 am to 4 pm. Admission to each is €9 or €17 for both on the same day.

Schloss Neuschwanstein (de:Benutzer:Softeis)

■ Schloss Neuschwanstein

This was the ultimate fantasy castle of Mad King Ludwig. It was built between 1869 and 1886 in the Historicist style. It was supposed to resemble a medieval knight's castle and thus follows the Romanesque style to a large extent. It looks magical, high on a hill against an Alpine background. The briefest of glances tells you where Disney's castle came from.

The interior, which can only be seen on a guided tour, mostly resemble scenes from Wagnerian operas such as *Tannhäuser* and *Lohengrin*. The Singers' Hall is a smaller copy of the one in the Wartburg near Eisenach and its walls are decorated with scenes from *Parzival*. Only about 20 rooms are on view, as the castle was never completed. King Ludwig spent less than six months here.

Several routes lead to the top of the hill where Schloss Neuschwanstein is perched. The most interesting route goes up through the **Pöllatschlucht** (Pöllat Gorge). Others go more directly and are less strenuous. Walking up requires 20 to 45 minutes, depending on the route chosen. It is also possible to take a minibus or horse-drawn carriage to the top.

The best views of the castle are from the **Marienbrücke** (Mary Bridge), which is 148 ft above the Pöllat waterfall, and absolutely worth the 15-minute walk from the castle. (Note that the

Bavaria

hike that continues on the far side of this bridge is beautiful, but it takes several hours.)

■ Schloss Hohenschwangau

Schloss Hohenschwangau gate

The other royal castle in Schwangau, Schloss Hohenschwangau, was also built in a Historicist style but by Maximilian II in 1832-36. It is a Neo-Gothic building with wall paintings of German sagas. Ludwig spent happy childhood years here and was almost certainly influenced by what he saw on these walls. He also first met Richard Wagner here. The interior can only be seen on a guided tour, which generally is less fully booked than those for Neuschwanstein.

Cultural Events & Festivals

Concerts are held each September in the **Sängersaal** in Schloss Neuschwanstein. Tickets go on sale from the first Monday in February and the program is available from the tourist office from January.

Alphorns are blown at the Alpsee from May to September on Monday at 8 pm.

Adventures

■ On Foot

Countryside Hikes: The natural beauty of the area invites hiking. A popular hike is from Schwangau up the Pöllat Gorge, over the Marienbrücke with views of Schloss Neuschwanstein, and then onwards through the mountains to the Bergstation of the Tegelberg cable car. From here, take the cable car or, more interestingly, follow the Schutzengel (Guardian Angel) route back to the valley. The walk takes three to five hours.

■ On Wheels

By Bicycle: A popular cycling route is the 19 miles around the **Forggensee**. You are allowed to take bicycles on the lake boats. Cycling to the Wieskirche is also popular.

Many hotels have bicycles available for guests but otherwise try at **Aktiv Flugschule**, An der Tegelbergbahn-Talstation, ☎ 08362-921-457; **Auto Köpf**, Münchner Straße 11, ☎ 08362-930-271; or **Campingplatz Bannwaldsee**, ☎ 08362-93-000.

■ In the Air

The Tegelbergbahn

Cable Cars: The **Tegelbergbahn**, 87645 Schwangau, ☎ 08362-98-360, www.tegelbergbahn.de, uses an enclosed cable car to hoist passengers from Schwangau's 2,690-ft altitude to the Tegelberg peak at 5,641 ft.

The Bergstation is the starting point for many popular hikes. In winter, a downhill ski slope is available. It operates daily from 9 am to 4:30 pm. A round-trip ticket is €15 or €9 one-way. Day-tickets are available for skiers.

Hot-Air Ballooning: Balloon flights are arranged by **Bavaria Ballonfahrten**, Hitzleriederstraße 15, 87637 Seeg, ☎ 08364-986-068.

Paragliding: For tandem flights from the Tegelberg, contact **Aktiv Flugschule**, Tegelbergstraße 33, 87645 Schwangau, ☎ 08362-921-457, www.flugschule-aktiv.de.

■ On Water

Fishing is allowed in most waters of the area. Permits and exact details are available from the tourist office.

Boat Rental: Rowboats and pedal boats can be rented without reservations at the **Bootsverleih Alpsee**,

☎ 08362-8782, or from the **Campingplatz Bannwaldsee**, ☎ 08362-93-000. A larger selection, including windsurfers, sailboats, canoes, and family-size kayaks, is available from **Surfschule Forggensee** in Brunnen, ☎ 08362-924-386.

Lake Boats: Städtische Forggensee-Schifffahrt, ☎ 08362-921-363, www.fuessen.de, operates lake boats on the Forggensee from mid-June to early October. Excursions last from 50 minutes to two hours.

■ On Snow

Alpine Skiing: The **Allgäu-Tirol Vitales Land**, www.vitalesland.com, ski area encompasses not only the area around Schwangau, but also other mountains in the region and in Austria – 82 ski lifts and 87 miles of downhill slopes are available. In Schwangau, in addition to the Tegelbergbahn, another four ski lifts operate near the Talstation. A Vitales Land ski pass costs €48 for two days.

Cross-Country Skiing: The Füssen area is considered one of the best in Germany for cross-country skiers. In Füssen alone, 36 miles of cross-country trails are open freely.

An interesting trail is at an altitude of 3,772 ft on the Buchenberge. It allows cross-country skiing at a high altitude with wonderful views and guaranteed snow while the lower regions are still green.

Where to Stay & Eat

Most visitors to Schwangau are day-trippers, but there are a few hotels in town.

The **Lisl Schlosshotel und Jägerhaus** are close to Schloss Hohenschwangau. The Jägerhaus is by far the more luxurious but both are very comfortable. Many rooms have views of the castle. The **Wittelsbacher Restaurant** (€-€€) serves international cuisine and hearty

Lisl Schlosshotel und Jägerhaus

local dishes at pleasantly low prices. Neuschwansteinerstraße 1, 87645 Hohenschwangau, ☎ 08362-8870, fax 08362-81-107, www.lisl.de. (€€€-€€€€)

Hotel Müller

The early-20th-century **Hotel Müller** is directly below Schloss Hohenschwangau. Most of the individually furnished rooms have balconies or terrace access. Some suites are very luxurious. Alpseestraße 16, 87645 Hohenschwangau, ☎ 08362-81-990, fax 08362-819-913, www.hotel-mueller.de. (€€€-€€€€)

The **Alpenhotel Meier** is a small, 12-bedroom pension. Rooms are comfortable and some have balconies. The rustic **restaurant** (€-€€) serves international cuisine, as well as hearty local specialties. Schwangauer Straße 37, 87645 Hohenschwangau, ☎ & fax 08362-81-889, www.alpenhotel-allgaeu.de. (€€)

■ Camping

Campingplatz Bannwaldsee is beautifully located next to the Bannwald Lake. It has on-site bicycle and boat rentals, a natural beach and is close to ski areas. There are 520 lots for tourists and another 190 for long-term campers. It is open year-round. Münchner Straße 151, 87645 Schwangau, ☎ 08362-93-000, fax 08362-930-020, www.camping-bannwaldsee.de.

Camping Brunnen is right next to the Forggensee Lake, only 2.4 miles from Neuschwanstein. It has excellent facilities and many shady lots. There are 230 lots for tourists and 70 for long-term campers. It is open from late December to early November. Seestraße 81, 87645 Schwangau, 8273, fax 08362-8630, www.camping-brunnen.de.

Camping Hopfensee is a first-class campsite with excellent facilities. It is open from mid-December to early November, with its own ski lift and direct access to 36 miles of cross-country skiing trails. It has 380 lots. 87629 Füssen, ☎ 08362-917-710, fax 08362-917-720, www.camping-hopfensee.com.

◆ Bavarian Alps

The Bavarian Alps are generally lower than their Austrian and Swiss counterparts but equally beautiful. The Alps suddenly rise out of green meadows, making any approach from Munich or the north spectacularly beautiful. The mountains are easily reached from Munich by road or rail and are popular for day-trips. The east-west connections in the mountain areas themselves are less well developed and a private car makes traveling much simpler.

In addition to the mountains, the area teams with history and interesting buildings, many lakes and rivers, and countless hiking and cycling opportunities. Many ski resorts are popular with families as slopes are generally less challenging than in neighboring countries.

Garmisch-Partenkirchen

This is the most visited Bavarian Alpine resort. It became internationally famous after hosting the 1936 Winter Olympic Games and several international competitions since. The town of just under 30,000 is not partic-

Above Garmisch-Partenkirchen

ularly high. Although its altitude is only 2,370 ft, it is surrounded by Germany's highest mountains. These allow for excellent skiing conditions as well as popular summer hiking.

The whole region is stunningly beautiful, with its mountain panoramas. Interesting excursions include the amazing Baroque monastery in Ettal, Oberammergau with its woodcarving tradition, King Ludwig II's fabulous Linderhof palace, the Baroque Wieskirche, and, of course, the mountain peaks, including Zugspitze. Schloss Neuschwanstein is easily accessible by car.

Information Sources

Tourist Office: Tourist Information, Richard-Strauss-Platz 2, 82467 Garmisch-Partenkirchen, ☎ 08821-180-700, www.garmisch-partenkirchen.de.

Transportation

Garmisch-Partenkirchen has a good bus system that connects to all sights and adventure areas. Ettal and Oberammergau can be reached in 40 minutes by at least two buses per hour, while Mittenwald is a 20-minute train ride away. Bus services to the Wieskirche, Schwangau, and Füssen are available but double-check return schedules – the services are especially limited on weekends.

Driving is easy in the region and the best way to get to several sights on the same day. It is often sensible to take shortcuts through Austria – where fuel is significantly cheaper – but stay off the highways or purchase a vignette (toll pass).

Garmisch-Partenkirchen can be reached from Munich in 90 minutes on at least hourly trains. Driving along the Autobahn A95 can be slightly faster in light traffic.

Sightseeing

■ Garmisch Partenkirchen

This is such a lovely area that indoor sights are best left for rainy days. In addition, the excursions are generally more interesting than the sights in the town itself.

In the Garmisch part of town is the **Neue Pfarrkirche St Martin** (New Church), a single-nave church with two half-round chapels. It was erected in 1730-34 in a Rococo

Alte Kirche

style with stuccowork and wall paintings. The **Alte Kirche Garmisch** (Old Church) has a Romanesque core (1280) but was altered into a mainly Gothic structure during the 15th century. It has two equal naves with a single central column supporting the Gothic vaulting. Some 15th- and 16th-century wall paintings were preserved. Historic houses are in Loisach, Frühlings, and Kreuzstraße.

Ludwigstraße leads from the Bahnhof east through Partenkirchen. It makes a sharp right turn to become the **Historische Ludwigstraße** (Historic Ludwigstraße), with many historic buildings and painted façades. More historic buildings are in

Ludwigstraße

Sonnenbergstraße and Ballengasse.

The **Werdenfels Museum**, Ludwigstraße 47, ☎ 08821-2134, has an interesting exhibition of masks, furniture and decorative items. It is in a former 17th-century grocer's house – the only building in the street that survived a town fire in 1865 intact. Opening hours are Tuesday to Friday from 10 am to 1 pm and from 3 to 6 pm, weekends from 10 am to 1 pm only. Admission is €1.50.

■ Mittenwald

Mittenwald is around 15 miles east of Garmisch-Partenkirchen. It is generally considered the most picturesque of all Bavarian Alpine villages. Parts of it look as if they came straight from a tourist brochure.

Mittenwald

Goethe described the town as a living picture book and the attraction remains despite the huge number of visitors.

The main attractions of Mittenwald are its beautiful location and the Alpine houses, many with painted façades. Hiking, cycling, and skiing are popular activities. The **Karwendel ski area** has Germany's second-highest cable-car route and a 4.2-mile downhill ski slope.

Mittenwald is also famous for violins. In 1684, Matthias Klotz, a former pupil of Stradivarius, settled here and started the violin-making industry that continues to the present. The **Geigenbau-und Heimatmuseum** (Violin and Local History Museum), Ballenhausgasse 3, ☎ 08823-2522, tells the story. It is open Tuesday to Friday from 10 am to 1 pm and 3 to 6 pm. On weekends, it is open from 10 am to 1 pm. Admission is €2.

■ Ettal

Kloster Ettal

Ettal is a small village nine miles north of Garmisch-Partenkirchen. The main sight is **Kloster Ettal** (Monastery), Kaiser-Ludwig-Platz 1, 82488 Ettal, ☎ 08822-740, which is next to the main through-road.

In 1330, Emperor Ludwig the Bavarian founded a Benedictine monastery here. The original Gothic church has the only example in Germany of a figure-8 floor plan – it is still the basis of the present church. The monastery was relatively obscure in its first centuries, but became more prominent in the 18th century due to an increase in pilgrims and the foundation of a school. In the 18th century, the monastery and especially the church were converted to a Baroque style. Following a major fire in 1744, the marvelous current cupola was added. The interior is an excellent example of Bavarian Baroque excess, with the cupola fresco by Johann Jakob Zeiller. Some of the stuccos are by

Johann Baptist Zimmermann. The church is open daily from 8 am to 6 pm.

Part of the monastery is still functioning and brews an excellent beer, as well as a famous liqueur. Ettal also houses a prestigious private school.

Schloss Linderhof

■ Linderhof

Schloss Linderhof, Linderhof 112, 82488 Ettal, ☎ 08822-92-030, fax 08822-920-311, www.linderhof.de, is the only one of Mad King Ludwig's palaces that was actually completed. It is the smallest and least pretentious of one of all. Still, it uses a wide range of conflicting styles and is over-decorated inside. The Petit Trianon in Versailles was probably an inspiration. It has many references to French King Louis XIV, with whom King Ludwig became obsessed. Highlights of the interior include the sumptuous bedroom, a magnificent hall of mirrors, and King Ludwig's favorite: a table that could be hoisted from a floor below so he could eat his dinner in peace without servants hovering around.

The Schloss is in a beautiful English-style landscaped park with wonderful Alpine backdrops. There are several interesting features in the park. Directly in front of the Schloss is a fountain with a gilded Neptune statue that spouts water up to 100 ft high. In the park are a Moorish Pavillion and a Moroccan House that King Ludwig bought at world exhibitions in Paris. Several other structures remind one of Wagner operas, which Ludwig loved: a grotto of Venus (*Tannhäuser*), a Hundingshütte pavilion (*The Valkyries*), and the Gurnemanzklause hermitage (*Parzifal*).

The Schloss is open daily from April to September, 9 am to 6 pm, and from October to March, 10 am to 4 pm. In winter, the structures in the garden are closed. Admission is €7 (€6 in winter), which includes a compulsory guided tour of the palace, available in English. Advance reservations are possible in writing or by fax. That requires a small service fee worth paying when visiting in the high season.

The Schloss is six miles west of Ettal on the B23. It can be reached by car, hiking, cycling, or bus. The B23 is a convenient shortcut through Austria to Füssen. The road is, however, one of the first in the region to close when weather is inclement.

■ Oberammergau

Oberammergau is a small village about 12 miles north of Garmisch-Partenkirchen. It is most famous for its **Passion Play** but is also a major woodcarving center. The village is pretty but at times very commercial and full of religious kitsch.

The town has many painted façades in the local *Lüftlmalerei* (trompe l'oeil) style. The theme of the paintings is mostly religious, but some façades are secular, with fairy tales and beer hall scenes. The **Pilatushaus**, Ludwig-Thoma-Straße 10, ☎ 08822-92-310, is a particularly good example. It houses a gallery and workshops of carved wood items. Before buying woodcarvings from the wide range of shops in town, look here to see what true skill can produce. A shop next to the Pilatushaus sells items produced here. Opening hours are weekdays from May to October, 1 to 6 pm. Admission is free.

Pilatushaus

In 1633, the villagers of Oberammergau made a pledge to perform Christ's Passion if the approaching plague passed the town by. The first play was staged in 1634. Presently, the **Passion Play** is performed every 10 years in a huge open-air theater specially built for the play. Around 2,000 performers are needed for the 100 performances between May and September. About 1,000 performers are used for each performance, which lasts six hours. All actors are amateurs who either were born in Oberammergau or have lived here at least 20 years. The next performance is in 2010 and tickets will go on sale in 2008.

In recent years, the theater has also been used in summer to stage major operas such as *Nabucco* and *Aida*. For details, contact **Oberammergau Tourismus**, Eugen-Papst-Straße 9a, 82487 Oberammergau, ☎ 08822-92-310, www. oberammergau.de.

■ Wieskirche

The magnificent **Wieskirche** (Church in the Meadow), Wies 12, 86989 Steingaden, ☎ 08862-932-930, www.wieskirche.de, is generally seen as the definitive Rococo church in southern Bavaria. This glorious construction in a meadow, literally in the middle of nowhere, is a UNESCO World Cultural Heritage Site.

The Wieskirche was designed by master Rococo architect and stucco artist Dominikus Zimmermann (1685-1766). His equally talented brother Johann Baptist Zimmermann (1680-1758)

Wieskirche

did much of the interior painting. The exterior is typical of a Rococo church – rather plain and serving mainly to keep the interior from falling apart. Approaching the Wieskirche from the parking lot a few hundred yards down a gentle hill, the pale yellow exterior reveals nothing of the glorious interior. Inside, the church is oval, with a narrow apse extension. The huge cupola is also oval and ideally suited for the Rococo painting of the Second Coming. The lower parts of the church, associated with

Wieskirche altar

earth, are sparsely decorated, at least for a Rococo church, and mostly white. The upper reaches represent heaven and are typical Rococo with stuccowork, paintings, and gilded decorations. The choir is a symphony of color, with frescoes, gilded stuccos, statues, and marble balustrades. Large windows insure ample light and the church is best appreciated on a sunny day. Opening hours are daily from 8 am to 7 pm, closing at 5 pm in winter. Admission is free.

It is hard to imagine today how such a magnificent church could have been financed by such a small agricultural community. It was all due to a statue of Christ that was considered too pitiful for use in processions. In 1738, a farming couple saw this Christ in tears. Subsequent prayers were answered and the pilgrims and donations started to come in droves. It currently attracts around a million visitors annually. Dominikus Zimmermann saw the church as his greatest accomplishment and spent the last 10 years of his life in a small house almost at its doorstep.

Several series of concerts are held in the church, especially in summer. Each series is organized by different organizations –

the details and where to buy tickets are available on the church's English-language website. Entrance to many concerts is free and without reservations.

The Wieskirche is 30 miles north of Garmisch on a small country lane near Steingaden. It can be reached by irregular bus from Füssen or Garmisch-Partenkirchen.

Adventures

■ On Foot

 Countryside Hikes & Mountaineering: Garmisch-Partenkirchen is in a lovely area with many hiking opportunities. Popular starting points are at the mountain stations of cable cars. Often walks with spectacular views are possible without strenuous inclines. Excellent hiking maps are available from the tourist information office or any bookshop.

A popular walk is in the **Partnachklamm gorge**. This narrow gorge has bizarre rocks and arcades carved by the thundering Partnach Alpine stream. Take rain gear in summer. It is also open, but mostly frozen, during winter. A round-trip from the Partenkirchen ski area takes around 90 minutes.

A similar walk is in the **Höllentalklamm** from Hammersbach towards Zugspitze. A small entrance fee is payable before entering a half-mile gorge with tunnels, arcades, and bridges.

The tourist office arranges guided mountain hikes from mid-June to September on most Tuesdays and Thursdays. The route depends on the weather and details are provided only a day in advance.

HOLIDAY PASS

During the summer season, the Holiday Pass allows free entry to some sights and local transportation as well as one cable car per day in the Classic area. The train or bus can be taken to Eibsee but the final assault on Zugspitze itself is not included. It costs   35 and is available from the tourism office.

Mountain guides are available through the **Bergsteigerschule Zugspitze**, Am Gudiberg 7, ☎ 08821-58-999, www.

bergsteigerschule-zugspitze.de. Guided trips ranging from a few hours to several days are offered and range from hiking to rock and ice climbing.

■ On Wheels

By Bicycle: Bicycle rentals are available in Garmisch-Partenkirchen from **Trek-Pro-Shop**,Rathausplatz 11, ☎ 08821-79-528, www.trekproshop.de, and from **Multi Cycle**, Bahnhofstraße 6, ☎ 08821-948-994, www.multicycle.de. Mountain bikes only are offered by **Sport Total**, Marienplatz 18, ☎ 08821-1425, www.agentursporttotal.de.

■ In the Air

Cable Cars: The mountains around Garmisch-Partenkirchen are divided for practical purposes into two main areas: Zugspitze and the Classic area, which includes Alpspitz, Kreueck, Hausberg, and Wank. All the cable cars are operated by **Bayerische Zugspitzbahn Bergbahn**, Olympiastraße 27, ☎ 08821-7970, www.zugspitze.de.

Zugspitze: At 9,715 ft, Zugspitze is Germany's highest mountain, with the only glacial skiing area in the country. It is a popular all-year destination.

Other than climbing, the peak can be reached in two ways: via the Bayerische Zugspitzbahn or the Eibsee-Seilbahn. The **Bayerische Zugspitzbahn**, ☎ 08821-7970, is a cogwheel train that runs from Garmisch-Partenkirchen via Eibsee to the Gletscherbahnhof (Glacier Station) at 8,495 ft. Part of the journey is in a tunnel carved through the mountain rock. The journey takes 75 minutes from Garmisch-Partenkirchen, or 40 minutes from Eibsee. From the Gletscherbahnhof, the 3,280-ft-long **Gletscherbahn** cable car goes to the Bergstation near the top in four minutes. (€4 one-way if not used in conjunction with the Zugspitzbahn.)

A much faster alternative is to take the **Eibsee-Seilbahn**, ☎ 08821-7970, from Eibsee directly to the Bergstation. The large cable car gondolas take only 10 minutes. (Due to the rapid changes in air pressure, children under 18 months are not allowed in the gondolas.)

Round-trip tickets are €43 in summer and €34 in winter. One-way tickets are €25. A combination of the cable car and train can be used on round-trip tickets. The service is available year-round from 8 am to 4:45 pm, with longer hours in the high season.

 A one-day ski pass costs €34.

THE CLASSIC AREA

■ The **Alpspitzbahn** cable car goes from Garmisch to the 6,722-ft Osterfelderkopf peak in nine minutes. It operates daily from November to February, 8:30 am to 4:30 pm, from March to June, 8:30 am to 5 pm, and from July to October, 8 am to 5:30 pm. Round-trip journeys are €20, or €15 one-way.

■ The **Hochalmbahn** cable car goes from Hochalm to Osterfeldkopf in four minutes. It operates the same times as the Alpspitzbahn and costs €4 one-way.

■ The **Kreuzeckbahn** cable car connects Garmisch and the 5,379-ft Kreuzeck in seven minutes. It operates year-round from 8:15 am with the final ride 15 minutes after the Alpspitzbahn. Round-trip journeys are €16, or €11 one-way.

■ The **Hausbergbahn** cable car operates only in winter and connects Garmisch with the 4,395-ft Hausberg in five minutes. Operation hours are daily from November to April, 8:30 am to 5 pm. Round-trip journeys are €11, or €8 one-way.

Combination tickets with hikes between the mountain stations are available. The Kreuzberg-Hausberg combination is €15.50 and requires an hour's hike. An Alpspitz-Rundfahrt combines the Alpspitz, Hochalm, and Kreuzeck cable cars with hikes of between 30 minutes and an hour between the mountain stations. It costs €23.50.

A one-day ski pass valid on all Classic area cable cars costs €28.

The **Wankbahn** operates only in summer and connects Partenkirchen with the Bergstation (5,756 ft) on the Wank (5,838 ft) in 18 minutes. It operates daily from May to November, 8:45 am to 5 pm (4:30 pm in October and November). Round-trip journeys are €16.50, or €11.50 one-way.

Hang-gliding & Paragliding: Tandem flights are arranged by **Sport Total**, Marienplatz 18, ☎ 08821-1425, www.agentursporttotal.de; **Gleitschirmschule Garmisch-Partenkirchen**, Am Hausberg 8, ☎ 08821-74-260, www.gleitschirmschule-gap.de; and **Aerotaxi**, Beim Gerber, 82481 Mittenwald, ☎ 0171-281-9199, www.aerotaxi.de. Winter and summer flights are available from various peaks in the region.

■ On Snow & Ice & Ice

 The ski season is long and lasts from November to May, with Zugspitze's snow usually guaranteed. For actual snow conditions call the snow telephone, ☎ 08821-797-979.

Alpine Skiing: Garmisch-Partenkirchen is one of Germany's premier Alpine skiing areas, with 71 miles of downhill slopes. Zugspitze is the only glacial skiing area in Germany. The *Kandahar* is Germany's only downhill run with a World Cup License.

If the adjacent Austrian slopes are added, 126 miles of downhill runs, serviced by 105 ski lifts and cable cars are available. The Holiday Pass, from €83 for three days, gives access to the whole area. Up to 120,000 people per hour can be transported, meaning very few lines and short waiting times.

Cross-Country Skiing: For cross-country skiers, 66 miles of trails (*Loipen*), both traditional and freestyle skating, are available for free. Kainzenbad has a floodlit trail.

Ice Skating: Ice skating is possible in the **Olympia-Eissport-Zentrum**, ☎ 08821-52-578, www.gemeindewerke-garmisch-partenkirchen.de. It is open to the public from July to Easter.

RENTAL EQUIPMENT & SKI SCHOOLS

■ Garmisch-Partenkirchen has many ski schools – all also rent out equipment. Alpine and cross-country ski schools include **Skischule Alpin**, Reintalstraße 8, ☎ 08821-945-676, www.skischulealpin.de and **Skischule Garmisch-Partenkirchen**, Am Hausberg 8, ☎ 08821-4931, www.skischule-gap.de.

■ **Erste Skilanglaufschule Garmisch-Partenkirchen**, Olympia-Skistadion, Osteingang, ☎ 08821-1516, www.ski-langlauf-schule.de, is a school for cross-country skiing only.

■ **Snowboardschule Erwin Gruber**, Mittenwalder Straße 47d, ☎ 08821-76-490, www.snowboard-schule.de, is a school for snowboarding.

■ **Skiing equipment** can be rented from **Skiverleih Ostler**, at the Hausbergbahn, 08821-3999; **Welt des Sports**, Fürstenstraße 20, ☎ 08821-72-601, www.skiverleih-garmisch.de; and **Snowboard & Skicenter Zugspitzplatt**, on Zugspitze, ☎ 08821-74-505.

■ **Snowshoes** can be rented from **Schneeshuh Verleih**, Reintalerstraße 8, ☎ 08821-945-676, www.schneeschuh-verleih.de.

Snowboarding: Around 12 miles of slopes are open to snowboarders. The most popular area is on the **Zugspitzeplatte**. The area is a freestyle paradise with a super pipe 394 ft long, 52 ft wide, and 16 ft high, a line with four straight jumps and leaps, and a rail-combo.

Tobogganing: There are several challenging tobogganing courses in the area. **Rodelbahn am Kainzenbad** (3,477 ft with a 590-ft drop) is a natural tobogganing course, **Partnachalm** (6,560 ft/915 ft) and **St. Martin am Grasberg** (5,248 ft/1,050 ft) are on streets that are not cleared in winter. The longest course with the highest drop is on the **Hausberg** (12,792 ft/2,132 ft). First ascend the peak with the cable car and then use the summer hiking trail, which is prepared as a tobogganing course in winter. On Wednesdays from 5 to 8 pm, the cable car is €9 for unlimited rides. **Skiverleih Ostler** next to the Hausbergbahn rents out equipment, or contact any of the ski schools

Where to Stay & Eat

■ Partenkirchen

The **Reindl's Partenkirchner Hof** is luxury country-style hotel in the heart of town close to the station. Rooms are comfortable and romantic with solid wood furniture. Some are luxurious. Many rooms have balconies with views of the Wetterstein Mountain.

The **restaurant** (€€-€€€) serves local as well as international cuisine and has a long wine list. Bahnhofstraße 15, 82467 Garmisch-Partenkirchen, ☎ 08821-943-870,

Reindl's Partenkirchner Hof

fax 08821-9438-7250, www.reindls.de. (€€-€€€€)

The **Post-Hotel Partenkirchen** is in the heart of the Old Town. It has a Baroque façade and inside combine antiques with mod-

Post-Hotel Partenkirchen

ern furniture. Rooms are comfortable and some have great mountain views. Four **restaurants** (€-€€€) on the premises serve international and regional cuisine. Ludwigstraße 49, 82467 Garmisch-Partenkirchen, ☎ 08821-93-630, fax 08821-9363-2222, www.post-hotel.de. (€€-€€€)

■ Garmisch

Hotel Zugspitze is a typical Bavarian Alpine hotel with balconies. Rooms are comfortable with country-style furniture. The hotel is halfway between the station and the Kurpark. Klammstraße 19, 82467 Garmisch-Partenkirchen, ☎ 08821-9010, fax 08821-901-333, www.hotel-zugspitze.de. (€€-€€€€)

The **Clausings Posthotel** is in the heart of Garmisch at the edge of the major shopping street. Rooms are individually furnished and some are very comfortable. Many have views of the

Clausings Posthotel

Zugspitze. The **restaurant** (€-€€€) serves regional as well as international cuisine. It has a pleasant terrace as well as a historic bar area. Marienplatz 12, 82467 Garmisch-Partenkirchen, ☎ 08821-7090, fax 08821-709-205, www.clausings-posthotel. de. (€€-€€€)

The **Hotel Vier Jahreszeiten** is a block from the station. It has comfortable rooms with solid wood furniture. All rooms have mountain views and some have balconies. The large **restaurant** (€-€€) is decorated with hunting trophies and serves hearty local dishes. Bahnhofstraße 23, 82467 Garmisch-Partenkirchen, ☎ 08821-9160, fax 08821-4486, www. vierjahreszeiten.cc. (€€)

The **Alpenhof Restaurant**, Am Kurpark 10, ☎ 08821-59-055, serves hearty local dishes as well as Mediterranean cuisine. (€-€€)

■ **Ettal**

Hotel Ludwig der Bayer

The huge **Hotel Ludwig der Bayer** is run by the Benedictine order. Although there are plenty of carved wood religious objects in the hotel, life here is anything but monastic. Rooms are comfortably furnished in solid wood furniture. The hotel has a huge **restaurant** (€€) popular with bus parties, which can mean serious waiting times for service.

Kaiser-Ludwig-Platz 10, 82488 Ettal, ☎ 08822-9150, fax 08822-74-480. (€€)

The much smaller **Hotel Zur Post** is on the same square. It is a typical Alpine guesthouse with flowers on the balconies and ample unpainted wood in the interior. Rooms are comfortable. The hotel is popular with families. The **restaurant** (€-€€€) is open for dinner only and serves regional cuisine. Kaiser-Ludwig-

Hotel Zur Post

Platz 18, 82488 Ettal, ☎ 08822-3596, fax 08822-6399, www. posthotel-ettal.de. (€€)

■ Camping

Camping Zugspitze is on the road to Grainau. It has many shady spots but can be noisy. Facilities are rather basic. It has 130 lots for tourists and 50 for long-term campers. Reservations are required in winter and it's open year-round. Griesener Straße 4, 82491 Garmisch-Grainau, ☎ 08821-3180, fax 08821-947-594.

Much more pleasant are the two campsites near Mittenwald. **Alpen Caravanpark Tennsee** is a five-star site with excellent facilities. It bills itself as the campsite with hotel flair. In winter, it has a shuttle bus to the ski areas. There are 267 lots and it's open from mid-December to early November. 82494 Mittenwlad-Klais-Krün, ☎ 08825-170, fax 08825-17-236, www. camping-tennsee.de.

Equally well located, only 1.8 miles outside Mittenwald, is **Naturcamping Isarhorn**. It's in a natural setting with excellent facilities. There are 200 lots for tourists and another 130 for long-term campers. It is open from mid-December to October. Isarhorn 4, 82481 Mittenwald, ☎ 08823-5216, fax 08823-8091, www.camping-mittenwald.de.

Chiemsee

Chiemsee is the largest lake in Bavaria. It is a popular vacation area but foreign visitors come mainly on daytrips from Munich to see King Ludwig's Schloss Herrenchiemsee Palace. It is a popular stop en route to Berchtesgaden or Salzburg.

Information Sources

Tourist Office: Chiemsee-Tourismus, Felden 10, 83233 Bernau, ☎ 08051-965-550, www.chiemsee. de.

Transportation

Chiemsee is easily reached by road or rail. Trains from Munich run hourly to Prien. From May to September, an original steam tram engine with wagons from 1887 operates between Prien train station and the boat landing. A shuttle bus operates on the same route all year.

The lake is next to the Autobahn A8, about an hour's drive from Munich or 30 minutes from Salzburg. Although ferry services are available from several towns, the most frequent and shortest rides to the islands are from Prien.

Sightseeing

The main attractions in the area are on the two largest islands in the lake: Herrenchiemsee (Men's) and Frauenchiemsee (Women's) islands. These are named after the monastery and nunnery that were originally on the islands. Both islands are traffic-free and easily reached by frequent boats from Prien.

Chiemsee Schifffahrt, Seestraße 108, 83209 Prien, ☎ 08051-6090, www.chiemsee-schifffahrt.de, operates ferries from Prien to Herrenchiemsee and continues to Frauenchiemsee. Boats depart year-round every 20 minutes

■ Herrenchiemsee

The Herrenchiemsee Island is the more famous and popular because King Ludwig II erected the magnificent **Schloss Herrenchiemsee** (New Palace), 83209 Herrenchiemsee, ☎ 08051-68-870, www.herren-chiemsee.de, here in the late 19th century. Ludwig admired his French namesake, Louis XIV. They were equally vain but, in contrast to the Sun King, Ludwig had no actual power and limited talent. His Schloss Herrenchiemsee was to be the new Versailles. It lacks none of

Schloss Herrenchiemsee (Werner Hölzl)

the French palace's pomp or splendor and actually has a Great Hall of Mirrors larger than the original. Only 20 of the rooms were completed, but that alone cost more than Ludwig's two other follies, Schloss Linderhof and Schloss Neuschwanstein, combined. Other highlights include the ambassadorial staircase, a huge bath, a dining table that was hoisted from a floor below so the King could eat in complete privacy, and a ceremonial bedroom with a 9.84- by 8.5-ft bed.

The interior can only be seen on a 40-minute guided tour – frequent English tours are available. Opening hours are daily from April to October 3, 9 am to 6 pm, from October 4-31, 9:40 am to 5 pm, and from November to March, 9:40 am to 4 pm. The fountains in the park play daily from May to September, every 15 minutes between 9:35 am and 5:25 pm.

Inside the palace is the **King Ludwig II Museum**. It has exhibits on the king's life and plans. Several more castles were planned in addition to the ones he actually started. It also has a section on his friendship with Richard Wagner, with portraits and stage sets. Opening hours are daily from April to October 3, 9 am to 6 pm, from October 4-31, 10 am to 5:45 pm, and from November to March, 10 am to 4:45 pm.

Bavaria

In the **Altes Schloss** (Old Palace) is the Museum im Augustiner-Chorherrenstift Herrenchiemsee (Museum in the Augustinian Monastery), 83209 Herrenchiemsee, ☎ 08051-68-870, www.herren-chiemsee.de. A Benedictine monastery was founded on the island in the eighth century but replaced in 1130 by an Augustinian Order. The current palace building was later remodeled in a Baroque style. It was secularized in 1803 and King Ludwig stayed here after acquiring the island in 1873. The museum has an exhibition on the history of the island as well as the history of the German constitution. An art gallery has 80 paintings by Munich artist Julius Exeter (1863-1939). Opening hours are similar to those above. The Julius Exeter collection is closed from November to March. Admission is €2.50, but included in the combination ticket with the New Palace.

VISITORS' INFORMATION

Admission to the island and parks is free. A combination ticket of €6.50 gives access to the Herrenchiemsee (New) Palace, King Ludwig II Museum, and the Museum in the Old Palace (Monastery). The latter can also be seen separately for €2.50.

The former Augustine Monastery is directly at the boat landing. It is now a hotel and has a large restaurant. The new palace is a pleasant 15-minute stroll from here. Cars and bicycles are banned from the island.

■ Frauenchiemsee

Frauenchiemsee has around 300 inhabitants and is famous for its nunnery and smoked fish. The monastery was founded in 766 by the last Agilolfinger Duke Tassilo III. It was secularized in 1803, but King Ludwig I later opened a new Benedictine monastery.

Romanesque church (Rufus46)

The monastery is still in operation with the nuns running a popular conference center.

In addition to the Baroque monastery, the main sight on the island is the 1,000-year-old Romanesque church. Its freestanding, onion-domed campanile was erected in the 11th century as the first high building in southern Bavaria. During the 1950s, frescoes dating back to 1130 were rediscovered. The nearby **Carolingian Torhalle** (Gate Portal), Frauenchiemseestraße 41, ☎ 08054-7256, is one of the oldest buildings in Bavaria and has an angel cycle painted in 860. There is an exhibition of mainly medieval art works. It is open daily from May to October from 11 am to 6 pm. Admission is €1.50.

Where to Stay & Eat

■ Herrenchiemsee Island

It is possible to spend the night on King Ludwig's traffic-free island. Unfortunately, the opulent palace is not available, but the **Schlosshotel Herrenchiemsee** is in a mansion older than Ludwig's fantasy palace. Rooms are comfortable, but not particularly luxuri-

Schlosshotel Herrenchiemsee

ous or spacious. The **restaurant** (€€-€€€) is famous for its fish. The hotel is only a few minutes walk from the boat landing. The hotel is only open from Easter to October; the restaurant is open all year. 83209 Herrenchiemsee, ☎/fax 08051-1509, www.schlosshotel-herrenchiemsee.com. (€€-€€€)

■ Camping

Various campsites are scattered around the lake and region. Two of the best are in Prien.

Panoramacamping Harras is quietly and beautifully located on a small peninsula near Prien. It has wonderful views of the lake. The site has 180 lots, many with shade. Facilities are very good. The site is open from mid-April to mid-October. Harrasser Straße 135, 83209 Prien am Chiemsee, ☎ 08051-90-460, fax 08051-904-616, www.camping-harras.de.

Camping Hofbauer is at the southern edges of Prien, just under a mile from the lakeshore. It has excellent facilities and 120 lots. Bicycle rental is available on-site. It is open from April to October. Bernauerstraße 110, 83209 Prien am Chiemsee, ☎ 08051-4136, fax 08051-62-657, www.camping-prien-chiemsee.de.

Berchtesgaden

The Berchtesgaden area is one of the most beautiful parts of Germany. The Alps are a constant presence, the towns are small and picturesque, and the natural beauty serene. The area is very popular, with the high season in July and August for families, autumn and spring for hikers and cyclists, and December to March for winter sports fans.

In addition to outdoor pursuits, the area is also infamous as the favored retreat of Adolf Hitler. Although most of the buildings erected by the Nazis as holiday villas for the top leaders have been destroyed, some interesting sites survived, including bunkers and Hitler's Eagles Nest.

The Watzmann peak, at 8,899 ft, Germany's second-highest, forms the backdrop to many parts of Berchtesgaden. It is particularly impressive where it drops around 5,900 ft almost straight into the beautiful Königssee Lake.

Information Sources

Tourist Office: Tourist information is available from Berchtesgaden Tourismus, Königssee Straße 2, 83471 Berchtesgaden, ☎ 08652-967-270, www.berchtesgadener-land.com.

Transportation

Public transportation is available to all parts of the region, making one-way hiking trips easy. In addition, many transportation modes are geared for easy connections, e.g. from bus to cable car to boat. Except for the high season, driving is a very pleasant option too with ample parking lots at major attractions.

From Munich, at least hourly trains take around 2½ hours and require a changeover at Freilassing, or a change in Salzburg to a bus.

By car, the fastest way from Munich to Berchtesgaden is along the Autobahn A8 passing through Austria at Salzburg. However, do note that an Austrian highway vignette (toll pass) is required. Otherwise turn off at Bad Reichenhall and use the beautiful country road.

URLAUBSTICKET

Overnight guests in the Berchtesgaden area have to pay spa taxes. These allow some free and reduced admission prices. However, the best deal is the Urlaubsticket (Vacation Ticket) – it costs €15 and allows unlimited transportation for five days on the RVO local bus network. Included in this deal are buses to the Roßfeld area, Salzburg, Bad Reichenhall, and Schönau-Königssee, among others.

Sightseeing

■ Berchtesgaden Town

Berchtesgaden has a lovely Old Town with an interesting Schloss and museum. However, overall the indoor sights here are best left for bad weather days. They are interesting, but the natural beauty of the area has much more to offer.

The **Königliches Schloss Berchtesgaden** (Royal Palace), Schlossplatz, ☎ 08652-947-980, www.haus-bayern.com, was a monastery from the 12th century up to secularization in 1803. Thereafter, it became a royal residence and still has the art collection of Crown Prince Rupprecht. The interior can only be seen on a 50-minute guided tour that includes some 30

Königliches Schloss

Bavaria

rooms. Most are furnished with Renaissance or Baroque furniture and art. Opening hours are Sunday to Friday from Pentecost to mid-October, 10 am to noon and 2 to 4 pm. From mid-October to Pentecost, it is open weekdays only for tours at 11 am and 2 pm. Admission is €7.

Very popular with children is the **Salzbergwerk** (Salt Mines), Bergwerkstraße 83, ☎ 08652-6002, www.salzbergwerk-berchtesgaden.de. The mine was in operation from 1517 and brought great wealth to the region. Tours include a barge ride on the underground salt lake. It measures 328 by 100 ft and is illuminated. Opening hours are daily from May to mid-October, 9 am to 5 pm. From mid-October to April, it is open from Tuesday to Saturday, noon to 3 pm. Admission is €12.50.

Maria Gern has a famous Wahlfahrtskirche (pilgrims' church) seen on all postcards and brochures in the region. It was built in 1709 and has a very rich interior. You reach it via narrow, but well signposted, country roads. Parking at the church is very limited, but it is more the setting that attracts the visitors than anything else. The interior is rich but usually fenced off and can be seen in minutes.

■ Obersalzberg

In the 1920s, following an early release from prison for his attempted coup d'état in Munich, Adolf Hitler settled in Obersalzberg outside Berchtesgaden. After he eventually came to power in 1933, the area became a second seat of government. His house, the **Berghof**, was enlarged and other senior party leaders acquired properties in the area. Locals, including party faithful, were forced off their land.

Virtually all the buildings were destroyed by the Allies during or shortly after the war. However, a **Documentation Center Obersalzberg**, Salzbergstraße 41, 83471 Berchtesgaden, ☎ 08652-947-960, www.obersalzbergweg.de, opened in 1999 to explain the role of the area in the Nazi regime. Unfortunately, virtually all the information is in German only, although the photos and videos are graphic and shocking. English audio guides are available. Very interesting is the bunker complex that was constructed to protect the leadership during air raids. A vast network of tunnels gave access to the outlying properties.

Opening hours are Tuesday to Sunday from April to October, 9 am to 5 pm, and from November to March, 10 am to 3 pm. Admission is €2.50. A large parking lot is available at the center and Bus 38 from Berchtesgaden station stops here too.

At the instigation of Martin Bormann, a "diplomatic house" was erected on the Kehlstein peak (6,015 ft) as a 50th-birthday gift from the party to Adolf Hitler. In German this building, with absolutely stunning views, is known as the **Kehlsteinhaus**, www.kehlstein.info. In English, it is generally called the **Eagle's Nest** – a term never used by the Nazis. Hitler never liked the place much. Officially, he thought the elevator mechanism on top of the building would act as a lightening rod. Unofficially, some thought he suffered from vertigo, while there is also evidence that he thought the British Royal Air Force might bomb it. Ironically, when the the Berghof complex was bombed at the end of the war, the bombers either thought the Eagle's Nest was too unimportant to strike, or it was so small that they missed it.

It is possible to hike up to the top, but it is easier to take the shuttle bus from behind the Documentation Center. The access road, open only to the shuttle buses, is an incredible feat of engineering. From the bottom, it climbs 2,296 ft over a distance of 3.9 miles, making only a single turn in the process. From the upper bus station, a horizontal tunnel was carved 407 ft though solid rock; then an elevator sweeps you up another 407 ft in 41 seconds. The elevator is the original one from the 1930s. The whole project was completed in an impressive 13 months – Bormann never had to bother with accounting or budgets.

At the top, in the former diplomatic guesthouse, is a **restaurant**, ☎ 08652-2969, serving mostly local dishes. The views from here are magnificent and you can take a short hike to the peak as well. Note the absence of safety railing – in Germany *not* falling off a mountain remains the individual's responsibility.

It is necessary to make return reservations on arrival at the top bus station. Ignore the recommended times; even if you have a drink at the top, it is hard to spend more than an hour. Opening hours are mid-May to October, but they depend on snowfall. The bus and elevator round-trip cost €12.

The only sanctioned tours of the Kehlsteinhaus are in English and offered by **Eagle's Nest Tours**, Vorbergstrasse 12, 83471

Schönau, ☎ 08652-64-971, www.eagles-nest-tours.com. The tour usually departs daily at 1:30 pm from the Berchtesgaden Visitors' Center. Reservations are required.

■ Königssee

In 1978, the **Alpine National Park** was formed to protect the natural beauty of the area around the Königssee and Watzmann peak in Schönau. Nothing at the entrance to the park reveals any of the beauty that lies beyond the tollgate-like entrance, the enormous parking lot,

The Königssee

and the street of kitsch souvenir shops that leads to the lake. Once at the water itself, things improve quickly. The **Königssee** (King's Lake) is Germany's cleanest lake, with water of drinking quality. Measuring 4.8 miles long, up to 1.2 miles wide, and 620 ft deep, it is almost fjord-like, and surrounded by mountains. The Watzmann peak rises 5,904 ft straight up from the lake to form a wall on the eastern shore. It is impossible to hike around the lake, since it is edged with sheer walls of rock in many places. Electric boats do tour the lake, with a round-trip taking two hours.

The most popular stop is at the **St Bartholomä** enclave, about halfway down the lake. The first **Wahlfahrtskirche St Bartholomä** (Pilgrims Chapel) was erected in 1134. This Romanesque church was converted to the present Baroque structure between 1698 and 1710. Its triple apse is one of the most photographed buildings in Germany. The best view of it is from the lake – all three round apses can be seen in equal proportion shortly before landing. It is also visible from several viewing points in the region such as Jenner and Kehlstein. The St Bartholomä enclave was a favored hunting area for the rulers of Berchtesgaden in the 18th century and the Bavarian royals in the 19th century. A popular hike is the two-hour round-trip to see the ice chapel. The enclave can only be reached by boat or by hiking across the lake when it occasionally freezes over in winter.

At the far end of the lake is the **Salet** stop. From here, it is a 15-minute hike to see the spectacularly located little Obersee Lake. Also visible from here are the 1,300-ft-high Röthbach Waterfalls.

Where to Eat

In the larger building attached to the Wahlfahrtskirche St Bartholomä chapel is the **St Bartholomä Historische Gaststätte**, 83471 Schönau am Königssee, ☎ 08652-964-937. It serves traditional hearty food and has space for 370, with an additional 540 seats outdoors. (€-€€)

Shopping

Lederhosen and other Trachten (traditional dress) items can be bought from **Franz Stanassinfer**, Marktplatz 10, 83471 Berchtesgaden, ☎ 08652-2685.

Schönauer Krippenställe, Vorbergstraße 23, 83471 Schönau, ☎ 08652-5375, www.weihnachtskrippen-online.de, produces and sells Christmas nativity scenes and other wood-carved items.

Adventures

■ On Foot

 Countryside Hikes: Berchtesgaden has 120 miles of marked hiking routes. Good hiking maps are available from the tourist office and many hotels. Along the routes are huts and restaurants – opening times are available from the tourist information office or at www.huettenwirte.com.

Some of the most popular hikes are in the **Alpen (Alpine) National Park**, which includes the Königssee area and the Watzmann peak. The park has excellent hiking paths, but note that it is strictly forbidden, and dangerous, to wander off the marked trails.

From the National Park parking lot in Schönau, a one-hour circular route leads to the **Malerwinkel** (Painter's Corner), from where beautiful panoramas of the lake as well as St Bartholomä can be enjoyed.

From St Bartholomä, it is a two-hour round-trip walk to the **Ice Chapel**. The shape and size of the chapel depends on the season.

Several interesting trails lead from the stops along the **Jennerbahn cable car route**. These range from easy one-hour walks to challenging eight-hour hikes in the Alpine peaks. Walking downhill from the middle station takes around 90 minutes.

The tourism office in **Schönau**, Rathausplatz 1, ☎ 08652-1760, www.koenigssee.com, leads guided hikes, usually on Tuesday mornings. Other guided hikes are also available – schedules are available from any tourist office in the region.

Mountaineering: Bergschule Watzmann, Am Forstamt 3, 83486 Ramsau, ☎ 08657-711, www.bergschule-watzmann.de, offers a wide range of mountain climbs and walks in the region. Climbs for families and children are also available.

Outdoor Club, Am Gmundberg 7, 83471 Berchtesgaden, ☎ 08652-97-760, www.outdoor-club.de, offers guided climbs of the Watzmann and other peaks. Overnight hikes with sleeping in mountain huts are also available.

■ On Wheels

By Car: Most of the Berchtesgaden area is fantastic to drive through, with marvelous views of the mountains. However, the **Roßfeld Panorama Straße** (Panorama Road) is in a class of its own. It reaches an altitude of 5,248 ft, making the Roßfeld road the highest public road in Germany. En route, ample parking areas allow drivers to enjoy the marvelous panoramas safely. The road is open all year, but a small toll is payable. It starts a few miles past the Documentation Center Obersalzberg and ends near Berchtesgaden.

By Bicycle: The area is famous for its mountains and it should come as no surprise that cycling routes are available with altitude differences of up to 6,500 ft. However, it is also possible to enjoy cycling on relatively flat routes. Good cycling maps are available from the tourist information offices or bookstores. Many hotels and holiday homes have bicycles for guests. Rentals are also available from **M&R Brandner**, Bergwerkstraße 52, Berchtesgaden, ☎ 08652-1434; **M & R Brandner**, Im Tal 64, Ramsau, ☎ 08657-790; and **BGD Radl Verleih**, Am Rehwinkl 3, Schönau, ☎ 08652-96-870, delivers to hotels. Bicycles may be taken on local trains at no charge.

By Bus: Many a German spouse or partner with no interest in hiking, skiing, or other outdoor pursuits has been forced to accompany their better-halves to Berchtesgaden. People who tire of the mountains quickly will be happy to know that a wide range of daytrips is available to other destinations. **Omnibus Biller**, Zentrale Schönau, ☎ 08652-95-660, and **Bus Schweiger**, Vorbergstraße 5, Schönau, ☎ 08652-2525, www.bus-schwaiger.de, operate daytrips with different destinations most days of the week. The most popular destinations include Salzburg, Munich, and Chiemsee, but trips to Vienna and even Venice are also possible.

Eagle's Nest Tours, Vorbergstrasse 12, 83471 Schönau, ☎ 08652-64-971, www.eagles-nest-tours.com, offers an English-language tour of Salzburg and the *Sound of Music* sights in the region. It usually runs Monday to Saturday from 8:30 am to 12:30 noon. Participation is restricted to eight persons and reservations are required.

■ In the Air

Hot-Air Ballooning: Hot-air balloon flights and tandem paragliding are offered by **Outdoor Club**, Am Gmundberg 7, 83471 Berchtesgaden, ☎ 08652-97-760, www.outdoor-club.de.

Cable Cars: A popular cable car is the **Jennerbahn**, Jennerbahnstraße 18, Schönau, ☎ 08652-95-810, www.jennerbahn.de. In less than half an hour, two-seater gondolas lift passengers up to an altitude of 5,904 ft. A 10-minute walk leads to the top of the plateau and affords a view that includes 100 German and Austrian Alpine peaks. Walking down from the halfway station takes 90 minutes. The cable car operates daily from May to September, 9 am to 5 pm. The round-trip fare is €18.

The **Obersalzbergbahn**, ☎ 08652-2561, www.obersalzbergbahn.de, ascends to 3,280 ft above sea level. At this point are several marked hiking paths, with little or no further variations in altitude. The car operates daily from 9 am to 5:20 pm. Round-trip journeys are €7.50.

Tandem Paragliding & Parachuting: The steep mountain cliffs make for excellent paragliding. Several companies offer tandem flights and parachuting: **Aero-Taxi Watzmann**, ☎ 0171-894-6394, www.aero-taxi.de; **Flieg mit Para-Taxi**, ☎ 08652-948-450; **Gleitschirm-Taxi**, ☎ 0171-314-2898; and **Tandem Flight Fun**, ☎ 0171-616-9048.

■ On Water

Boat Rental: Rowboats can be rented without reservations on the Königssee and Hintersee lakes.

Lake Boats: Bayerische Seenschifffahrt, ☎ 08652-963-618, www.bayerische-seen-schifffahrt.de, has a fleet of 19 electric motorboats on the Königssee. Boats operate daily from May to late October, starting at 8 am and running at 30-minute intervals. From late October to April, boats depart at least hourly from 9:50 am onwards. Round-trip journeys to Salet are €13.80 and to St Barholomä €10.80. It is wise to take the earlier boats. In summer, discounts are offered for departures before 9 am. Note the final return time of the day – missing it either means spending the night in the open or paying an enormous fee to charter a special boat.

Occasionally, night cruises are available on the Königssee to St Bartholomä. The cruise includes a dinner in the restaurant and a concert in the chapel.

■ On Snow & Ice

The Berchtesgaden area has 30 miles of Alpine skiing slopes at 1,900 to 6,146 ft altitude. For cross-country skiers, 36 miles of trails are available, and winter hikers can enjoy up to 90 miles of cleared winter hiking paths.

For updates on actual snow conditions, call the **Schneetelefon** (snow telephone), ☎ 08652-967-297. The season is generally from December to April.

Alpine Skiing: The **Königssee-Jenner ski area**, ☎ 08652-95-810, www.jennerbahn.de, in Schönau can transport up to 3,500 skiers per hour. Around 6.6 miles of prepared slopes are available with lengths up to 1.9 miles and drops up to 2,000 ft. Most slopes are classified as intermediate. A day ski-pass costs about €25.

The **Roßfeld** ski area, ☎ 08652-3538, www.rossfeld.info, has the highest probability of natural snow of all skiing areas in the region. It is at 5,248 ft and is easily reached on public transportation. The area is popular with families as it has just over 4.2 miles of beginners' level slopes and 1.2 miles of intermediate. The lifts operate daily from 10 am to 4 pm, with floodlit skiing on Wednesday from 6:30 to 9:30 pm. Day passes are €12.50.

The **Hochschwarzeck** ski area, ☎ 08567-368, www.jennerbahn.de/hsb.htm, in Ramsau is also very popular with families. The four main slopes are between 1,600 and 8,200 ft – all rated beginners' level. The long tobogganing course is also popular. Rental equipment is available. The lifts operate daily from 9 am to 4 pm. Day passes are around €16.

Bobsledding: The bobsled course at Berchtesgaden was the world's first artificial ice course when it opened in 1969. It is 4,920 ft long with 18 turns and still considered one of the most challenging in the world.

It is possible to hurtle down this course in a "Bob-Raft," which is less high-tech, and less slick-looking than a real bobsled. In the **Gästebob** (Guest Bob), three passengers join a professional in a raft for a 4,264-ft downhill ride, reaching speeds up to 50 mph. Each ride is €30. Information and reservations through the **Verkehrsamt Schönau**, Rathausplatz, Schönau, ☎ 08652-1760. On most weekends from November to February, it is also possible to be a passenger in a real four-seater bobsled with professional pilot and co-pilot supplied by **Rennbob-Taxi Königssee**, ☎ 08652-95-880. No running start, but everything else is the real thing. These rides cost €80.

Cross-Country Skiing: In **Schönau**, four cross-country skiing courses are available, ranging from 1.2 to 2.4 miles each. Ramsau has five courses between one and 3.6 miles long. However, the best area for cross-country skiing is **Aschauer Weiher**, with eight courses ranging from 1.2 to 5.4 miles. Some are classified very difficult and one is a skating route.

Ice Skating: The **Eishalle Berchtesgaden**, An der Schießstätte, ☎ 08652-61-405, is open during winter, from late September to April, on weekdays from 10 am to 12:30 pm and 2 to 4:30 pm, on weekends from 2 to 4 pm and 8 to 10 pm. Rental skates are available on-site. Admission is €3.

Ice skating is also allowed on the Hintersee and Böcklwieher lakes when sufficiently frozen.

Ski School & Equipment Rentals: Several ski schools (downhill and snowboarding) operate in the area – all listed below also rent out equipment. Five-day group courses, four hours per day, cost about €90 for adults.

Ski- und Snowboardschule Jenner-Königssee, Franz Graßl, ☎ 08652-66-710; **Skischule Schönau**, Skilift Kohlhiasl, Oberschönauerstraße, ☎ 08652-948-406, www.ski-schoenau.de; **Skischule Berchtesgaden**, Schornstraße 34, ☎ 08652-61-197.

Winter Hiking: Up to 72 miles of hiking routes are cleared to allow safe hiking in winter.

Where to Stay & Eat

■ Berchtesgaden

The **Hotel Vier Jahreszeiten** is at the edge of the town close to the station. Rooms are comfortable with wood furniture. South-facing rooms have excellent views of the mountains. The **Hubertusstuben Restaurant** (€€-€€€) serves local and international dishes. Maximilianstraße 20, 83471

Berchtesgaden, ☎ 08652-9520, fax 08652-5029, www. berchtesgaden.com/vier-jahreszeiten. (€€-€€€)

The **Hotel Rosenbichl** is outside the town in the National Park. The comfortable rooms are modern and have great views. The whole hotel is non-smoking. The hotel operates its own ski school.

Hotel Rosenbichl

Rosenhofweg 24, 83471 Berchtesgaden, ☎ 08652-94-400, fax 08652-944-040, www.hotel-rosenbichl.de. (€€)

Alpenhotel Denninglehen

The **Alpenhotel Denninglehen** is quietly located along the Roßfeld ring road and has spectacular views. (It is at 2,952 ft as opposed to Berchtesgaden's altitude of 1,771 ft.) Rooms are spacious, comfortable, and partly furnished with traditional hand-painted furniture. The rustic dinner-only **restaurant** (€€) serves international cuisine. Am Priesterstein 7, 83471 Berchtesgaden-Oberau, ☎ 08652-5085, fax 08652-64-710, www.denninglehen.de. (€€-€€€)

■ Schönau am Königssee

Hotel Alpenhof is idyllically located at 2,296 ft in a green area with meadows and forests. Most of the comfortable rooms have balconies and mountain views. Richard-Vos-Straße 30, 83471 Schönau, ☎ 08652-6020, fax 08652- 64-399, www. alpenhof.de. (€€€-€€€€)

Hotel Zechmeisterlehen is at the edge of the town sur-

Hotel Alpenhof

Hotel Zechmeisterlehen

rounded by a large meadow. Rooms are comfortable and most have balconies and mountain views. The hotel has an indoor and outdoor swimming pool. Wahlstraße 35, 83471 Schönau, ☎ 08652-9450, fax 08652-945-299, www.zechmeisterlehen. de. (€€-€€€)

The **Stolls Hotel Alpina** is in a quiet spot inside a large garden. It is a typical Alpine resort building and has comfortable rooms. The rustic **restaurant** (€-€€) serves regional and international dishes. Dinner reservations are recommended. Ulmenweg 14, 83471 Schönau, ☎ 08652-65-090, fax 08652-61-608, www. stolls.hotl-alpina.de. (€€€)

Waldhauser-Bräu Restaurant, Walshauserstraße 12, ☎ 08652-948-943, is a rustic locale with a wide-ranging menu from hearty local dishes to Chinese and Spanish favorites. On weekdays, it is open for dinner only, but is open from 10 am on weekends. (€-€€)

■ Camping

There are a surprising number of campgrounds in the Berchtesgaden vicinity. All the sites listed below are open year-round, but some require prior reservations in the winter season.

Camping Allweglehen is one of the best, with excellent facilities. It has 130 lots on seven levels with marvelous views. 83471 Bechtesgaden-Salzberg, ☎ 08652-2396, fax 08652-63-503, www.alpen-camping-allweg.de.

Camping Grafenlehen also has excellent facilities and 180 lots. It is on the beautiful Königssee. Königsseer Fußweg 71, 83471 Berchtesgaden-Königssee, ☎ 08652-4140, fax 08652-690-767, www.camping-grafenlahen.de.

In the same area is **Camping Mühlleiten**, with good facilities and 100 lots. 83471 Berchtesgaden-Königssee, ☎ 08652-4584, fax 08652-69-194, www.camping-muehlleiten.de.

Index